West Virginia Hiking Trails

Hiking the Mountain State

2d edition

Allen de Hart

APPALACHIAN MOUNTAIN CLUB BOOKS
BOSTON, MASSACHUSETTS

Cover Photograph: Steve Swingenstein
Book & Cover Design: Elisabeth Leydon Brady
All photographs by the author unless otherwise noted.

Published by the Appalachian Mountain Club, 5 Joy St., Boston, MA 02108.

Distributed by the Globe Pequot Press, 6 Business Park Rd., PO Box 833, Old Saybrook, CT 06475.

Library of Congress Cataloging-in-Publication Data
De Hart, Allen.
    West Virginia hiking trails: hiking the mountain state / Allen de Hart. —2nd ed.
        p.   cm.
    Rev. ed. of: Hiking the mountain state. c1986
    Includes index.
    ISBN 1-878239-56-2 (alk. paper)
    1. Hiking—West Virginia—Guidebooks. 2. Trails—West Virginia—Guide-
books. 3. Campsites, facilities, etc.—West Virginia. 4. West Virginia—Guidebooks. I. De Hart, Allen. Hiking the mountain state. II. Title
GV199.42.W4D4 1997
917.5404'43—dc21   97-4398
                                                                            CIP

The paper used in this publication meets the minimum requirements of the American National Standard for Information Sciences—Permanence of Paper for Printed Library Materials, ANSI Z39.48–1984.∞

**Due to changes in conditions, use of the information
in this book is at the sole risk of the user.**

Printed on recycled paper using soy-based inks.

Printed in the United States of America.

10 9 8 7 6 5 4 3 2 1   97 98 99 00 01 02 03

Contents

*To the volunteers who design, construct, and maintain
the hiking trails of West Virginia.*

Acknowledgments

This book has been made possible by the assistance of federal, state, and local government personnel, university research assistants, and hiking friends. Because half of the trails are in the Monongahela National Forest, I depended on Joe Robles, forest recreation specialist in Public Services. He provided me with a list of new trails, some relocated trails, some in the planning stages, and others that were abandoned. Others in Public Services who provided assistance were Steve Chandler, land-use planning specialist, and William Kerr, landscape architect.

Linda White, forester in the Cheat Ranger District, provided information about not only her district, but on forests in general. Gary Willison, district ranger of Cheat Ranger District, also assisted. In the Gauley Ranger District help came from Acting Ranger Don Kinerson, Integrated Resource Analyst Bill Schiffer, and Supervisory Forester Gail Lantz. Cindy Schiffer, district ranger for the Marlinton and White Sulphur Ranger Districts, and Nancy Feakes, district ranger of the Potomac Ranger District, provided information. Also assisting was Anne Downing, forester of White Sulphur Ranger District. Help was also received from Patrick Sheridan, district ranger of the Greenbrier Ranger District. Assisting from the George Washington and Jefferson National Forests was Harry Fisher, forest recreation specialist.

Because of the new trails in the New River Gorge National River area, I depended on help from Kelly Bridges, Tina White, and Shirley Grant, park rangers. Additionally, Tom DeCesar, trail-crew supervisor, gave me guidance to the most remote trails. Among others who provided me with information was Donald Campbell, superintendent of Harpers Ferry National Historical Park; Kim McHenry, programming services coordinator for West

Virginia Parks and Recreation; Mark Clarke, area manager of Elk River WMA; Doug Wood and the Warrior Trail Association; Robert E. Driscole, forest ranger of West Virginia University; and Jan Wilkins of Coolfont Resort and Park.

Sharing in the fifteen years of fieldwork was a dedicated team of hikers and backpackers. They hiked with me in all seasons, whether in perfect weather or storms and snow; they assisted in logistics, supplied photos, and made notes on trail relocations. To the following I am profoundly grateful: Chris Addison, Andrea Alter, Tim Averette, Robert Ballance, Pat Barnes, Mike Batts, Michael Beaman, Stuart Boyd, Dale Bowman, Jimmy Boyette, Jeff Brewer, Cliff Brummitt, Richard Byrd, Ray Carpenter, Charley Carlson, Gary Cliett, John Cohn, Vance Collom, Don Cox, Paula Crenshaw, David Critz, Don Davis, Loree Davis, Richard Davis, John Dean, Skip Deegans, Kirk Dickerson, Tony Droppleman, Frank Duke Jr, Alvin Edwards, Brooke Faircloth, David Fisher, Jeff Fleming, Beth Garner, Wayne Gibbs, Ellen Haney, Steve Harris, Don Hayes, Stephanie Hickey, Rob Hight, Greg Hippert, Kelly Horton, Dick Hunt, David Hutson, Charles Isley, Mark Ivey, Jeff Jeffreys, Lisa Kiley, Charles Knowles, Sheri Lanier, Sharon Leonard, Ed Liberatore, Leslie Marchant, Jason Mason, Reuben Massey, Daren Matthews, John Matthews, Steve Miller, Scott Morris, Greg Murphy, Dennis Parrish, Jimmy Paulakuhn, Bob Peterson, Tommy Pike, David Porter, Wade Potter, George Rosier, David Salling, Scott Sanders, Joe Smith, Clint Snow, Gene Spears, Gary Stainback, Scott Stalls, Gwen Struzik, Mark Suelflohn, Chip Suttles, Eric Tang, Greg Taylor, Carol Ann Thompson, Jon Toppen, Jena Trent, Ryan Watts, Wayne Williams, Travis Winn, Doug Wood, Jeff Wood, and Kevin Zoltek.

I am deeply indebted also to the late Dr. Maurice Brooks, professor emeritus of wildlife management at West Virginia University. For thirty of the fifty years I have been hiking West Virginia trails, Dr. Brooks (known as "Dr. Appalachia") has been my inspiration. He died January 10, 1993, at the age of ninety-three. His legendary contributions to those of us who love the outdoors are unequaled.

Introduction

Walking is the prescription without medicine, the fountain of youth that is no legend.

—Aaron Sussman

West Virginia, the Mountain State of 24,282 square miles, is approximately 75 percent forest (11.6 million acres). On thousands of rugged, wild mountain ridges; steep hills; and cloistered hollows grow what N. Bayard Green called "one of nature's greatest miracles": the magnificent stands of cherry, oak, hickory, beech, birch, maple, spruce, hemlock, and pine. Although these forestlands are 90 percent privately owned, there are three national forests, which together cover a total of 1,028,708 acres; nine state forests, with 79,018 acres; fifty-nine wildlife management areas, with 1.3 million acres managed by the state; and 73,789 acres of preserved forest in the state's thirty-eight parks. Aesthetically inviting and commercially valuable, the state's woodlands annually provide more than 800 million board feet of timber, 27 million of which are cut in the Monongahela National Forest (MNF). It is in these woodlands that I have been hiking for nearly sixty years, and I have found there a priceless heritage. This is where Maurice Brooks experienced "nature as it was intended to be" and where Peter Josimovich found a "natural flavor of life and values." "A culture is no better than its woods," wrote W. H. Auden in *Bucolics*.

Timber harvesting has long been the concern of citizens' groups that advocate wildlife protection and careful management of natural resources. This concern was demonstrated nationwide in 1984, when the U.S. Forest Service (USFS) proposed a fifty-year long-range plan to increase timbering, mining, and road construction by approximately 70 percent. Estimates were that reforestation and natural succession were perpetuating one-third more trees than were being harvested.

In West Virginia, the Monongahela National Forest, in compliance with the USFS directive, distributed its Draft Plan and Environmental Impact Statement (EIS) for public review in December 1984. Within a year the public rejected it and claimed that the forest should retain its natural character, conditions, and remoteness, and that excessive roads and timbering would damage the environment. The final, more protective plan was accepted in 1986. The George Washington National Forest Land and Resource (GWNF) Management Plan also faced considerable public resolve to minimize roads and timbering. Its final revised plan was made in 1993. Nearly 40 percent of the GWNF has experienced at least one defoliation by the gypsy moth. Timbering was necessary for efforts at salvage. In 1996 a settlement was made between the West Virginia Highlands Conservancy and the Monongahela National Forest over timbering and roads in East Gauley Mountain, a wilderness-type area. It was the first time in thirty years the MNF had been taken to court on behalf of the environment. However, it should be noted that in 1996 only 12 million board feet were sold, in contrast to 39 million board feet in 1991. Plans are to average about 25 million board feet annually for the next five years.

Recent surveys indicate that West Virginians wish to keep the mountains and hills green with trees, a goal of great significance if examined in terms of global forest conditions. For example, in the summer of 1985, *CBS News* reported that the world's forests were disappearing at an average rate of 50 acres each minute; that is 3,000 acres an hour, 504,000 acres a week, or 26,208,000 acres each year—more than twice the total acreage of all West Virginia forests.

Although the Mountain State has a valuable and expendable resource in timber, its major natural resource is minerals. It leads the nation in annually exporting 44 million tons of coal from a total mining of 126 million tons. It has been estimated that coal lies under 65 percent of the state and that it will last for another 400 years. In 1996 the *Sunday Gazette-Mail* reported that strip mining is another cause for the loss of the state's forests. "Between 1987 and 1995, nearly 250,000 acres of state timberland was lost to strip mining, farming, rights of way and housing developments. This was the first decrease in state timberland acreage in more than 50 years." Petroleum and natural gas are found in thirty-three of the fifty-five counties. Other prominent minerals are limestone, sandstone, sand, clays, and salt. Hikers will see considerable evidence of coal mining, oil and gas drilling, salt and stone quarries, timber harvesting, and a few pristine places unchanged since the days of the American Indians and early explorers.

The first known white explorer to stand on the Blue Ridge Mountains and look over the Shenandoah valley toward the Alleghenies was John Lederer, who reported in his *Journal* (1669–70) that among the plants, geology, and animals he saw "lions and peacocks." With less imagination, but with more hiking stamina, Thomas Batts and Robert Fallam, professional explorers searching for the "waters on the other side of the mountains...and discovery of the South Sea," went as far as the east boundary of current Monroe County in 1671. In 1763, James Needham and Gabriel Arthur were successful, after a first attempt was repulsed by the Occaneechees Indians, in reaching the Kanawha and Cumberland valleys. In *Elderberry Flood*, Louise McNeill, a West Virginia poet laureate, describes the explorer's forest from the Shenandoah to the Ohio River as "15,000,000 acres, span-on-span of leafy distance / Like a hunter's dream." Trans-Allegheny exploration began in earnest after 1710, when Virginia's governor-explorer Alexander Spotswood organized expeditions westward. Members of his party were called "Knights of the Golden Horseshoe."

Indian tribes that claimed areas that became West Virginia were the Shawnees, Tuscaroras, Cherokees, Delawares, and Mingos, but their infrequent settlements (because they mainly hunted and fished in the area) had disappeared before the major English settlements. After the Indian battle of 1774, when General Andrew Lewis repelled Chief Cornstalk and his warriors, Indian power claims ceased on the frontier. Hunting, fishing, and trade routes the Indians had followed became access routes across the mountains for the migration of white settlers. Among the routes was the famous *Seneca Trail* (also called *Shawnee Trail*), with a network of connecting trails along the rivers. From the South Branch of the Potomac it followed the North Fork to Seneca Rock, where it branched east into the Shenandoah and west to cross the Cheat Mountains and Shavers Fork to Elkins. Here it turned north to Parsons and on to Oakland, Maryland. The southern trailway from Elkins was to Mingo Flats in Randolph County. Again, it divided; the western route followed the *Little Kanawha Trail*, which went west to join the *Scioto-Monongahela Trail* into Ohio. The southern route of the *Seneca Trail* followed a route similar to US-219 to Marlinton, Lewisburg, and on to Bluefield. Other Indian trails were the *Warrior Path* in the present eastern panhandle and the *Buffalo Trail* (also called *Kanawha Trail*), which followed the Kanawha River along what later became US-60 from Ohio to White Sulphur Springs.

Except for early settlers clearing land for pastures and crops, the forest changed little until the turn of the twentieth century, when the original timber was devastated by logging companies. Ralph Widner, in his *Forests and Forestry in the United States*, said that by 1920 the "cream of the virgin forest crop has been taken with only scattered tracts remaining." The peak year had been reached in 1909, when a record 1.473 billion board feet were cut. In *Tumult on the Mountains*, Roy B. Clarkson described trees in the primeval forest that "grew to six or seven feet in diameter." Fortunately, a group of enormous trees remain in the 118-acre Cathedral State Park in Preston County. The state's largest hemlock is here.

The state's named trail system has 2,029 miles, of which 941 miles are in the national forests. For many years the hills and valleys on which these trails wind, wave, and curve have been admired by tourists, hunters, fishermen, naturalists, poets, and composers. For example, one of the state's late poet laureates, Roy Lee Harmon, wrote that "the hillman, though he's young or old / Enjoys life's finest frills / When springtime puts her magic touch / On West Virginia hills" in "Roses in December" (*Poems of a Mountaineer*). Other poets have written about the hills in William Plumley's anthology *Poems from the Hills*. The first song to be adopted as an official state song was Colonel Julian G. Hearne Jr.'s "West Virginia, My Home Sweet Home," "where mountains and hills and valleys too...all have charm." Another official song is "The West Virginia Hills," written by the Reverend David King in 1879 and set to music by Henry E. Engle in 1885. "How majestic and how grand, / with their summits bathed in glory...How I love these West Virginia hills."

All these hills are part of the geographic features of a state whose average altitude of 1,500 feet is higher than any other state east of the Mississippi River. The state lies wholly in the Appalachian region, a large land province that extends from southeast Canada to central Alabama. As a result, the state is often described as the "land of 10,000 valleys." It is also called the "Panhandle State" because of its irregular arms extending east and north. The easternmost tip, at Harpers Ferry, has the same longitude as Rochester, New York. The western boundary is as far west as Port Huron, Michigan, and the north panhandle extends farther north than Pittsburgh. The southern border is 60 miles below Richmond. It is 237 miles from the north to the south of the state and 265 miles from east to west. The Allegheny Plateau has 6,500 square miles and the Allegheny Highlands have approximately 6,000 square miles. The prominence of these scenic areas led to suggestions by delegates at the state's first constitutional convention in 1861 to name the seceding part of Virginia "Allegheny." Other Indian names such as Kanawha and Potomac were suggested, but on June 20, 1863, western Virginia became West Virginia, the thirty-fifth state. On the reverse side of the great seal the new government chose a Latin logo, *Montani semper liberi* ("Mountaineers are always free").

How to Use This Book

The purpose of this book is to describe the foot trails clearly enough for you to locate the trailheads and follow the trails with reasonable security of direction. It is recommended that you read the information about the trails before you leave home. This will enable you to plan your supplies, road directions and conditions, and campsites. The book has been designed so you can easily carry it with you in a pack or jacket pocket. All the trails described are grouped in five parts: national forests; national parks and Corps of Engineers; state parks and forests; counties and municipalities; and college, private, or special trails. Each chapter and section has an introduction to acquaint you with the area and to provide information on access, address, and support services.

Ten national forest districts are covered. Each district has been assigned trail numbers by the USFS. I have used these throughout the book because many of the Forest Service trailheads and intersections have them for guidance. The Cheat Ranger District of the Monongahela National Forest has numbers 100–199; Gauley, 200–299; Greenbrier, 300–399; Marlinton, 400–499; Potomac, 500–599; and White Sulphur, 600–699. (One exception to the numbered sequence is that the *North-South Trail* #688 is in the Gauley District and another *North-South Trail* #688 is on Shavers Mtn in the Greenbrier District. The latter is now also #701, the *Allegheny Trail*.) The *Allegheny Trail* is #701 because it traverses more than one district. The George Washington National Forest numbers in West Virginia are 1001–1050. There are no group numbers on the partial trails in West Virginia for the Jefferson National Forest, except #71 for the *Virginia's Walk* in the Blacksburg District and *Allegheny Trail* in the New Castle District.

The first trail in the book is the *Plantation Trail* #101. Under it are listed connecting trails. When grouped in this manner all trail lengths are in parentheses with an open total length. An effort has been made to follow a numerical sequence from low to high numbers rather than an alphabetical sequence of trail names. In some groups, however, the trail numbers are not in sequence.

You will see numerous trails described singly, such as *Tablerock Overlook Trail* #113, because they do not connect with other trails. Some trails, usually two or three, such as *Mountainside Trail* #114 and *Bennett Rock Trail* #112, may be listed under one heading because the main trail does not have a group of appendages or because it is difficult to make satisfactory loops. They do, however, connect at some point. In connecting trail groups the main or primary trail description is interrupted by material in parentheses to describe the spur or connecting trail. The objective in this arrangement is to give you options on how far you wish to hike before backtracking, making a loop, or following only the main trail. If you select the last option, the sections in parentheses can be ignored, but the information will always be there if you change your mind. In the Gauley District, the *North-South Trail* #688 has eight connecting trails. The parentheses around the name of the connecting trail also mean it has been covered before or will be covered down the list in more detail. You will notice this arrangement also with the *Pocahontas Trail* #263. The index is arranged alphabetically, but only the national forest trails will have both a USFS number and a page number.

Although I have copious notes on each trail, I have been brief in trail descriptions for two reasons: to save book space and to leave some options for your feelings of discovery. Because you will likely be on the trail at a different season from the time I was there, you will experience a different show of plant and animal life. Where I found rare or endangered plants and animals I have omitted describing their exact location.

Roads to the trailheads are described according to the Department of Highways road names, signs, and numbers. The CO roads are significant because they are the chief access to the trailheads. Each CO is described by its official name and number (though the local citizens may call it by another name). You will find exceptions. For example, in Monroe County, CO-15 is named Limestone Hills Road on the state list, but the state sign at the Waitesville Road junction is Gap Mills Road. County road name and number may change at the county line. It is wise to expect a remote and isolated road to be rough, eroded, or rutted and difficult for passenger vehicles. Another type of county road is the Delta road, with a triangular sign, designated *D*; it is usually short and receives minimal maintenance. An example is Workman Road (D-l9) at Stony Bottom in Pocahontas County.

The forest road (*FR*) may also be difficult for passenger vehicles, locked, or unplowed in winter. Nevertheless, the condition of some forest roads is superior to that of the adjoining CO roads.

Abbreviations

An effort has been made to save space in this book by using abbreviations wherever possible. Most of these are part of everyday usage; specialized ones follow:

AT	Appalachian National Scenic Trail
ATC	Appalachian Trail Conference
ATV	all-terrain vehicle
Ave	Avenue
Bldg	Building
CO-	county road
D-	Delta road
DNR	West Virginia Department of Natural Resources
elev	elevation
4WD	four-wheel-drive vehicle
FR-	USFS forest-development or protection road
ft	foot, feet
GWNF	George Washington National Forest
I-	Interstate highway
in	inch(es)
jct	junction(s)
JNF	Jefferson National Forest
L, R	left, right
mi	mile(s)
mtn	mountain
mt	mount
MNF	Monongahela National Forest
ORV	off-road vehicle
PATC	Potomac Appalachian Trail Club
PO	post office

Rd	Road
RR	railroad
RV	recreational vehicle
SR-	secondary road
St	Street(s)
US-	United States highway
USFS	United States Forest Service
USGS	United States Geological Survey (map)
USGS-FS	USGS map showing USFS boundaries
WMA	Wildlife Management Area
WV-	West Virginia primary highway
WVHC	West Virginia Highlands Conservancy
WVSTA	West Virginia Scenic Trails Association
yd	yard(s)

Maps

The first map you should have is a West Virginia official highway map. It is available at service stations, chambers of commerce, and free from the West Virginia Department of Highways, Public Information Division, Charleston, WV 25305; 304-348-0103. Other sources are the state travel councils, listed in the introduction to chapter 6 State Parklands and Historic Sites, or the Office of Economic and Community Development, Capitol Building, Charleston, WV 25305; 800-624-9110. A more detailed map of each county is available at county courthouses, local chambers of commerce, and from the Department of Highways for a nominal cost. Descriptions, directions, and trail map designs in this book are based on the state highway and county maps to simplify the process of finding the trailheads. Some county and U.S. Geological Survey (USGS) maps do not show all the national forest roads. An update, with additional access points, follows the index. The trail narrative should be sufficient without use of the USGS topographic maps. In addition to these basic maps, there are special multicolored contour maps of the Monongahela National Forest for a small cost. Write or call USFS/Monongahela National Forest, PO Box 1548, Elkins, WV 26241; 304-636-1800. Addresses and telephone numbers are listed for other forests and parks in the chapters where they are described. The most detailed maps are the USGS maps. They are on the scale of 1:24,000 (1 inch = 2,000 feet), 7.5-minute series. Where I have referred to USGS-FS it means the regular USGS map is modified for the US Forest Service and shows only the forest areas in green. It is preferred over the standard map if you plan to be in the national forest. Some of the USGS maps are vintage and you will find their trail lines in question. If a local blueprint company does not have your desired map, write to Branch of Distribution, US Geological Survey, Box 25286 Federal Center, Denver, CO 80225. Because you must pay in advance, write for free information, West Virginia Index Map, and order form. A list of stores in West Virginia that stock USGS maps is in the index here. State parks and forests also have maps of their areas. Write to them at the addresses given in chapters 6, 7, and 8.

Markers, Signs, Numbers, and Blazes

For directional purposes, trailheads usually have a lettered sign or a number, or both. This also applies to intersections. Blazes, usually painted on trees, are along the trails at irregular intervals. Some trails have neither a blaze nor a sign. Because of this, I have described the trails with more emphasis on such other factors as trees, streams, bridges, or mileage in the event the markers are missing. Signs may be wood or metal. Wood is usually routed and painted, but some signs (now in the Wilderness areas) may be only routed, as in Cranberry Wilderness. Others are only painted. Some signs are bolted on posts or trees, as on *Shavers Mtn Trail* (*Allegheny Trail*). Where there is a discrepancy between the sign mileage and this book, depend on the book because many trails, particularly in the national and state forests, have not been measured. The Forest Service claims to have rounded off the trail mileage to the nearest half-mile or quarter-mile.

MNF blazes are always blue. The *AT* blaze is always white; side trails are blue. The *Allegheny Trail* is always yellow, and multiple colors exist in the George Washington National Forest and in state parks and forests. All USFS blazes are supposed to be a 2" x 6" vertical rectangle. Some have an unnecessary 2" x 2" square above the blaze (a nationwide procedure), but the newest trails have only the 2" x 6" rectangle and in many cases only splotches of blue paint much larger than 2" x 6". A few trails have other designs, such as circles in Cacapon State Park, where as many as four different colors on a tree indicate trail overlap. Some trails have the diamond-shaped metal or plastic or painted marker for cross-country skiing. If you find a trail sign in error, please report it to the ranger or superintendent rather than trying to redesign it yourself.

Trail Types, Length, and Difficulty

Most trail types are called primary or main because they are maintained, blazed, or marked. The opposite is true of primitive trails. An abandoned trail may or may not be blazed or passable; it is not maintained. A *side* or *spur* trail is usually shorter than the main trail and may serve only as an access route to a water source or point of interest. A *multiple-use trail* is authorized for people, horses, and wheels. A *jeep* trail may be used by hikers, horses, ORVs, and ATVs, or it may be posted for foot travel only. A *gated* trail may be a foot trail for pedestrians during a protective season for wildlife but open to both hikers and vehicles at other times. A *wilderness* trail is for foot traffic only. An unnamed *hunters'* trail or *fishermen's* trail may be easy to hike, though it is not maintained by the park or Forest Service. Other hunters' access roads have trail names, for example those at Lewis Wetzel or Sleepy Creek Wildlife Management Area. A number of *ski* trails and trail-roads are easy and accessible for cross-country skiing. The major ones are mentioned this book. I have described trails as *scenic* if they have impressive views of the natural environment in or out of the forest, *recreational* if used mainly for exercise, *historical* if emphasizing a heritage area, and *nature* if they are interpretive. Special-use trails are for such special populations as the visually handicapped.

The length of the trails has been measured by a Model 400 Rolatape measuring wheel. Although it measures each foot, I have rounded the trail length off to the nearest 0.1 mi. Where you have to backtrack, I have described the distance and used *round-trip* in the length. Miles are used without kilometers, because none of the state's trails is marked or signed with kilometers only.

Each trail is listed as *easy*, *moderate*, or *strenuous*, and it is based on the ratings for average hikers, not athletes or the very old and very young. *Easy* means that if you are in good health you can hike the trail without fatigue or exertion. *Moderate* means there may be some exertion involved and you will probably need to rest occasionally. Trails featuring steep climbs/descents or rough and long traverses are classified as *strenuous*—greater exertion and more-frequent rest stops. Of course, the size and weight of a pack can make a difference in any classification.

Animal and Plant Life

Wildlife is abundant almost everywhere and particularly in the national forests. The state animal is the black bear (*Euarctos americanus*) and the state bird is the cardinal (*Cardinalis cardinalis*). I have mentioned some of the species I saw on the trails, and your chances of seeing wildlife are good. For the best observation, know the animals' watering and feeding places, leave the dog at home, and walk softly in the woods. You may be closer to them than you think. In some state parks, such as Canaan Valley, deer (*Odocoileus virginianus*) and woodchuck (*Marmota monax*) graze by the dozen, generally ignoring the public. On the *Meadow Mtn Trail* an amiable striped skunk (*Mephitis mephitis*) glanced at our feet and fortunately continued his dig for grubs. At the junction of *County Line Trail* and *District Line Trail* in the Cranberry Wilderness a bear sat chewing on a signpost. He stared at me but continued to chew on the post. Some recommended books about the area's wildlife are *West Virginia Birds and Mammals of West Virginia*, both by George Hall, and *A Field Guide to Reptiles and Amphibians of Eastern and Central North America*, by Roger Conant, of the Peterson Field Guide series.

The state's fifty-nine Wildlife Management Areas, described in section 8, have hundreds of wildlife food plots. If you are hunting or fishing, a license can be secured at most of the rural general stores. Alternatively, contact the Wildlife Resources Division of the Department of Natural Resources (DNR), 1900 Kanawha Blvd. E, Bldg. 3, Room 819, Charleston, WV 25305; 304-558-2771. Addresses and telephone numbers for the nearest DNR officers are: District I, 1304 Goose Run Rd. Fairmont, WV 26554, (304-367-2720); District II, 1 Depot St., Romney, WV 26757 (304-822-3551); District III PO Box 38, French Creek, WV 26218 (304-924-6211); District IV, 2006 Robert C. Byrd Dr., Beckley, WV 25801 (304-256-6947); District V, McClintic Wildlife Sta, Box 484, Pt. Pleasant, WV 25550 (304-675-0871); District VI, 2311 Ohio Ave., Parkersburg, WV 26101 (304-420-4550). The telephone number of the Elkins Operations Center is 304-637-0245. Be sure to ask for *West Virginia Hunting and Trapping Regulations* and *West Virginia Fishing Regulations*. Also ask for the *West Virginia Fishing Guide*, *West Virginia Impoundment Fishing Guide*, and *West Virginia Stream Map*. Fishing is a popular sport in the state. In the MNF alone there are 576 miles of trout streams, where state and federal hatcheries stock more than 500,000 catchable-size trout annually. Izaak Walton summed up the sport in *The Compleat Angler* when he said "God never did make a more calm, quiet, innocent recreation than angling."

If you are a vascular-plant enthusiast, the estimated 2,200 species in the state await your study. I have mentioned some of them in this book, but this list is minuscule in comparison to what I saw. Within the MNF at least 1,500 plants have been cataloged. The state tree is the sugar maple (*Acer saccharum*) and the state flower is the pink-white great laurel (*Rhododendron maximum*). Your bible for plant study is *Flora of West Virginia* by P. D. Strausbaugh and Earl L. Core. It is available in a combined volume or in four separate volumes. Other books are the *Audubon Society Field Guide to North American Wildflowers* (Eastern Region) by W. A. Niering and Nancy C. Olmstead; *Ferns* by Norma J. Venable of the Center for Extension and Continuing Education at West Virginia University; *Spring Wild Flowers of West Virginia* by Earl L. Core; *Dictionary of Useful Plants* by Nelson Coon; *A Field Guide to Edible Wild Plants of Eastern and Central North America* by Lee Peterson; and *Mushrooms of North America* by O. K. Miller. A number of brochures are distributed by the West Virginia Department of Agriculture, State Capitol Bldg, Charleston, WV 25305; 304-293-4411. Among them are "West Virginia Mid-Summer Wild Flowers," "Common Mosses of West Virginia," "Rare and Endangered Plant Species of West Virginia," "Edible Wild Plants," and "Poisonous Plants." Additional information may be secured from the Division of Forestry, West Virginia University, Morgantown, WV 26506; 304-293-4411. The harvesting of some plants such as ramp, ginseng, wild fruits, berries, and nuts is allowed by the national forests. For information contact the headquarters of the MNF, P.O. Box 1548, Elkins, WV 26241; 304-636-1800; for the GWNF and the Jefferson National Forest, now administratively consolidated, the address is: 5162 Valley Pointe Pkwy, Roanoke, VA 24019; 540-265-5100.

Health and Safety

It is recommended by forest and park officials that you hike with one or more companions to reduce the danger of hypothermia, poisonous snakebite, injury from a fall, being lost, or becoming sick. Accidents happen to the most cautious hikers, and even minor mishaps can ruin an otherwise exciting and pleasant journey. Carry pure drinking water on all trails, and use water officially designated safe by the forest or park. My listing of springs and clear streams in this book does not mean the water has been tested. Properly boiling the water remains one of the best ways to be sure, or use water purifiers. Be sure someone in your party has a good first-aid kit.

Two poisonous snakes, the timber rattler and the copperhead, exist in the state. The largest rattler I have seen in the state was on a trail in Coopers Rock State Forest. The best precaution against snakebite is to watch where you place your feet and where you use your hands around rocks and logs. Hypothermia—the number-one cause of death for outdoor recreationists—is caused by the lowering of body heat. It can be fatal even in the summertime. Sweaty and wet clothes lose about 90 percent of their dry insulating value, and windchill increases the danger. The best lines of defense are to stay dry; get out of the wind, rain, or snow to avoid exhaustion; and know the symptoms and treatment. The symptoms are uncontrollable shivering; vague, incoherent speech; frequent stumbling; and drowsiness. The victim may be unaware of all of these. Treatment for a mildly impaired victim is to place him or her in a dry place, in dry clothes, and in a warm sleeping bag, and give warm drinks; if the victim is semiconscious, try to keep the victim awake, and provide person-to-person skin contact in a warm sleeping bag.

Lightning is another danger in the outdoors. Some precautions in an electrical storm are: stay off sharp, prominent peaks; avoid standing under a cliff or in the entrance of a cave; avoid vertical cracks or crevices in the rocks, and avoid standing under prominent trees or other tall objects. Sit or lie down and insulate yourself from the ground if possible. Exposure also can be dangerous; a 2-inch snow in Bartow may be an 18-inch snow on Spruce Knob. You should be prepared for sudden changes in the weather in all seasons. Flash floods and snowstorms can maroon you and your vehicle. In remote areas some hikers take a small radio in their backpacks for weather reports. Mean Fahrenheit temperature in the state in winter is 36°; spring, 55°; summer, 74°; and fall, 57°. The number of clear days averages 110 partly cloudy, 105; and cloudy, 150. Snow may be more than 20 percent of the precipitation in Randolph County and less than 5 percent in Mingo County. The average snowfall is more than 70 inches in Preston, Tucker, Pendleton, and Grant Counties, with Pickens in Randolph County having the highest seasonal average: 127 inches. The Canaan Valley area has recorded below-freezing temperatures in all months of the year; the same is true for Spruce Knob. Some of the counties with the greatest rainfall are Grant, Harrison, Upshur, Gilmer, Taylor, Marion, Lewis, and Randolph. Fall is the driest season. On the trails, it is a good idea to carry warm clothes, rain gear, notepaper and pencil, waterproof matches, compass, map, first-aid kit, and a dependable flashlight with extra batteries and a bulb. If you get lost off the trail use the universal distress signal of three of anything—shouts, whistles, light flashes. A recommended book on this subject is *Field Guide to Wilderness Survival* by Tom Brown.

Support Facilities

When camping is not allowed on the trails, I have mentioned the nearest campground, public or commercial. If full service is indicated it means there are spaces for tents, RVs, and trailers that use electricity, water, and probably sewage lines. Such camps also have hot showers, public phones, and possibly a store or restaurant. Free brochures are available from the Travel Division, Department of Commerce: 800-CALL WVA. Among the brochures are "West Virginia Camping Directory," "West Virginia Lodging Directory," and "West Virginia Park and Forest Lodging Rates and Reservations," and "West Virginia State Parks and Forests." A comprehensive directory is *Woodalls Campground Directory* (Eastern edition), available at most bookstores. A free brochure, "Recreation Areas and Schedules," is available from the MNF: 304-636-1800. In the appendix I have listed support organizations and addresses for mountain climbing, spelunking, whitewater sports, and skiing. Other trail guides are the *Monongahela National Forest Hiking Guide* by Allen de Hart and Bruce Sundquist, West Virginia Highlands Conservancy, P.O. Box 306, Charleston, WV, 25321; *Hiking Guide to the Allegheny Trail* by Doug Wood and George Rosier, 633 West Virginia Ave., Morgantown, WV; *Guidebook to Hiking the Kanawha Trace* by Charles L. Dundas and John A. Gibson, Tri-State Area Council, BSA, 733 Seventh Ave., Huntington, WV 25701; 304-523-3408.

Planning the Trip

Unless you are an experienced hiker, I recommend that you acquire a guidebook on backpacking and camping. An example is *Walking Softly in the Wilderness*, a Sierra Club guide by John Hart. Its main focus is on supplies and gearing up, preparing for the trip, trail travel, managing camp, family hiking, and how to deal with problems. Your trail-shop personnel will have other guidebooks and the most current information on equipment quality and specific outfitting needs (see Resources in the appendix).

Many of the trails are isolated and nearby stores may be seasonal or may close early in the evening; it is wise to make yourself as self-sufficient as possible. If there are questions about road conditions and weather, call the rangers, superintendents, or managers at the numbers listed in each section or chapter. After you have chosen your trails and equipment, do not forget to service your vehicle with plenty of gasoline, a guaranteed battery, spare tire and jack, jumper cable, toolbox, and distress kit. Park only at designated places, remove all your valuables from sight, and lock your vehicle. Other standard suggestions for all of us are to take a highway map and compass, let someone know where we are going, have a leader in our group, do not cut any live trees or shrubs, carry out what we carry in, take warm clothing and rain gear, use a propane stove for food preparation, boil or purify drinking water, bury human waste properly, carry a first-aid kit, respect the rights and privacy of others, help preserve the plants and animals, and do not feed the bears.

Walking in Wild, Wonderful West Virginia

Part of my childhood was spent in Raleigh County between Coal City and Lillybrook. It was there I learned to walk, and my mother has said that the first time I was allowed to walk on the lawn I headed for the woods. When I was five, my older brother, Moir, took me on an exciting hiking trip in Virginia. The woods of the world have since been a source of physical and emotional health for me. Dr. Paul D. White has stated that "walking is as natural as breathing." To Margot Doss, "walking is a way of living." But many walkers do not think of themselves as hikers. How does it start? George Rosier of the West Virginia Scenic Trails Association described it this way:

> Being a hiker comes from having gone for a walk with someone, probably older than yourself, when you were quite young. It was a happy experience and is a happy memory. Then, when you are old enough, you go walking alone. Soon you realize that if you carry a sandwich you will not have to come back quite so soon. Before you know it you have your pockets so full of sandwiches and identification books for flowers and birds and trees that there is almost no room for a camera! So you decide to buy your first day-pack. Then you realize that if you had a larger pack and a sleeping bag you could stay out even longer. Eventually someone asks, very innocently, "How long have you been a hiker?" and you realize that you are.

From the stroller to the explorer, there is a long trail or a short trail for everyone. The five longest trails are the *Allegheny Trail* (300 miles, of which 124 are in the MNF); *Greenbrier River Trail* (75.2 miles); *Tuscarora*

Trail (formerly the *Big Blue Trail*)—144 miles, of which 65.9 miles are in West Virginia; *North Bend Trail* (58 miles); and *Kanawha Trace* (31.7 miles)

Another long trail is the *American Discovery Trail* (*ADT*). Its route through West Virginia is about 275 miles on back roads and other trails. Examples are *North Bend Trail* and routes through the Cheat and Potomac Ranger Districts of the Monongahela National Forest. The *ADT* was a joint project by the American Hiking Society (sponsor of the dramatic HikaNation in 1980–81) and *Backpacker* magazine, in 1990–91 with a team of hikers to scout a coast-to-coast hiking and bicycle trail from the Pacific Ocean to the Atlantic Ocean. Through 12 states and more than 6,000 miles it also provides an alternate route in the heart of America. For detailed information request *The American Discovery Trail, Explorer's Guide* and updated information at 4838 MacCorkle Ave, SW, South Charleston, WV 25309; 304-768-0441. Other tel numbers are 804-340-5948 or 800-851-3442.

The two shortest trails are the 85-yard *Garden Trail of the Five Senses* and the 100-yard *Gentle Trail*, both the results of local citizens providing trails for special populations. The longest asphalt trail (2.8 miles) is the *Wigginton Arboretum Trail*. The highest trail is the 0.5-mile *Whispering Spruce Trail* (4,861 feet in elevation), and the lowest is the 1.0-mile *Virginius Island Trail* (255 feet in elevation). The trail with the greatest increase in elevation (a climb of 2,380 feet) is the 5.1-mile *Flatrock Run Trail*.

I have been hiking the trails of West Virginia for more than fifty years. In the pages ahead I have described more than 650 trails. (I have also hiked another 174 trails that have been abandoned or that are on private property.) I have my favorite trails. You will, too, with your own choice of superlatives; there are some trails whose welcome is so magnetic that you will return again and again. Welcome to the wild, wonderful walking trails of West Virginia—trails of natural history, mystery, incomparable beauty, and challenge.

Gandy Creek, west of Spruce Knob Lake

PART ONE

National Forest Trails

1. Monongahela National Forest

Hiking is to see Nature as it was intended to be.

—Maurice Brooks

The 901,000-plus-acre Monongahela National Forest (MNF) received its name from the Monongahela River, whose headwaters drain the northwestern area of the forest. The Indian word *Monongahela* means "river of sliding banks." The first land acquired in the state by the US government for national forest purposes was the 7,200-acre Arnold Tract in Tucker County. This purchase took place on Nov 26, 1915. Half of the original tract, 3,640 acres, was set aside in 1934 to form the Fernow Experimental Forest in memory of Bernhard E. Fernow, a pioneer in forestry research. The other half is the NW tip of the Otter Creek Wilderness. Both areas are in the Cheat Ranger District.

Following the Arnold Tract the acquisition of land expanded into the Alleghenies to encompass parts of Grant, Greenbrier, Nicholas, Pendleton, Pocahontas, Preston, Randolph (the state's largest), Tucker, and Webster Counties. The magnificence of the forest is accentuated by its natural landmarks, some of which are lofty mtn summits such as Spruce Knob (4,863 ft), the state's highest mtn, and Bald Knob (4,842 ft), the second highest; the four wildernesses—Otter Creek, Dolly Sods, Laurel Fork, and Cranberry—with 77,965 acres preserved forever; the natural botanical wonder of Cranberry Glades; and Seneca Rocks, a towering natural sculpture of Tuscarora sandstone.

Within the splendor of the MNF are 1,350 mi of forest roads (often more scenic than the major highways); more than 700 mi of hiking trails (including 124 mi of the *Allegheny Trail*); 19 developed campgrounds;

more than 600 mi of stocked trout and bass streams for anglers; and abundant wildlife for hunters. The forest has 72 species of fish, 374 vertebrate wildlife species, and 1,500 species of plants. There are three "pioneer zones"—Seneca Creek, with 11,000 acres; Hopeville Gorge, with 4,500 acres; and Smoke Hole, with 5,800 acres—chiefly under MNF administration for semiprimitive, nonmotorized recreational environments.

Under the Multiple Use–Sustained Yield Act of 1960, the US Forest Service (USFS) has equal responsibilities for the appropriate use of such basic resources as wood, water, wildlife, historic values, and recreation. In 1996 approximately 25 million board ft of saw timber were harvested. Recently the MNF distributed $1,328,017 to 10 counties and to the Department of Highways from receipts generated by timber sales, mineral leases, grazing permits, land-use permits, and recreation user fees. By congressional order, about 30 percent of this fund can be used only for schools and roads. Other funding to counties comes from the "payment in lieu of taxes" (PILT) program established by Congress in 1976. These funds, in the amount of $627,751, may be used by county commissioners for government purposes.

Perhaps less emphasized are other renewable resources provided by the MNF. There are approximately 54 grazing allotments for sheep and cattle in 6,100 acres, and assigned areas for firewood harvesting. The public may harvest berries (strawberries, blackberries, elderberries, blueberries, and serviceberries); nuts (walnuts, butternuts, and filberts); grapes; mushrooms; ramps and wild onions; and herbs for folk medicine at no charge.

In a recent survey the MNF headquarters office in Elkins reported that more than 2.3 million people use the MNF annually. Their activities in order of preference were camping, motoring, hunting, fishing, hiking and walking, picnicking, swimming, and "viewing outstanding scenery."

Most of the recreational areas charge nominal user fees, and a license is required for hunting or fishing. The revenue is used to improve game and fish habitat and for trout stocking.

Hikers will immediately notice that many trails in the MNF are in need of maintenance. Rangers have stated that a reduction in funds and limited staff are the reasons. For a period in the late 1970s the Youth Conservation Corps (YCC), the Young Adults Conservation Corps (YACC), and the Student Conservation Program (SCP) assisted in trail maintenance, but with federal cuts the YACC was eliminated, the YCC severely reduced, and some other services reduced. The budget allowance for the Senior Citizen's Program is for 71 full-time employees. Their work is mainly at recreation areas. Because of the reductions in paid staff, the MNF is increasing its dependence on volunteers. Adopt-A-Trail agreements were signed for volunteers. Examples of volunteerism are the work by the West Virginia Scenic Trail Association on the *Allegheny Trail* and the "adoption" of trails and footbridges for maintenance by the West Virginia Sierra Club and other organizations.

If you are planning to visit any of the four wilderness areas in the forest be aware of the following information: Wilderness areas have low maintenance; they are rough, not blazed or signed. Facilities are not provided unless to protect the resources; horse use is discouraged, and no motorized or wheeled equipment is allowed. Camp stoves are strongly encouraged, but use only dead and down wood for a campfire. Make an effort to camp 150 ft away from streams and trails; leave-no-trace backcountry ethics is the way of life. Getting lost is a real possibility. Plan to have a topo map, compass, or hike with someone familiar with the area.

INFORMATION: Contact the district offices (listed at the beginning of each section) or the main office. The MNF main office is on Sycamore Street near the main entrance to Davis-Elkins College. Its address is PO Box 1548, Elkins, WV 26241; 304-636-1800. The MNF publishes a newsletter titled *Monongahela National Forest*; it is recommended that hikers ask to be placed on the mailing list.

SECTION 1: CHEAT RANGER DISTRICT

There are 126,890 acres in the Cheat Ranger District. The largest and most central acreage is in Tucker County, and the most southern section is in Randolph County. In the northeast corner small tracts are in Preston County, with one tract adjoining Garrett County, MD. A small acreage also exists in Barbour County. The district is the most northern of the six districts and is also the oldest. Its major section on the E boundary is between Blackwater Falls State Park and Canaan Valley State Park W of WV-32. On the S side the boundary is N of US-33 from Wymer to the Stuart Recreation Area. The W side is more irregular, with a boundary along Shavers Fork River, Cheat Mtn, and Laurel Mtn. On irregular N lines it follows Limestone Mtn, the Preston County line, and Stemple Ridge. River drainage is N, with major flows from Shavers Fork and Dry Fort converging at Parsons to form the Cheat.

The district has two special management areas: the 4,700-acre Fernow Experimental Forest (described here), and the 20,000-acre Otter Creek

Otter Creek Trail at Dry Fork footbridge.

Wilderness (described later in the chapter). Management of the Fernow Experimental Forest is for research in timber harvesting and regeneration practices, water quality and quantity studies, aquatic habitat studies, and bird and small mammal research. Several roads through the experimental forest are open year-round and provide opportunities to bird-watch, identify wildflowers, picnic, and hunt. (For hunting information call 304-558-2771, Department of Natural Resources in Charleston.) Camping is not permitted. There is only one trail, the 0.25-mi *Zero Grade Trail*, which takes visitors through several harvested areas and explains the reasoning behind each method. It is accessible to people with disabilities. Access is from downtown Parsons off US-219/WV-72 on Fernow Loop Road (FR-701) for 5.6 mi to a parking area at *Big Springs Gap Trail.* For more information on Fernow Experimental Forest contact Information Services, Timber and Watershed Laboratory, Nursery Bottom, Parsons, WV 26287; 304-478-2000.

The district has more than 150 mi of hiking trails; the four longest are the *Allegheny Trail* (26.0 mi; see chapter 11), the *Otter Creek Trail* (10.9 mi), the *Shavers Mtn Trail* (10.0 mi), and the 10.2-mi *Blackwater Canyon Railroad Grade Trail.* The 233 mi of forest roads also provide some excellent trail connections, hiking circuits, easier treadway, and scenic routes. The Otter Creek Wilderness is the district's major hiking attraction. Other hiking areas are Canaan Mtn Backcountry, Pheasant Mtn, and Horseshoe Run. All trails, except those in the Wilderness, are marked with blue plastic diamonds and receive light brushing every 1–3 years; heavy maintenance (brushing, widening, tread improvement) is done as funding is available. Trail usage is rare on some of the most remote trails. Vandals and bears may have destroyed some of the trail signs.

Wildlife in the district includes 51 species of mammals, such as deer, bear, wildcat, red and gray squirrel, raccoon, beaver, muskrat, and chipmunk. There are 31 species of amphibians and 21 species of reptiles. Among the reptiles are the copperhead and the timber rattler. An endangered mammal, the Indiana bat (*Myotis sodalis*), and a less endangered species, the Virginia big-eared bat (*Plecotus townsendii virginianus*), are protected in the Shavers Lick area. For anglers a number of streams are stocked with rainbow, golden rainbow, and speckled trout. More than 130 species of nesting birds may be found in the district. Flora is widely varied (a remarkable 1,100 species) because of the deep, shady valleys, bogs, open fields, and high mtns with their northern evergreens and hardwoods.

There are three recreational areas with campgrounds: Bear Heaven, near the S entrance of Otter Creek Wilderness Area; Stuart, E of Elkins on FR-91; and Horseshoe, E of Saint George on CO-7. There are also two picnic areas that have lookout towers: Bickle Knob, on FR-91, has an observation platform on top of a shortened fire lookout tower; and Olson tower, on FR-717 off US-219 between Parsons and Thomas, without a platform. (Both towers are to be climbed at your own risk.) The district's third picnic area, Alpena Gap, at the top of Shavers Mtn on US-33, is now a memorial site to

Franklin D. Roosevelt's CCC. The pavilion formerly on the site is now at Stuart Recreation Area.

ADDRESS AND ACCESS: District Ranger, Cheat Ranger District, PO Box 368, Parsons, WV 26287; 304-478-3251. In downtown Parsons go E on US-219/WV-72 across the Dry Fork bridge and turn R at the sign.

MAPS: Numbers 1–5

CANAAN MOUNTAIN AREA (Tucker County)

Canaan Mtn is a high E-W plateau, ranging from 3,000 ft to 4,000 ft in elev between Blackwater Falls State Park and the Blackwater River on the N to Mozark Mtn and Canaan Valley State Park on the S. The Canaan Loop Rd (FS-13) connects WV-32 on the E to Blackwater State Park on the W. Its passage from the Blackwater Falls State Park for 6.6 mi may be impassable for passenger cars. High water on Lindy Run also may prevent fording. Passage is easy for passenger cars from WV-32 for 9.3 mi on a gravel road to a gravel parking area. It is another 0.5 mi on a rocky and less passable road to the crest of the mtn and the W terminus of the *Plantation Trail*. The improved gravel section of the road was made possible by the Amoco Production Co. of Texas, when it spent approximately $750,000 on the road in its unsuccessful $2 million search for oil. The *Allegheny Trail* runs N-S (jointly with the *Davis Trail* for a few mi) through the area, as does the Columbia Gas Co. pipeline. The most prominent trail in the area, the *Plantation Trail*, runs E-W. Because the area is rocky and frequently wet, tent sites are scarce; there are two shelters.

Before 1885 Canaan Mtn had a red spruce forest of unbelievable grandeur; then the West Virginia Central Railroad and the lumber companies arrived. Two major companies were the West Virginia Pulp and Paper Co. (Wesvaco) in 1892 and the Babcock Lumber and Boom Co. in 1907. The town of Davis (named after railroad and coal entrepreneur and US senator [1871–83] Henry Gassaway Davis) suddenly became a boomtown of more than 3,000 inhabitants. Most of them worked at the sawmills, pulp mills, and tanneries, and on the timber railroads. For 38 years Davis was an example of the timber feast that depleted the state's virgin hardwood and conifer forests. One company in Davis manufactured more than 1.5 billion board ft of spruce, hemlock, and hardwoods. After 1920, however, the population fell sharply.

Nearly 200 mi of timber railroads were like tentacles out of Davis to Canaan Mtn, Canaan Valley, Cabin Mtn, and Dobbin Ridge. With the competitive challenge of the timber industry came also the railroads and the competition to run the best trains. Safety records were usually good, but a single curve was the nemesis of a speeding train at least once. On Feb 5, 1924, as described in Homer Fansler's *History of Tucker County* (1962), Fred Viering of the Babcock Lumber and Boom Co. went on an inspection trip over Cabin Mtn (E of Canaan Mtn). In order to be back in Davis at the time he had promised his wife, he told his fireman, George Kline, to speed up the train. Kline said it was not safe, but Viering said, "I'll eat my supper with the old woman in Davis tonight or eat it with the devil in hell." Kline and two workers safely jumped from the speeding train before it left the track, overturned, and killed Viering in a Blackwater swamp.

ACCESS: Northwest entrance is on FR-13 at the end of the paved road near the ski warming hut in Blackwater Falls State Park. The E entrance is on WV-32, 3.1 mi S of Davis at Canaan Heights at the Wilderness Rd sign on FR-13.

SUPPORT FACILITIES: The nearest campground is Blackwater Falls State Park in Davis (see chapter 6). Davis also has restaurants, grocery store, motel, hardware store, service station, and bank.

Plantation Trail (8.4 mi; USFS #101)

CONNECTING TRAILS:
>
> *Fire Trail #3* (0.8 mi; USFS #104)
> *Allegheny Trail* (*Davis Trail*) (5.2 mi; USFS #701)
> *Fire Trail #6* (1.1 mi; USFS #108)
> *Lindy Run Trail* (2.8 mi; USFS #109)
> *Railroad Grade Trail* (3.1 mi; USFS #110)

TOTAL LENGTH: 21.4 mi

DIFFICULTY: moderate

FEATURES: red spruce plantation, forest history

TRAILHEADS AND DETAILS: The *Plantation Trail* is named for a 2,462-acre plantation of red spruce (*Picea rubens*) in Canaan Mtn Spruce Plantation. It is the result of work accomplished by the Civilian Conservation Corps (CCC) in the 1930s to reforest one of the best spruce forests that had ever existed. In addition, the CCC planted a few stands of Norway spruce (*Picea abies*) and red pine (*Pinus resinosa*). They also built fire lanes and a number of cement dams called "water points" or "pump changes" for watering the seedlings and for foot-trail firefighters. The connecting trails to the *Plantation Trail* may be used for loops between the trail and Canaan Loop Rd.

The E (3,580 ft) trailhead is 2.0 mi S on WV-32 from the Blackwater River bridge in Davis. Park beside the road. Enter a young forest of maple, birch, and spruce. White snakeroot (*Eupatorium rugosum*) borders the trail in the summertime. Descend to and cross Devil's Run at 0.5 mi. Ascend gradually in rocky areas with spruce, mtn laurel, hemlock, and rhododendron. Ferns are prevalent. Reach the jct, L, with *Fire Trail #3* at 1.1 mi. (*Fire Trail #3* ascends through the spruce plantation, generally straight but rocky with dense undergrowth and dense stands of spruce. Sections of treadway are usually wet, with carpets of ferns and mosses. The S trailhead is on FR-13, 1.4 mi from WV-32.)

Continue on the *Plantation Trail*, cross a drain with a small dam built by the CCC, and reach the Columbia Gas Co. pipeline at 1.8 mi. Reach another small dam at 2.3 mi at Engine Run. At 2.7 mi reach the jct with the *Allegheny Trail* (formerly *Davis Trail*, USFS #107, was on this route). A six-person Adirondack shelter is here (constructed by the Youth Conservation Corps in 1981) and a dependable spring is nearby, W, on the *Plantation Trail*.

(The *Allegheny Trail* crosses here, 1.6 mi from its N beginning at the horse stables in Blackwater Falls State Park, and 1.2 mi S to the Canaan Loop Rd [2.7 mi W from WV-32]. It follows W on the Canaan Loop Rd for another 1.2 mi before it turns L and S toward its entry into Canaan Valley State Park at 5.2 mi. The blaze is yellow, but a diamond blue marker indicates the trail is also a cross-country ski trail for the first 6.3 mi. See chapter 11.)

The *Plantation Trail* continues ahead on a level contour with a number of drains from the L. Sections of the trail are rocky. Yellow blazes are seen for the former or alternate route of the *Allegheny Trail*. At 3.8 mi is the jct L with the *Fire Trail #6*. This is the W end of the Canaan Mtn Red Spruce Plantation. The trail continues under this name, and so do numerous stands of spruce.

(*Fire Trail #6* goes 1.1 mi S to Canaan Loop Rd, 4.2 mi W from WV-32. Pass through rhododendron, yellow birch, spruce, mtn ash, and mtn laurel. Hay-scented fern and club moss are part of the ground cover. At 0.7 mi cross a fire lane and follow a wide trail that had been damaged by 4WD vehicles until the USFS recently installed a "tank trap," a rock barrier, at the Canaan Loop Rd entrance near the north fork of Red Run.)

Ahead on the *Plantation Trail*, cross a small drain, Shays Run, with a miniature cement dam at 4.3 mi. Ascend a rocky area into a hardwood stand and level off in spruce at 4.6 mi. (Yellow blazes on the trail are from the former route of the *Allegheny Trail*.) At 5.1 mi reach a crossing with the *Lindy Run Trail*.

(It is 1.5 mi N on the *Lindy Run Trail* to Canaan Loop Rd. From there to Blackwater Falls State Park it is 1.2 mi. Going S on the trail it is 1.3 mi to Canaan Loop Rd, 4.5 mi W from WV-32. The N section descends gradually on the R side of Lindy Run and crosses the stream at 0.8 mi. The most frequent species of trees are hemlock, maple, cherry, and yellow birch. Rhododendron arbors are common. On the S section ascend slightly on a wide but rough treadway. Thick patches of sphagnum, ferns, and mtn laurel occur on a level area at 0.9 mi. Descend gently through a wet area and reach Canaan Loop Rd at 1.3 mi.)

Continue W on the *Plantation Trail* and immediately cross Lindy Run. Follow the trail on a level contour through an increase of hardwoods and a decrease of conifers. Reach the N-S jct with the *Railroad Grade Trail* in a flat area at 6.3 mi.

(On the N side of the *Plantation Trail*, the *Railroad Grade Trail* descends gently for 1.4 mi to the Canaan Loop Rd, 2.6 mi S of Blackwater Falls State Park. There are obvious signs of the old RR grade along the way. On the S side the *Railroad Grade Trail* also descends gently, but is in a more deciduous forest. At 0.6 mi reach a stream crossing and a six-person Adirondack shelter with a picnic table and grill. This exceptionally attractive area is in a cove once spanned by a 0.1-mi RR trestle. At 1.4 mi cross a small drain and continue descent. Reach the Canaan Loop Rd at 1.7 mi, 6.5 mi W from WV-32.)

The *Plantation Trail* crosses the *Railroad Grade Trail* obliquely, SW. Trail signs here are frequently chewed by the bears. Follow a level, mossy, and occasionally wet treadway. A hardwood forest is more dominant, and there are thickets of mtn laurel, usually blooming in late June. Pass through a boggy area at 8.0 mi and reach the Canaan Loop Rd at 8.4 mi (3,312 ft), only 268 ft elev difference from the beginning. Here is the W terminus, 6.6 mi R to the Blackwater Falls State Park and 9.8 mi L to WV-32. Within 65 yd to the L on the road is the trailhead of *Tablerock Overlook Trail* (described below), and 1.2 mi to the R on the road is the trailhead for the *Mountainside Trail*. (*USGS-FS Maps:* Blackwater Falls, Mozark Mtn)

(Nearby are three fire trails that do not connect with other trails in this area and whose main purpose is for fire access. *Fire Trail #1* [0.4 mi; USFS #102] has termini 0.8 mi W on the Canaan Loop Rd from its jct with WV-

32 and 0.4 mi N on WV-32. *Fire Trail #2* [0.4 mi; USFS #103] has termini 0.8 mi W on the Canaan Loop Rd from its jct with WV-32 and 1.0 mi N on WV-32. *Flag Run Trail* [1.0 mi; USFS #106] has termini 1.9 mi W on Canaan Loop Rd from its jct with WV-32 and 1.7 mi S on WV-32. The latter trail was relocated in 1984 and is now entirely on national-forest land.)

Tablerock Overlook Trail (1.1 mi; USFS #113)

LENGTH: 2.2 mi round-trip

DIFFICULTY: easy

FEATURE: Tablerock Overlook

TRAILHEAD AND DETAILS: From WV-32, drive W on Canaan Loop Rd for 9.8 mi to the trailhead on the L (65 yd before you reach the W end of the *Plantation Trail*). Ascend slightly and follow a rocky tread in a basic hardwood forest. Pass through a damp area arbored by rhododendron at 0.9 mi for the final 0.2 mi. From the magnificent overlook you can see the Red Run Valley and Mozark Mtn Range SE and Shavers Mtn and the Otter Creek Wilderness SW. The naturally sculpted rocks have indentations and fissures. Wintergreen and huckleberry hold tight to each other. Backtrack. (*USGS-FS Map*: Mozark Mtn)

Mountainside Trail (4.1 mi; USFS #114); Bennett Rock Trail (0.7 mi; USFS #112)

LENGTH: 9.6 mi round-trip

DIFFICULTY: moderate to strenuous

FEATURE: wildlife

TRAILHEAD AND DETAILS: This is a longer trail than 4.1 mi because you will have to backtrack or hike out to Canaan Loop Rd for 2.5 mi on FR-244-A and FR-244, both of which are gated. With a vehicle shuttle on the Canaan Loop Rd, 3.1 mi E from the trailhead, your hiking mileage will be 6.6 mi. To reach the trailhead from WV-32, drive 11.0 mi on Canaan Loop Rd to *Mountainside Trail*, L. (It is 5.4 mi on the Canaan Loop Rd N to Blackwater Falls State Park on a rugged road frequently unsuitable for passenger cars.) Begin on an old road that soon becomes an old RR grade. Cross a small stream, Laurel Run, at 0.4 mi. Cross it again four times and leave the stream area L at 0.7 mi. Descend gradually through a hardwood forest of yellow birch, cherry, and maple. Vistas of the Dry River Valley are best when the leaves are off the trees. Pass L of an old logging road at 1.7 mi. At 2.8 mi reach a jct with *Bennett Rock Trail*.

(The *Bennett Rock Trail*, R, descends on an exceptionally steep grade, dropping more than 1,000 ft in elev in 0.7 mi to WV-72, 2.3 mi S of the Blackwater River bridge in Hendricks. Entrance here is R of large boulders in a forest of hemlock, rhododendron, maple, and beech. The trail has been listed by the USFS as abandoned for the past few years, but soon it will be blazed and reinstated.)

On the *Mountainside Trail* curve around the Canaan Mtn arm at 3.1 mi and reach the end of the trail at 4.1 mi and the beginning of FR-244-A. Backtrack or continue ahead to the Canaan Loop Rd as described above. (*USGS-FS Map*: Mozark Mtn)

Pointy Knob Trail (USFS #139)

LENGTH: 4.2 mi

DIFFICULTY: moderate

FEATURE: plant life

TRAILHEAD AND DETAILS: The E terminus is 4.1 mi from WV-32 on the Canaan Loop Rd, and the W terminus is 1.9 mi farther on the Canaan Loop Rd. At the E terminus begin on a jeep road through a meadow, enter a forest of red spruce, cross a small drain at 0.1 mi, and turn L off the jeep road. Ascend gradually on a ridge with rocky treadway through dense areas of mtn laurel, rhododendron, and conifers. Sections of the trail are overgrown, but the district office has promised to maintain them in the future. At 2.2 mi reach White Raven Rocks. (An overgrown, faint, blue-blazed spur trail goes S toward *Pointy Knob Trail* to private property.) Turn NW and begin a descent to the headwaters of the south fork of Red Run. Rock-hop the stream a number of times and follow a section of an old RR grade, with beds of ferns and running cedar and a canopy of birch and hemlock. At 4.2 mi cross both the S and N forks at the confluence of Red Run and up an embankment of Canaan Loop Rd. A hike R to the point of origin is 6.2 mi for a loop. (*USGS-FS Maps*: Blackwater Falls, Mozark Mtn)

BACKBONE MOUNTAIN AREA (Tucker County)

Although there is no campground at the Olson Recreation Area (3,736 ft) on Backbone Mtn, there are picnic tables, grills, vault toilets, and a hand water pump. The 130-step Olson Lookout Tower provides spectacular views of the entire Cheat district. This magnificent scenery is on any hiker's "must see" list. Views W are of the Cheat and Dry Fork basins and the Laurel Mtn Range. North is the extension of Backbone Mtn into Maryland. To the E are

Canaan Mtn and Cabin Mtn, and to the S, McGowan Mtn and the Otter Creek Wilderness Area. The tower was dedicated in 1963 to Ernest B. Olson for his 28 years of service in forest fire control.

Canyon Rim Trail (3.0 mi; USFS #117); Fansler Trail (1.0 mi; USFS #118)

LENGTH: 5.0 mi round-trip, combined
DIFFICULTY: easy
FEATURES: scenic, wildlife

TRAILHEADS AND DETAILS: The E terminus is at the scenic area of Big Run on the Canyon Rim Rd (FS-18), 0.2 mi E of the W terminus of the *Boundary Trail* and 1.9 mi SE of US-219. The W terminus is 0.1 mi N of the Olson Lookout Tower. Trail elev range is from 3,100 ft to 3,600 ft. If hiking from the E terminus, park at the side road on Canyon Rim Rd. Descend into a hemlock grove to rock-hop the cascading Big Run. Ascend, cross a small fork of Big Run, and follow an old RR grade. A decorative border of rocks is a reminder of the CCC's trail work. Pass through rhododendron, spruce, hemlock, mtn laurel, maple, birch, and red pine. The treadway is mossy, grassy, and wet in the springtime. Cinnamon and hay-scented ferns and club moss are prominent. A number of natural vistas of the Blackwater Canyon follow at 0.5 mi, 0.9 mi, 1.0 mi, 1.2 mi, and 1.4 mi. Cross a small drain at 0.5 mi where deer are likely to be seen. At 1.7 mi pass a jct L with the abandoned *Flat Rock Trail*. Curve R and slightly ascend, level off, and reach the W terminus at 3.0 mi on the Olson Lookout Tower Rd (FR-717). To the L it is 0.1 mi to the Olson Recreation Area. To the R it is 1.6 mi on the road to a jct with Canyon Rim Rd (FR-18) and another 0.3 mi to US-219.

The *Fansler Trail* begins on the S side of the picnic area by entering a wall of naturally sculpted rocks and follows the blue blazes. The trail is arbored with hemlock, oak, spruce, and maple. Mtn laurel and rhododendron form a border in sections, and club moss and ferns form part of the ground cover. Follow an even grade on the Backbone Mtn ridge for 0.7 mi before descending to a dead end at FR-717 at 1.0 mi. Backtrack. (*USGS-FS Map:* Mozark Mtn)

Boundary Trail (USFS #116)

LENGTH: 3.5 mi
DIFFICULTY: easy
FEATURE: old strip mines

TRAILHEAD AND DETAILS: In the town of Thomas turn off WV-32 (near the post office) on Douglas Rd (CO-27) and drive 2.4 mi to the MNF boundary line. Here the road becomes graveled Canyon Rim Rd (FR-18) and also the route of the *Allegheny Trail*. On the R of the road is the E terminus of the *Boundary Trail*. (The red blazes are MNF boundary marks.) Ascend and descend gradually in a hardwood forest to a strip mine area at 1.3 mi. Cross Finley Run at 1.4 mi. Scotch pines are along the boundary. Climb a strip mine headwall in a spruce stand and descend first to cross Tub Run Rd and then Tub Run at 2.2 mi. Enter another strip mine area and reforestation area of red pine. Sections of the trail through here are overgrown and difficult to follow. At 3.0 mi enter a boggy section, go through rhododendron and yellow birch, and reach the W terminus on Canyon Rim Rd at 3.5 mi. To the R it is 1.7 mi to US-219, 6.3 mi W of Thomas. To the L it is 0.2 mi to the jct with the *Canyon Rim Trail*. Also to the L an 8.7-mi loop can be made by following the scenic Canyon Rim Rd (FR-18) for 5.2 mi to the point of origin. (*USGS-FS Map*: Mozark Mtn)

Limerock Trail (*USFS #142*)

LENGTH: 4.0 mi
DIFFICULTY: moderate
FEATURES: remote, scenic, RR history

TRAILHEAD AND DETAILS: The NE trailhead is on Canyon Rim Rd (FR-18), 0.2 mi W of the Tub Run crossing and 5.6 mi from WV-32 in Thomas on the Douglas Rd (CO-27). At a narrow parking area descend between a cherry tree and a birch tree on an unmarked, unblazed path through spruce and hemlock. In less than 0.1 mi turn R to follow an old RR grade. (On the 1968 Mozark Mtn quad map this entrance is listed as trail #144. Trail #143 is in the wrong place; it should be trail #142.) This sylvan route through the gorge is rich in RR history. Where once you would have heard logging or, more recently, the Western Maryland Railroad trains on the wall of Blackwater Canyon, you now hear only the sound of Blackwater River and the cascading tributaries. At 0.7 mi go R of the old RR grade fork, and at 1.3 mi reach the E end of a vanished RR trestle that spanned the thundering Big Run. Rock-hop Big Run, whose waters can be impassable in wet seasons. At 1.4 mi rejoin the RR grade. Black cohosh, ferns, and mosses thrive in this damp, shady area. At 2.2 mi leave the Big Run Canyon and return to the N wall of the Blackwater River. Reach a jct with the abandoned *Flat Rock Trail* at 3.7 mi. Rock-hop Flat Rock Run and leave the old RR grade to connect with the *Blackwater Canyon Railroad Grade Trail*, R and L at 4.0 mi. Backtrack, or hike out R 2.1 mi on the *Blackwater Canyon Railroad Grade Trail* to Hendricks and WV-72 (see below). A switch box, signal light, and the beginning of double tracks are at 1.4 mi. Ironweed, soapwort, joe-pye weed, jewelweed, and virgin's-bower are thick on this scenic route by the Blackwater River. (*USGS-FS Maps*: Mozark Mtn, Parsons)

Blackwater Canyon Railroad Grade Trail (USFS #115)

LENGTH: 10.2 mi

DIFFICULTY: moderate to strenuous

FEATURES: scenic, historic, wildlife

TRAILHEAD AND DETAILS: This trail is a section of the former Western Maryland Railroad that passed through the town of Parsons in its ascent to the town of Thomas and beyond. Its elevation change is 1,290 ft, and it connects with the *Allegheny Trail* and *Limerock Trail* in the process. The N trailhead is off WV-32 S in the town of Thomas, about a block N of the post office. Look for a USFS gate with a brown-and-white sign: Foot Travel Welcome. Hike S and after 300 yd cross the North Fork of the Blackwater River on an old RR bridge. Cross a natural-gas line at 0.6 mi, then pass the N and S switch of the Coketon RR spur. Cross SR-27 at 0.9 mi. (The *Allegheny Trail* follows SR-27 from Thomas and onto USFS-18 S of the community of Douglas.) Pass the Douglas Highwall #2 Project (a reclamation project to remove acid from strip mine drainage into the Blackwater River). At 2.0 mi cross Long Run on a plate girder bridge.

From here the rugged remoteness is noticeable as the RR drops into the steep-walled canyon. Sounds of cascades can be heard and sometimes seen in the wintertime. Tall oak, maple, cherry, yellow poplar, hemlock, and rhododendron are dominant. The area is a black bear habitat. Some other animals here are deer, squirrel, birds, and snakes. Cross bridges with spectacular scenery of cascades over Tub Run at 4.8 mi, Big Run at 5.9 mi, and Flat Rock Run at 7.4 mi.

Meet *Limerock Trail* R, at 7.6 mi (see *Limerock Trail* above). (It is reported that several rattlesnake dens exist in this area of the canyon.) Cross Hickory Lick Run at 8.4 mi; at 9.0 mi are former RR double tracks. Such wildflowers as soapwort and jewelweed are common along the route. Reach the crossing of WV-72 in Hendricks at 9.7 mi. From here you will pass through residential areas of Hendricks and Hambleton to parallel Dry Fork of the Cheat River. Cross Roaring Run (near the US-219 and WV-72 jct), and after 0.1 mi connect with an access road to Cheat Ranger District Office. You can park near the gate, but do not block its entrance. (A vehicle return to Thomas on US-219 is about 12.0 mi.) (*USGS-FS Maps*: Davis, Lead Mine, Mozark Mtn, Parsons)

PHEASANT MOUNTAIN AREA (Tucker County)
Pheasant Mtn Trail (4.7 mi; USGS #120)
> CONNECTING TRAILS:
>> *Shingletree Trail* (4.5 mi; USFS #121)
>> *Clover Trail* (1.9 mi); USFS #124)
> TOTAL LENGTH: 11.1 mi
> DIFFICULTY: moderate
> FEATURES: wildlife, RR history

TRAILHEADS AND DETAILS: In the town of Parsons at the jct of WV-72 and US-219, drive N for 0.4 mi on WV-72 to Mt Zion Rd (CO-17) and turn L. After 1.7 mi reach the ridge crest and park on the R. The *Pheasant Mtn Trail* ascends L and curves S of the ridge through hardwoods of black birch, hickory, oak, maple, and sassafras. Trail bikes and ATVs use the entire trail; except for some erosion the treadway is smooth. At 1.1 mi reach the jct with *Shingletree Trail*.

(The *Shingletree Trail* crosses here with 3.1 mi L to US-219 and 3.6 mi SW of Parsons, and 1.4 mi R to Clover Run Rd [CO-21] and 3.7 mi W of Parsons. If hiking the L section, follow the old RR grade for 0.6 mi to a saddle between two ridges. Former RR trestles were at 0.8 mi and 1.4 mi. At 1.5 mi leave the old RR grade from Sugarcamp Run drainage and turn S on an old wagon road. At 1.7 mi ignore the old trail on the R that shows on the Parsons topo map as *Shingletree Trail*. Instead continue ahead, pass the abandoned *Hawk's Run Trail* on the L, and take the R trail. Follow around a knoll, weave in and out of coves, some with small drainage, and descend through long sections of rhododendron. At 3.0 mi cross Shingletree Run and follow an old woods road arbored with wild roses and elderberry out to US-219 in the community of Moore. If taking the R [N] section of the *Shingletree Trail*, begin on an old RR grade but after 0.1 mi leave the grade and bear L. The first of four switchbacks begins at 0.9 mi; exit under a stand of white pine and hemlock by a branch at Clover Run Rd at 1.4 mi.)

Continue ahead on the *Pheasant Mtn Trail*. At 1.7 mi is a small wet-weather water hole. Bear and deer tracks have been seen here and elsewhere along the ridge. At 3.0 mi is a jct R with *Clover Trail*.

(The 1.9-mi *Clover Trail* is in a historic area. For many years until 1930 a RR grade served to haul timber from Clover Run Valley over Pheasant Mtn [for 500 ft in elev] and down to Moore for the D. D. Brown Lumber Company. The train would pull up to one switchback and back up the next until reaching the top. Because of a timber clearcut in 1990–91, parts of the original trail were moved off the route to FR-937. For a few years the clearcut will provide scenic vistas across the Clover drainage toward Mt Zion.

Descend 0.1 mi among hardwoods on the old RR grade to intersect and follow L on FR-937. [On the forest road R, it descends about 2.4 mi to near the N trailhead of *Shingletree Trail* on Clover Run Rd.] After 1.0 mi leave the road and switchback R at a log landing; then another switchback L. At 1.4 mi leave the old RR grade area for a narrow path on two switchbacks to cross a small stream near a parking area at CO-21, Clover Run Rd. From here it is 4.3 mi E (R) on the Clover Run Rd and Mt Zion Rd to Parsons.)

Ahead on the *Pheasant Mtn Trail* reach a jct L with the former (and closed) *Ridge Trail* at 3.1 mi. The area has mainly oak, maple, dogwood, beech, and black birch. At 3.5 mi enter Mail Route Hollow. (There is space for campsites here within the USFS boundary.) Vehicular entrance is R on a rough road through private property. After 90 yd on the old road, turn L at a white oak tree. Cross a stream, ascend through a hardwood forest of oaks, black birch, and maple. Wildflowers and ferns are in watershed ravines. At 3.9 mi the trail joins a logging road cul-de-sac in a clearcut. It follows the road on an easy descent to a gate, then reaches Valley Fork Rd (CO-23) at 4.7 mi. There is roadside parking here. To the R it is 0.3 mi to Clover Run Rd (CO-21) where a R turn (E) takes you 5.7 mi back to Parsons via Mt Zion Rd. (*USGS-FS Maps*: Montrose, Parsons)

OTTER CREEK WILDERNESS AREA
(Randolph and Tucker Counties)

The Otter Creek Wilderness is a 20,000-acre oval-shaped forest of Allegheny hardwoods, red spruce, hemlock, and rhododendron thickets. Ferns, wildflowers, and mosses cover its floor. There are rock outcrops on the canyon walls and plateaus on the ridge tops. In its center flows cascading Otter Creek, fed by tributaries whose headwaters are high in Shavers Mtn and Green Mtn on the E rim and McGowan Mtn on the W and N. Elevation ranges from 1,829 ft to 3,811 ft.

The wilderness is a haven for wildlife. There are 19 species of amphibians, which include the Cheat Mtn salamander and gray tree frog. Among the 12 species of reptiles are the northern redbelly snake and two poisonous snakes—the copperhead and timber rattler. At least 42 species of mammals have been identified; the most frequently seen are bear, deer, squirrel, raccoon, woodchuck, rabbit, fox, and chipmunk. Mink and beaver are in the creeks, but the river otter (*Lutra canadensis*), for which the creek was named by the early settlers, is conspicuously missing. Blue crayfish are frequently seen along damp trails. Nesting birds number 76 species, which include 6 species of owl and the black-billed cuckoo, grouse, and wild turkey. Neither the hummingbird nor the mockingbird lives here.

Designated by Congress in 1975 as a place of solitude and personal challenge, the trails are not signed or blazed. Hunting, fishing, hiking, and camping are allowed but the use of all motorized vehicles or equipment is prohibited. Although permits are no longer required, it is requested by the USFS that you register at the access points. The maximum number allowed per party is 10. Pack out all refuse and treat or boil all drinking water. For hunting and fishing it is necessary to check the special regulations for the Otter Creek area. In keeping with the wilderness character, the area is primitive, wild, and rugged. You are encouraged to carry topo maps and a compass, and follow "no-trace" campsite usage. Safety is an essential consideration because the weather can change suddenly; flash floods and snowstorms are particular hazards.

ACCESS: From the S at the jct of US-33 and FR-91 at Alpena Gap drive N on Stuart Memorial Dr (FR-91) 1.3 mi and FR-303 for 0.6 mi to a parking area. From the N on US-219 and WV-72 in downtown Parsons at a side street, S, follow the sign for Fernow Experimental Forest for 5.6 mi to Big Springs Gap. Another access is off WV-72 at a parking lot 2.0 mi S of Hendricks. (This access has a high footbridge over Dry Fork at the S side of Otter Creek.) Other accesses are described with trail narratives.

SUPPORT FACILITIES: Bear Haven Recreation Area has 7 camping units, picnic area, hand water pump, and vault toilets (no hookups). Access is 2.8 mi on Stuart Memorial Dr (FR-91) from US-33 in Alpena Gap. Open Apr 1–Nov 30. Stuart Recreation Area has 27 camping units, 51 picnic units, spigot water, and vault toilets, but no hookups. Open May 18–Sept 9. Access is from Alpena Gap 2.6 mi W on US-33, R on Old US-33 (CO-33/8) for 3.7 mi, and R on CO-6 for 0.4 mi. A commercial campground, Alpine Shores, is 2.0 mi W on US-33 from Alpena Gap. It has full service, recreational facilities, restaurant, and hot showers. It is open Apr 15–Nov 15 (304-636-4311). Shopping malls, banks, motels, service stations, and restaurants are in Elkins, 10.0 mi W on US-33 from Alpena Gap.

Otter Creek Trail (10.9 mi; USFS #131)

CONNECTING TRAILS:

> Hedrick Camp Trail (1.0 mi; USFS #165)
> Yellow Creek Trail (1.3 mi; USFS #135)
> Mylius Trail (2.4 mi; USFS #128)
> Moore Run Trail (4.1 mi; USFS #138)
> Possession Camp Trail (3.2 mi; USFS #158)
> Green Mtn Trail (4.0 mi; USFS #130)
> Big Springs Gap Trail (0.9 mi; USFS #151)

TOTAL LENGTH: 27.8 mi

DIFFICULTY: easy to strenuous

FEATURES: nature study, scenic, history, isolated

TRAILHEADS AND DETAILS: The Otter Creek Trail parallels Otter Creek, fords it three times (3.6 mi, 4.2 mi, and 7.1 mi) for 10.9 mi from its main trailhead at Condon Run in the S to its N terminus at Coal Run. Steadily descending for 1,170 ft in elev, its treadway is on sections of logging RR grades that were abandoned early in the century. Its natural beauty through a wilderness forest of mixed hardwoods and conifers is unsurpassed in the Cheat Ranger District. Always audible and usually in sight, the creek sometimes roars as it cascades over large boulders and sometimes ripples at pools where polished stones rest from nature's tumbling box. A popular trail, it is the trunk line for seven immediate and six other connecting trails.

(From the parking area the first connecting trail, R, is the Hedrick Camp Trail. It goes 0.1 mi through a hemlock and rhododendron grove to Otter Creek where flash floods have washed out the footbridge. Wade across and ascend SE on an abandoned woods road with a gentle contour level on the N side of the stream. Reach the site of the vanished Hedrick logging camp and meet the Shavers Mtn Trail at 1.0 mi.)

From the parking area cross the footbridge over Condon Run, follow a graveled road for 0.2 mi to a registration sign on the Otter Creek Trail. Continue straight on an old RR grade (the road to the R descends to the Otter

Creek Fishing Water Improvement Station, where limestone is ground to neutralize the stream acid). Drainage on the L frequently makes a wet treadway under yellow birch and hemlock. Dense rhododendron is an understory. At 1.0 mi rock-hop Yellow Creek (excellent campsites here), and at 1.1 mi meet the *Yellow Creek Trail,* L.

(The *Yellow Creek Trail* follows an old RR grade W, parallel with Yellow Creek, under hemlock and yellow birch. At 0.7 mi is a jct, R, with *McGowan Mtn Trail.* Rock-hop Yellow Creek at 0.8 mi, and at 1.2 mi reach a saddle and a small open area in the ridge where a sign indicates the Wilderness boundary. Here the 3.0-mi *Baker Sods Trail* forks L and leads to the 4.0-mi *Little Black Fork Trail* and the 1.6-mi *Middle Point Trail.* The *Yellow Creek Trail* proceeds ahead for 0.1 mi to its W terminus with McGowan Mtn Rd [FR-34]. The McGowan Mtn Rd entrance at 6.8 mi in Fernow Experimental Forest is gated to vehicle traffic Apr 15–Aug 15.)

Continue on the *Otter Creek Trail* through a heavy stand of hemlock and red spruce. At 2.2 mi is an excellent grassy campsite area, R. On the L at 2.9 mi is a spring and on the R is a jct with *Mylius Trail.*

(The 2.4-mi *Mylius Trail* crosses Otter Creek, ascends for 0.7 mi to a saddle on Shavers Mtn, crosses *Shavers Mtn Trail,* and descends 835 ft in elev for 1.7 mi to the Kuntzville Rd [FR-162] and Galdwin Rd [CO-12]. See *Shavers Mtn Trail* below.)

On the *Otter Creek Trail* at 3.6 mi cross Otter Creek either by wading or rock-hopping. A sign here warns of the danger of flash flooding and high water in the stream bed. At 4.0 mi intersect with *Moore Run Trail,* L, and *Possession Camp Trail,* R. The *Otter Creek Trail* continues ahead.

(The *Moore Run Trail* immediately crosses Otter Creek to the R of Devils Gulch—a forbidding, impenetrable rhododendron coppice where water splashes from a maw of darkness. Follow the old RR grade around the E slope of the mtn in a gradual ascent through a splendid forest of cherry and maple. Rhododendron is common; ferns and wood shamrocks cover the treadway. Grouse are often seen. At 1.2 mi cross a small stream; pass an old RR timber loading dock, L, at 1.7 mi. At 2.1 mi rock-hop Moore Run in an area of boulders, rhododendron, and hemlock. Ascend steeply to the S and N forks to another RR grade, but turn off the grade at 2.4 mi to skirt the wide glade. Reach a jct with *Turkey Run Trail,* R, at 2.7 mi. [See *Turkey Run Trail* below.] Cross a small tributary at 3.1 mi and enter a soggy open area where thick sphagnum can hide a watery path on the old RR grade. At 3.5 mi reach the end of the bog and pass through a rhododendron thicket to a jct with the *McGowan Mtn Trail*, L at 4.0 mi. [See *McGowan Mtn Trail* below.] Continue for 0.1 mi to a jct with the McGowan Mtn Rd [FR-324]. From here it is 3.9 mi L on the road to the W terminus of *Yellow Creek Trail* and 2.9 mi R to Fernow Loop Rd [FR-701] in the Fernow Experimental Forest.)

(From the jct with the *Otter Creek Trail* and the *Moore Run Trail*, the *Possession Camp Trail* ascends on an old RR grade through a hardwood forest with an understory of rhododendron. At 0.5 mi turn E to cross a stream in a deep cove. Continue on the W slope of the mtn and curve E again at 1.0 mi to parallel the S fork of Possession Camp Run before crossing the stream in another cove. Remains of a stone RR bridge are at 2.1 mi. Birch, beech, maple, and scattered hemlock and spruce tower over rhododendron thickets. Pass through a section of large boulders at 2.6 mi and reach a jct with the *Green Mtn Trail* at 3.2 mi.)

To continue on the *Otter Creek Trail* at the *Moore Run Trail* and the *Possession Camp Trail* jct, go downstream to the six-person Adirondack shelter at the site of an old logging camp at 4.1 mi. From here veer L and wade or rock-hop Otter Creek at 4.2 mi. At 4.4 mi pass a scenic area called Pothole Falls, the highest falls in the river, where powerful whitewater has churned pebbles to carve shafts in the rocks. Forest cover is birch, hemlock, rhododendron, and witch hazel. Rock-hop or wade the mouth of Moore Run at 5.5 mi. Pass near Otter Creek at 5.7 mi and move temporarily away from it; rejoin it at 6.2 mi. Wade across Otter Creek again at 7.1 mi and reach the site of an old logging camp called Camp Two at 7.3 mi. Beyond the camp 0.1 mi on the R is jct with the *Green Mtn Trail*.

(The *Green Mtn Trail* follows an old timber road SE on an exceptionally steep climb for the first 1.2 mi [more than 1,000 ft in elev] to the top of Green Mtn. It joins an old RR grade in a forest of maple and yellow birch and curves E at 1.6 mi. At 2.0 mi reach a jct with another RR grade and turn sharply S. Pass through rhododendron thickets and under yellow birch and cherry. Reach an old logging campsite, Possession Camp, and a jct with *Possession Camp Trail* at 2.7 mi. From here ascend gently E to the ridge crest and turn SE on an easy contour level of 3,600-ft elev. Ferns and moss cover the treadway. Follow S of an open glade and reach a jct with *Shavers Mtn Trail* at 4.0 mi. See description of *Shavers Mtn Trail* below.)

Continue on the *Otter Creek Trail* and cross a drain immediately beyond the jct with the *Green Mtn Trail*. At 7.8 mi reach a rock overhang called Camping Rock, R. The canyon becomes narrow here but widens after 8.3

mi. Hardwoods, hemlock, and rhododendron are mixed. Ferns and black cohosh are frequent. Reach a jct with *Big Springs Gap Trail*, L, at 8.6 mi.

(To hike *Big Springs Gap Trail*, ford the creek, L. Follow an old rocky wagon road up a gulch of Spring Run on whose mountainside remain apple trees from a pioneer's vanished homesite. A wet summer can change the hollow into a rain forest. Tall cinnamon ferns drape the trailside, and large, curling grapevines hang nearby. At the trailhead is the boundary of the Fernow Experimental Forest, a parking area, and a registration stand. From here it is 5.6 mi on the Fernow Loop Rd [FR-701] to US-219/WV-72 in Parsons. Also at the trailhead is a convenient alternate loop back to Otter Creek. If taking this route, go L on the road and ascend to a gated road jct on the L at 0.5 mi to the N terminus of the 5.0-mi *Turkey Run Trail*. The *Turkey Run Trail* joins the *Moore Run Trail* for another 2.8 mi back to the *Otter Creek Trail*.)

The *Otter Creek Trail* now begins a curve E around the toe of Green Mtn. There are four former meadows where deer are frequently seen at 8.9 mi, 9.2 mi, 10.5 mi, and 10.7 mi. Heart-leaved skullcap (*Scutellaria ovata*) grows in the rich, damp soil. There are also beds of club moss under locust, spicebush, sycamore, and maple. At 10.9 mi rock-hop Coal Run, and at 11.2 mi ascend a sculpted cliff among maidenhair fern and blue cohosh. Descend to cross Dry Fork footbridge at 11.3 mi. Across the river turn L (NE), to the parking lot off WV-72, 2.0 mi S of Hendricks. (The current footbridge was constructed in 1991 but was damaged by flooding in 1994 and in 1996. It has been reconstructed to its original safe condition.) (*USGS-FS Maps*: Bowden, Parsons, Harmon, Mozark Mtn)

Shavers Mountain Trail (USFS #129)

LENGTH: 10.0 mi
DIFFICULTY: strenuous
FEATURES: wildlife, scenic

TRAILHEAD AND DETAILS: At the jct of US-33 in Alpena Gap (3,022 ft) and FR-91 park at the picnic area L, and enter the trail across the road near the picnic shelter. Ascend on three steep switchbacks through a hardwood forest to a curve W around a knob. At 0.9 mi and 1.3 mi skirt L of the forest boundary line and USGS bearing trees. Rattlesnakes have been seen on the trail. Reach the Otter Creek Wilderness boundary at 1.8 mi. Begin a descent on an old logging road, make a number of turns, and reach the headwaters of Otter Creek at 2.4 mi. There is a rhododendron copse near the stream area. At 3.0 mi reach the jct, L, with *Hedrick Camp Trail*.

(The 1.0-mi *Hedrick Camp Trail* follows the Otter Creek on a gentle contour line for 0.9 mi before fording the stream. The footbridge has been washed out. Follow the trail through a hemlock grove to the Condon Run parking area and entrance to the *Otter Creek Trail* described above.)

Continue ahead on the *Shavers Mtn Trail* and climb to the mtn ridge on four switchbacks in a rocky and sometimes wet area. On the crest, pass L of a fence and private property at 4.7 mi. Deer and red squirrel are often seen here. At 5.0 mi a series of ridge-crest undulations begins, continuing for 1.0 mi. Hardwoods predominate, with striped green maple common to the understory. Occasionally there are thick stands of hemlock, red spruce, and rhododendron. At 6.8 mi on Rough Ridge is a vista of Middle Mtn. Begin the descent on switchbacks to the forest boundary sign at 6.7 mi. Reach the jct with *Mylius Trail* at 7.3 mi.

(The *Mylius Trail* crosses here in a gap. To the L it descends 0.7 mi to the *Otter Creek Trail*. The trail goes through three small fields and a hemlock stand to reach Otter Creek. Rock-hop or wade the creek, pass a good camping area in red pine on the L near the riverbank, and connect with the *Otter Creek Trail*. The R section of *Mylius Trail* drops 835 ft in elev from Shavers Mtn to Glady Fork. The descent is on a well-graded footpath for 0.6 mi, then joins an old, open logging road. Cherry, poplar, maple, and oak dominate. Ferns and wildflowers are prevalent. Pass through three wildlife food plots and reach Quarry Rd [FR-228] at 1.2 mi and the registration box at Kuntzville Rd [FR-162] at 1.7 mi. It is 0.1 mi R to Galdwin Rd [CO-12] and a parking area. Right on Galdwin Rd it is 4.7 mi to US-33 at the Alpine Springs Lodge. Right on US-33 it is 1.0 mi to Alpena Gap picnic area and the *Shavers Mtn Trail* point of origin.)

Continue ahead on the *Shavers Mtn Trail*; ascend steeply for 0.4 mi to the ridge top in a hardwood forest. At 8.5 mi enter a section of rhododendron, hemlock, and virgin red spruce. At 9.4 mi reach a 150-yd spur trail E to a six-person Adirondack shelter at the rim of the ridge. (The USFS will remove the shelter [in keeping with the wilderness environment] if it becomes unsafe.) Unless trees have grown to obstruct the views, you can see the Middle Mtn Range across the first valley—Glady Fork—and SE to Briarpatch Mtn (4,430 ft) and part of Spruce Knob (4,861 ft). Thunderstruck Rock is visible, NE, on Mt Porte Crayon (4,770 ft). Springs are nearby for a water supply. Descend and reach the end of *Shavers Mtn Trail* at a jct with *Green Mtn Trail* L at 10.0 mi. Backtrack or make a loop.

(The 4.0-mi *Green Mtn Trail* proceeds NW on an easy descending grade S of the swamp and headwaters of Shavers Lick Run. At 1.3 mi is a jct with *Possession Camp Trail*, L, that leads 3.3 mi to the *Otter Creek Trail*. Ahead, the *Green Mtn Trail* slightly descends on an old RR grade through a mixed forest and dense fern beds. At 2.8 mi begin a 1.2-mi, steep descent on an old skid road to an old logging camp, Camp Two, and the end of *Green Mtn Trail*. Here is a jct with the *Otter Creek Trail* that goes S for 7.4 mi. A N exit is 1.2 mi farther downstream to a jct with *Big Springs Gap Trail*, L, and 0.9 mi up to Big Springs Gap and the Fernow Loop Rd [see *Big Springs Gap Trail* above]). (*USGS-FS Maps*: Bowden, Harmon, Mozark Mtn, Parsons)

McGowan Mountain Trail (USFS #136)

LENGTH: 3.5 mi
DIFFICULTY: moderate
FEATURES: red spruce forest, wildlife

TRAILHEAD AND DETAILS: Access from the S is by *Otter Creek Trail* 1.1 mi and *Yellow Creek Trail* 0.7 mi, or 0.6 mi on the *Yellow Creek Trail* from McGowan Mtn Rd (FR-324), gated Apr 15–Aug 15. Access from the N is by McGowan Mtn Rd, 3.1 mi from the Fernow Loop Rd (FR-701), and *Moore Run Trail*, 0.1 mi. If using the N access, park at the *Moore Run Trail* jct, go 0.1 mi to the jct, R, for the *McGowan Mtn Trail*. Immediately cross a woods road and ascend steeply on rocky treadway to a large rock formation on the top of the ridge at 0.3 mi. At 1.1 mi pass L of the high point of McGowan Mtn (3,912 ft) and turn SE. Sections of the trail are arbored by rhododendron. Red squirrels are frequently seen. Maple, ash, cherry, and yellow birch form a high canopy, and ferns form a velvet green ground cover. (Caution: In 1994 and 1996 heavy rains scoured the treadway in the middle section of the trail. The USFS does not plan maintenance. Therefore, if you feel lost use a topo map and stay E, but parallel, of Yellow Creek.) At 1.6 mi pass through a naturally sculpted sandstone formation. Enter a dense red spruce forest at 1.9 mi that continues for 0.7 mi. Descend rapidly on a footpath through hemlock and conifers to a RR grade at 2.7 mi. At 3.5 mi arrive at the end of the trail and jct with *Yellow Creek Trail*. It is 0.6 mi R to McGowan Mtn Rd; 3.7 mi N to the point of origin. (*USGS-FS Maps*: Parsons, Bowden. The trail has been relocated since the 1976 maps were printed.)

Turkey Run Trail (USFS #150)

LENGTH: 5.0 mi
DIFFICULTY: moderate
FEATURE: wildlife

TRAILHEAD AND DETAILS: The S access is by *Moore Run Trail*, 2.8 mi from the *Otter Creek Trail*, or 1.3 mi from the McGowan Mtn Rd (2.9 mi from Fernow Loop Rd, FR-701) in the Fernow Experimental Forest. Access from the N is on Fernow Loop Rd, 0.5 mi from *Big Springs Gap Trail* and 5.6 mi from downtown Parsons. If choosing the N access, park near the gated abandoned road. A registration box is near the gate. Follow the old road and ascend gradually in a forest of cherry and maple. Enter the Otter Creek Wilderness Area at 0.3 mi. Follow the old road through a forest of hardwoods around the E slope of McGowan Mtn, and at 2.0 mi pass R of an old trail. At 2.3 mi take the L road fork, immediately cross Turkey Run, and follow a switchback W. At 2.7 mi reach another road fork; turn L and climb to the ridge top. Ferns and mosses are plentiful. Leave the old road and enter an old skid trail at 3.1 mi. Continue the ascent to the top of the ridge (3,730 ft) and after 0.3 mi begin a slow descent through red spruce, hemlock, and rhododendron. Rejoin the old trail at 4.0 mi, continue descent (more rapidly) at 4.7 mi to the S terminus, and reach a jct with *Moore Run Trail* at 5.0 mi. Backtrack, make the loop R as described above, or descend L for other loops on the Otter Creek via the *Otter Creek Trail*. (*USGS-FS Map*: Parsons)

Middle Point Trail (1.6 mi; USFS #140); Baker Sods Trail (3.0 mi; USFS #132)

LENGTH: 4.6 mi combined
DIFFICULTY: moderate to strenuous
FEATURES: wildlife, botany

TRAILHEADS AND DETAILS: Although these trails are not in the Wilderness, they serve as access routes to the Wilderness on *Yellow Creek Trail*. The relocated *Middle Point Trail* begins on the Stuart Memorial Dr (FR-91), 1.7 mi E from the Bickle Knob Recreation Area and 2.2 mi W from the Bear Haven Recreation Area. Park on the S side of the road, climb the bank, and follow the E slope of Stuart Knob in an open hardwood forest of huge oak, maple, beech, and birch. A wide range of ferns—including cinnamon, hay-scented, Christmas, shield, and winged—are on the trail. Wild lily of the valley (*Malanthemum canadense*) is among the ground cover.

After crossing a rocky ridge descend 800 ft in elev on a spur ridge N to the trail terminus in a saddle at 1.6 mi, and reach a jct with the E and W *Baker Sods Trail*. To the L (W) the *Baker Sods Trail* descends 0.2 mi to a jct, L, with the Rattlesnake Run Rd (FR-774). (FR-774 is a 2.0-mi walk out to the Stuart Memorial Dr, where another L turn at 0.9 mi makes a loop of 4.7 mi to the point of origin.) On the *Baker Sods Trail* continue R at the Rattlesnake Run Rd jct and follow a timber road on the S slope of the mtn for 1.1 mi to the Baker Sods wildlife grazing fields, the trail's W terminus. Here it joins Baker Sods Rd (FR-798), a 3.8-mi route to Rocky Mtn High June Bug's Cabin at Shavers Fork Rd (CO-6) and 5.6 mi L (S) on CO-6 to Stuart Campground. A turn R (E) on the *Baker Sods Trail* from the jct of the *Middle Point Trail* is 1.7 mi to its E terminus and jct with the *Yellow Creek Trail*. Along the way the trail is a scenic narrow footpath in an open hardwood forest, except for a brief use of an old RR grade in a descent to the jct with abandoned *Little Black Fork Trail*. Beyond the jct ascend and parallel the R of Little Black Fork, but cross it at 50 yd before the jct with the *Yellow Creek Trail*. (*USGS-FS Map*: Bowden. The 1976 map needs updating on these trails.)

HORSESHOE RECREATION AREA (Tucker County)

Located beside Horseshoe Run in Lead Mine Valley, this attractive area has 10 campsites with both flush and vault toilets, hand pump, and spigot water. Each campsite has a table and fireplace. There are 29 picnic units and a large shelter for group occasions. Activities include fishing and swimming in the Horseshoe Run and hiking up both mountainsides. The season is May 20–Sept 10.

ACCESS: From the W jct of US-219 and WV-72 in Parsons, go N 1.4 mi on WV-72, turn R on Holly Meadows Rd (CO-1), and go 5.9 mi to Horseshoe Run Rd (CO-7). Turn R and go 3.6 mi to the campground, L. For a NE access descend on Lead Mine Mtn Rd (CO-9) for 4.7 mi from US-219 to Lead Mine and 1.3 mi L to the campground, R.

SUPPORT FACILITIES: Drive 1.3 mi NE on Horseshoe Run Rd to a country store in the community of Lead Mine.

Maxwell Run Trail (2.2 mi; USFS #157); McKinley Run Trail (1.0 mi; USFS #154)

LENGTH: 6.3 mi round-trip
DIFFICULTY: moderate

FEATURE: wildlife

TRAILHEADS AND DETAILS: The *Maxwell Run Trail* is 1.0 mi SW from the campground on the Horseshoe Run Rd. Park opposite the trailhead. Enter the forest on the L side of the run on a footpath. Pass through a stand of white pine followed by a pasture, and at 0.2 mi follow a narrow footpath on a slope by the stream. At 0.5 mi cross the S side of the stream near a small K-dam followed by another K-dam. Scenic cascades are at 0.7 mi and 0.9 mi. Pass through a wildlife grazing field, re-enter the forest, and cross the stream four more times on an old logging road. Pass two waterfalls and at 2.0 mi cross the R fork, then after 75 yd the L fork, of Maxwell Run. Ascend Close Mtn to a switchback at 2.1 mi and reach the end of FR-903 at 2.2 mi. (A loop can be made by walking 1.8 mi on FR-903 to *McKinley Run Trail* and returning to the campground, for a circuit of 5.8 mi.)

The unblazed *McKinley Run Trail* begins where McKinley Run flows through the campground. Go upstream, ascend the highway embankment, go 150 yd on an old paved road, and ascend the slope L of a sycamore tree. Pass through rhododendron and a hardwood forest. Cross an old woods road and ascend on a blue-tagged footpath to the headwaters of McKinley Run after passing a hunter's deer stand. Ascend on a switchback to FR-903 at 1.0 mi. Backtrack or turn L and go 0.2 mi to a locked gate and to FR-16. Turn L on FR-16 and descend on the road through a scenic group of conifers and hardwoods to Horseshoe Run Rd for 0.6 mi. Turn L again and return to the campground for a loop of 2.2 mi. (*USGS-FS Map*: Lead Mine)

Horseshoe Run Nature Trail (0.5 mi); Losh Run Trail (2.3 mi; USFS #155); Dorman Ridge Trail (1.3 mi; USFS #153)

LENGTH: 4.1 mi combined

DIFFICULTY: easy to moderate

FEATURE: nature study

TRAILHEAD AND DETAILS: At the S edge of the campground near site #2 is a trail-design board. From there proceed on the *Horseshoe Run Nature Trail* through a forest of sycamore, hemlock, white pine, maple, ironwood, and yellow birch. Flowers include mandrake, jewelweed, and true forget-me-not (*Myosotis scorpioides*). Ferns and ground ivy cover portions of the forest floor. After 0.4 mi the *Nature Trail* continues L for 0.1 mi to the Horseshoe Run. (Slightly upstream from the *Nature Trail*, the construction of a footbridge over Horseshoe Run is planned for the *Losh Run Trail*.) After wading the creek, follow Losh Run upstream in a deep hollow with an open forest of yellow birch, white pine, hemlock, and oak. White snakeroot and ferns are along the trail. Ascend gradually, cross a number of drains, and at 0.8 mi enter a thick grove of rhododendron. Reach a saddle of Drift Ridge, L, at 1.5 mi. Continue R, pass W of a knob in the ridge, and pass E of the headwaters of Mike's Run to ascend to a ridge crest and hemlock stand. At 2.3 mi reach a forest of white pine and the jct with *Dorman Ridge Trail* and *Mike's Run Trail*. A six-person shelter is L of this jct. (See *Mike's Run Trail* below.)

The *Dorman Ridge Trail* goes N for 0.4 mi through a hardwood forest to a field. Follow the trail through the field and a stand of white pine to a border of silverberry. Continue on an old farm road through fields where sections are growing up with young trees. Reach Lead Mine Mtn Rd (also called Hiles Run Rd) (CO-9) at 1.3 mi. Backtrack or use a vehicle shuttle. From here it is 0.7 mi W on CO-9 to Location Rd (CO-5) at a jct with three wooden crosses. It is 6.0 mi SW on Location Rd to the community of Saint George. For an E route on Lead Mine Mtn Rd descend 3.1 mi to Horseshoe Run Rd and turn R for 0.5 mi back to the campground. (*USGS-FS Maps*: Lead Mine, Saint George)

Mike's Run Trail (USFS #156)

LENGTH: 4.0 mi (or a loop of 8.1 mi)

DIFFICULTY: strenuous

TRAILHEAD AND DETAILS: At the jct of the *Losh Run Trail* and *Dorman Ridge Trail*, *Mike's Run Trail* crosses the run in front of the shelter to cross a graveled timber road (FR-930). Follow the stream on the N side through hardwoods and rhododendron, and cross to the S side of the run at 1.1 mi. Pass through a hemlock grove and pass a number of cascading ledges at 2.1 mi. After crisscrossing the stream in a beautiful and remote hollow, enter an old field with scattered apple trees and hawthorn at 3.4 mi. Pass through another field and into private property on the W side of the run. The trail ends at the confluence of Mike's Run and Horseshoe Run at 4.0 mi. Backtrack, or ford Horseshoe Run to a private farm road. Follow it 0.3 mi to CO-7, turn L, and follow it 2.0 mi to Horseshoe Recreation Area for a loop of 8.1 mi if using *Losh Run Trail* to the shelter where *Mike's Run Trail* began. (*USGS-FS Maps*: Lead Mine, Saint George)

SOUTH HADDIX AREA (Tucker and Randolph Counties)

South Haddix Trail (USFS #126)

LENGTH: 10.0 mi

DIFFICULTY: strenuous

FEATURES: wildlife, wildflowers

TRAILHEAD AND DETAILS: To gain access to the NE trailhead drive 4.0 mi S of Parsons on US-219 to Moore and turn off on South Haddix Rd (CO-219/10). Follow the road for 1.6 mi to a fork at Haddix Run South Branch. Parking here may be a problem because of space. (Do not block either road or obstruct private property on the L.) Hike past the gated FR-116 on the R and at 0.4 mi pass a water experiment station. Reach the trailhead at 0.5 mi up a steep road embankment. For the next 0.2 mi the trail is arbored with rhododendron.

At a wildlife food plot pass L (W) in an ascent to an old fire road. Turn R (N) and after 0.2 mi turn L, off the road on a footpath. Through hardwoods you may see deer, turkey, or bear. There are some traffic sounds from US-219, but as the trail curves S at 3.9 mi near a pipeline, the sound disappears. From the pipeline you can see the Cherry Fork drainage to the W and Haddix Run drainage to the E. At 5.2 mi the trail leaves the ridge, descends to join an old logging road, and has views of Pheasant Mtn to the SE (unrelated to *Pheasant Mtn Trail*, USFS #120). Dogwoods, blueberries, and trailing arbutus are among the wildflowers.

Arrive at grassy FR-861, R and L, in a gap. (To the R it formerly served as a 0.8-mi section of the *South Haddix Trail*, with the exception of a 0.3-mi footpath to avoid private property. It can still be used as a shortcut. Access to its S terminus is 1.6 mi E from US-219 on Cherry Fork Rd (CO-129/3), 1.0 mi S of the community of Montrose.)

Continue on *South Haddix Trail*, SE, on FR-861, but after 0.4 mi turn R in a curve to FR-862. Follow it for the remaining 3.8 mi. Along the way the trail follows close to the ridge line of Pheasant Mtn (of the Cheat Mtn Range), and has three major horseshoe curves, the first at 6.6 mi. Pass logging roads at 7.3 mi (FR-861B), at 7.5 mi (FR-862B), and at 8.7 mi (FR-862A), all of which are on the E side of the ridge. Descend to the S trailhead, SR-47, at 10.0 mi. Access from the W is off US-219 (1.1 mi N of the community of Kerens) on Wilmoth Run Rd (SR-3). After 2.0 mi on SR-3 the road becomes SR-47; the parking area is another 0.4 mi at the trailhead. Another access is 6.1 mi S of Porterwood (off US-219), 2.8 mi on Shavers

Fork Rd (SR-3), and 3.3 mi on Pleasant Run Rd (SR-47). (*USGS-FS Map:* Montrose)

SECTION 2: GAULEY RANGER DISTRICT

Within the 158,147-acre Gauley Ranger District are four developed campgrounds: Big Rock, Bishop Knob, Cranberry, and Summit Lake. Additionally, 23 numbered and restricted campsites exist along the Williams River and 12 on the banks of the Cranberry River. Both of these streams and the North Fork Cherry River are stocked with trout. Large and small game hunting is allowed in all areas except developed recreational areas, and bear hunting is not allowed in the Black Bear Sanctuaries. There are two developed picnic areas, North Bend and Woodbine. The district may be best known for the famous 750-acre Cranberry Glades Botanical Area, but equally significant are the 35,864-acre Cranberry Wilderness, the Highland Scenic Highway, and the Falls of Hills Creek. There is also another special place, the 26,000-acre Cranberry Back Country, where for 60 years the area traditionally has been closed to public motorized vehicles. The Back Country has nearly 75 mi of hiking trails and six Adirondack shelters by the Cranberry River. Access to all of the above will be described later in this section.

The geography of the trails can be categorized as Cranberry Glades at the headwaters of Cranberry River; N and NE of Cranberry River; S of Cranberry River; and Bishop Knob, NW of Cranberry River. The trails will be described in that order except the *Nature Trail* at the Cranberry Mtn Nature Center and the water falls at *Falls of Hills Creek Trail*, which are described in this introduction.

Although hiking, backpacking, and camping are prominent on nearly 190 mi of trails, there are other activities for the outdoor-sports enthusiast. For example, the lower Cranberry and the Gauley Rivers are suitable for canoeing, kayaking, and rafting. For cross-country skiing there are nearly 75 mi of trails, some marked with the standard diamond-shaped US Ski Association signs. Area information on outdoor sports for all seasons is available from the Richwood Chamber of Commerce. The chamber also has information on Richwood, the home of the National Ramp Association, which sponsors the annual Feast of the Ramson the first Saturday in April. A spring nature tour is the second Saturday in May and a Cranberry Glades tour is the second Saturday in July. (Chamber address: Box 267, Richwood, WV 26261; 304-846-6790.) Exceptionally scenic vistas are on the Highland Scenic Highway, the *Forks of Cranberry Trail*, and the *Nature Trail* behind

Evidence of black bear near Frosty Gap Trail.

the Cranberry Mtn Nature Center (800-655-4826). The Cranberry Mtn Visitor Center (at the jct of WV-39/55 and WV-150, 6.3 mi W of US-219 at Mill Point) provides visitor information and audiovisual programs on the history and natural phenomena of the area. It is open daily, 9:30 A.M.–5:00 P.M., from Memorial Day to Labor Day; and from Oct 1 through fall color season, usually Oct 20, and weekends the rest of the year except December. From the center is a *Nature Trail* that begins E of the building and circles the mtn rim (elev 3,605 ft) through a hardwood forest for remarkable vistas of the Greenbrier River valley, Beaver Lick Mtn, and Bald Knob, Virginia. Some of the understory is striped maple and witch hazel (*Hamamelis vir-*

giniana). The trail follows the *Pocahontas Trail* for 0.1 mi to a picnic area and loops back to the center parking area at 0.6 mi.

Another popular area for a short trail is at the Falls of Hills Creek Scenic Area, 5.3 mi W from the nature center on WV-39/55/150 and L for 0.2 mi to the parking area. From the parking area descend on the 0.8-mi round-trip *Falls of Hills Creek Trail* into a narrow sandstone and shale gorge covered by northern hardwood, hemlock, and rhododendron. Among the wildflowers are Dutchman's-breeches (*Dicentra cucullaria*), trillium, wild orchids, and Canada violets. The 114-acre scenic area has three waterfalls: 25-ft Upper Falls, 45-ft Middle Falls, and 63-ft Lower Falls (the second highest in the state). Above the Upper Falls the *Fork Mtn Trail* crosses the creek on its E route to the *Pocahontas Trail*. For a number of years after the 1985 flood the lower section was closed, but it is now reconstructed with several boardwalks, stairs, two towers and a bridge.

It is recommended that you write for, or pick up at the nature center or district office, the "Recreation Guide for the Gauley District." It has information on activities as well as a map.

ADDRESS AND ACCESS: District Ranger, Gauley Ranger District, PO Box 110, Richwood, WV 26261; 304-846-2695. District office is 1.0 mi E of Richwood on WV-39/55. The nature center is 21.4 mi E of the district office and 6.3 mi W from US-219 at Mill Point. (WV-55, the Highland Trace, is a 165-mi route from the West Virginia–Virginia border near Wardensville in Hardy County to Muddlety in Nicholas County. Named the Highland Trace by Margaret Temple West, a member of a task force appointed by Governor John D. Rockefeller IV, the scenic route is a guide to dramatize the state's skiing areas.)

MAPS: Numbers 6–11

CRANBERRY GLADES BOTANICAL AREA
(Pocahontas County)

The Cranberry Glades Botanical Area receives its name from the cranberry (*Vaccinium macrocarpon* and other species) and from wet sphagnum bogs, also called glades. The area is similar to the arctic tundra of the Canadian bogs or "muskegs" in floristic composition, but dissimilar in that the West Virginia glades are unglaciated. The glades are the southernmost breeding area for a number of bird species. The area contains four glades; the 0.5-mi boardwalk *Cranberry Glades Botanical Trail* loops through two of them, Flag Glade and Round Glade. Ten interpretive signs explain the flora and fauna, formation, geology, and future of this natural garden. Among the more than 100 identified plants are the snakemouth orchid (*Pogonia ophioglossoides*) and grass pink orchid (*Calagogon pulchellus*). Both bloom in late June or early July. Sundew (*Drosera rotundifolia*), monkshood (*Aconitum uncinatum*), and sarsaparilla (*Aralia nudicaulis*) also grow here. Access to the glades is 0.6 mi W on WV-39/55 from the nature center to paved FR-102, R, for another 1.5 mi.

The glades area has two parking lots. The first is paved with asphalt at the entrance to the boardwalk trail described above, and the second is graveled, 0.9 mi downstream for an easy connection with the *Cow Pasture Trail* and the nonmotorized, 16-mi Cranberry River Rd (FR-102/76), which connects with nine trails into the Cranberry Wilderness and the Cranberry Back Country.

Cranberry Volkswalk

LENGTH: 6.0 mi

DIFFICULTY: easy

FEATURES: scenic, wildlife, ferns, historic site

TRAILHEAD AND DETAILS: Park at the Cranberry Mtn Nature Center at the intersection of WV-39/55 and WV-150, and walk across the road to the NW corner of the intersection. The trail was created in 1991; interconnecting loops are marked with plastic white diamond blazes to Cranberry Glades Botanical Area and black insets in the blazes for return routes.

Follow a wide trail through a forest of cherry, maple, hemlock, and red spruce for 0.5 mi. Turn R and at 0.7 mi turn L. Cross Charles Creek, and follow an old gravel road through the historic site of Millpoint Federal Prison (active from 1938 to 1959). Reach FR-102 at 1.5 mi. Turn R and follow FR-102 to the parking area at Cranberry Glades at 2.4 mi.

A return route can be to 0.1 mi S to *Cow Pasture Trail* (TR-253) and turn L. After 0.5 mi turn R on the *Cranberry Volkswalk* near a stream. The trail passes cascades in a forest of hemlock before ascending to a grassy meadow. Pass through the scenic area to reach FR-102 at 1.5 mi. From here follow the trail S along paved FR-102 for another 0.6 mi to WV-39/55. (A shortcut trail can be taken along the N side of WV-39/55 to the trail's origin.) For the remaining 1.1 mi, the trail crosses WV-39/55 and proceeds SE to *Pocahontas Trail* (TR-263). Here it turns L onto *Pocahontas Trail* and returns to the nature center. (*USGS-FS Map*: Lobelia)

Cow Pasture Trail (USFS #253)

LENGTH: 6.7 mi
DIFFICULTY: moderate
FEATURES: wildlife, scenic Cranberry Glades

TRAILHEAD AND DETAILS: From the paved parking lot walk up the entrance road for 0.2 mi to an old RR grade on the L. Pass the gate, enter the forest of birch and hemlock, and walk on a ground cover of buttercups. At 0.8 mi turn L at a gate and go through a boggy area. Beavers have been active here. At 1.5 mi veer away from the glades into a hardwood forest, cross two streams, and enter an old cow pasture among sparse hawthorn and elder. There are scenic views here of the glades. Excellent area for bird-watching. Leave the old road and cross the South Fork of the Cranberry River at 3.5 mi. Cross a tributary at 4.1 mi and enter an old pasture. For the next 1.0 mi cross tributaries, pass through pleasant pastures with beds of wild geranium (*Geranium maculatum*) and groves of yellow buckeye. After crossing a beaver dam area ascend to a ridge, descend into a boggy area, and cross a footbridge. Enter a hemlock stand and reach the Cranberry Rd (FR-102) at 6.5 mi. Turn L on FR-102 for 0.2 mi to a gate and the gravel parking area. Hike another 0.9 mi upstream to your point of origin for a loop of 7.8 mi. (*USGS-FS Map*: Lobelia)

CRANBERRY WILDERNESS AREA
(Pocahontas and Webster Counties)

In 1983 Congress passed Public Law 97-466, which created the 35,500-acre Cranberry Wilderness. The area included 26,500 acres from the original Cranberry Back Country and 9,000 additional acres. It is preserved forever without the sound of motorized vehicles or equipment. Trees will never be logged, minerals mined, or shelters built. Hunting, fishing, camping, hiking, and cross-country skiing will be allowed. There are nine hiking trails in the Wilderness and some of them extend or connect with other trails outside the Wilderness. The USFS has listed the following trails for "lower standard" maintenance as funding permits: *County Line Trail, Big Beechy Trail, Tumbling Rock Trail, Forks of Cranberry Trail, District Line Trail, Laurelly Branch Trail, Middle Fork Trail, North Fork Trail*, and the *North-South Trail*. Because the bears chew painted or treated signs, the USFS is replacing signs with routed natural material.

Animal life in the Wilderness includes 16 species of amphibians, 7 species of reptiles, 41 species of mammals, and 80 species of birds (among the most common are woodpeckers, vireos, warblers, and sparrows, but the cardinal is not listed). More than 900 species of flora have been identified.

The USFS requests that all hikers and backpackers register at the access points and that campers carry a tent, as the shelters in the adjoining Back Country may be filled. Licenses are required for fishing and hunting. The weather is drastically capricious, requiring proper clothing. The area is usually wet and the summer temperature ranges from 40° to 70°; the winter reaches subzero temperatures with "whiteouts" and deep snow. The nearest campground is the Cranberry Recreation Area described below.

At the NW edge of the Cranberry Back Country lies a scenic meadow campground by the Cranberry River. On carefully mowed lawns are 30 campsites with a picnic table and grill, hand-pump drinking water, and vault restrooms. Fishing, picnicking, camping, and hiking are its main activities. Because it is a popular campground, it fills up quickly, particularly in the spring and summer. Open Mar 15–Dec 8. The S terminus of the *North-South Trail* is here.

ACCESS: From Richwood at the jct of WV-39/55 and CO/FR-76 (across from Gales Restaurant) drive 12.0 mi on CO/FR-76 to the campground. (FR-76 beyond the campground is gated, restricted, and not open to vehicles.)

SUPPORT FACILITIES: Motels, restaurants, banks, service stations, and shopping centers are in Richwood.

North-South Trail (15.1 mi; USFS #688)

CONNECTING TRAILS:
   Lick Branch Trail (2.1 mi; USFS #212)
   Little Fork Trail (3.7 mi; USFS #242)
   Rough Run Trail (3.2 mi; USFS #213)
   Birch Log Trail (2.9 mi; USFS #250)
   Laurelly Branch Trail (3.4 mi; USFS #267)
   Tumbling Rock Trail (2.6 mi; USFS #214)
   North Fork Trail (9.0 mi; USFS #272)
   Middle Fork Trail (10 mi; USFS #271)

TOTAL LENGTH: 48.6 mi

DIFFICULTY: moderate to strenuous

FEATURES: wildlife, botany, wilderness, geology

TRAILHEADS AND DETAILS: The *North-South Trail* is unique and significant because it is more an east-west trail than north-south, particularly since the USFS has the trail now ending at WV-150 and 5.0 mi of its N route to Tea Creek Campground is no longer maintained. The trail is a master route through the Cranberry Back Country and the Cranberry Wilderness, with connecting trails in the Greenbrier and Marlinton Ranger Districts. Although the *North-South Trail* (formerly called the *Red and Black Trail*) is not a loop trail, the number of potential loops in its use is a hiker's dream. Elevation increase in the first 2.0 mi of the trail is 1,040 ft and follows a ridge line of nearly 4,000 ft elev for most of the distance.

The W trailhead is at Cranberry Campground. From its parking area pass the FR-76 gate and trail signs, turn L, and ascend on a narrow footpath in a forest of beech, birch, cherry, maple, and poplar. Wildflowers such as Indian cucumber root (*Medeola virginiana*), mandrake, and rose-colored twisted stalk are prevalent on the mountainside. At 0.5 mi begin the first of four switchbacks to the mtn ridge. At 1.6 mi and 2.1 mi cross tributaries of the Lower Twin Branch. A good campsite is R at 2.4 mi, followed by a jct with FR-272 (gated at Red Oak Knob). Cross the grassy road and ascend to an old woods road, which follows the ridge line through an open forest of tall cherry and maple. Ferns and trout lilies cover the path. Enter a short bog at 4.0 mi, followed by a mixed forest that includes hemlock and red spruce. Arrive at the jct with *Lick Branch Trail,* R, at 4.7 mi. Water is 0.1 mi on R.

(The 2.1-mi *Lick Branch Trail* drops 1,050 ft in elev to FR-76 at the Cranberry River. Pass the confluence of cascading streams. At 0.4 mi pass an old pot-bellied stove among other signs of an old lumber camp. Follow an old RR grade to a seeded road at 1.0 mi, leave the road after 0.5 mi, and descend into a rocky area with hemlock. At 2.1 mi is a large, two-tiered waterfall at the trail terminus. It is 2.2 mi back to the Cranberry Campground, a loop of 9.0 mi.)

Continue ahead on the *North-South Trail* and at 5.9 mi reach a jct with the 3.7 mi *Little Fork Trail,* L.

(The *Little Fork Trail* descends N from the headwaters of Little Fork. At 1.1 mi cross the drain and stay on the E side through the gorge. Pass through stands of tall poplar, beech, yellow birch, cherry, and hemlock. Cross the creek at 3.0 mi and again at 3.3 mi. Reach the middle fork of the Williams River at 3.6 mi, wade, cross a flood plain for 0.1 mi, and meet the N terminus of *Middle Fork Trail*, R. To the L is a cul-de-sac parking area, the terminus of FR-108. To the R is the W terminus of the *County Line*

Trail. Trail loops can be made here for a return to the *North-South Trail.* At the parking area are five numbered, restricted campsites. FR-108 goes 0.5 mi to FR-86, a point on the state highway map listed as Three Forks of the Williams.)

The *North-South Trail* continues ahead on the ridge, and at 6.4 mi is a jct with *Rough Run Trail,* R.

(The 3.2-mi *Rough Run Trail* descends 1,000 ft in elev for 3.2 mi to FR-76 and the Cranberry River. After 0.2 mi the trail begins to follow, and subsequently crosses, *Rough Run Trail* through rhododendron and hemlock for the first 1.8 mi. Follow an old RR grade as the trail leaves the stream and curves around the ridge spur to its exit at Little Rough Run for 3.2 mi. Right on FR-76, it is 4.5 mi back to Cranberry Campground—a loop of 14.2 mi.)

After another 0.9 mi on the *North-South Trail* reach the jct with the *Birch Log Trail,* R.

(The *Birch Log Trail* descends for 2.9 mi to FR-76 and to the Cranberry River. It follows an old logging road along the Birch Log Run through hemlock, oak, maple, and birch. Fern beds are frequent. Cross Birch Log Run five times and smaller drains in wet areas, particularly at 1.0 mi and 2.6 mi. On FR-76, R, it is 9.1 mi to Cranberry Campground—a loop of 18.9 mi.)

Ahead on the *North-South Trail,* ascend and descend slightly for 0.9 mi to a jct with the *Laurelly Branch Trail,* L, and enter the Cranberry Wilderness Area at 8.2 mi.

(The 3.4-mi *Laurelly Branch Trail* descends on an old RR grade with switchbacks through a hardwood forest to the middle fork of the Williams River and the abandoned FR-108, now *Middle Fork Trail.* An exit downstream to FR-86 at the Williams River is another 3.9 mi, or an ascent on the *Middle Fork Trail* is 6.1 mi to rejoin the former *North-South Trail,* now the *North Fork Trail,* 1.2 mi from the Highland Scenic Highway, WV-150.)

Remaining on the *North-South Trail,* the hardwoods become increasingly mixed with red spruce and dense undergrowth, mainly of rhododendron. Seeps are more frequent. At 10.2 mi arrive at the N terminus of *Tumbling Rock Trail,* R.

(The 2.6-mi *Tumbling Rock Trail* descends and crosses the stream a number of times. At 1.7 mi cross a tributary and descend on a slope W of the stream. Reach FR-76 at the Cranberry River at 2.6 mi. To the R (N) it is 0.1 mi to Tumbling Rock Shelter and 9.1 mi farther on FR-76 to Cranberry

Campground—a 22-mi loop. It is 6.0 mi L (S) on FR-76 and FR-102 to Cranberry Glades parking area.)

For the next 4.5 mi of the *North-South Trail* the treadway has more-frequent seeps, rocky areas, and red spruce stands, which form a canopy over moss-covered rocks, logs, and stumps. The elev is between 4,000 ft and 4,400 ft. Reach a significant trail intersection at 14.7 mi with the *North Fork Trail*, R (S) and L (N). The *North-South Trail* crosses the *North Fork Trail* (*USFS #272*) and goes through a magnificent display of spruce and thick, spongy moss to a parking area on the Highlands Scenic Highway, WV-150, 0.3 mi N of Little Spruce Overlook. Elev here is 4,556 ft. North on WV-150 it is 5.6 mi to the Tea Creek Campground, and S on WV-150 it is 8.6 mi to the Cranberry Mtn Nature Center.

(The S section of *North Fork Trail,* formerly FR-76, descends through a beautiful forest, first of red spruce and gradually changing to hardwood. At 2.5 mi the road crosses the left fork and later the north fork at 4.4 mi. White snakeroot, ferns, and cohosh border the road for the last 2.0 mi. Reach a jct with FR-102 at 6.6 mi. From here it is 4.3 mi upstream on FR-102 to the Cranberry Glades parking area. The N section of *North Fork Trail* follows the former FR-76 and former *North-South Trail* through seedlings and maturing red spruce.

Wildflowers are prominent in the open areas. At 1.2 mi reach a jct, L, with the *Middle Fork Trail*. The only sign here may be the old FR-108 sign, or there may be none at all.)

(The 10.0-mi *Middle Fork Trail* follows down the stream by the same name, crosses a number of small drains and tributaries, and then the main stream with a drop of 1,930 ft to the fork of the Williams River parking area. Once a graded road and open for vehicular traffic, it is now returning to the wilderness it once was. Cascades, pools, moss-covered rocks, and hardwood forests provide immense beauty, another prize of the Cranberry Wilderness. At 6.2 mi meet, L, the *Laurelly Branch Trail*. [The *Laurelly Branch Trail* ascends 3.5 mi to a jct with the *North South Trail* described above.] At 7.5 mi pass the *Big Beechy Trail*, R. [The 5.4-mi *Big Beechy Trail* ascends steeply in a hardwood forest with rhododendron for the first 1.3 mi and then follows a ridge line to a jct with the *District Line Trail*, L, at 4.3 mi in a stand of large red spruce. It continues ahead on the ridge for another 1.1 mi to Sugar Creek Mtn and a jct with the *North-South Trail*.] The *Middle Fork Trail* crosses the scenic Beechy Run with a waterfall to the L and continues downstream. Pools, rock tiers, and cascades are scenic parts of the

Middle Fork. At 8.6 mi cross a cement bridge. Among the hardwoods are witch hazel, bee balm, wild hydrangea, jewelweed, and flowering raspberry (*Rubus odoratus*). At 10.0 mi the *Middle Fork Trail* ends at the jct with *Little Fork Trail*, *County Line Trail*, and the three forks of the Williams River parking area.)

(From the E jct of the *Middle Fork Trail* the *North Fork Trail* continues N for 1.1 mi to a low gap, where it turns R. After 0.1 mi it ends at a registration box and parking area off the Highlands Scenic Highway, WV-150. It is 2.0 mi S on WV-150 to the E trailhead of *North-South Trail*. (*USGS-FS Maps*: Webster Springs SW and SE, and Woodrow may not show current trail routes.)

County Line Trail (9.2 mi; USFS #206); District Line Trail (2.8 mi; USFS #248)

TOTAL LENGTH: 12.0 mi

DIFFICULTY: strenuous

FEATURES: wildlife, remote

TRAILHEADS AND DETAILS: The *District Line Trail* and 9.2 mi of the *County Line Trail* (named for its proximity to Webster and Pocahontas Counties) are in the Wilderness. They can be used to form loops with the *Middle Fork Trail* and *Big Beechy Trail*. The description below offers one of those options. At the trailhead parking area near the *Middle Fork Trail* at the end of FR-108 (0.5 mi off FR-86 at three forks of the Williams River), ascend gradually on the *County Line Trail* for 1.2 mi on the S slope of the mtn to the ridge crest. The forest is composed of birch, beech, poplar, hickory, and oak. Nettles and white snakeroot are prominent in the summertime. Follow the trail over a mixture of rocky footpaths, old woods roads, and rugged sections of the N slope to arrive at a rock formation at 2.1 mi. Cross drains at 3.0 mi and 3.8 mi. The Williams River can be heard, L (N). At 5.0 mi ascend on a rocky and mossy N slope. Sections of dense red spruce are here. Signs of bear and deer are at 5.9 mi in a cherry and maple forest. At 7.0 mi reach a jct with *District Line Trail*, R, where bear have chewed former wire-framed signs.

(The 2.8-mi *District Line Trail* follows the ridge line R through hardwoods, red spruce, and hemlock to a jct with the *Big Beechy Trail*, where to the R a 16.6-mi loop can be made back to the point of origin by using 2.5 mi of the lower *Middle Fork Trail*.)

The *County Line Trail* turns L and at 7.6 mi reaches the ridge edge for a steep descent. From here there is 1,000-ft elev drop on 15 switchbacks with rugged treadway in a forest of cherry, maple, birch, and sparse hemlock to FR-86 and the Williams River at 9.2 mi. (*USGS-FS Maps*: Webster Springs SW and SE, Bergoo)

Black Mountain Loop Trail (USFS #412)

LENGTH: 4.7 mi
DIFFICULTY: moderate
FEATURES: wildlife, wildflowers, scenic views
TRAILHEAD AND DETAILS: On the Highlands Scenic Highway (WV-150), 6.2 mi N from the intersection with WV-39/55 at Cranberry Mtn Nature Center is the S trailhead at Big Spruce overlook. The N trailhead is at Little Spruce Overlook, 1.7 mi farther N on WV-150. The day-hike trail makes a loop with 2.4 mi on the E side in the Marlinton District and 2.3 mi on the W side of the highway in the Gauley District. (Because the trail's passage in the Gauley District is through the Cranberry Wilderness where construction and maintenance is minimal, you will need to be alert for tracking the pathway.)

If beginning at Big Spruce Overlook on the E side, enter a dense forest up the bank near the picnic shelter, and soon descend on rocky and mossy switchbacks. At 0.3 mi turn L (N) and follow sections of an old timber RR grade among birch, beech, rhododendron, and red spruce. At 2.1 mi ascend a rocky mountainside to a boardwalk and observation deck. Proceed L to an exit at Little Spruce Overlook at 2.4 mi.

Across the highway enter the forest of red spruce and descend gradually into a narrow, rocky, mossy passage. There are a few sections of seepage at 0.5 mi and 0.8 mi. The pathway levels before a rock pile at 1.0 mi. Lichen decorate the rocks and wood sorrel and Indian pipe are among damp and rich green moss fields. Scattered mtn ash and quaking aspen are among the birch. Pass through a patch of rhododendron and mtn laurel before reaching WV-150 at 2.3 mi and Big Spruce Overlook. (*USGS-FS Maps*: Hillsboro, Woodrow)

Forks of Cranberry Trail (USFS #245)

LENGTH: 5.7 mi
DIFFICULTY: strenuous
FEATURES: botanical study, geology

TRAILHEAD AND DETAILS: The E trailhead is on Black Mtn at a parking area on the Highlands Scenic Highway (WV-150), 5.2 mi N of the Cranberry Mtn Visitor Center. Trail elev change is 1,300 ft. Hike 0.2 mi to a scenic view L of the glades and the south fork of the Cranberry River drainage. Follow a rocky plateau for 1.0 mi through mtn ash (*Sorbus americana*), rhododendron, mtn laurel, huckleberry, ferns, and spruce. Begin descent; pass through beds of trout lily and pass a spring, R, at 2.1 mi. Reach a rocky knoll at 2.2 mi with limited vistas; descend into a spruce and rhododendron stand. Pass large boulders and the Elephant Rock at 3.3 mi. Trail becomes overgrown; descend steeply in sections and under tall maple, cherry, and birch to reach the Cranberry River Rd (FR-102). (A turn R is 0.1 mi to jct R with the *North Fork Trail* [abandoned FR-76] and across the bridge of the north fork of the Cranberry River is an Adirondack shelter. From here it is 11.6 mi downstream to the Cranberry Campground.) Turn L and hike upstream on the Cranberry River Rd for 4.2 mi to a jct with the *Cow Pasture Trail* and the Cranberry Glades gravel parking area. (*USGS-FS Maps*: Hillsboro, Lobelia, Webster Springs SE)

SUMMIT LAKE RECREATION AREA (Greenbrier County)

High in the N corner of Greenbrier County is beautiful 43-acre Summit Lake (3,388 ft). Adjoining it is a 33-site campground, one of the gateways to the Cranberry Back Country and an excellent base camp for planning hikes south of the Cranberry River and to the ridge line of Fork Mtn. The campground has hand-pump water, tables, grills, and vault toilets (no hookups). Activities include boating (nonmotorized); fishing for trout, bass, and bluegill; and hiking. The campground is open Mar 15–Dec 8.

ACCESS: From the town of Richwood drive 6.6 mi E on WV-39/55 to FR-77 on the L (5.8 mi from the district office). Drive 2.0 mi to the campground entrance.

SUPPORT FACILITIES: Accommodations and shopping centers are in Richwood.

Summit Lake Trail
LENGTH: 1.8 mi
DIFFICULTY: easy
FEATURE: lake vistas
TRAILHEAD AND DETAILS: From campsite #1 follow the trail sign or from the lake parking area follow L around the lake on a blue-blazed trail into a

forest of birch, oak, cherry, beech, and poplar. Rhododendron, ferns, club moss, and wildflowers are frequent. Cross a stream at 0.9 mi and another, Coates Run, on a footbridge at 1.3 mi. Pass the boat dock and complete the loop. (*USGS-FS Maps*: Webster Springs SW, Fork Mtn)

(In 1988 a short section of the *Pocahontas Trail* was relocated at Hills Creek; a number of short sections on the *Kennison Mtn Trail* were relocated for better cross-country skiing; and a major change in the *Frosty Gap Trail* placed its central route on the Frosty Gap Rd and shortened the NW terminus to the jct with the *Pocahontas Trail*, 1.5 mi SE of Mike's Knob. Relocations have also been made on the *Fork Mtn Trail* near Desert Branch, at both its mouth and its headwaters.)

Pocahontas Trail (20.2 mi; USFS #263)

CONNECTING TRAILS:
>> *Fisherman Trail* (1.2 mi; USFS #231)
>> *Frosty Gap Trail* (5.2 mi; USFS #235)
>> *Eagle Camp Trail* (1 mi; USFS #259)
>> (*Fork Mtn Trail* 21.4 mi; USFS #236)
>> (*Kennison Mtn Trail* 9.7 mi; USFS #244)

TOTAL LENGTH: 58.7 mi

DIFFICULTY: easy to strenuous

FEATURES: wildlife, wildflowers, history

TRAILHEADS AND DETAILS: The W terminus of the 20.2-mi *Pocahontas Trail* is on gated Pocahontas Rd (FR-99), a 1.0-mi walk-in access. The E terminus is at the Cranberry Mtn Nature Center parking area. It crosses the county lines of Nicholas, Webster, Greenbrier, and Pocahontas, as well as WV-39/55, and connects with a wide range of other trails for a short 1.0-mi hike to lengthy partial loops. Description here begins not at its termini but at its jct with FR-77/99, because of its proximity to a developed campground.

From Summit Lake Recreation Area drive or hike 1.0 mi on FR-77 to a saddle in the ridge at a parking area (3,655 ft). Here is the jct with the *Pocahontas Trail*, Pocahontas Rd (FR-99), L, and the W boundary of the Cranberry Back Country. Also here is the W trailhead for the *Fisherman Trail* at a graded parking area.

(The *Fisherman Trail* was reconstructed by the YCC in 1979, but you may find the trail eroded and in need of maintenance. It descends steeply for a drop of 900 ft in elev from the saddle into Pheasants Hollow, crosses the stream five times, and reaches the Cranberry River at 1.2 mi, its SE terminus. Across the river is Pheasants Hollow Shelter and FR-76. The river can be waded at normal water levels. From here it is 5.0 mi downstream on FR-76 to the Cranberry Campground.)

To hike L on the *Pocahontas Trail*, cross an open area and enter the forest by a large maple tree. Follow the E slope of the ridge through a hardwood forest. At 1.0 mi cross FR-99, and at 1.6 mi reach the Hanging Rock area, a tricounty point. Begin a gradual descent to cross Coats Run Rd (FR-786) at 2.0 mi. After curving N of the Hunter's Run headwaters and crossing a number of drains, join a wildlife road at 3.5 mi. A spring is on the L at 3.7 mi. Reach the W terminus of the trail at FR-99 at 4.2 mi. Backtrack or turn L on FR-99 and hike 1.0 mi to the gate and vehicle access. It is 6.1 mi from the gate to Richwood. Or turn R for 0.3 mi to a jct L with *Barrenshe Trail* and hike 4.5 mi to FR-76. It is another 4.5 mi L on FR-76 to Richwood.

To hike R on the *Pocahontas Trail* at the FR-77/99 jct, enter the forest on an old woods road near an old building foundation. Ascend and follow the ridge line (and the Cranberry Back Country border) through a forest of beech, cherry, maple, oak, hemlock, and rhododendron. At 0.6 mi and 1.3 mi are boggy areas. Reach a clearcut area at 1.9 mi and continue through the cut for 0.8 mi. There is another wet area at 3.2 mi. At 3.5 mi cross FR-77 and join FR-77 at 4.2 mi for 0.1 mi before turning R into the woods. (FR-77 ends 1.3 mi at Mike's Knob, 4,240 ft.) The W terminus of the 5.7-mi *Frosty Gap Trail* is here.

(*Frosty Gap Trail* begins at the sharp bend in the road that ascends to the top of Mike's Knob. It is an undulating ridge trail, almost exclusively between 4,000 ft and 4,400 ft elev for its entire distance. It follows old RR grades and timber routes, but is overgrown in spots. It is signed as both a hiking and cross-country ski trail. From FR-77 it parallels the *Pocahontas Trail* SE for 1.5 mi to a spur connection, after which it turns more to the E through a red spruce forest. At 5.2 mi it crosses Dogway Rd [FR-232], gated to the L but open to the R for vehicle access 1.2 mi from WV-39/55. Straight ahead, the trail goes 0.5 mi to its E terminus with *Kennison Mtn Trail*.)

Continue ahead on the *Pocahontas Trail*, which parallels the *Frosty Gap Trail* for 1.5 mi to a spur connection, L, at 6.8 mi. Descend slightly, turn S around a knob to a switchback for a descent on the SE slope. Reach the jct with the *Eagle Camp Trail*, R, at 8.2 mi.

(*Eagle Camp Trail* is a 1.0-mi access route between *Pocahontas Trail* and WV-39/55. It follows W of the Left Branch drainage on a gradual descent through a mixed forest to the North Fork of the Cherry River. There is a bridge across the North Fork. Across the river in a small field is a parking area. It is 10.1 mi W on the highway to the Summit Lake Campground and 13.9 mi to the district office.)

On the *Pocahontas Trail* cross the headwaters of the Left Branch at 8.4 mi and begin a 2.0-mi S and E curve around the slopes of Yew Mtn. A number of places are wet, such as a 0.3-mi section near the Left Branch and spots where there is natural drainage from the slope. The forest is chiefly hardwood, with rhododendron a part of the understory. At 10.4 mi arrive at WV-39/55. From here it is 16.0 mi R on the highway to the district office and 4.5 mi L to the Cranberry Mtn Nature Center. Parallel the road and Hill Creek for 0.3 mi to the *Pocahontas Trail* parking lot. From the parking lot cross a tributary and then Hill Creek. Enter a gardenlike area of rhododendron, hemlock, and wood shamrock. Ascend steeply on the N slope of Spruce Mtn and reach a jct, R, with the terminus of *Fork Mtn Trail* at 12.0 mi. Bears may have damaged the trail signs.

(The 21.4-mi *Fork Mtn Trail* descends W on the N slope of Spruce Mtn for 2.4 mi to Falls of Hill Creek Scenic Area, and beyond it ascends SW to Rocky Knob, where it turns W on the Fork Mtn ridge line. Its W terminus is on WV-39/55 at the North Fork of the Cherry River bridge, 1.1 mi E of the district office. It could serve as a long partial loop to return within 6.8 mi of the Summit Lake Campground. See details below.)

Ahead on the *Pocahontas Trail* at 12.5 mi turn sharply L; intersect with Spruce Mtn Rd (an old woods road) at 12.9 mi (4,000 ft). Bear tracks are often seen in this area, particularly near drains. Forest is cherry, oak, maple, birch, and, infrequently, red spruce. Among the wildflowers is a species of green unfringed (*Habenaria*) orchids. Arrive at the S terminus jct of *Kennison Mtn Trail* at 13.4 mi.

(The *Kennison Mtn Trail* ascends slightly, curves around Blue Knob, descends through a hardwood forest, and crosses WV-39/55 at 1.0 mi on its way to the Cranberry River and a jct with the *Frosty Gap Trail*. See description below. Use of these two trails can form a loop of 28.6 mi back to Summit Lake.)

Continuing on the *Pocahontas Trail*, go through a boggy area and R of a field at 13.8 mi; make a sharp L at 14.1 mi. Bears may have damaged the trail signs. After 0.3 mi begin E descent on four switchbacks through tall hardwoods. An understory is dense with jewelweed, ferns, striped maple, cohosh, nettles, love vine, and squawroot (*Conopholis americana*). Reach a picnic area and join the nature center's *Nature Trail* at 15.8 mi. At 16.0 mi arrive at the E terminus of the visitor center parking area. A few yd E on the *Nature Trail* provides a magnificent view of the Greenbrier River valley and the Allegheny Mtns. (*USGS-FS Maps*: Webster Springs SW, Lobelia, Fork Mtn)

Kennison Mountain Trail (9.7 mi; USFS #244)
CONNECTING TRAILS:
> (*Pocahontas Trail* 20.2 mi; USFS #263)
> *South Fork Trail* (1.6 mi; USFS #243)
> (*Frosty Gap Trail* 5.2 mi; USFS #235)

TOTAL LENGTH: 36.7 mi
DIFFICULTY: moderate to strenuous
FEATURES: outstanding spruce forest, isolation
TRAILHEADS AND DETAILS: The S trailhead is at the Blue Knob jct with the *Pocahontas Trail*, 2.6 mi W of the nature center, but 1.0 mi S of its crossing at WV-39/55. At this point on the highway it is more likely to be used N than from its S terminus at the nature center. A rarely used trail, it has at least a dozen overgrown sections and no water except at a small drain 2.0 mi from the highway. Its attractiveness, however, is in its open hardwood areas; dense hemlock, red spruce, and rhododendron stands; sections of ferns and wildflowers; and wildlife. If hiking the entire trail, begin at the nature center on the *Pocahontas Trail*. After descending from the *Pocahontas Trail* for 1.0 mi, cross the highway to a parking lot constructed in 1996. (It is 2.0 mi E on WV-39/55 to the nature center.)

From the parking lot follow the trail through cherry, birch, beech, maple, and patches of ground cedar and blue cohosh. After 0.3 mi there may be a streamlet in wet weather. At 0.1 mi farther join with the *South Fork Trail*, R, a former timber road. (The *South Fork Trail* is a grassy road. At 0.6 mi it makes a switchback R, then L for a more rapid descent to Cranberry River Rd [FR-102] at 1.6 mi, and a jct with *Cow Pasture Trail*. To the R, upstream it is 0.2 mi to a gate, and another 0.9 mi to the Cranberry River Rd parking area. A loop could be made by taking the *Cranberry Volkswalk* back to the nature center and the SE end of *Pocahontas Trail*.)

On the *Kennison Mtn Trail* ascend another 0.3 mi to the S of the Kennison Mtn Range (4,445 ft). The jct with *Frosty Gap Trail* is at 2.1 mi. (At this point a loop could be made on *Frosty Gap Trail* to its first spur connection with the *Pocahontas Trail* and a turn S for a return to the point of origin at the nature center for 18.7 mi.) Continue ahead through large stands of spruce forest with segments of hardwoods, hemlock, and rhododendron for 6.0 mi on slightly changing contour levels. Except in rainy seasons, the treadway is generally dry. At 8.3 mi descend 1,000 ft in elev to the S bank of the Cranberry River. Wading is necessary to reach FR-76 on the N side of the river to Houselog Run shelter at 9.6 mi. On FR-76 (where vehicle traffic is not allowed) it is 8.0 mi N to Cranberry Campground and 8.0 mi SE to Cranberry Glades parking area. (*USGS-FS Maps*: Webster Spring SE, Lobelia)

Fork Mountain Trail (21.4 mi; USFS #236)

CONNECTING TRAILS:
> (*North Bend Trail*, 2.4 mi; USFS #225)
> *Big Run Trail* (1.0 mi; USFS #237)
> *Falls of Hill Creek Trail* (0.8 mi round-trip)
> (*Pocahontas Trail*, 20.2 mi; USFS #263)

TOTAL LENGTH: 45.3 mi

DIFFICULTY: easy to strenuous

FEATURES: wildlife, botanical study, Falls of Hill Creek Scenic Area

TRAILHEADS AND DETAILS: From the district office drive E for 1.1 mi on WV-39/55 to the trailhead across the North Fork of the Cherry River bridge. (It is 6.8 mi W from Summit Lake Recreation Area.) Enter the forest at the bridge in a low area on an old RR grade and follow the easy blue-blazed trail downstream. At 0.1 mi is a precipitous passage by the river. At 0.9 mi turn L and follow an old RR grade. Watch for a sharp L turn in a rocky area and ascend to another switchback on an old logging road. A wide range of botanical species include maple, cucumber, poplar, yellow birch, cherry, wood shamrock, rhododendron, orchids, club mosses, bee balm, ferns, blue-bead lily (*Clintonia borealis*), bellwort, blue and black cohosh, and meadow parsnip (*Zizia trifoliata*). Wildlife frequently are seen. After paralleling Desert Branch reach the end of a glade and cross FR-946 at 3.6 mi. Ascend to Fork Mtn ridge at 4.1 mi. Follow the ridge line and pass N and above Shiras Run headwaters through a forest of cherry, maple, and beech. Turn S at 5.6 mi in a rocky but level area. Hike on the E slope. At 6.0 mi is a jct with *North Bend Trail* L (see separate description below). Continue SE near the top of the plateau and reach the N slope of Rock-camp Knob (3,933 ft) at 8.7 mi. In a more E direction on rocky treadway, arrive at the *Big Run Trail* jct, L, at 10.6 mi.

(The *Big Run Trail* is a 1.0-mi access spur that descends steeply and partly on an old RR grade on the E side of Big Run to WV-39/55. Parking space is narrow here. It is 11.1 mi W on the highway to the district office.)

Continue SE on rocky, sometimes extremely rocky, treadway for 1.5 mi before turning S. After another 2.4 mi turn E on the slope. The land has sections of wet areas, large rocks covered with thick moss, rhododendron thickets, and patches of moosewood (*Virburnum alnifolium*). Deer, wild turkey, and red squirrel are frequently seen. At 15.1 mi ascend to the ridge line on an old woods road and turn L. (The woods road continues R to a private-property road.) Follow the ridge and reach the S terminus of FR-223 at 16.0 mi. Cross the road and parallel the Quiggly Rd (a private road R) for 0.9 mi to a woods road L. Leave the mtn ridge at 16.9 mi in a forest of beech, maple, cherry, and sparse red spruce. Understory is ferns, striped maple, moosewood, woodland sunflowers, and pink turtlehead. Cross a small stream at 18.2 mi. (To the L it is 125 yd to the Falls of Hill Creek Scenic Area parking lot and 0.2 mi out to WV-39/55; to the R the *Falls of Hill Creek Trail* descends for 0.4 mi to the middle and lower falls.) Continue ahead for another 125 yd to the Upper Falls and a sharp turn L. Go upstream, rock-hop, and ascend in a forest of rhododendron, hemlock, and yellow birch. At 19.9 mi cross a small drain in a ravine; the treadway is rocky and mossy. At 21.1 mi descend to an old RR grade and arrive at the E terminus of the trail and the jct with the *Pocahontas Trail* at 21.4 mi. From here it is 4.0 mi R on the *Pocahontas Trail* to the Cranberry Nature Center, or L it is 1.6 mi to WV-39/55. (*USGS-FS Maps*: Richwood, Fork Mtn, Lobelia)

North Bend Trail (USFS #225)

LENGTH: 2.4 mi

DIFFICULTY: moderate

TRAILHEAD AND DETAILS: On WV-39/55, 5.8 mi E of the district ranger's office, park at North Bend Picnic Area. The blue-blazed trail begins at a high footbridge over the North Fork of Cherry River. Hike downriver for 0.3 mi and turn L to ascend five switchbacks in a forest of yellow poplar, maple, cherry, and birch. Ferns, trillium, ramps, and foamflowers are part of the ground cover. At 1.1 mi is a jct with FR-730. Turn L, go 75 yd, then turn R. Follow a narrow logging road through a clearcut. Level off and meet a jct with *Fork Mtn Trail* (USFS #236). (It is 6.0 mi R on *Fork Mtn Trail* to WV-39/55 [1.1 mi E of the district ranger's office], and 15.4 mi L to the jct with *Pocahontas Trail* [USFS #263]). (*USGS-FS Map*: Fork Mtn)

BISHOP KNOB RECREATION AREA (Webster County)

Located 11.7 mi N of Richwood, this area has 61 campsites in a spacious hardwood forest, hand-pump water, and vault toilets. Each campsite is equipped with picnic table, lantern post, and grill. The campground is open Mar 1–Dec 1.

ACCESS: From jct of WV-39/55 and Cranberry Rd (CO-76) (across the road from Gales Restaurant) in Richwood, drive N on Cranberry Rd and reach Big Rock Recreation Area at 5.7 mi. (Right it is 7.0 mi to Cranberry Recreation Area.) Turn L on FR-81 and drive 6.0 mi to FR-101; turn R on FR-101 to entrance, R.

SUPPORT FACILITIES: (The same as for Summit Lake Recreation Area.)

Adkins Rockhouse Trail (2.1 mi; USFS #228); Cranberry Ridge Trail (5.8 mi; USFS #223)

LENGTH: 7.9 mi combined

DIFFICULTY: moderate

FEATURES: Black Cherry Seed Orchard, wildlife

TRAILHEADS AND DETAILS: These trails connect on FR-81, 0.3 mi S from the jct of FR-81 and FR-101 at Bishop Knob Recreation Area. Hike W on blue-blazed *Adkins Rockhouse Trail* near the fence of the Black Cherry Seed Orchard. Descend gradually to a timber road at 0.6 mi. At 1.3 mi follow the N side of Adkins Rockhouse Branch on an old RR grade. Cross a tributary at 1.6 mi and reach the Gauley River Rd (FR-234) near the Gauley River at 2.1 mi. Backtrack or use a vehicle shuttle. (To the W trailhead drive FR-101, 3.1 mi from the Bishop Knob campground, to FR-234 and turn L. Drive 5.1 mi S to trailhead, L.)

The *Cranberry Ridge Trail* begins opposite the road from *Adkins Rockhouse Trail*. Cross a damp area and at 0.6 mi pass a spur trail, L, to Bishop Knob campsite #44. Follow an old woods road through a hardwood forest and begin a gradual descent at 1.3 mi. At 2.1 mi the headwaters of Glade Run flow partially underground. At 2.5 mi pass E of a scenic lake and follow the road across Glade Run, S of the dam. Ascend and veer L off the road at 3.1 mi. (A gated road ahead leads out 0.6 mi to FR-81.) Ascend steeply, pass over a hill with red spruce to the R, and arrive at FR-84 at 3.8 mi. Cross

FR-81 and follow a ridge line through a hardwood forest. Some clearcuts of timber are on the L. Painted trillium (*Trillium undulatum*) are on this ridge. At 5.7 mi reach a logging road, turn L, and reach the SW end of the trail at 5.8 mi on CO-7/6. (Left on CO-7/6 it is 0.6 mi to the trailhead of *Hinkle Branch Trail*, 2.1 mi to FR-81, and 7.4 mi back to Bishop Knob camping area.) (*USGS-FS Map*: Camden on Gauley, Webster Springs SW)

Hinkle Branch Trail (USFS #219)

LENGTH: 2.4 mi round-trip
DIFFICULTY: moderate
FEATURES: wildflowers, Cranberry River

TRAILHEAD AND DETAILS: From the jct of FR-76 and FR-81 at Big Rock Campground it is 0.7 mi on FR-81 to CO-7/6. Turn L and go 1.5 mi to a small parking area across Hinkle Branch. Follow the blue-blazed trail downstream under tall birch, beech, and hemlock. Large colonies of club moss, mandrake, and wild lily of the valley are prominent. Cross the stream at 0.4 mi, descend to another old road in a halcyon glen near the branch at 0.8 mi. Reach the bank of the Cranberry River at 1.2 mi. Backtrack. (*USGS-FS Map*: Camden on Gauley)

Barrenshe Trail (USFS #256)

LENGTH: 4.5 mi
DIFFICULTY: moderate
FEATURE: Barrenshe Run cascades

TRAILHEAD AND DETAILS: From the jct of FR-81 and FR-76 at Big Rock Campground drive 1.4 mi S on FR-76 (4.5 mi N from Richwood) to *Barrenshe Trail*. Park on the W side of the road. The blue-blazed trail ascends on the road bank, E, to follow an old RR grade upstream by large beds of foamflower (*Tiarella cordifolia*) to cascades of Barrenshe Run. Turn L, ascend steeply to the ridge at 0.7 mi, veer R, and follow an undulating ridge line with oak, hemlock, maple, and locust for 3.0 mi. Striped maple is frequent as an understory. Curve on the N slope of Briery Knob (3,765 ft). Reach gated FR-99 at 4.5 mi. Backtrack or go R on FR-99 for 0.3 mi to the *Pocahontas Trail* (see connecting information below) on the L. Another option is to continue on FR-99 for 1.0 mi to the gate and vehicle access, and 3.7 mi on Country Club Rd to the jct with F-7. (*USGS-FS Maps*: Camden on Gauley, Webster Springs)

SECTION 3: GREENBRIER RANGER DISTRICT

In comparison to the other districts, the Greenbrier is the largest (243,055 acres), has has up to four times as many miles of forest roads (528 mi), and contains the longest section (49 mi) of the *Allegheny Trail*. In addition to its size, it also leads in having the most headwater sources to some of the major rivers. Some reasons why this district is often called the "Birthplace of Rivers": the Tygart, Shavers, Glady, and Laurel flow N to the Monongahela River; the east and west forks of the Greenbrier start S to the New River; the Elk begins W to the Kanawha River; the Jackson drains E to the James River; and the south branch of the Potomac flows NE. The district also has more nesting birds (104 species) in the 12,195-acre Laurel Fork Wilderness than any other MNF wilderness and the largest preserve (140 acres in the Gaudineer Scenic Area) of virgin red spruce and northern hardwood.

Old railroad tunnel on West Fork Trail.

Recreation areas include three picnic grounds and two campgrounds. One picnic area is Old House Run on US-250, 2.5 mi E from WV-28 in Thornwood, and another is nearby at Buffalo Fork Lake on FR-54, 2.4 mi off WV-28 in Thornwood. (North on WV-28, 5.6 mi from Thornwood, is the Locust Springs Picnic Area on FR-60 in the George Washington National Forest.) The other picnic area is on Gaudineer Knob (4,440 ft) on FR-27, 2.3 mi off US-250/WV-92 and 7.4 mi W of the ranger station in Bartow. The Gaudineer area was dedicated in 1937 in honor of D. R. Gaudineer, a ranger for 12 years in the MNF who sacrificed his life in an attempt to save others. Farther N, 0.8 mi, on FR-27 is the parking area, R, for the *Virgin Spruce Trail*, a 0.5-mi interpretive loop that have exceptionally tall maple, beech, cherry, ash, birch, and spruce. An understory and ground cover have moosewood, rhododendron, new-growth spruce and birch, wood shamrock, trillium, and foamflower. Campgrounds are Laurel Fork (15 sites) on FR-423, 1.5 mi off FR-14, and Island Creek (six sites) on WV-28, 0.8 mi N from the S entrance of FR-14.

The W boundaries of the district are the Tygart Valley, a broad and beautiful farming area that invites an artist's brush, and a section of Glady Fork on the N panhandle. Across the N border is US-33, and the E boundary follows directly S from US-33 near Job to WV-28 and S along the Virginia state line to the Marlinton Ranger District. The S boundary is SE from Valley Head in the W to the N boundary of Seneca State Forest and to the Virginia state line in the E, N of Paddy Knob.

ADDRESS AND ACCESS: District Ranger, Greenbrier Ranger District, PO Box 67, Bartow, WV 24920; 304-456-3335. In Bartow, 0.3 mi W on US-250/WV-92 from its jct with WV-28/92.

MAPS: Numbers 12–19

MIDDLE MOUNTAIN AREA
(Randolph and Pocahontas Counties)

On the main ridge of Middle Mtn (over 3,500 ft in elev) is FR-14, engineered to wave like a colorful banner in the wind for 26.5 mi from Wymer in the N to Burner Mtn in the S, before it descends to Fivemile Hollow for 4.0 mi to the National Youth Science Camp at WV-28, N of Thornwood. Tall black cherry, red and sugar maple, yellow birch, green ash, beech, and other hardwoods, which Dr. Maurice Brooks said had "leafy crowns," tower over open, gentle understories. Deer, grouse, and wild turkey are often seen crossing the road. Trail signs indicate the frequent descent to deep and damp shady paths under conifers and rhododendron. And for 12 mi on the E side of the road the forest is forever preserved in the Laurel Fork Wilderness. For those who love the splendor of the deciduous forest and cannot go hiking, a leisurely drive on this road is the next best thing.

If you see Middle Mtn from the air, you can understand why it is named Middle Mtn. It is between Shavers Mtn, W, and Rich Mtn, E, but beyond those ranges are Cheat Mtn and another Rich Mtn in the W, and Spruce Mtn, Fork Mtn, and Shenandoah Mtn in the E, all appearing as huge garden rows with natural irrigation between. This view, if none other of the topography, sustains Louise McNeill's "The Forest": "And shadowed in the distance / From Allegheny westward there is rolled / As God first planted when the hills awoke." Because the Middle Mtn trails are linear in their directions, some will be described in connecting groups to offer the use of the forest roads for circuit routes. The USFS reports that all trails are maintained every three or four years, with the exception of those in the Laurel Fork Wilderness Area, which receive less attention.

ACCESS: The N entrance is from Wymer on FR-14 at the jct with US-33. The S entrance is from Thornwood on FR-14 at the jct with WV-28, and from the E there is Dry Fork Rd (CO-40), 5.0 mi from Osceola (Sinks of Gandy). A W route is from Glady on Elliots Ridge Rd (CO-22).

SUPPORT FACILITIES: A former CCC camp, the Laurel Fork Campground has six campsites, hand water pump, tables, and vault toilets in the middle of the Laurel Fork Wilderness Area. In Bartow there is a motel, a restaurant, grocery stores, a service station, and a post office. The nearest commercial campground with full service is 3.0 mi S of Bartow on WV-28/92. Address: Boyer Station, Rte 1, Box 51, Arbovale, WV 24915; 304-456-4667.

Laurel River Trail (17.2 mi [9.6 mi N, 7.6 mi S]; USFS #306)

CONNECTING TRAILS:
    Stone Camp Run Trail (1.5 mi; USFS #305)
    Middle Mtn Trail (1.2 mi; USFS #307)
    Forks Trail (1.1 mi; USFS #323)
    Beulah Trail (4.2 mi; USFS #310)
    Camp Five Trail (1.6 mi; USFS #315)
TOTAL LENGTH: 26.8 mi
DIFFICULTY: moderate to strenuous

FEATURES: Laurel Fork Wilderness, wildlife, plant life

TRAILHEADS AND DETAILS: (Because of the damage caused by the 1996 floods, a few short segments of the *Laurel River Trail* may be changed or relocated.) The N entrance of the *Laurel River Trail* is on the S side of Beaverdam Run, on FR-14, 5.0 mi S of Weymer and US-33. After 3.4 mi the trail enters the Laurel Fork Wilderness. (On FR-14 the Laurel Fork Wilderness begins 2.6 mi S of Beaverdam Run.) The Laurel Fork Wilderness is in two sections: the North with 6,081 acres and the South with 6,114 acres. They were established by a congressional public law in January 1983. The E boundary is on the slope of Rich Mtn and the W border is on the E side of FR-14 along the Middle Mtn ridge. Forming the S border is Burner Mtn and the headwaters of Laurel Fork, a trout stream that flows N through the center of Dry Fork in the Cheat District. Between the two sections are 10 acres not in the Wilderness on FR-423 for a semiprimitive Laurel Fork Campground. The Wilderness has a number of wildlife species not found in the other MNF district Wildernesses. They are the hellbender (*Cryptobranchus alleganiensis*) and the mud puppy (*Necturus maculosus*) among 19 species of amphibians; the eastern box turtle (*Terrapene carolina*) and the milk snake (*Lampropeltis triangulum*) among 15 species of reptiles; the red bat (*Lasiurus borealis*) and the least weasel (*Mustela nivalis*) among 38 species of mammals; the hooded merganser (*Lophodytes cucullatus*), the red-shouldered hawk (*Bauteo platypterus*), the yellow-billed cuckoo (*Coccyzus americanus*), the willow flycatcher (*Empidonax traillii*), the least flycatcher (*Empidonax minimus*), the brown thrasher (*Toxostoma rufum*), the cedar waxwing (*Bombycilla cedrorum*), the bobolink (*Dolichonyx oryzivorus*), and the dickcissel (*Spiza americana*) among 104 species of nesting birds. Both the copperhead and the rattlesnake are found in the hardwood and pine ecosystems. The rattlesnake also is found in the red spruce ecosystems.

To hike the 9.6 mi N section of the *Laurel River Trail*, park on the N side of Beaverdam Run near the entrance to *McCray Ridge Trail* and walk 0.1 mi S on FR-14 to a seeded woods road, L, and enter a forest of maple, cherry, and birch. Parallel the stream by an open area of old beaver dams, glades, and vegetation such as ninebark (*Physocarpus opulifolius*), meadowsweet (*Spiraea latifolia*), fireweed, and cinnamon fern. At 0.3 mi leave the road, turn sharply L, and enter a section of hemlock, spruce, and rhododendron. Pass L of a rocky area and at 1.2 mi reach the riverbank. Campsites are here. Go upstream through a flood plain to a crossing of Laurel Fork at 1.4

mi. The river can be waded in normal weather. After crossing the river the trail goes upstream for 8.2 mi to Laurel Fork Campground. It follows short sections of footpaths and some old RR grades, but mainly a woods road. After crossing Bennett Run, return to the side of the river but soon veer away. Reach a pipeline clearing and Mud Run at 2.8 mi. Here is the N boundary of the Laurel Rock Wilderness. Deer are frequently seen here. Turn R and follow the pipeline swath for 0.2 mi. Turn L and gradually ascend and then descend on the old road through rhododendron and mtn laurel. Cross Stone Camp Run at 4.1 mi (this is an E tributary and not the Stone Camp Run with the trail). Cross Scale Lot Run after another 0.5 mi and pass through a forest of hemlock. At 5.3 mi reach a jct with the *Stone Camp Run Trail,* R, in a meadow of bellflower, ironweed, asters, and golden Alexander.

(The 1.5-mi *Stone Camp Run Trail* [650-ft gain in elev] crosses the river. Follow the blue-blazed trail up a deep hollow on portions of an old RR grade that weaves back and forth across the stream. Treadway is wet in sections. Black cohosh, ferns, and saxifrage grow on the trailside. Conifers are infrequent in a forest of beech, cherry, birch, and maple that become unusually tall from 1.2 mi to the top of the Middle Mtn ridge and the jct with FR-14. It is 3.8 mi N on FR-14 to the beginning of *Laurel River Trail* for a loop of 10.6 mi.)

Ahead on the *Laurel River Trail,* immediately after the jct with the *Stone Camp Run Trail,* cross Three Bear Run and follow a generally straight trail for 1.8 mi. Campsites are along the way. There are considerable signs of beaver activity on the W side of the river. Cross Bill White Run at 6.4 mi and Adamson Run at 7.1 mi. At 8.0 mi reach the jct with the blue-blazed *Middle Mtn Trail,* R.

(On the *Middle Mtn Trail* descend from the road, cross a small boggy area in hardwoods of maple and ironwood for 0.1 mi, and wade across Laurel Fork. Follow an old woods road in a hardwood forest to the stream's headwaters at 0.8 mi. Ascend on a footpath of switchbacks to the W terminus at FR-14. Elevation gain is 584 ft. The FR is too narrow to park here, so leave your vehicle 0.2 mi S at the jct with FR-422. It is 6.5 mi N on FR-14 to the N entrance of the *Laurel River Trail.*)

Continuing on the *Laurel River Trail,* pass through a stand of hemlock and join an old RR grade at 8.7 mi. Reach the riverbank where large hawthorn grow on the edge. Cross Five Lick Run and pass through a grassy field with wildflowers to re-enter the forest. At 9.2 mi arrive at a parking area on Dry Fork Rd (CO-40). Turn R and go 0.4 mi on CO-40 to the bridge; cross the bridge to the Laurel Fork Campground. Here is the S terminus of the N section of the *Laurel River Trail*.

The grassy Laurel Fork Campground has 15 campsites, hand water pump, tables, and vault toilets on the W side of the river. Primitive camping is also allowed anywhere in the adjoining open areas. (The USFS continues to improve the facilities at the campground as funds become available.) The managed season is from Apr 15 through November. The nearest grocery store, post office, and gasoline (open 11 A.M.–3 P.M., Mon–Sat) is in Glady, 6.2 mi on FR-423 W for 1.5 mi, FR-14 N for 0.3 mi, and FR-422 W for 2.5 mi to Elliots Ridge Rd (CO-22). Wymer also has a grocery store, post office, and gasoline; they are open each day with more hours. (See other support facilities above.)

The 7.6-mi S section of the *Laurel River Trail* is within the Laurel Fork Wilderness and receives little maintenance, but some improvements were made in 1984 by the Sierra Club. Nevertheless, the trail is well blazed, scenic, and generally easy on old RR grades, forest roads, and foot trails. From the Laurel Fork Campground go upstream by the restrooms and enter the forest in a red pine grove. Pass remnants of a water supply used by the CCC in the 1930s and reach a jct, R, with *Forks Trail* at 0.6 mi.

(The 1.1-mi *Forks Trail* ascends in a hollow and a S slope in a hardwood forest for 0.6 mi to FR-14. It crosses FR-14 and descends for 0.5 mi on a spur ridge and hollow of hardwoods, ferns, and club mosses to a gated gas-well access road, FR-183. Here it could be used as a loop S on FR-183 to the *Beulah Trail* and a return to the *Laurel River Trail* and *Forks Trail* jct for 4.6 mi, or FR-14 could be used for 0.9 mi to make a shorter loop of 3.5 mi.)

On the *Laurel River Trail,* cross a small drain in a meadow with scattered hemlock, pass a patch of skunk cabbage, and ascend slightly on a rocky area. To the L are sections of rapids and pools in the river. Reach a jct, R, with the *Beulah Trail* at 1.5 mi.

(The scenic 4.2-mi *Beulah Trail* ascends 440 ft in elev for 0.9 mi to cross FR-14 on its way to FR-44, where it provides the only practical trail route from this area to Shavers Mtn. Ascend on a partial old RR grade in a hardwood forest. At 0.5 mi it passes a water hole, favored by deer and surrounded by beds of ferns and wood shamrocks. It crosses FR-14 and can be used as a loop trail with the *Forks Trail* described above, or it can be used as access to FR-44 and Shavers Mtn. It is described in more detail below.)

Continue ahead on the *Laurel River Trail* on a more open slope and make a horseshoe curve near the mouth of Crawford Run, a tributary E of Laurel Fork, at 2.2 mi. Cross a number of drains where hemlock and spruce dominate, and arrive at the jct of *Camp Five Trail*, R, at 4.1 mi near a stand of red pine.

(The 1.6-mi *Camp Five Trail* ascends gently along Camp Five Run to FR-14. Outstanding features of this lush area are large fern and club moss beds and a charming mixture of hardwoods and conifers. Grouse and songbirds are prominent. Pass an inactive beaver dam at 0.2 mi and a small impoundment near the Middle Mtn Cabins at 1.4 mi.)

On the *Laurel River Trail* follow a grassy trail past old beaver dams, L. At 4.4 mi cross Laurel Fork (for the first time since the campground). It can be rock-hopped in normal weather. Leave the old RR grade on a slope; pass more old beaver dams. Summer butterflies are copious here. At 4.7 mi pass the remains of a large sawdust pile and enter a spruce and red pine grove. Pass through a boggy area at 5.1 mi. Prairie cordgrass (*Spartina pectinata*), bulrush, sedge, and speckled alder are prevalent. Because of beaver dams, the trail may be difficult to follow through swamps and high water. A departure from the trail to find a suitable crossing upstream may be necessary. The open area is scenic, and wild turkey are often seen. At 5.3 mi curve away from the main stream and ascend into a forest of conifers, maple, and birch. Join a seeded road (gated FR-97) at 6.3 mi. A section of the forest here has been set aside for testing and demonstrating silviculture practices for Allegheny hardwoods. Reach FR-14 at 7.6 mi. It is 10.5 mi S on FR-14 to WV-218 near Thornwood, and 1.4 mi N on FR-14 to *Camp Five Trail*, where a loop of 6.5 mi can be made for a return to the *Laurel River Trail* jct. (*USGS-FS Maps*: Glady, Sinks of Gandy, Whitmer)

Spring Box Loop Trail (1.8 mi; USFS #336)

CONNECTING TRAIL:
(*Camp Five Trail*, 1.6 mi; USFS #315)

DIFFICULTY: easy to moderate

TRAILHEADS AND DETAILS: Access is at Middle Mtn Cabins on FR-14 (18.7 mi S from the community of Wymer on US-33 and 10.5 mi from Camp Pocahontas off WV-28, N of its jct with US-250). Parking is roadside, and entrances to gated roads must not be blocked. (This area with Middle Mtn Cabins has a few cabins for rent from April through October.) *Camp Five Trail* (*USFS* #315) is also accessible here.

If beginning upstream from FR-14 follow a grassy forest road among ever-greens, ferns, and cool mtn air (average elev is 3,777 ft). Curve L (S), pass L of the spring boxes, and enter a forest path. At 0.9 mi reach the former *Lynn Knob Trail* and turn L. (To the R is a 0.5-mi connector to FR-179, the N trail-head for *Lynn Knob Trail* (*USFS* #317). Ascend easily to a knob, descend, cross a grassy opening, descend to FR-14, and cross at 1.6 mi. Pass through a dense forest to exit at a cabin restroom. Turn L, follow the driveway, and complete the loop at 1.8 mi at FR-14. (*USGS-FS Map*: Sinks of Gandy)

McGray Run Trail (USFS #302)

LENGTH: 4.7 mi
DIFFICULTY: easy to moderate
FEATURES: Glady Fork, wildlife, scenic
TRAILHEAD AND DETAILS: The *McCray Run Trail*, rather than crossing the ridge, follows the McCray Creek that runs from Middle Mtn to Glady Fork. Its steady contour is between 2,800 and 3,000 ft the entire distance. It is the only trail that directly connects Middle Mtn to the *Allegheny Trail*. The E terminus is 5.0 mi S of Weymer on F-14 to a parking area a few yd N of Beaverdam Run, at a gated road of the Columbia Gas Trans Corp. Follow the blue-blazed trail on the road through an assorted hardwood forest with scattered hemlock and red spruce; pass L of a wildlife food plot and R of the Beaverdam Run glades. Slightly ascend and reach a jct with a woods road, R, at 1.1 mi. Cross an old RR grade and descend gently on an old road for 0.5 mi to a jct; turn L to parallel McCray Creek. Cross a pipeline swath at 2.3 mi and remain on the L side of the stream. Pass through a mixture of hardwood, hemlock, and rhododendron. At 3.5 mi reach a jct with the *Allegheny Trail*. Turn L on jointly running trails for 0.5 mi, where *McCray Run Trail* descends R to the Glady Fork. Wading will be necessary, but impossible during spring runoffs or other high water. Across the river, fol-low upstream for 0.4 mi, veer R and parallel a drain on a footpath, pass through a hemlock grove, and reach the W terminus at Glady Fork Rd (CO-27) at 4.7 mi. It is 4.3 mi L to Glady and 5.1 mi R on CO-27 to Alpena and US-33. (*USGS-FS Map*: Glady)

Beulah Trail (4.2 mi; USFS #310); County Line Trail (4.1 mi; USFS #311)

LENGTH: 8.3 mi combined
DIFFICULTY: moderate to strenuous

FEATURES: wildlife, scenic forest, gas wells

TRAILHEADS AND DETAILS: In John Bunyan's *Pilgrim's Progress*, the land of Beulah was a tranquil land of peace and rest. The *Beulah Trail* has been named correctly. Its E trailhead is at the jct with the scenic *Laurel River Trail* (1.5 mi S from the Laurel Fork Campground). It ascends W in a moist glen where hardwoods shade the fern beds, mossy rocks, and a cascading tributary. At 0.5 mi it passes a small water hole, favored by deer, and ascends a S slope to reach FR-14 at 0.9 mi. (It is 0.9 mi N on FR-14 to a jct with the *Forks Trail,* and 3.9 mi S on FR-14 to a jct with *Camp Five Trail.*) Across the road it descends steeply on a N slope to a cove and drain at 1.2 mi. Birch and maple are the dominant hardwoods. Colorful and poisonous baneberry (*Actaea pachypoda*) is seen among the rich fern beds. Reach FR-183B at 1.9 mi. Follow the road for 1.1 mi to a jct uphill with the N terminus of the *County Line Trail.* Here the *County Line Trail* follows the road and the *Beulah Trail* turns a sharp R on a footpath to descend in an open hardwood forest. Cross two drains where wildlife is frequently seen and gradually descend on a N slope to the main stream crossing at 4.1 mi. Reach FR-44 at 4.2 mi. (It is 0.5 mi L on FR-44 to the *High Falls Trail,* and 3.5 mi R on FR-44 to Glady.)

At the N terminus of the *County Line Trail* at the jct with the *Beulah Trail,* hike up the road (FR-183B) to the crest of the ridge and descend to a curve where the road ends at a gas well and the blue-blazed trail remains on the ridge at 0.5 mi. Ascend to the first (3,610 ft) of five major knobs on Little Beaver Mtn, a ridge of hardwoods shaped like a crescent high above the headwaters of the east fork of the Glady Fork. Arrive at the unmarked county line of Randolph (L) and Pocahontas (R) at 2.0 mi. After a plateau begin a descent on switchbacks into an impressive open cove of cherry and maple to cross an old RR grade in a saddle at 2.5 mi. Ferns and wildflowers are abundant and a drain begins on the L. Ascend on two switchbacks to a knob (3,686 ft), descend to another saddle, and ascend again to another knob. At 3.7 mi reach a clearing with a gas well and a pipeline crossing at the end of FR-35A. There is plenty of space here to park. The trail's S terminus is 0.4 mi farther down the road to a jct in a sharp curve with Snorting Lick Rd (FR-35). To the L it is 0.7 mi to FR-14. (*USGS-FS Maps*: Widell [1977], Sinks of Gandy [1970], and Glady [1976] do not show trail relocations.)

Lynn Knob Trail (3.1 mi; USFS #317); Hinkle Run Trail (3.7 mi; USFS #367)

LENGTH: 6.8 mi combined

DIFFICULTY: moderate to strenuous

FEATURES: scenic, diverse animal and plant life

TRAILHEADS AND DETAILS: These two N-S trails are grouped because they connect on FR-17. The N terminus of the *Lynn Knob Trail* is on Elklick Run Rd (FR-179), 0.6 mi W from FR-14. (On FR-14 it is 1.4 mi N to Middle Mtn Cabins, and 10.5 mi S to WV-28 near Thornwood.) There is parking space at the trailhead. Ascend to Lynn Knob (3,990 ft) in a beech and cherry forest at 0.4 mi. Deer, turkey, red squirrel, and grouse are often seen here. At 1.8 mi begin a descent, steep in sections, on switchbacks. Reach an old logging road at 2.2 mi and descend through a beautiful maple forest. Pass a number of drains with ferns and club moss. Arrive at the S terminus at the Little River Rd (FR-17) at 3.1 mi. (It is 1.4 mi E to FR-14 and 4.2 mi W to FR-44.)

Across the road is the N terminus of the *Hinkle Run Trail* (USFS #367). Descend slightly on a grassy road, make a sharp L, cross a small stream, and rock-hop or wade the Little River at 0.1 mi. Liverwort grows on mossy rocks. Parallel the stream for 0.5 mi to the mouth of Hinkle Run. Pass R of an open field at 0.8 mi. After the third crossing of Hinkle Run, leave the stream and parallel a tributary drainage. At 2.3 mi turn sharply L off the old grassy road and rock-hop the tributary on an old road. Immediately turn R off the road to join another old logging road. At 3.0 mi pass through a stand of hemlock. Pass a large and steep grassy field that is on the N side (former route of this trail), and make a curve L (S) at 3.2 mi. Here the road becomes level, passes through birch and maple, then for the last 0.2 mi goes through a stately red pine plantation. At 3.7 mi reach the S terminus at the jct of FR-14 and FR-15. Elevation gain is 646 ft. (It is 5.0 mi L on FR-14 to FR-17 and 4.0 mi R on FR-14 to WV-28.) (*USGS-FS Maps*: Wildell, Sinks of Gandy)

Burner Mountain Trail (USFS #322)

LENGTH: 3.6 mi

DIFFICULTY: moderate

FEATURE: nature study

TRAILHEAD AND DETAILS: (In 1997 the USFS announced plans to relocate this trail. Contact the district ranger's office for an update.) The E trailhead of the *Burner Mtn Trail* is 1.0 mi S on FR-14 from the jct of FR-14 and FR-15 at the S terminus of the *Hinkle Trail*. (However, at the FR jct there is a spur access trail up the Burner Mtn ridge for 0.7 mi to the *Burner Mtn Trail*. A posted, seeded road is unmarked and unblazed through a forest of red pine, hawthorn, cherry, and maple. It passes through a wildlife food plot on the ridge top to join the blue-blazed *Burner Mtn Trail*.) From the jct of WV-28 and FR-14 at the National Science Youth Camp, drive up FR-14 for 3.0 mi to the trailhead sign, L, and parking on the R. Ascend Burner Mtn on the wide pathway and reach the ridge top at 0.2 mi. Pass L of the wildlife food plot and follow the blue-blazed trail on the ridge line of 4,000 ft or more elev. Treadway is on a wide woods road. The forest has maple, ash, oak, cherry, birch, spruce, ferns, and wildflowers. The wildlife includes deer, turkey, red squirrel, owls, and songbirds. At 1.1 mi pass an old woods road L; begin a slight ascent and reach a knob (4,285 ft) at 2.0 mi. After 0.2 mi turn W, then NW, and finally N in a slight descent on the ridge. Enter a red pine grove at 3.4 mi and a grassy area at the trailhead on FR-15. From here it is 0.6 mi L to the *Span Oak Trail* and 4.1 mi R to FR-14. (*USGS-FS Maps*: Thornwood, Durbin)

Span Oak Trail *(USFS #321)*

LENGTH: 3.7 mi

DIFFICULTY: strenuous, elev gain 1,175 ft

FEATURE: nature study

TRAILHEAD AND DETAILS: From US-250 on Highland St in Durbin go N on FR-44 for 7.0 mi to the trailhead on the R (before the Little River bridge and FR-17 jct). (It is 16.2 mi N on FR-44 to Glady.) Follow the blue-blazed trail on an old wagon road through red pine, maple, birch, and serviceberry, past attractive views of the Little River. Cross a small drain at 0.3 mi and ascend gradually through cherry, witch hazel, rhododendron, and ferns. Turn R at 0.4 mi on an old RR grade and pass the site of a former RR trestle at 0.6 mi. Turn off the RR grade; ascend to the top of the ridge at 1.1 mi. Follow the ridge in a gradual climb for 2.6 mi through a beautiful forest of birch, maple, cherry, and oak. Deer, turkey, grouse, owls, and songbirds frequent the ridge. At 3.0 mi parallel FR-477, pass a wildlife food plot and reach the E terminus for 3.7 mi at FR-15. (FR-15 is usually rutted and narrow.) It is 0.6 mi L on FR-15 to *Burner Mtn Trail* and 4.1 mi farther on FR-15 to FR-14. (*USGS-FS Map*: Durbin)

ISLAND CAMPGROUND AREA (Pocahontas County)

This small picturesque campground is on an island of the east fork of the Greenbrier River at the SW toe of Poca Ridge and the mouth of Long Run. It has only four campsites with tables and vault toilets, but it is an excellent base for hiking the *East Fork Trail, Poca Run Trail,* and other nearby trails.

ACCESS: In Bartow, at the jct of US-250 and WV-28/92, drive N on WV-28 for 4.7 mi to entrance, L.

SUPPORT FACILITIES: In Bartow there is a motel, restaurant, service station, post office, and grocery stores. The nearest commercial campground with full service is 3.0 mi S of Bartow on WV-28/92. Address: Boyer Station, Rte 1, Box 51, Arbovale, WV 24915; 304-456-4667.

East Fork Trail (USFS #365)

LENGTH: 7.9 mi

DIFFICULTY: easy

FEATURES: scenic, botanical study

TRAILHEAD AND DETAILS: This luxuriant, luminous pathway is a paradise for wildflower enthusiasts. From the ragwort and violets of springtime to the wreath goldenrod (*Solidago caesia*) in the fall, there is color, fragrance, and beauty. At the S trailhead in Island Campground, enter at the trail sign and follow an old RR grade through a hemlock grove for 0.3 mi to parallel the east fork of the Greenbrier River. The stream has both native and hatchery trout. It is one of those streams observed by poet laureate Roy Lee Harmon in "Summer River": "For carefree days, for happiness sublime, I know that there are things to find, along a summer river any time." Yellow birch, beech, hemlock, ironwood, maple, alder, and red spruce are along the trail. Reach an island at 0.7 mi, but hike on the E bank if the water is high. At 2.0 mi cross a tributary and pass through a field with St John's wort, asters, elderberry, and golden Alexander. Although the blue blazes indicate a fording of the stream at 2.4 mi, the forest is open enough to hike 0.3 mi to rejoin the trail without crossing. Make a horseshoe turn after another 0.3 mi but soon return to a N direction. At 4.0 mi begin a longer curve on the mountainside to small meadows and a red pine plantation. Rock-hop Abe's Run and immediately arrive at Abe's Run Rd (FR-51). Here is an open area good for campsites. To the R, it is 2.4 mi to WV-28 and 4.0 mi farther S to Island Campground. To the L is a cement bridge and gate. Serviceberry, wildflowers, and ferns are prominent. Continue upstream on a pleasant path through a number of red spruce borders. At 5.8 mi cross Burning Run and at 6.8 mi cross Simmons Run. For the last 0.8 mi the trail is close to the stream bank. Wildflowers and mosses are prolific. At 7.9 mi reach the N terminus of the trail and jct with the Pigs Ear Rd (FR-254). It is 1.6 mi E to FR-103 and 1.9 mi farther to WV-28 for a total return R on WV-28 of 9.3 mi to Island Campground. (*USGS-FS Map*: Thornwood, Sinks of Gandy)

Poca Run Trail (USFS #335)

LENGTH: 2.5 mi
DIFFICULTY: easy

TRAILHEAD AND DETAILS: From Island Campground drive 1.3 mi NE on WV-29 to gated FR-286, L at Poca Run (that flows under WV-28) for the W trailhead. (The trail makes a crescent to return to WV-28.) The E trailhead is 2.2 mi farther NE (and 0.3 mi W from entrance to Locust Springs Picnic Area in Virginia) on the W side of the road.

Follow a blue blaze on an old woods road through yellow birch, basswood, cherry, ferns, and such flowers as blue cohosh and sweet cicely. At 0.6 mi curve R. (Down an embankment, across a stream, and upstream on FR-286 is an unnamed, 1.8-mi, blue-blazed trail to the top of Poca Ridge.) At 1.2 mi is a red cedar forest near the headwaters of Poca Run. From here the trail follows FR-271A 0.5 mi to FR-806, where it follows down a ridge to a gate at WV-28. (*USGS-FS Map*: Thornwood)

Smoke Camp Trail (USFS #324)

LENGTH: 2.6 mi
DIFFICULTY: strenuous, elev gain 1,327 ft
FEATURE: Rothkugel Forest Plantation

TRAILHEAD AND DETAILS: From Island Campground, drive S on WV-28 for 2.0 mi to the Max Rothkugel sign, L, and park. Walk S on WV-28 for a few yd to the trailhead, L. Ascend into the forest where in 1907 Rothkugel planted Norway spruce, European larch, and black locust under the supervision of George F. Craig, a close friend of the famous forester Gifford Pinchot. Originally, Craig acquired 13,000 acres; later, 9,965 of those acres became one of the first tracts for the MNF. At the lower elev are conifers, but after 0.6 mi enter a hardwood forest of cherry, beech, ash, and maple. Pass a spring at 0.8 mi. Ascend steeply on a N slope, reach a ridge line, and exit at the E terminus with Smoke Camp Rd (FR-58) at 1.8 mi. To the R is the site of the former Smoke Camp fire tower. Backtrack. (FR-58 is closed from April to mid-August for wildlife protection. The road connects with

Long Run Rd, FR-57, which begins 0.1 mi S on WV-28 from Island Campground.) (*USGS-FS Map*: Thornwood)

Buffalo Fork Lake Trail (USFS #368)

LENGTH: 1.1 mi

DIFFICULTY: easy

FEATURES: scenic, wildflowers

TRAILHEAD AND DETAILS: Access is from the jct of WV-28 and FR-54, 1.3 mi N from WV-28 and US-250 jct, and 2.3 mi S from Island Campground. Drive 2.4 mi on FR-54 to parking area L, midway on Buffalo Fork Lake. The 22-acre impoundment was completed in 1969. Swimming, motorboats, and the use of live minnows for fishing are prohibited. Facilities include picnic area, vault toilets, and drinking water. Hike down the road, cross the dam, and enter the forest. At 0.7 mi reach a boardwalk and a bridge in a marshy area. (The bridge over Buffalo Fork may be washed out.) Reach the road and return to the parking area. Vegetation on the trail includes hemlock, beech, birch, trillium, club mosses, columbine, and waterleaf (*Hydrophyllum virginianum*). (*USGS-FS Map*: Thornwood)

SHAVERS MOUNTAIN AREA
(Randolph and Pocahontas Counties)

Shavers Mtn is a long (more than 20 mi), high (4,000 ft), narrow (3.0 mi), remote, and scenic SW-NE ridge between two rivers. On its ridge line are the former *Shavers Mtn Trail* and *North-South Trail*, now the *Allegheny Trail* (see Chapter 11). For 10.0 mi on the S half, the county line of Randolph (W) and Pocahontas (E) weaves across the ridge top, and on the E slope for this same distance is a 0.8-mi-wide swath of private land. On the E slope the elev drops 1,000 ft for 1.5 mi to the West Fork of the Greenbrier River, which flows S, and on the W slope the elev drop is 500 ft for 2.0 mi to the Shavers Fork, which flows N. Wildlife, particularly bear and deer, is abundant in a forest of mixed hardwoods, spruce, hemlock, and pine. The Gaudineer Knob Picnic Area is 2.3 mi into the forest on FR-27 from US-250/WV-92, and it is another 0.8 mi on FR-27 to the Gaudineer Scenic Area and *Virgin Spruce Trail* described in the introduction to this section.

The *Allegheny Trail* follows the ridge in forest property for 20.4 mi. Its N access is in Glady and the S access is on US-250/WV-92, 2.0 mi W of Durbin. It has two shelters, one vehicle access point, and three foot-trail access points on this long stretch. The farthest N is the *High Falls Trail* from FR-44. In the S is *Johns Camp Run Trail* from FR-317; at the Gaudineer Scenic Area it touches FR-27, and near the jct of FR-27 and US-250/WV-92 is a 0.2 mi-spur trail for an access. The only vehicle access to the ridge is on FR-27, 4.0 mi W of Durbin.

SUPPORT FACILITIES: Slightly SE and across the road from the Gaudineer Rd (FR-27) entrance off US-250/WV-92 is a seasonal restaurant, and public telephone. In Durbin, 4.0 mi E on US-250/WV-92, there is a service station, grocery store, restaurant, and laundromat.

High Falls Trail (USFS #345)

LENGTH: 5.0 mi round-trip

DIFFICULTY: moderate to strenuous

FEATURES: scenic, beaver dam, High Falls

TRAILHEAD AND DETAILS: Entrance to the E terminus is on FR-44, 4.0 mi S of Glady and 19.0 mi N on Little River Rd (FR-44) from Durbin. The road is too narrow for parking at the trailhead but there is space nearby, N on the W side of the road. Follow the blue blazes on an old woods road in a wet area and cross the west fork of Glady Fork at 0.2 mi. A beaver dam is upstream. Cross the abandoned Western Maryland Railroad at 0.4 mi. Pass through a pasture with grasses, hawthorn, and such wildflowers as Deptford pink, daisy, and selfheal. Cross a stream and then enter the forest at 0.5 mi. Deer, raccoon, turkey, and numerous songbirds have been seen here. Climb a stile and ascend steeply to an intersection with the *Allegheny Trail* at 1.0 mi in a forest of maple and cherry. (On the *Allegheny Trail* it is 1.1 mi S to Widell shelter and 8.3 mi to Johns Camp shelter. It is 5.0 mi N to Glady.) Continue ahead, W, descend, cross Deer Lick to a S slope, and reach the Western Maryland Railroad after 1.0 mi. Elev drop is 700 ft. Turn R and follow the RR 0.5 mi to a horseshoe bend in Shavers Fork to scenic High Falls (approx 12 ft high) at 2.5 mi. Backtrack. (*USGS-FS Maps*: Wildell, Beverly East)

West Fork Trail (25.5 mi; USFS #312)

CONNECTING TRAILS:

      (*High Falls Trail*, 2.5 mi; USFS #345)

      (*Allegheny Trail*, 20.4 mi; USFS #701)

DIFFICULTY: easy to moderate

FEATURES: scenic old RR grade, tunnel, trestle, wildlife, wildflowers

TRAILHEADS AND DETAILS: This former CSX Railroad was purchased by the USFS in 1986 and now is one of the district's most exciting hiking routes. Scattered campsite space is available along the way and hiking, biking, and cross-country skiing are allowed. Motorized vehicles are prohibited. Its change in elev is hardly distinguishable at its high point between the headwaters of Glady Fork (flows N) and the West Fork of the Greenbrier River (flows S) near the crossing of *High Falls Trail.*

Its N trailhead is at a jct with the CSX Railroad near Shavers Fork at Greenbrier Jct. To reach the location, drive 0.7 mi W from Glady on CO-22 to the top of the ridge and an old RR loading dock L (S). Descend to old RR grade and hike R (W) 2.7 mi to Greenbrier Jct near Shavers Fork canyon. Then backtrack to proceed E through the tunnel and S to Durbin. The S trailhead is at the jct of US-250 and CO-250/15, E of the US-250 bridge over West Fork.

If choosing to avoid the backtracking at the N trailhead, make an 11.2-mi loop by using *High Falls Trail* described above. Instead of backtracking on the *High Falls Trail,* continue downstream on CSX Railroad 1.4 mi to Greenbrier Jct, leave the RR tracks, and begin the *West Fork Trail.* At the tunnel (where you will need a flashlight) climb over earthen barriers at 3.1 mi and exit the tunnel at 3.3 mi. (You may decide not to wade the water inside the tunnel, and instead ascend N near the old loading dock to CO-22, turn R, and rejoin the trail on the E side. If not easy to locate, simply hike the road down to Glady and turn R (S) on Glady Fork Rd, CO-27, to the trail.)

At 3.8 mi pass private houses and arrive at a parking area near other private houses. Begin a narrow channel of RR grade on scenic hillside pasturelands. Cattle, sheep, and deer graze together on both sides of the fenced and gated trail. Pass a gate and graveyard at 4.1 mi and a jct with *High Falls Trail* at 7.3 mi. (To the L [E] it is 0.4 mi to FR-44.) At 8.1 mi cross a glade, a forest logging road at 8.6 mi, and reach a meadow with a hawthorn grove at 10.0 mi. Wildflowers are commonplace along the trail, and through forest sections are ash, maple, hemlock, and cherry. Cattails border some former and current beaver dams. The former Wildell Railroad jct is at 10.5 mi, where a gate and parking area are near a dirt road, 0.2 mi L (E) to FR-44.

Trestles over the West Fork of the Greenbrier River are crossed at 13.5 mi and 13.7 mi before a gate crossing to Mill Run Rd at 15.5 mi. (The dirt road goes E 0.1 mi to FR-44 and a popular spring.) Other trestles are crossed near the confluence with Iron Bridge Run at 16.5 mi, at 18.7 mi with Little River, and at 23.9 mi with Mtn Lick Run. Between the trestle crossings are excellent views of the river, pools for fishing, wildflower meadows, and rock formations. At 21.5 mi is a trail access a few yd to FR-44 (Braucher on topo maps). Pass under US-250 bridge at 25.0 mi, pass a gate, and reach the end of the trail at 25.5 mi at a parking area off Pocahontas Rd (CO-250/13). (Across the street, US-250, is Highland St that connects with FR-44.)

Another loop option using the *West Fork Trail* is to include the *Allegheny Trail*. Follow the *High Falls Trail* 1.0 mi from FR-44 to the jct with the *Allegheny Trail*, turn R (N), and after 3.9 mi arrive at CO-22 at Glady. Turn R to follow the *West Fork Trail* and return to *High Falls Trail* for a loop of 9.3 mi. It is 4.0 mi on FR-44 (which becomes CO-22/2) between the *High Falls Trail* and Glady. A small store may be open at irregular hours in Glady. (*USGS-FS Maps*: Bowden, Glady)

Johns Camp Run Trail (USFS #341)

LENGTH: 0.8 mi

DIFFICULTY: easy

FEATURE: wildlife

TRAILHEAD AND DETAILS: From the jct of US-250/WV-92 and FR-27, 4.0 mi W of Durbin, take FR-27 for 6.1 mi to a jct with FR-317, R. Drive 0.5 mi on FR-317 to a dead end. Begin the trail on a wet old woods road that parallels Johns Camp Run. The forest is mainly birch and spruce. At 0.7 mi cross a small stream and follow a footpath to the *Allegheny Trail* and Johns Camp shelter. There is evidence that deer, red squirrel, chipmunk, raccoon, and other small animals frequently visit this campground. On the *Allegheny Trail* S it is 9.5 mi to US-250/WV-92; N, it is 8.3 mi to the jct with *High Falls Trail*. (*USGS-FS Map*: Wildell)

CHEAT MOUNTAIN AREA (Randolph County)

The high, scenic Cheat Mtn area is the westernmost section of the district. Altitudes range from 3,700 ft to 4,700 ft on its long ridge line. Its W drainage is to the Tygart River and its E waters flow to the trout-filled Shavers Fork. The mtn range is rich in timber, minerals, vascular plants, and wildlife, particularly bear, deer, and turkey. There is a 5.5-mi "Fish for Fun" section of Shavers Fork, from Whitmeadow Run downstream to McGee Run, which is stocked twice annually. Four trails have their W termini on the Cheat Mtn Rd (FR-92), the main artery across the ridge. The trails descend like tributaries to Shavers Fork. One other trail, *Chestnut*

Ridge Trail, has its E terminus on FR-92 and goes down the W slope. There are no designated campgrounds or picnic areas, but there are excellent campsites on the trails and backcountry roads.

ACCESS: The S access is at the jct of FR-92 and US 250/WV-92 at Cromer Top (3,803 ft), 9.8 mi W of Durbin and 8.4 mi E of Huttonsville. The N access to FR-92 is by Back Rd (CO-37), which begins 1.6 mi S of Beverly on US-219/250.

SUPPORT FACILITIES: Motels, restaurants, service stations, banks, grocery stores, and a post office are in Huttonsville and in or near Durbin.

Stonecoal Ridge Trail (USFS #360)

LENGTH: 4.0 mi
DIFFICULTY: moderate
FEATURE: wildlife
TRAILHEAD AND DETAILS: From the jct of US-250/WV-92 and FR-92, drive N on FR-92 for 3.2 mi to the W trailhead, R. Follow the undulating ridge in a mixed forest dominated by red spruce. Deer and turkey are seen at the wildlife food plots, such as at 1.8 mi, and chipmunk are prevalent throughout. Ferns, mosses, and new growth are common ground covers. From 2.2 mi the blazes may be absent, but the trail begins a descent on the S slope of the ridge toward a drain. At 3.1 mi curve away from the stream and reach FR-760 at 3.8 mi. Turn R and descend on a gated road to FR-209, the E trailhead at 4.0 mi. Across the road is a thick stand of rhododendron by Shavers Fork. The exit is 1.0 mi upstream on FR-209 to US-258/WV-92, 2.5 mi E of FR-92. (*USGS-FS Maps*: Mill Creek, Wildell)

Chestnut Ridge Trail (USFS #327)

LENGTH: 5.5 mi
DIFFICULTY: strenuous, elev gain 1,548 ft
FEATURES: scenic, wildlife
TRAILHEAD AND DETAILS: (Some relocations are planned or in process.) The E trailhead is on FR-92 (opposite the jct with FR-47), 4.2 mi from US-250/WV-92. Descend in a hardwood forest of cherry, maple, and yellow birch with sparse conifers on a rocky and sometimes wet, eroded treadway for 0.7 mi to FR-1560. Turn R. (At 0.8 mi the abandoned and unmaintained *McGee Run Trail* is L.) Follow FR-1560 for 0.7 mi and turn L on an old woods road along Chestnut Ridge. At 2.4 mi is a jct with *Laurel Run Trail*, L. (The *Laurel Run Trail* is no longer maintained by the USFS.) Deer, turkey,

and grouse are often seen on the ridge. Pass through a wildlife food plot at 2.6 mi. ATVs use the trail. Turn L at 4.0 mi on a footpath and descend to a secluded cabin with a scenic view at 4.1 mi. Cross another ATV route at 4.3 mi. Leave the ridge, L, and descend in a cove of nettles, white snakeroot, wild azaleas, and ferns. At 4.9 mi arrive at a drain and pass through a mixed forest with poplar, dogwood, bush dogwood, and locust. Wild sunflowers, goldenrod, asters, and vines grow in the meadow. Arrive at Shavers Run Rd (CO-39/1) and a wooden bridge over Shavers Run at 5.5 mi, the trail's W terminus. Access here is from the town of Mill Creek at the jct of US-219/250/WV-92 and Back Rd (CO-39) at the Mill Creek Methodist Church. Follow CO-39 over the Tygart River bridge and go 0.6 mi to Mud Run Rd (CO-39/2), R (old barn is L). Follow Mud Run Rd for 2.0 mi and turn R on Shavers Run Rd (CO-39/1). After another 0.8 mi reach the trailhead, R. (*USGS-FS Map*: Mill Creek)

Whitemeadow Ridge Trail (USFS #361)

LENGTH: 4.6 mi

DIFFICULTY: moderate

FEATURES: wildlife, scenic

TRAILHEAD AND DETAILS: The trail entrance is 1.4 mi N on FR-92 from the *Chestnut Ridge Trail* at the FR-92 and FR-47 jct. Follow the blue blazes, though some are faint, uphill on a wide, seeded road to a knob at 0.4 mi. Turn L on the ridge that remains about 4,000 ft in elev for 2.3 mi. The forest has birch, maple, red spruce, and hemlock. Wildlife is prominent. Sections of the trail are unblazed. At 2.7 mi begin a descent that becomes steeper after 0.5 mi. On a rocky treadway, descend to an old RR grade at 3.6 mi. Bear have been sighted here. (To the L is an access route through a birch and rhododendron forest for 0.5 mi to the E terminus of FR-49 at scenic Shavers Fork.) A turn R on the old unblazed RR grade leads through a verdant, tranquil, and sometimes gardenlike route of rhododendron, birch, ferns, mosses, and the sound of the river. After 1.0 mi reach the E terminus of the trail and the E terminus of FR-47. Here is an excellent campsite area near the trout-stocked Shavers Fork. It is 2.2 mi on FR-47 up Whitemeadow Run to FR-92. (*USGS-FS Maps*: Mill Creek, Wildell)

Crouch Ridge Trail (2.9 mi; USFS #362); Turkey Trail (0.7 mi; USFS #364)

LENGTH: 3.6 mi combined

DIFFICULTY: moderate

FEATURE: wildlife

TRAILHEADS AND DETAILS: The W trailhead is a few yd N on FR-92 at the jct of FR-92 and FR-49. Follow the ridge line over knobs. In sections, walking is rough over rocks and roots. Ferns are copious and the forest is red spruce, hemlock, birch, and maple. At 2.0 mi reach a fork in the trail: *Turkey Trail* goes L and *Crouch Ridge Trail* goes R. (The *Turkey Trail* descends 0.7 mi in a damp ravine area to cross Yokum Run and exit at FR-188.) To the R is a new gated road for coal mining that has access across Shavers Fork to the Western Maryland Railroad. (To the L on FR-188, go 0.5 mi to a parking area and pass the jct with *Yokum Ridge Trail*, R, on the way. From here it is 1.9 mi on FR-188 to FR-92.) Continue descent on *Crouch Ridge Trail*, cross a number of wet spots, and pass through a forest of exceptionally tall and large red spruce in an open forest. Rock-hop Crouch Run and reach FR-49 at 2.9 mi. To the L it is 1.2 mi up Crouch Run to the jct with FR-92. (*USGS-FS Maps*: Mill Creek, Wildell)

Yokum Ridge Trail (1.4 mi; USFS #365); Yokum Ridge Spur Trail (0.8 mi; USFS #369)

LENGTH: 2.2 mi combined

DIFFICULTY: moderate

FEATURES: wildlife, scenic

TRAILHEADS AND DETAILS: From the FR-92 and FR-188 jct, drive N on FR-92 for 0.9 mi to trailhead, R. Enter forest of red spruce, maple, birch, and cherry with an understory of new growth and ferns. Club moss and other mosses form a ground cover. At 0.9 mi is a trail fork. The *Yokum Ridge Trail* goes L. (An old damaged sign indicates the L fork is the *Bear Trail*, but the USFS has taken this off their list for maintenance.) (To the R the unblazed, 0.8-mi *Yokum Ridge Spur Trail* descends through a forest of tall red spruce, birch, and maple. At 0.6 mi pass through a boggy area to an open grassy area that has a good campsite. Follow an old RR grade over remnants of bridges, cross Yokum Run in a damp, dark green mossy area to reach FR-188 at 0.8 mi, the trail terminus. To the R it is 0.2 mi to a parking area and 1.9 mi farther on FR-188 to FR-92.) On the *Yokum Ridge Trail* descend through a beautiful forest of tall maple, red spruce, and beech where wood shamrock and moosewood are abundant. Turkey, deer, and bear are in the area. Pass R of a small stream and ravine and descend to exit at 1.4 mi. To the R is the riverbank of Shavers Fork. To the L it is 50 yd to a cul-de-sac, the E end of McGee Run Rd (FR-210), and 1.8 mi W to FR-92. At FR-92 it is 9.0 mi S to US-250/WV-92. (*USGS-FS Map*: Wildell)

CHEAT SUMMIT FORT AREA (Randolph County)
Strip Mine Trail (USFS #350)

LENGTH: 3.5 mi

DIFFICULTY: easy to moderate

FEATURES: history, scenic, strip mines

TRAILHEAD AND DETAILS: The E trailhead is accessible by driving 9.4 mi W on US-250 from the Greenbrier Ranger District office in Bartow. Immediately after crossing the Shavers Fork bridge turn L off US-250 onto FR-245. After 0.5 mi turn R on a steep and rough road 0.5 mi to a parking area for Cheat Summit Fort Historical Site. Here is a picnic area and a signboard of information about the walk N up to White Top (4,100 ft in elev). The summit was a strategic lookout at the beginning of the Civil War. Confederates lost the fort to Col Nathan Kimball, but the fort was abandoned after the winter of 1861–62 when soldiers died from disease and cold weather. South of the parking area up toward a viewing area is Fort Milroy Cemetery, partially destroyed by strip miners. Since the USFS purchase of the property in 1986, the 40,827-acre Mower Tract has had white crosses placed at the cemetery. A short path leads to the cemetery.

From the parking area drive S, ascend 0.2 mi past the cemetery, and drive another 0.3 mi through Scotch pine to a parking area for viewing. In 1996 a vault toilet was constructed here by the USFS. The E trailhead of *Strip Mine Trail* begins at the parking area opening into Scotch pines. (In early 1997 the trail was not blazed, but this is the general direction. Hike through the pines on a flat area, then follow the S slope of a ridge in a forested area. Descend on two switchbacks at 2.1 mi to follow R (W) on a strip mining road. For the next 1.4 mi the route is on the old road in an open area to the jct with FR-227. Contact the ranger's office for an update on the trail's status.)

To reach the W trailhead by vehicle, drive 4.0 mi farther W on US-250 and turn L at Cromer Top on FR-227 (FR-92 is R [N]). Follow FR-227 2.2 mi to a strip mine road L and a flat area for parking. (There may not be a trail sign here.) (FR-227 continues R steeply to cross a bridge over Lambert Run, up to FR-227B, R for 3.6 mi to FR-233, and another 3.0 mi to Beaver Creek.) To have a lofty view of the general route of *Strip Mine Trail,* drive E on FR-227B. The lack of vegetation from strip mining gives an eerie, surrealistic feeling of artificial landscaping: neatly created pools of dark water and bleak, remote vastness. You can also see Barton Knob (elev 4,434) to the N. (*USGS-FS Map*: Snyder Knob [includes 4,700-ft Snyder Knob] [the 1977 topo map does not show either the FRs or the trail location])

NORTH FORK OF DEER CREEK AREA
(Pocahontas County)
Rattlesnake Trail (2.5 mi; USFS #366); North Fork Trail (2.9 mi; USFS #333)

LENGTH: 5.4 mi combined

DIFFICULTY: *North Fork Trail* is moderate; *Rattlesnake Trail* is strenuous with elev gain of 1,548 ft

TRAILHEADS AND DETAILS: (During the mid-1980s these trails were in need of maintenance, and by the end of the decade the USFS considered them abandoned and requested the description be removed from the *Monongahela National Forest Hiking Guide*. In 1996 the USFS requested the *North Fork Trail* be included in the guide and in *West Virginia Hiking Trails*. Maintenance continues as a problem, but hunters use the *Rattlesnake Trail,* and you may find the trail worth exploring.) To reach the W trailheads, turn off WV-28/92 in Arbovale on Back Draft Rd (CO-6), opposite the National Radio Astronomy Observatory (NRAO), and drive 0.6 mi. Turn L on North Fork Rd (CO-6/1) and go 1.6 mi to a fork in the road. Veer L on gravel road for 0.4 mi to FR-197. Cross a cement bridge over the North Fork of Deer Creek, pass L of Sutton Run Rd (FR-1678), and reach the end of FR-197 at a group of hunter's cabins after 1.4 mi.

Begin the *Rattlesnake Trail,* R, on the abandoned FR and cross Tacker Run at 0.2 mi. Through hemlock, witch hazel, maple, and birch reach Rattlesnake Run at 0.5 mi. Turn L up Rattlesnake Hollow and ascend steeply on four switchbacks to a ridge line at 1.2 mi. Deer, grouse, turkey, skunk, and red squirrel are on this trail. Continue constant ascent in oak, hickory, ash, beech, cherry, and mtn laurel for another 1.2 mi to a grassy area and Elleber Sods Rd (FR-1681). Ahead 0.1 mi is Elleber Knob (4,595 ft), with superb views of Deer Creek Valley, Little Mtn, and other distant ridges. Backtrack or plan a vehicle shuttle. To the R, FR-1681 is 9.0 mi to US-250 at the West Virginia–Virginia state line, on the Virginia side. There are two gates on the road; the first (usually open), is 1.0 mi from US-250, and the other gate, 1.0 mi E of Elleber Knob, is closed except for the fall game season.

The *North Fork Trail* goes upstream by the North Fork. Cross Tacker Run at 0.1 mi in a hemlock and maple forest. Cross an overflow of North Fork, R of gentle section of cascades. Follow an old RR grade and pass R of another old RR grade at Block Run at 0.8 mi. At 1.6 mi there are sections that are eroded and need relocating. There are a number of beaver ponds here; deer and raccoon tracks are noticeable. Cross the North Fork a number of times and reach the Elleber Sods Rd (FR-1681) at 2.9 mi, the NE trail terminus. Here is the confluence of North Fork and Elleber Run. Backtrack or use a vehicle shuttle 2.2 mi S on FR-1681 from US-250 at the West Virginia–Virginia state line. It is 7.0 mi W on US-250 to the jct with WV-28 near Thornwood. (*USGS-FS Maps*: Green Bank, Hightown)

(While close to the National Radio Astronomy Observatory, you may wish to visit and take a tour. Of high significance is a 140-ft telescope completed in 1965, the largest equatorially mounted telescope in the world, and the Green Bank Telescope, 100 meters in diameter, also the largest of its type in the world. The guided tour also includes audiovisuals. If the NRAO office is closed, you may park at the parking lot near the gate and take an authorized 1.0-mi walking tour to the 140-ft telescope. For safety reasons do not walk under any telescope or equipment. Call 304-456-2011 for information.)

LITTLE MOUNTAIN AREA (Pocahontas County)

The following two trails at separate locations ascend to end and connect with the *Allegheny Trail* on Little Mtn, a forested N-S ridge between WV-28/92, E (S of Bartow), and the Greenbrier River, W. Wildlife is prominent on both trails. (See chapter 11 for *Allegheny Trail*.)

Little Mountain Trail (USFS #332)

LENGTH: 2.5 mi

DIFFICULTY: moderate

TRAILHEAD AND DETAILS: Access to this area of sylvan remoteness is on WV-7, 3.0 mi E from the bridge in Cass and 2.3 mi W from the jct of WV-28/92. Limited parking is on the S side of WV-7 near Deer Creek. (In 1997 this trail was infrequently used and blue blazes were sparse.) At the trail sign ascend 45 yd to turn L. Ascend gradually on an old and narrow road for 0.8 mi to a streamlet (that may be dry in summer). Twenty feet beyond turn sharply R off the old road and ascend in a rocky area. At 1.2 mi among an oak/hickory forest reach the top of Little Mtn ridge. (Here may be sounds of the Cass Railroad steam whistles from the W.) In winter there are views of Deer Creek Valley E at 1.4 mi. Make a sharp R turn and descend at 1.6 mi. The trail undulates for the next 0.4 mi, and at 2.0 mi plunges into a hollow on five switchbacks. At 2.5 mi is a jct with the *Allegheny Trail*, R and L, in a dense and dark grove of hemlock and rhododendron. (*USGS-FS Map*: Cass)

Hosterman Trail (USFS #337)
CONNECTING TRAIL:
   Allegheny Trail (57.9 mi in Greenbrier R.D.)
LENGTH: 5.2 mi round-trip
DIFFICULTY: easy to moderate
FEATURES: Greenbrier River swinging bridge, wildlife
TRAILHEAD AND DETAILS: Access from Durbin is W on US-250 across the bridge and L on Grant Vanderventer Rd (CO-250/11). After 1.0 mi turn L on Back Mtn Rd (CO-1) for 6.8 mi to L turn on Hosterman Rd CO-1/24). Descend 1.2 mi, turn R, cross old RR ties, and go through a rutted meadow for 0.2 mi to Greenbrier River, L. Another approach is from Cass off WV-7 on CO-1 for 6.2 mi to Hosterman Rd, R.

Begin your hike across the scenic 208-ft swinging bridge. (Bridge was repaired from damage by 1996 floods that rose near the top of guardrails.) Turn R and enter a rocky and dense passage of rhododendron and hemlock to a wide and old road at 0.3 mi. Turn L. (In 1997 there were no blazes or signs here.) Ascend a gentle grade among a mixture of hardwoods and evergreens, beautiful, remote, and peaceful any season of the year. Deer, fox, owls, and songbirds are among the wildlife. Sounds of the river can be heard at 1.3 mi. At 1.8 mi is old open field and pines, R. Cross a culvert washout at 1.9 mi. Ascend; meet a jct with the *Allegheny Trail* (R and ahead) at 2.6 mi. After 175 ft the *Hosterman Trail* ends at gated Slavin Hollow Rd (boundary of National Radio Astronomy Observatory). Backtrack. (The *Allegheny Trail* continues L [N] 10.0 mi to Durbin. Going S on the *Allegheny Trail* it is 7.2 mi to Cass.) (*USGS-FS Map*: Green Bank)

Peters Mountain Trail (5.5 mi; USFS #359); Bar Ford Trail (1.5 mi; USFS #370)
LENGTH: 7.0 mi combined
DIFFICULTY: moderate
FEATURE: nature study

TRAILHEADS AND DETAILS: The E trailhead for *Peters Mtn Trail* is on WV-92, 0.6 mi S of the jct with WV-7. The W trailhead is on WV-7, 0.6 mi E from the Greenbrier River bridge in Cass. On WV-92 (2,610 ft) ascend gradually from the trail sign on a blue-blazed trail through white oak, white pine, hickory, and dogwood to the ridge top at 0.2 mi. Wintergreen, Indian plantain, wild azalea, and thyme-leaved speedwell (*Veronica serpyllifolia*) border the trail. Descend and ascend knobs, first in a SW direction, then W, and then S to a fork at 2.7 mi (3,078 ft) with *Bar Ford Trail*.

(*Bar Ford Trail* forks R and descends to Clay Hollow, where it follows the stream to its mouth at Deer Creek at 1.0 mi. Follow upstream on the R of Deer Creek to the creek crossing. Only a cable remains of a former cable line crossing; wading is necessary. Ascend steeply on a large rock formation to a sharp curve on WV-7, 1.0 mi E from the Greenbrier River bridge in Cass.)

Continue L on the *Peters Mtn Trail,* which undulates through a hardwood forest with scattered Virginia pine and evidence of wildlife. At 4.3 mi curve N and begin descent at 4.6 mi. Wade across Deer Creek at 5.4 mi and ascend to WV-7, 0.6 mi E from the Greenbrier River bridge in Cass. (Trail sign may not be here.) Parking is difficult here. (*USGS-FS Maps*: Cass, Clover Lick, Green Bank)

SECTION 4: MARLINTON RANGER DISTRICT

The Marlinton Ranger District has 135,170 acres and 285 mi of system forest roads. Its W boundary adjoins the Gauley Ranger District along the Highlands Scenic Highway (WV-150) for 13.3 mi from the Cranberry Mtn Visitor Center to the Williams River. This area also includes the Tea Creek drainage, the remote Gauley Mtn Range, and such magnificent high points as Sharp Knob (4,532 ft), Little Spruce Knob (4,128 ft), Big Spruce Knob (4,673 ft), Gauley Peak (4,584 ft), and Red Spruce Knob (4,703 ft). The Greenbrier Ranger District is on the N boundary from Valley Head to Cass and the N edge of Seneca State Forest. On the E boundary the Marlinton Ranger District adjoins the George Washington National Forest along the Virginia–West Virginia state line on the Allegheny Mtn ridge. The S border is from the Calvin Price State Forest to High Top on the state boundary and adjoins the White Sulphur Ranger District. The *Allegheny Trail* runs N-S for 40 mi through the E center of the district (see chapter 11). Such trails as the *Bear Pen Ridge Trail* and the *Red Run Trail* are significant examples of remoteness in the Tea Creek Area. The most remote area is the N section of

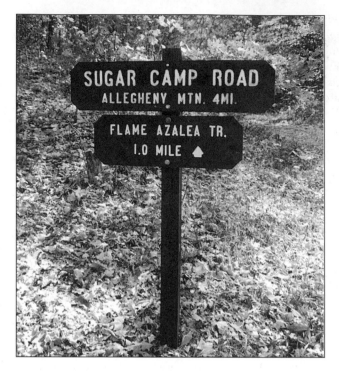

Entrance to Flame Azalea Trail.

Gauley Mtn. Old timber roads off FR-24 (access W off US-219, 2.4 mi S of Slaty Fork) takes hikers and hunters to rugged backcountry near Sharp Knob (4,532 ft) and Rocky Point (4,364 ft). The district has four semiprimitive recreational areas with campgrounds, none of which it plans to expand. They are Bird Run, Day Run, Pocahontas, and Tea Creek, open year-round, but services are closed between Dec 15 and Mar 15. There are more than 70 mi of hiking trails plus the *Allegheny Trail.*

Passing through the district is the 75.2-mi *Greenbrier River Trail,* a state park, but only 3.6 mi of it are on district property, between Marlinton and Clover Lick. (See chapter 6 in this book for more information.)

ADDRESS AND ACCESS: Marlinton Ranger District, Marlinton, WV 24954; 304-799-4334. The office headquarters are at the E edge of Marlinton on WV-39.

MAPS: Numbers 6,9,20, and 21

SUGAR CAMP AREA (Pocahontas County)
Flame Azalea Trail (USFS #410)

LENGTH: 0.3 mi (or 2.3 mi)

DIFFICULTY: easy (or moderate)

FEATURES: concentration of flame azaleas

TRAILHEAD AND DETAILS: Access from the jct of WV-92 and WV-84 in the community of Frost is N on WV-92 for 1.5 mi to the entrance R at a sign and gate on FR-441. (Parking for two cars.) If the gate is unlocked drive 1.0 mi to the trail entrance, L. Otherwise hike the road. The uniqueness and beauty of this short loop in a cove is the more than 150 azaleas in a timber cut of the early 1980s. Profusely blooming near the last week of May, the wild azaleas (*Rhododendron calendulaceum*) have hues of yellow, red, and orange. Growing among the azaleas are rosebay rhododendron, dogwood, white pine, locust, minnie-bush, ferns, and more than 50 species of wildflowers. The trail is maintained by an outing club of professors and students from Louisburg College in North Carolina. (*USGS-FS Map*. Paddy Knob)

> SUPPORT FACILITIES: The nearest store for gasoline and groceries is at the jct of WV-92/WV-84 in Frost. From the jct it is 1.6 mi NE on WV-84 to Bird Run Campground, R. It has 12 shaded campsites with central vault toilet and water pump.

POCAHONTAS RECREATION AREA (Pocahontas County)

The Pocahontas Recreation Area is in the SE corner of the district and accessible to nearby trails in the White Sulphur District also. It is 4.0 mi SE of famed Minnehaha Springs and Camp Minnehaha, where the mineral springs bubble from the hillside between Kapp Creek and Douthat Creek. (The area was named to honor Minnehaha, meaning "laughing water," wife of Dakota Indian Hiawatha in Longfellow's fictional *The Song of Hiawatha*.) The recreation area is cloistered in rhododendron and exceptionally tall hemlock and white pine. There are nine campsites with picnic tables, vault toilets, and a manual water pump for drinking water.

> ACCESS: From the jct of WV-39/92 at Remel Forest Plantation, go S for 1.8 mi on WV-92 to the entrance, L.

> SUPPORT FACILITIES: The nearest general store for groceries, gasoline, and public telephone is in Minnehaha Springs, 4.0 mi NW on WG-39/92.

Two Lick Trail (USFS #456)

LENGTH: 4.3 mi

DIFFICULTY: moderate

FEATURES: remote, botany

TRAILHEAD AND DETAILS: At the entrance of the Pocahontas Campground, at the immediate L, follow a blue-blazed foot trail and cross a footbridge over Cochran Creek in a hemlock forest. After 0.1 mi the trail forks around the headwaters of Two Lick Run. If turning R, after 0.2 mi pass through beds of such club mosses as *Lycopodium flabelliforme* and *Lycopodium obscurum*. Ascend a ridge in a hardwood forest with sparse Virginia and white pine, and at 1.6 mi turn sharply L to the side of another ridge. After a rocky footway, descend and ascend slightly between the ridges and turn L again at 2.6 mi for a descent by switchbacks to Two Lick Run. Pass L of a grazing field at 4.1 mi and complete the loop at 4.3 mi. (*USGS-FS Map*: Mtn Grove)

Laurel Creek Trail (USFS #466)

LENGTH: 8.0 mi

DIFFICULTY: moderate

FEATURES: nature study, history, remote

TRAILHEAD AND DETAILS: From the Pocahontas Campground drive N 2.3 mi on WV-92 to a jct with WV-39. Turn L and go 0.4 mi to the Rimel parking circle and picnic area, R. (From Minnehaha Springs drive S on WV-39/92 for 3.6 mi.) The trail was a former National Recreation Trail (1975–85), and was constructed by the Older American Workers under the supervision of the USFS. Follow the blue-blazed trail R, cross the Lockridge Mtn Road and reach an old RR grade at 0.4 mi. Proceed upstream, L of the trout-stocked Laurel Creek, on a wide, grassy, and sometimes wet trail under a magnificent canopy of hemlock, oak, and white pine. The route is bordered by rhododendron, witch hazel, and hay-scented fern. Cross streamlets from the L; enter a long meadow at 1.1 mi. At 2.2 mi there is a skunk cabbage patch. Turn L off the grassy road at 2.5 mi by Lockridge Run, and follow on the SW side. Begin an ascent at 3.8 mi in young forest growth from a mid-1980s clearcut. Curve S around the slope and pass an Adirondack shelter (sleeps eight), R, at 4.5 mi. Continue to curve around a number of Lockridge Mtn spur ridges in a hardwood forest to cross Lockridge Mtn Road at 7.5 mi. Begin a descent to a drain and reach the parking area at 8.0 mi. (*USGS-FS Map*: Minnehaha Springs)

Middle Mountain Trail (North Section, USFS #408)

LENGTH: 4.6 mi (of 17.7 mi)
DIFFICULTY: moderate
FEATURES: flora and fauna
TRAILHEAD AND DETAILS: (The 13.1-mi S section is described in the White Sulphur District, part 2, section 6.) Entrance to the N trailhead is across the road (WV-39/92) from the Rimel parking circle and trailhead for the *Laurel Creek Trail*. Follow the blue blazes through a stand of white pine for 0.1 mi to Laurel Creek. Rock-hop or wade because the footbridge has been washed out. (The USFS does not plan to replace the bridge due to budget constraints. During high water, another access is possible by entering the pine forest in the SW corner of the WV-39/92 jct and hiking downstream 0.5 mi to cross Cochran Creek near its confluence with Laurel Creek.) Begin ascent on a well-graded treadway through a garden of violets and ferns—Christmas, sensitive, maidenhair, cinnamon, and hay-scented. Tall hemlocks drape over rhododendron before the trail enters an oak forest with mtn laurel. At 0.5 mi reach a jct with a grassy road. Turn R and continue the ascent. The air is filled with the medicinal odor of pennyroyal. Reach the Middle Mtn crest line and a wildlife water hole at 1.5 mi and follow SW. Pass another wildlife water hole and food plot at 2.5 mi, and at 3.5 mi arrive at a shelter (sleeps eight). (There is a lack of water on the ridge crest.) At 4.4 mi reach a jct with the newly constructed Divide Rd (FR-790), which descends E for 3.0 mi to a gate at WV-92. The trail ascends 0.2 mi farther to the White Sulphur District, where the trail number changes from 408 to 650. Backtrack and hike down the Divide Rd, or continue ahead. If continuing ahead it is 2.7 mi to connect with the *Allegheny Trail*, another 5.8 mi to Boles Run Rd (FR-875), which exits E to WV-92, and another 4.6 mi to North Fork Rd (CO-14/FR-96) for an exit E to WV-92 at Neola. (*USGS-FS Maps*: Minnehaha Springs, Mtn Grove, Lake Sherwood)

BEAVER CREEK AREA (Pocahontas County)
Beaver Trail (USFS #458)

LENGTH: 2.8 mi round-trip
DIFFICULTY: strenuous, elev gain 1,165 ft
FEATURE: panoramic view
TRAILHEAD AND DETAILS: From the jct of Beaver Creek Rd (CO-21) and Pyles Mtn Rd (CO-21/4), at the E entrance of Watoga State Park, go N on Beaver Creek Rd for 1.8 mi to a curve L and a cabin R. (Request permission

from the occupant of the cabin to park near the unmarked trail entrance.)
Follow the private road, pass R of a house, reach the forest boundary, and
cross Mary Sharp Run footbridge at 0.3 mi. Among the flora are hemlock,
white pine, rhododendron, trailing arbutus, wintergreen, fern, oak, and
maple. Cross the creek again at 0.7 mi, turn sharply L, and ascend steeply
to the crest of a ridge. Ascend steeply on switchbacks to the top of Beaver
Lick Mtn (3,645 ft; Beaver 2 on the topo map), site of a dismantled fire
tower, for a superb panoramic view at 1.4 mi. Backtrack. (A parking area is
here, accessible during the hunting season on Beaver Lick Tower Rd [FR-
343]. See Middle Mtn Area in White Sulphur District.) (*USGS-FS Maps*:
Marlinton, Lake Sherwood)

Beaver Creek Trail

LENGTH: 0.4 mi

DIFFICULTY: easy

FEATURE: scenic

TRAILHEAD AND DETAILS: At the Beaver Campground on the E side of the
Watoga State Park, drive to campsite #27 and a gate. (The trail formerly
began here and went 2.1 mi to FR-343.) If the gate is open, drive upstream
to a large meadow (a former light-plane landing strip) in the Calvin Price
State Forest. At 0.1 mi reach a jct, R, with *Jacob's Well Trail*, which goes W
into Watoga State Park. After another 0.3 mi, park at the graveled cul-de-
sac. Rock-hop Beaver Creek and follow an old wagon road through a scenic
and dark forest of hemlock, maple, and rhododendron for 0.4 mi to a jct
with the *Allegheny Trail* R and L. (The *Allegheny Trail* is being relocated
here to follow the *Jacob's Well Trail*.) A turn L on the *Allegheny Trail* is 1.3
mi up the hollow and ascends the headwaters to Beaver Lick Tower Rd
(FR-343), the boundary of White Sulphur District. (*USGS-FS Map*: Lake
Sherwood)

HIGHLANDS SCENIC HIGHWAY (PARKWAY) AREA
(Pocahontas County)

Highlands Scenic Highway

The Highlands Scenic Highway is a 45-mi, two-lane paved corridor through
the Gauley and Marlinton Ranger Districts of the Monongahela National
Forest. Without billboards and housing developments this high (2,235 ft to
over 4,500 ft in elev) highway is also called the National Forest Scenic
Byway. Its 22-mi section from Richwood to Cranberry Mtn Nature Center

parallels the meandering and cascading North Fork of Cherry River and Hills Creek on WV-39/55. The other 23 mi from the nature center N and E to Elk Mtn and US-219 is shaped like a skyline crescent. On WV-150 it is the parkway section, the only system of its type in the nation managed by a national forest. (In contrast Virginia's Skyline Drive and the Blue Ridge Parkway in Virginia and North Carolina are managed by the US Park Service, though these scenic highways pass through sections of national forests.) In addition to the highway numbers, the scenic highway also has green and yellow logo markers.

The Gauley Ranger District is on the W side of the parkway section and the Marlinton Ranger District is on the E and N. In the Gauley Ranger District is Cranberry Wilderness and on the E side is the Black Mtn Range, a sanctuary for black bear. The entire highway is exceptionally colorful with spring flowers and flowering trees, and foliage colors in autumn. The parkway is not plowed in the winter and may be closed from late December into March. Listed below are some of the landmarks on the parkway, beginning with Cranberry Mtn Nature Center at the jct of WV-39/55 and WV-150 (6.5 mi W from US-219 at Mill Point on WV-39/55).

Location	Milepost
High Rock Trail and parking area (E)	3.3 mi
Cranberry Glades Overlook and parking area (E)	4.8 mi
Forks of Cranberry Trail and parking area (W)	5.2 mi
Big Spring Overlook and parking area (E) and *Black Mtn Loop Trail* (E & W)	6.2 mi
Little Spring Overlook and parking area (E) and *Black Mtn Loop Trail* (E & W)	7.9 mi
North-South Trail and parking area (W)	8.6 mi
North Fork Trail and parking area (W)	10.0 mi
FR-86 jct and Williams River Bridge (NW & SE)	13.3 mi
Williams River Trail and parking area (SE)	13.4 mi
Little Laurel Overloop and parking area (SE) and *Tea Creek Mtn Trail* (N)	16.8 mi
Gauley Mtn Trail and parking area (N)	17.3 mi
Red Spruce Knob Trail and parking area (S)	17.7 mi

Location	Milepost
Red Lick Overlook and parking area (S)	20.1 mi
US-219 at Elk Mtn (6.6 mi S to Marlinton	
and 9.6 mi N to Slaty Fork)	23.0 mi

High Rock Trail
LENGTH: 3.2 mi round-trip
DIFFICULTY: moderate
FEATURE: scenic
TRAILHEAD AND DETAILS: From the Cranberry Mtn Visitor Center, drive on the Highlands Scenic Highway (WV-150) for 3.3 mi to a parking area, R. Trail enters open woods of maple, beech, and oak with a ground cover of ferns, trillium, blue-bead lilies, and other wildflowers. Follow the High Rock ridge, cross an old timber road at 1.3 mi, and reach a precipitous rock formation for a splendid view at 1.6 mi. A chestnut fence is a protective barrier at a cliff. Views are of Bald Knob (4,289 ft), directly ahead, and in the far distance, Beaver Lick Mtn and the Allegheny Mtns. Backtrack. (*USGS-FS Map*: Hillsboro)

Cranberry Glades Overlook Trail
LENGTH: 0.5 mi round-trip
DIFFICULTY: easy
FEATURE: cranberry glades
TRAILHEAD AND DETAILS: From the *High Rock Trail* parking area described above, go N 1.5 mi to another parking area, R. Follow the sign and ascend through birch, maple, moosewood, and ferns to a spectacular view of Cranberry Glades Botanical Area and the Kennison Mtn Range. Backtrack. (*USGS-FS Map*: Hillsboro)

Black Mountain Loop Trail (USFS #412)
LENGTH: 4.7 mi round-trip
DIFFICULTY: Moderate
FEATURES: wildlife, wildflowers, scenic views
TRAILHEAD AND DETAILS: On the Highlands Scenic Highway (WV-150), 6.2 mi N from the intersection with WV-39/55 at Cranberry Mtn Nature Center, is the S trailhead at Big Spruce overlook. The N trailhead is at Little Spruce Overlook, 1.7 mi farther N on WV-150. The day-hike trail makes a loop with 2.4 mi on the E side in Marlinton Ranger District and 2.3 mi on

the W side of the highway in Gauley Ranger District (Because the trail's passage in the Gauley Ranger District is through the Cranberry Wilderness where construction and maintenance is minimal, you will need to be alert for tracking the pathway.)

If beginning at Big Spruce Overlook on the E side, enter a dense forest up the bank near the picnic shelter, and soon descend on rocky and mossy switchbacks. At 0.3 mi turn L (N) and follow sections of an old timber RR grade among birch, beech, rhododendron, and red spruce. At 2.1 mi ascend a rocky mountainside to a boardwalk and observation deck. Proceed L to an exit at Little Spruce Overlook.

Across the highway enter the forest of red spruce and descend gradually into a narrow, rocky, mossy passage. There are a few sections of seepage at 0.5 mi and 0.8 mi. The pathway levels before a rock pile at 1.0 mi. Lichen decorate the rocks and wood sorrel and Indian pipe are among damp and rich green moss fields. Scattered mtn ash and quaking aspen are among the birch. Pass through a patch of rhododendron and mtn laurel before reaching WV-150 at 2.3 mi and Big Spruce Overlook. (*USGS-FS Maps*: Hillsboro, Woodrow)

Red Spruce Knob Trail (USFS #405)

LENGTH: 2.3 mi round-trip

DIFFICULTY: easy

TRAILHEAD AND DETAILS: On the parkway, 0.9 mi E of Little Laurel Overlook and 2.4 mi N of Red Lick Overlook, enter the trail at a parking lot sign. Ascend gradually on switchbacks. In a forest of hardwoods, conifers, and mosses, this area is a habitat for Virginia flying squirrels. Make a short loop at the top (4,703 ft in elev—the highest peak in the district) among dense red spruce at 1.2 mi. Once the site of a fire tower, views are now limited, mainly E to Crooked Fork Valley and Old Field Fork Valley. (From the parking area another 1.0-mi walk descends to gated FR-115.) (*USGS-FS Map*: Woodrow)

TEA CREEK RECREATION AREA (Pocahontas County)

Here is a rich meadow filled with the spring fragrance of black locust and apple blossoms. Once an old logging camp with a church and school, it now is a campground with yellow buckeyes, elderberries, raspberries, and wild plums growing by the entrance. Canada lily (*Lilium canadense*) grows by the stream banks. The area is bordered on the E and the S by the splashing waters of Tea Creek and the trout-filled Williams River. Towering 1,000 ft above it are Sugar Creek Mtn, Turkey Mtn, and Tea Creek Mtn. The campground is open all year with 29 camping sites, tables, vault toilets, and a hand pump for drinking water, but service is closed from Dec 15 to Mar 15. Because the concrete bridge over Williams River at the campground entrance is constructed low, the campground may be isolated during high water and flooding. Flooding also can endanger campsites, particularly on the access near Tea Creek. Examples of severe flooding have been in 1981, 1984, 1985, and 1996.

In 1985 five trails were accessible from the campground, all of which were on the E side of Tea Creek. Since then the USFS has constructed 12 more trails, with six on the W side of Tea Creek for the purpose of expanding usage away from the most popular *Tea Creek Trail*. (One of these six, *Tea Creek Interpretive Trail*, has been abandoned by the USFS.) In the current network of 45 mi of multiple loops you will have a choice for popular campsites or remote solitude. A land of flood and fire, soggy old RR beds, cascading streams, rock outcrops with dense rhododendron, and prowling bears, there is also space for serendipity. To assist in keeping it wild and clean, promote no-trace camping. Below are three examples of how to form long loops with the guidance of the Tea Creek Area hiking map, free at the campground (or from the district office).

ACCESS: At the jct of WV-150 and WV-39/55, at the Cranberry Mtn Nature Center, drive N on WV-150 for 13.3 mi to FR-86, turn W, and drive 1.0 mi to the campground entrance, R, over a cement bridge.

SUPPORT FACILITIES: In Marlinton, 15.5 mi E on WV-150 and S on US-219, there are banks, shopping centers, restaurants, motels, and service stations.

Option #1: Turkey Mountain Loop, 8.8 mi

Bannock Shoals Run Trail (4.4 mi; USFS #446); Saddle Loop Trail (1.6 mi; USFS #448); Turkey Point Trail (1.1 mi; USFS #447); Turkey Point Connector Trail (1.3 mi)

CONNECTING TRAIL:

(*Boundary Trail*, 3.8 mi; USFS #449)

DIFFICULTY: strenuous

FEATURES: gorge, wildlife, serenity

TRAILHEADS AND DETAILS: In the campground, walk up the road that parallels Tea Creek to a dead end and gated *Bannock Shoals Run Trail* (formerly graveled FR-135). Ascend gradually. At 0.3 mi is a jct with former *Tea Creek Interpretive Trail*, R (an access to *Turkey Point Connector Trail*). After another 0.5 mi curve N up Upper Bannock Shoals Run in mainly a hardwood forest of yellow and black birch, beech, maple, and oak. Ferns and wildflowers are copious. In a horseshoe curve cross the stream in a gorge at 1.5 mi. At 2.3 mi make a switchback in another horseshoe curve and continue to ascend on the mountainside, W of the gorge but increasingly close. Near the top of the mtn curve R and at 4.4 mi meet *Saddle Loop Trail*, R, and *Boundary Trail*, also to the R. (There are signs here unless the bears have destroyed them.) (Ahead, NE, is FR-135, previously gated but now only posts remain. The road leads to FR-24, where FR-135 may be gated at private property. FR-24 descends to US-219, 2.4 mi S of Slaty Fork.)

Follow *Saddle Loop Trail* (not actually a loop unless using part of *Boundary Trail* and *Turkey Point Trail*) on an old grassy FR for 0.6 mi to cross a bridge and stream, but leave the road, L, for a footpath. At 0.8 mi pass through groves of hemlock and red spruce on Turkey Mtn. Among the wildlife are turkey, bear, bobcat, and owls. At 1.6 mi reach a jct with *Turkey Point Trail* L and R. (To the L it is 0.5 mi with scenic views of Tea Creek Valley to the jct with *Boundary Trail*.) Turn R on *Turkey Point Trail*, which has some rocky sections. After 0.5 mi arrive at a fork where you may see a sign, Turkey Loop. Choose either direction. If going R reconnect after 0.3 mi, where you may see a sign, Turkey Point Connector. From here the forest has maple, birch, and hemlock with beautiful patches of sorrel and ferns. Descend steeply among sections of new forest growth to reach a grassy logging road (the former *Tea Creek Interpretive Trail*) at 1.9 mi. Turn R, follow the old road, and after 0.6 mi meet the *Bannock Shoals Run Trail*, R and L. Turn L and after 0.3 mi reach the gate for a loop of 9.4 mi. (*USGS-FS Maps*: Woodrow, Sharp Knob)

Option #2: Perimeter Loop, 21.4 mi

Bannock Shoals Run Trail (1.1 mi; USFS #446); Boundary Trail (3.8 mi; #449); Tea Creek Trail (6.9 mi; USFS #454); Gauley Mtn Trail (5.2 mi; USFS #438); Right Fork Connector Trail (0.6 mi); Tea Creek Mtn Trail (4.6 mi; USFS #452)

CONNECTING TRAILS:
>   (*Saddle Loop Trail*, 1.3 mi)
>   (*Turkey Point Trail*, 1.0 mi)
>   Tea-Gauley Connector Trail (0.6 mi)

Bear Pen Ridge Trail (3.5 mi; USFS #440)
Red Run Trail (2.5 mi; USFS #439)
Right Fork of Tea Creek Trail (3.4 mi; USFS #453)
North Face Trail (3.1 mi; USFS #450)
(*Williams River Trail*, 3.0 mi)

DIFFICULTY: strenuous

FEATURES: gorge, old RR grades, streams, shelter, wildlife, highest peak, some solitude, mainly dry treadway

TRAILHEADS AND DETAILS: Follow the *Bannock Shoals Run Trail* as described above. At its jct with *Saddle Loop Trail* and *Boundary Trail* proceed on *Boundary Trail* (named for the USFS boundary with private property on the N side). Ascend among moss-covered rocks and into a hemlock grove. Pass large rocks with crevices and through rhododendron thickets. At 1.1 mi reach a jct with *Turkey Point Trail*, R. (Here is the third highest point, 4,369 ft, on the Perimeter Loop. *Turkey Point Trail* with scenic views of the Tea Creek valley goes 0.5 mi to a jct with *Saddle Loop Trail*, R.) Descend gradually on a rocky flank. At 2.1 mi are large boulders in a mixed forest with striped maple in the understory. An old strip mine road from Yew Mtn adjoins the trail L near red pines at 2.4 mi. At 3.1 mi is an old RR grade, followed by a crossing of a rocky stream bed. Cross another rocky drain scoured by floods. Cross Tea Creek to another old RR grade and *Tea Creek Trail*, R and L, at 3.8 mi. (After 75 yd R is a jct with *Bear Pen Ridge Trail*, L, which ascends to *Gauley Mtn Trail*. Downstream *Tea Creek Trail* goes 4.5 mi to Tea Creek Campground.)

Turn L on the *Tea Creek Trail*, upstream in a marshy meadow of ferns, yellow birch, and red spruce. Cross the E fork of Tea Creek after 0.9 mi, and follow a switchback in an ascent to a jct with *Tea-Gauley Connector Trail* at 1.4 mi. (It is an easy shortcut to avoid 1.0 mi by FR-24.) Ascend to a shelter (sleeps six) on a flat area created by former strip mining at 1.7 mi. Bear, deer, turkey, hawks, owls, chipmunk, and red squirrel have been seen here. Follow an easy treadway with carpets of club mosses through red and Scotch pine to a small strip mine pond at 2.3 mi. In the pond are red-spotted newts (*Notophthalmus viridescens*). Arrive at Sharp Knob Rd (FR-24) at 2.4 mi (halfway, 10.6 mi of option #2 loop).

Turn R on FR-24 and go 0.2 mi before turning R, off FR-24, on *Gauley Mtn Trail*. (It is 3.6 mi down the mtn on rocky FR-24 to US-219, which is 2.4 mi S of the community of Slaty Fork.) Climb an earthen barrier to the RR grade and follow it through yellow birch, maple, and red spruce. The treadway is frequently wet. Elevation remains steady between 4,200 and 4,400 ft for the entire distance of the trail. At 0.9 mi reach a jct with the 0.6-mi *Tea-Gauley Connector Trail,* R. (An old RR grade, the shortcut has some of the original crossties in wet spots.) Ahead, reach a wildlife field at 1.0 mi. Wildflowers on the trail include wood shamrock, foamflower, bluebead lily, and painted trillium. Mosses and ferns are prominent. At 1.5 mi meet *Bear Pen Ridge Trail,* R.

(The 3.5-mi *Bear Pen Ridge Trail* follows an old RR grade, ascending gradually to the ridge line N of Red Run. After slight level areas at 1.5 mi the route becomes a foot trail through a rocky area. Cherry, maple, hemlock, and red spruce are among the tree species. From a knob it joins a timber road and steeply descends to a jct with *Tea Creek Trail* R and L. Here is also the E end of *Boundary Trail.* It is 1.7 mi R to the shelter, and 4.5 mi L to Tea Creek Campground.)

Continuing on the *Gauley Mtn Trail,* pass a wildlife field at 2.0 mi, follow a straight section of the trail on the ridge top, and after a turn W meet the *Red Run Trail* R at 2.6 mi.

(The 2.5-mi *Red Run Trail* has red spruce, yellow birch, rhododendron, and cherry with a ground cover of ferns and wood shamrock. The trail descends moderately to the headwaters of Red Run at 0.5 mi; it follows an old RR grade for 1.0 mi through hardwoods and red spruce in a rocky area on the N slope from the stream. Near the end it follows a switchback L to a jct with *Right Fork of Tea Creek Trail* at the confluence of Red Run and Right Fork. To the R it is 1.7 mi downstream to *Tea Creek Trail* and L it is 1.7 mi upstream to *Tea Creek Mtn Trail.*)

Continuing on the *Gauley Mtn Trail* as it curves S (in a barely noticed saddle), follow the trail into a wide cove. At 3.7 mi is a wildlife field. Enter another cove and reach a jct with *Right Fork Connector Trail* R at 4.8 mi. (Ahead the *Gauley Mtn Trail* crosses a stream and at 5.2 mi reaches a parking area at WV-150, where L it is 5.7 mi to US-219, and R [S] 3.9 mi to William Creek Rd [FR-86].)

At the jct with the *Right Fork Connector Trail* follow it 0.6 mi to the jct with *Right Fork of Tea Creek Trail,* R and L.

(To the R the *Right Fork of Tea Creek Trail* descends 2.9 mi on an old RR grade to jct with *North Face Trail* and *Tea Creek Trail,* R and L. [Downstream, L it is 2.9 mi to Tea Creek Campground, and R it is 1.5 mi to *Boundary Trail.*] A popular access to Tea Creek basin, the *Right Fork of Tea Creek Trail* crosses the cascading stream a number of times. Flash-flood damage is noticeable, particularly at 1.0 mi and 1.6 mi. There are dense patches of rhododendron and hemlock. At 1.7 mi is a jct with the W end of *Red Run Trail*.)

Continue on option loop #1; turn L on *Right Fork of Tea Creek Trail* and ascend 0.5 mi to a jct with *Tea Creek Mtn Trail* and access to WV-150, across the highway from Little Laurel Overlook. (On the highway L it is 0.5 mi to the Gauley Mtn trailhead and parking area.) Continue ascending on the *Tea Creek Mtn Trail* by switchbacks to reach a knob (4,561 ft), the highest point on the Tea Creek network of trails. Here, as at other rock outcroppings on the mtn crest, are rhododendron and red spruce thickets. On this dry trail descend on a rocky surface and at 3.1 mi reach the jct with *North Face Trail*, R.

(The 3.1-mi *North Face Trail* is a rocky, usually wet, old RR grade whose N end is at the jct with *Right Fork of Tea Creek Trail* and *Tea Creek Trail*. Along the way it crosses cascading Lick Creek at 1.8 mi, but there are other small streams. Vegetation is cherry, birch, and rhododendron. After Lick Creek the descent is steep, but the trail levels off for the last 0.5 mi.)

Continuing on the *Tea Creek Mtn Trail*, descend to the last knob at 4.0 mi, then descend on switchbacks to a jct with the *Tea Creek Trail* R and the *Williams River Trail*, R and L. Turn R on the *Williams River Trail*, cross a footbridge over Tea Creek, and return to Tea Creek Campground after 0.1 mi for the completion of the loop. (*USGS-FS Maps*: Woodrow, Sharp Knob.)

Option #3: Tea Creek Loop, 17.7 mi

Tea Creek Trail (6.9 mi; USFS #446); Gauley Mtn Trail (5.2 mi; USFS #438); Right Fork Connector Trail (0.6 mi); Tea Creek Mtn Trail (4.6 mi; USFS #452)

CONNECTING TRAILS:
> (*Williams River Trail*, 3.0 mi)
> (*North Face Trail*, 3.1 mi)
> (*Right Fork of Tea Creek Trail*, 3.4 mi)
> (*Bear Pen Ridge Trail*, 3.5 mi)
> (*Boundary Trail*, 3.8 mi)
> (*Tea-Gauley Connector Trail*, 0.6 mi)

DIFFICULTY: strenuous

FEATURES: stream bank, beaver dams, wildflowers, wildlife, pools and cascades, shelter, high rock outcrops

TRAILHEADS AND DETAILS: The description of this option is the same as option #2, except the lower 4.5 mi to *Tea Creek Trail* are described and all trails W of Tea Creek are omitted. Tea Creek received its name from its tea-colored waters. The creek and its tributaries are made amber by tannin from such conifers as spruce and hemlock and are influenced by sedimentary rock acidity. *Tea Creek Trail* is among the oldest in the network, and like some of the other trails follows an old RR grade. The stream and the trail have received severe damage and route alterations by flooding, a natural occurrence. Sometimes the trail is impassable after flooding.

Begin from the campground entrance at the signboard. Cross the Tea Creek footbridge on the *Williams River Trail,* but after 0.1 mi turn L at the trail signs where there is a jct with *Tea Creek Mtn Trail,* R. After 0.4 mi descend through rhododendron to creekside. Cross two tributaries along the way before reaching a scenic area of wildflowers and ferns at 2.7 mi. Among the wildflowers are purple-fringed orchid (*Habenaria psycodes*), wood betony, and yellow root. Hardwoods include ironwood, maple, and beech. At 2.9 mi cross Right Fork of Tea Creek where there are cascades and pools. After 150 yd reach the jct with *North Face Trail* and *Right Fork of Tea Creek Trail,* R. (*North Face Trail* ascends S to a jct with *Tea Creek Mtn Trail,* and *Right Fork of Tea Creek Trail* ascends parallel with Right Fork E to *Tea Creek Mtn Trail.*) Continue upstream, frequently rock-hopping or wading the creek near maples and yellow birches, off and on sections of the old RR grade and by large boulders at 3.5 mi. Pass R of rocky section of pools and rapids and at 4.4 mi pass a jct with *Bear Pen Ridge Trail* (which ascends to *Gauley Mtn Trail*), R, and 75 yd ahead to a jct with *Boundary Trail,* L (described in option loop #1). (Including access of 0.1 mi on *Williams River Trail,* you have hiked 4.5 mi from the campground. To complete the loop follow the descriptions in option #2, Perimeter Loop.)

Williams River Trail (USFS #487)

LENGTH: 3.0 mi

DIFFICULTY: easy

FEATURES: Williams River dead waters, waterfowl

TRAILHEAD AND DETAILS: From the Tea Creek Campground follow the trail sign across the Tea Creek on a footbridge to an old RR grade. After 0.1 mi pass a jct with *Tea Creek Trail* and *Tea Creek Mtn Trail.* Pass through a hardwood forest and open fields on the N side of Williams River. At 1.0 mi pass under WV-150 bridge and reach a spur trail at 1.2 mi to a nearby parking area, L, and access to WV-150. Continue ahead and pass the Williams River dead waters; cross Little Laurel Creek at 2.4 mi and enter Handley WMA to join Williams River Rd (CO-17/1) at 3.0 mi, the E terminus. Backtrack or use a vehicle shuttle by driving on FR-86 E from the campground to a jct L with CO-17/4 and to CO-17/1 for a total of 9.2 mi. (*USGS-FS Map*: Woodrow)

SECTION 5: POTOMAC RANGER DISTRICT

Each district has its special significance, but none excels the 134,482 acres of mtns and meadows in the Potomac District. It is named for the Potomac River, whose North Fork of the South Branch flows NE through the Allegheny Mtns. Its N boundary is N of the Dolly Sods Wilderness Area. On the W the line follows the waters of Dry Fork to border both the Cheat and the Greenbrier Districts. The S boundary is the West Virginia–Virginia state line and the George Washington National Forest, and the E border is along US-220 N from near Franklin to Petersburg. There are three prominent recreation areas that are portions of a National Recreation Area: Smoke Hole/Seneca Rocks, Spruce Knob/Seneca Creek, and Dolly Sods/Roaring Plains.

More than 150 mi of superb trails and 108 mi of winding forest service roads grace the district's priceless scenery, from the state's highest point on Spruce Knob (4,861 ft) to the pristine depths of Red Creek gorge in Dolly Sods. The district's natural monuments of sandstone, such as Champe Rocks, Seneca Rocks, Eagle Rock, Chimney Rock, and Bear Rocks, are only a few of the many geological formations. Within the district boundary, but not in the forest, are two commercially owned caverns—Seneca and Smoke Hole—both on WV-28. Between the forest properties are rich, cultivated bottom lands with crops, cattle, and sheep on manicured farms. Country stores, country roads, and country houses remind the hiker that those whom Jack Weller characterized as "yesterday's people" have a heritage as stable as the sandstone mtns.

The district has five campgrounds: Beg Bend (47 units, flush toilets, no showers); Seneca Shadows (80 units, flush toilets, hot showers, and some sites with electricity); Red Creek (12 units, vault toilets, hand pump at well); Spruce Knob Lake (43 units, vault toilets, hand pump at well); Gatewood (six units, vault toilets, no water). Judy Springs is a walk-in primitive camp. For the purpose of trail grouping, trails are described below in three geographical areas: Seneca Rocks Area, Dolly Sods Area, and Spruce Knob Area. The longest trail is the 23.8-mi *North Fork Mtn Trail*, and the shortest is the 0.3-mi *Northland Loop Trail*.

View of the South Branch of the Potomac River.

ADDRESS AND ACCESS: District Ranger, Potomac Ranger District, HC59, Box 240, Petersburg, WV 26847, 304-257-4488; or Seneca Rocks Visitor Center, 304-567-2827.
MAPS: Numbers 22–28

SENECA ROCKS NATIONAL RECREATION AREA
(Grant and Pendleton Counties)

Within the area boundaries are Seneca Rocks Visitor Center on WV-28/4 at the Mouth of Seneca and two recreation areas—Big Bend Campground and Smoke Hole Picnic Area—both in the Smoke Hole Canyon on Smoke Hole Rd (CO-2). Seneca is thought to be an Indian word meaning "stone" or "rock."

Big Bend is a large horseshoe bend of the North Fork of the South Branch of the Potomac River, in a tranquil meadow rimmed by a high ridge of Cave Mtn. There are 47 campsites with picnic tables, grills, and tent pads. Drinking water and flush toilets are available from mid-April to mid-October. Fishing is allowed. *Big Ben Trail* loops around the campground. One easy entrance is on the gated service road at campsite #12, toward the river. Turn L and hike through a border of oak, walnut, sycamore, and papaw by the river. At 0.4 mi pass an old log cabin site; ahead, cross the campground road and ascend to a knob for scenic views of the riverbend. Descend and pass by rock formations, enter the edge of a meadow, and return to the point of origin at 1.4 mi.

ACCESS: From the jct of US-220 and Smoke Hole Rd (CO-2) in the community of Upper Tract, take Smoke Hole Rd for 4.0 mi to Smoke Hole Picnic Area and 5.0 mi farther to Big Bend Campground.

SUPPORT FACILITIES: There is a general store at the jct of CO-2 and FR-79, 0.3 mi N of the Smoke Hole Campground, near St George's log cabin Methodist Church, built in the 1850s. In Franklin, 16.5 mi farther S on US-220, are motels, restaurants, banks, service stations, and stores.

South Branch Trail (USFS #539)

LENGTH: 3.5 mi

DIFFICULTY: moderate

FEATURES: scenic, history

TRAILHEAD AND DETAILS: From Big Bend Campground drive S on Smoke Hole Rd for 5.0 mi to Smoke Hole Picnic Area, L. From the parking area walk back to the picnic entrance and ascend on the E slope for 0.5 mi to the N slope of the mtn, and cross an old wagon road at 0.6 mi. The area has oak, hickory, dogwood, maple, beech, ferns, redbud, and wildflowers. At 1.2 mi reach an opening swath from a gas pipeline and a power line opening at 1.4 mi. Scenic views W are of North Fork Mtn. Near a stand of red cedar and Virginia pine bloom blue viper's bugloss (*Echium vulgare*). Reach an open farm road and sinkhole at 1.8 mi. Cross an abandoned farm field and descend on a jeep road. At 2.5 mi turn L off the road and descend through mtn laurel and rhododendron to the river. Follow upstream on a rocky area, cross a footbridge, and complete the loop trail at 3.5 mi in the picnic area. (*USGS-FS Map*: Upper Tract) (From Smoke Hole Picnic Area, S on Smoke Hole Rd for 0.5 mi, is the legendary Smoke Hole Cave, used by Indian and early settlers for curing meats. The 0.3-mi climb is exceptionally steep and slippery. Take a flashlight.)

North Fork Mountain Trail (23.8 mi; USFS #501)

CONNECTING TRAILS:
> Redman Run Trail (1.6 mi; USFS #507)
> Landes Trail (1.4 mi; USFS #502)

TOTAL LENGTH: 26.8 mi

DIFFICULTY: moderate to strenuous

FEATURES: superb vistas, wildlife, wildflowers, Chimney Top

TRAILHEADS AND DETAILS: If hiking the *North Fork Mtn Trail* from the S, park on the N side of US-33 at the top of North Fork Mtn (3,592 ft), 5.0 mi E of Judy Gap and 9.0 mi W of Franklin. The district's longest trail follows the E and leeward slope of North Fork Mtn near the ridge line, except occasional sections on the ridge top. For 4.6 mi the trail is on sections of private land. (These and other S sections may be closed. Check with the district ranger [304-257-4488]. Obey all No Trespassing signs.) At the N end the trail leaves the ridge and rapidly descends NE to FR-74. It is generally rocky through a hardwood forest with scattered stands of Virginia pine, and does not have any springs or streams on its immediate route. Scenery is more than spectacular.

After 0.4 mi the mossy jeep road through hardwoods becomes a footpath. Excellent views of Germany Valley and Spruce Mtn are L. (Germany Valley was the site of Hinkle's Fort, built in 1761–62. It was the last defense post after the Shawnee Indians had destroyed Fort Upper Tract and Fort Seybert in April 1758.) At 2.1 mi the foot trail becomes a woods road, which is less rocky. The road becomes more rocky and wider at 2.9 mi. At 3.3 mi pass under a power line; timbering is noticeable on the L for the next 0.7 mi. At 4.0 mi are large chestnut oak and black birch, with striped maple as part of the understory. Reach a jct at 4.3 mi; timber road L descends 2.0 mi to Germany Valley and the timber road R descends 2.3 mi to Reeds Creek Rd (CO-8). (A spring, L, is 0.8 mi down the mtn on this road.)

A clearing and turnaround is at 4.5 mi, and a hang-gliding ramp is on the W side of the ridge line. (Vehicle access to this point is from a private road on the W slope.) The trail becomes a footpath; skirt E of a rocky knob on private lands. The trail is well designed and naturally decorated with ferns, mosses, lichen, spring beauty (claytonia), mtn laurel, and blueberries. A vista is at 5.8 mi. White markers on L at 7.5 mi indicate development on private property, a disturbing obstruction to the amenity of the trail. Ascend steeply through a dense area of mtn laurel, Virginia pine, wintergreen, and bracken. An overview at 8.2 mi has a superb view of Seneca Rocks. Skirt E of High Knob, continue through open woods and for the only time on the trail cross the ridge line and descend slightly on the W slope to a saddle at 9.5 mi. Here the trail is an old woods road that leads into a jeep road. Ascend steeply and at 10.0 mi reach the pipeline swath and gravel road. At 10.5 mi pass a radio tower, the highest point on the trail (3,795 ft), and descend on FR-79 to reentry of the forest at 11.9 mi. (FR-79 is passable for passenger cars. It is 3.5 mi farther down the mtn on FR-79 to Smoke Hole Rd for exit N on FR-74 to WV-28 or S on CO-2 to US-220.) A large rock formation and numerous wildflowers, including thousands of spring beauty that bloom in April, are at 14.2 mi. An abandoned trail (1.5-mi *Kimble Trail*) is at a jct R at 14.3 mi. Ascend to ridge at 14.8 mi. Pass huge anthills at 14.9 mi. The trail forks at 15.7 mi with *Redman Run Trail*, R.

(At first the *Redman Run Trail* descends gradually but becomes steep near the N terminus for 1.6 mi to FR-74 [also called Smoke Hole Rd]. Here are a hikers' sign and USFS boundary markers in a young forest of ash and locust. It is 4.7 mi from here N on FR-74 to the N trailhead of *Landes Trail*, and 2.0 mi farther to N trailhead of the *North Fork Mtn Trail*.)

Continue ahead, pass E of a large rock formation, descend below 3,000 ft elev, then begin a steep ascent at 1.6 mi and reach a rhododendron thicket at 17.2 mi near the ridge line. There is a large section of wild azaleas here. At 18.7 mi, L, is a huge honeycombed sandstone wall with two other rock monoliths. The overlook is impressive. Pass through open hardwood forest and weave from the E slope to the ridge for more than 1.0 mi. Reach fork with *Landes Trail*, R, at 20.0 mi.

(The 1.4-mi *Landes Trail* descends on grassy switchbacks and is steep in spots on rocky treadway set in moss. Reach the N terminus in oak and stands of maple on FR-74 near a hikers' sign. It is 2.0 mi N on FR-74 to the N jct of the North *Fork Mtn Trail*.)

Ahead on the *North Fork Mtn Trail* reach the ridge top and a lookout at 20.3 mi. At 21.0 mi arrive at a small plateau. At 21.1 mi, a 0.1-mi spur trail is L to Chimney Top, with exceptional scenic views of Fore Knobs and the Dolly Sods Wilderness. Back on the main trail, descend by switchbacks; cross a large rock formation in a steep area at 21.5 mi. Pass a lookout at 22.0 mi for view of New Creek Mtn and NE canyon below. Continue on switchbacks and reach FR-74 at 23.8 mi. It is 0.3 mi N on FR-74 to WV-28. (*USGS-FS Maps*: Circleville, Franklin, Upper Tract, Hopeville, Petersburg West)

Seneca Rocks Hiking Trail (1.3 mi; USFS #563)

LENGTH: 2.6 mi round-trip
DIFFICULTY: strenuous to easy
FEATURES: impressive vistas, history

TRAILHEAD AND DETAILS: This interpretive trail is one of the most frequently used in the Monongahela National Forest. Begin the hike from the S parking area of Seneca Rocks Visitor Center. Cross a meadow and a high footbridge over the North Fork of the South Branch of the Potomac River. Curve R, then L in a forest of hardwoods and hemlock. Ascend gradually on switchbacks and occasional steps. There are at least seven benches for resting during the 700-ft-elev climb. The trail ends at an observation platform. Here are views of Seneca Rocks, North Fork Valley and W to the Allegheny Mtns. (Seneca Rocks is popular for rock climbers. Hikers should stay away from the climbing areas—there have been fatalities.)

The Seneca Rocks Visitor Center provides an information staff, exhibits, films, and programs on the Seneca Rocks and the nearby area. A picnic area is also provided. Outdoor display markers record some of the geological history of West Virginia. For example, it is estimated that the state was at the bottom of a vast sea 450 million years ago. Layer upon layer of silt, sand, and gravel became 50,000 ft deep. Such compressions became beds of rock. About 250 million years ago the pressure from within the earth lifted the former sea's area to some of the highest mtns in North America. Rivers carved the uplifted plains into valleys and ridges, so that what we see today are the foundations of the original mtns. In the process some hard ridges of sandstone, such as Seneca Rocks, were slower in wearing down.

ADDRESS AND ACCESS: Seneca Rocks Visitor Center, Seneca Rocks, WV 26884; 304-567-2827. The center is open Memorial Day through Labor Day, Mon-Fri 9 A.M.–6 P.M. and year-round Sat-Sun, 9 A.M.–4 P.M. It is located on WV-28/4, near its jct with US-33 at Seneca Rocks.

SPRUCE KNOB NATIONAL RECREATION AREA
(Randolph and Pendleton Counties)

Within this system are 17 individual trails, all of which connect with at least one other trail, for a network of more than 60 mi. The two longest trails— the 7.9-mi *Allegheny Mtn Trail* and the 8.3-mi *Seneca Creek Trail*—could be longer, but a chunk of private property limits their continuity. The trails are described in groups for loop options, and the Spruce Knob Lake Campground is chosen as a main base for camping. It has 45 sites, some of which are on a hillside and require prop blocks for RVs. There are 12 walk-in campsites. There are vault toilets, hand water pumps, picnic tables, and grills. The season is Mar 15 to the first weekend in December. Nearby is the 25-acre Spruce Knob Lake (3,840 ft), the highest lake in the state. Only campers may moor their nonmotorized boats on the lake. Swimming is prohibited. Trout, bass, and sunfish are stocked. Across the road from the campground entrance is the 0.5-mi *Short Trail,* a walk-through in a beechnut grove and past a row of red spruce and other conifers to FR-112 and a jct with the *Gatewood Trail.* (See below.)

ACCESS: To reach Spruce Knob National Recreation Area from the N, take Whitmer Rd (Co-29) S from US-33 (1.0 mi W of Harmon) to Whitmer for 8.3 mi. From Whitmer continue S on Whitmer Rd for 10.3 mi and turn L on FR-1 for 2.5 mi to the campground. A route from the S is on Sawmill Run Rd (CO-28/10), (2.8 mi S of Cherry Grove on WV-28). Ascend on a crooked road for 8.6 mi to FR-112 and follow the campground signs for another 1.3 mi. From the E, take Briery Gap Rd (CO-33/4 at Gateway General Store, 1.0 mi N of Judy Gap) off US-33, for 2.5 mi to FR-112 and follow the campground signs for another 14.0 mi.

SUPPORT FACILITIES: The nearest stores for groceries, gasoline, and hunting and fishing licenses are Sites Community Store in Whitmer, 12.8 mi N

(304-227-9928), and Gateway General Store on US-33, 16.5 mi E on FR-112 (304-567-2810).

Seneca Knob Lake Trail
LENGTH: 1.0 mi
DIFFICULTY: easy
TRAILHEAD AND DETAILS: Access is off FR-1 near the Spruce Knob Lake Campground. From the parking lot circle the lake on a foot trail (no bikes or horses). If going counterclockwise, cross the earthen dam in a scenic area. Cross a boardwalk at 0.3 mi, then ascend a tiered boardwalk through red spruce. Pass through a meadow at the lake's headwaters at 0.5 mi. The remainder of the trail has wildflowers, shrubs, yellow birch, red spruce, and ferns. After another boardwalk return past picnic tables (a popular place for lakeside fishing) to the parking lot. (*USGS-FS Map*: Spruce Knob)

Gatewood Trail
LENGTH: 2.3 mi
DIFFICULTY: moderate
TRAILHEAD AND DETAILS: Trailhead access is either to take the *Short Trail* across the road from the entrance to Spruce Knob Lake Campground, or drive 0.6 mi E on FR-1 to FR-112, turn R, go 0.8 mi, turn L on Sawmill Rd (CO-10), and go 0.5 mi to park in a wide curve. If the latter, enter the forest in a slight saddle. If clockwise, turn L, ascend 0.3 mi in hardwoods to a jct with access to *Short Trail,* near a small pond. Curve R, descend SE, cross a stream, and follow L by a fence in a field to go over a gate. Follow a field road to an old RR grade to a R turn alongside Big Run at 1.2 mi. After 0.3 mi, in which the RR bridge is over a stream, turn R and up through a red pine plantation to complete the loop. (*USGS-FS Map*: Spruce Knob)

Big Run Trail (3.1 mi; USFS #527); North Prong Trail (2.8 mi; USFS #528); Leading Ridge Trail (5.2 mi; USFS #557); Elza Trail (2.0 mi; USFS #556); Bee Trail (1.4 mi; USFS #555)
TOTAL LENGTH: 14.5 mi combined
DIFFICULTY: moderate
FEATURES: wildlife, wildflowers, bird-watching
TRAILHEADS AND DETAILS: These trails are grouped because of their circuit potential. (Footbridges may be washed away by flash floods, but Gandy Creek can be waded in normal conditions.) From the Spruce Knob Lake

Campground, drive E on FR-1 for 0.6 mi to a jct with FR-112, turn L, and drive another 0.5 mi to a side road, L. Here is the SE terminus of *Big Run Trail,* L, and the S terminus of the *Allegheny Mtn Trail,* R. The *Big Run Trail* descends NW to its terminus at Gandy Creek and Whitmer Rd. (The 7.2-mi *Allegheny Mtn Trail* follows N on a gated wildlife road along the ridge line. It is described below.)

On the *Big Run Trail* descend gradually through a forest of tall yellow birch, beech, cherry, and red and striped maple. At 0.2 mi a drain begins on the L; it becomes the S tributary of Big Run. At 1.5 mi the *North Prong Trail* connects from the R, near the confluence with Big Run, in a grassy meadow of old apple trees and wildflowers. Follow the *Big Run Trail* downstream partly on an old RR grade for another 1.6 mi and rock-hop the steam frequently. A number of good campsites are along the way; others have been washed away by the floods. Exit the forest at 2.9 mi in a wildlife grazing field. Cross the Gandy Creek footbridge or wade to the parking area on Whitmer Rd (CO-29) at 3.1 mi. Backtrack or, if using a shuttle, it is 6.1 mi S on Whitmer Rd and FR-1 and FR-112 to the point of origin. If a loop is preferred, some of the options are described below.

Loop Option #1 (9.6 mi): From the parking area walk N on Whitmer Rd (downstream) for 0.4 mi to the entrance of the *Leading Ridge Trail,* R. Cross the Gandy Creek footbridge, or wade and reach a gated wildlife road at 0.1 mi. Ascend on an excellent treadway through a fine forest of cherry, maple, and hemlock to a horseshoe curve at 0.9 mi. In the summer, fritillary butterflies are seen on roadside banks with wildflowers. At 2.0 mi is a grazing field. Continue a mild ascent through open woods dominated by beech to another wildlife plot and intersection with the *Elza Trail* at 2.9 mi. Deer are likely to be seen here. If you turn R on the *Elza Trail,* descend on a wildlife road through an open forest and grazing field for 0.5 mi to its E terminus and the jct with the *North Prong Trail* at a vehicle wooden bridge; turn R, downstream, and go 1.2 mi farther to a jct with, and return on, the *Big Run Trail,* L, to complete a loop of 9.6 mi.

Loop Option #2 (10.5 mi): (To the L of the *Leading Ridge Trail,* the 1.5-mi W section of *Elza Trail* descend S to Whitmer Rd.) If you continue ahead on the *Leading Ridge Trail,* ascend through a hardwood forest for 2.3 mi to the *Allegheny Mtn Trail,* turn R on the *Allegheny Mtn Trail* for 2.8 mi, and return to the point of origin for a loop of 10.5 mi.

Loop Option #3 (9.6 mi): A third loop option that is also 9.6 mi is to walk downstream on Whitmer Rd for 1.8 mi from the *Big Run Trail* parking area to the W terminus of the *Elza Trail*, R. Cross a footbridge over or wade across the Gandy Creek, and enter a grassy area with hay-scented ferns for 0.1 mi. Cross a small stream at 0.5 mi in a hollow of hardwoods, ferns, and club mosses. Pass the headwaters; at 1.5 mi reach a jct with the *Leading Ridge Trail*. From here follow the *Elza Trail* S for 0.5 mi to the *North Prong Trail* and the *Big Run Trail* as described in the first option.

Loop Option #4 (10.7 mi): A fourth circuit option is to walk downstream on Whitmer Rd 2.5 mi from the *Big Run Trail* parking area to the W terminus of the *Bee Trail*, R. Cross a footbridge over or wade across the Gandy Creek; enter a meadow of ferns and wildflowers before passing through a red spruce grove at 0.2 mi. Ascend on the R side of the cascading Bee Run. At 0.8 mi leave the old woods road and turn R on a footpath across a ridge slope. Pass stream headwaters at 1.1 mi. (There may be faint evidence of a former effort by the USFS to route the *Bee Trail* R [S] to a jct with *Elza Trail*.) Ascend straight and steeply up the mtn in an open forest for 0.4 mi to the jct with *Leading Ridge Trail*, R and L. (If making a loop R follow Loop Option #4; if going L follow Loop Option #5.) Go R on *Leading Ridge Trail* for 0.7 mi. Turn L on *Elza Trail* for 0.5 mi. Then turn R on *North Prong Trail* for 1.2 mi to a jct with *Big Run Trail*. Turn L and return at 10.7 mi.

Loop Option #5 (11.4 mi): If taking *Leading Ridge Trail* L from the E end of *Bee Trail*, go 1.6 mi to the jct with the *Allegheny Mtn Trail*, R and L. Turn R and go 2.8 mi to return at the SE end of *Big Run Trail*.

Loop Option #6 (6.6 mi): If the 2.8-mi *North Prong Trail* is chosen for a short loop after the 1.5-mi descent on the *Big Run Trail*, turn R at the meadow jct. Pass through 100 yd of ferns, grasses, and wildflowers such as bee balm, sunflowers, thistle, fleabane, asters, wild basil, and musk mallow (*Malva moschata*). Cross Big Run a number of times and pass through other small meadows. Excellent spaces for campsites. At 1.2 mi is a jct, L, with the *Elza Trail*. (The *Elza Trail* crosses a vehicle wooden bridge to ascend to and cross *Leading Ridge Trail*, described above.) The *North Prong Trail* continues upstream on the wildlife road and at 1.9 mi veers away from the stream for an easy ascent to the *Allegheny Mtn Trail* at 2.8 mi. A return, R, on the *Allegheny Mtn Trail* for 2.3 mi to the point of origin on FR-112 is a 6.6-mi loop. (*USGS-FS Maps*: Spruce Knob, Whitmer)

Allegheny Mountain Trail (7.9 mi; USFS #532)

> CONNECTING TRAILS:
>> *Tom Lick Trail* (1.1 mi; USFS #559)
>> (*North Prong Trail,* 2.8 mi; USFS #528)
>> (*Leading Ridge Trail,* 5.2 mi; USFS #557)
>> *Swallow Rock Trail* (3.2 mi; USFS #529)
>> *Bear Hunter Trail* (1.0 mi; USFS #531)
>> *Spring Ridge Trail* (3.2 mi; USFS #561)
>> (*Horton Trail,* 3.5 mi; USFS #530)
>> *Little Allegheny Mtn Trail* (4.5 mi; USFS #535)

TOTAL LENGTH: 24.4 mi

DIFFICULTY: moderate to strenuous

FEATURES: scenic, wildlife, plant life

TRAILHEADS AND DETAILS: The directions to the S terminus of the *Allegheny Mtn Trail* from the Spruce Knob Lake Campground are the same as described above for the *Big Run Trail.* Follow the *Allegheny Mtn Trail* by the gated wildlife road through beech, yellow birch, cherry, red maple, and oak with slight elev change from 4,000 ft. A wildlife field, R, is at 0.9 mi, and a wildlife road, L, is at 1.6 mi. Autumn colors are outstanding. At 2.1 mi is jct, R, with the *Tom Lick Trail.*

(The *Tom Lick Trail* descends 1.1 mi on the N side of the Tom Lick Run to Seneca Creek, where it crosses on a footbridge to a jct with the *Seneca Creek Trail.*)

Ahead on the *Allegheny Mtn Trail* reach a fork and jct with the signed *North Prong Trail,* L, at 2.3 mi in a grassy open area. Water sources are near-by on both sides of the ridge.

(The 2.8-mi *North Prong Trail* passes through a wildlife clearing by a grove of red pine, descends, and connects with the *Elza Trail* and the *Big Run Trail* described above.)

Continuing on the *Allegheny Mtn Trail,* reach a jct with the *Leading Ridge Trail,* L, at 2.8 mi.

(The 5.2-mi *Leading Ridge Trail* is a wildlife road that follows a ridge line to a wildlife clearing at 2.3 mi for an intersection with the *Elza Trail* and the *Bee Trail.* It continues through the clearing and descends to Camp Seven Hollow for an exit at the Gandy Creek and Whitmer Rd as described above.)

At 3.3 mi on the *Allegheny Mtn Trail* reach a clearing and crossing with the signed *Swallow Rock Trail.*

(The 3.2-mi *Swallow Rock Trail* goes R for 0.9 mi to the *Seneca Creek Trail,* and L for 2.3 mi to the Gandy Creek and Whitmer Rd. West on the trail descend through a hardwood forest to the drainage of Swallow Rock Run, where a breeze is almost constant. At 1.5 mi pass L of a N tributary. Bordering the trail are bellflowers, white snakeroot, ferns, and club mosses. Rock-hop the stream at 2.1 mi, and turn sharply R into a good campsite area. Ascend through a rhododendron stand and descend to Whitmer Rd on the N side of the road bridge at a parking area. This area is part of the Gandy Creek Experimental Stream Improvement Project and is 4.0 mi S of Whitmer. It is 1.4 mi N of the *Bee Trail* entrance, another possibility for a circuit hike.)

Continue N on the *Allegheny Mtn Trail* on the leeward side of the ridge and reach a clearing, L, and jct, R, with *Bear Hunter Trail* at 4.7 mi.

(The *Bear Hunter Trail* descends E through a remarkably open forest of tall cherry, beech, maple, and ash for 0.3 mi. Large patches of blue cohosh are part of the sparse ground cover. Cross a small stream at 0.8 mi and reach Judy Springs and *Seneca Creek Trail* at 1.0 mi. There are good campsites here. A circuit trail of 10.9 mi can be made here by following *Seneca Creek Trail* S to *Tom Lick Trail* and back to the *Allegheny Mtn Trail* for a return to the point of origin.)

Ahead on the *Allegheny Mtn Trail* ascend gradually to a higher ridge level. At 5.0 mi is a view, R, of Spruce Mtn, and at 5.4 mi is a thick grazing field, L, with wild basil, butter-and-eggs, yarrow, and silverberry. Wild turkey, deer, grouse, and raccoon are often heard or sighted in this area. Exit from the forest to the end of the road at 6.2 mi in a grazing field where the signed *Spring Ridge Trail* (wildlife road) is L and the *Allegheny Mtn Trail* descends steeply through the L side of the field.

(The *Spring Ridge Trail* has an easy treadway and passes through two grazing plots in the first 1.2 mi before descending on the N slope of the ridge. Curve R at 2.0 mi from the ridge line and curve L at 2.2 mi for a continuation of the N slope. A drain begins on the R. At 2.6 mi curve L into a scenic hollow and cross a small drain where hemlocks are part of the hardwood forest. Reach a locked post gate and the Whitmer Rd at 3.2 mi. From here it is 0.8 mi N on Whitmer Rd to the *Horton Trail* W entrance and 2.0 mi N to the town of Whitmer.)

The 3.4-mi *Horton Trail* descends W for 2.4 mi to the Whitmer Rd and E for 1.1 mi to the *Seneca Creek Trail*. A separate description is detailed below.)

Although 4WDs have been using the *Allegheny Mtn Trail* from its S entrance, their use is more noticeable here as the *Allegheny Mtn Trail* becomes more of a footpath. Descend into a saddle and ascend to the ridge line through a hardwood forest and reach a jct, R, with the *Little Allegheny Mtn Trail* at 7.9 mi. To avoid trespass problems on the *Allegheny Mtn Trail* to a private property road, take the *Little Allegheny Mtn Trail* to Whites Run Rd (CO-33/3).

The *Little Allegheny Mtn Trail* follows a ridge line 2.0 mi to a gas pipeline crossing. Here are vistas of the Seneca Creek valley and Kisamore Mtn (E) and the Dry Fork area (W). Follow the ridge, gradually descending through scenic sections of mtn laurel, Virginia and white pine, birch, oak, hemlock, huckleberry, wintergreen, and wild orchids. A number of outcrops on the ridge spine provide scenic views of the valleys. At 2.5 mi is one of a number of small saddles. On the R, and far below, the sound of Seneca Creek is audible. Continue the descent and begin the first of four switchbacks in groves of rhododendron at 3.3 mi. At 4.4 mi is a jct with a 60-yd spur trail R to Seneca Creek Rd (FR-1580) and a huge (9 ft in circumference) apple tree. Turn L and cross a footbridge over Whites Run to Whites Run Rd at 4.5 mi. A parking area is 0.1 mi downstream. It is 1.6 mi from here downstream to the former Seneca Creek Campground and another 0.5 mi to US-33. The nearest store for groceries, gasoline, and a post office is Phares Store in Onego, 2.7 mi E (from the former campground) on US-33 (304-567-2285). (*USGS-FS Maps*: Spruce Knob, Whitmer, Onego)

Horton Trail (USFS #530)

LENGTH: 3.5 mi

DIFFICULTY: strenuous

FEATURES: scenic, history, nature study

TRAILHEAD AND DETAILS: The trail receives its name from its NW trailhead on Whitmer Rd near the community of Horton. For the NW trailhead, park in the parking area on Whitmer Rd, 1.0 mi S of Whitmer at the Potomac Cooperative Wildlife Management Area sign. Follow an old wagon road into the forest, remain R of the Lower Two Spring Run, and cross over an earthen barricade. The forest is mainly beech, maple, and birch with a few hemlocks. Rock-hop the stream at 1.0 mi and again at 1.1 mi. Curve more to the SE at the confluence of the two runs at 1.5 mi and again at 1.7 mi. For the next 0.5 mi the stream disappears twice underground. The area is exceptionally scenic in the autumn; good campsites are at 2.1 mi. Ascend steeply on rocky and eroded treadway to a jct with *Allegheny Mtn Trail* at 2.4 mi. (It is 6.4 mi R on the *Allegheny Mtn Trail* to FR-112 and 6.0 mi L to Whites Run Rd. The correct distance for the Judy Springs sign is 2.6 mi.) Continue E at the sign and descend 800 ft in elev for 1.1 mi on the E slope of the ridge to Seneca Creek. On the descent are scattered views of Spruce Mtn Range. (The 1968 Whitmer topo map has an incorrect trail drawing of this descent.) Cross Seneca Creek on a footbridge (rock-hop or wade if the footbridge is washed away) and reach a jct with the *Seneca Creek Trail* on an old RR grade, the SE end of *Horton Trail*. (To the R it is 5.0 mi on *Seneca Creek Trail* to its S terminus at FR-112. On the way, upstream, it is 0.2 mi to the enchanting Upper Seneca Creek Falls. Here is also the NW trailhead of *Huckleberry Trail*, which ascends L and goes 5.2 mi to its S end at Spruce Knob.

Seneca Creek Trail *(5.0 mi; USFS #515)*

CONNECTING TRAILS:

> (*Tom Lick Trail,* 1.1 mi; USFS #559)
> (*Swallow Rock Trail,* 3.2 mi; USFS #529)
> *Judy Springs Trail* (0.7 mi; USFS #312)
> (*Bear Hunter Trail,* 1.0 mi; USFS #531)
> (*Huckleberry Trail* 5.2 mi; USFS #533)
> (*Horton Trail,* 3.5 mi; USFS #530)

TOTAL LENGTH: 19.7 mi

DIFFICULTY: easy to strenuous

FEATURES: scenic, waterfalls, nature study, Judy Springs, RR history

TRAILHEADS AND DETAILS: From the Spruce Knob Lake Campground drive 2.6 mi E on FR-1 and FR-112 to the parking area on the L. Before beginning the hike it is advisable to read the information board at the trail entrance. You will be entering the former USFS Seneca Creek Pioneer Zone, which provides only nonmotorized recreation facilities. The former 13.0-mi *Seneca Creek Trail* now dead-ends after 5.0 mi at the *Horton Trail* jct. (The Lower Falls of Seneca are on private property.) All of the footbridges and parts of the trail were washed away in the 1985 and 1996 floods. There are no immediate plans to restore all the bridges. Hiking will require rock-hopping or wading.

From the parking area pass through a gated forest road; descend gently through a forest of hardwood and hemlock. Serviceberry and gooseberry are on the road banks. Cross Trussel Run, a streamlet at 0.5 mi; pass an old beaver dam and at 0.9 mi reach a jct L with the moderate 1.1-mi *Tom Lick Trail.* (The *Tom Lick Trail* ascends to connect with the *Allegheny Mtn Trail.*) At 2.1 mi cross Beech Run, another small stream. A jct with the 3.2-mi

Swallow Rock Trail L is at 2.2 mi. (The *Swallow Rock Trail* is a moderate trail that ascends 0.9 mi to cross the *Allegheny Mtn Trail* and descend to Whitmer Rd.) Cross Seneca Creek on a footbridge (or rock-hop) at 3.0 mi and reach Judy Springs at 3.4 mi. There are good campsites here. Across the footbridge is the *Judy Springs Trail*. At a fork the *Judy Springs Trail* goes L and a footpath R goes to Judy Springs, a gushing fount of water from the rocky mountainside in a cove of hemlock, birch, fern, and liverwort. (Judy is the surname of pioneer families who first lived in the area.)

(The *Judy Springs Trail* ascends through the forest for 0.2 mi, over a stile to a grazing field, and follows cairns up the mountainside to the NE corner. This is an exceptionally resplendent area any season of the year. In the summer there are St John's wort, daisy, red clover, wild basil, Deptford pink, bird's-foot trefoil [*Lotus corniculatus*], and bittersweet nightshade [*Solanum dulcamara*]. Song sparrows, indigo buntings, and fritillary butterflies frequent the field. Reach the end of the trail at 0.7 mi at a jct with the *Huckleberry Trail*, described above. Backtrack or turn L on the *Huckleberry Trail* and descend for 1.2 mi, connect with the *Seneca Creek Trail,* and hike upstream for 1.4 mi to the campground for a loop of 3.3 mi.)

Continue downstream on the *Seneca Creek Trail* and meet the *Bear Hunter Trail,* L, at 3.5 mi. (The 1.0-mi *Bear Hunter Trail* is a strenuous ascent by a small stream through hemlock and birch to the *Allegheny Mtn Trail* described above.) Continue on the old RR grade by cascades and an ideal bathing pool. Cross a footbridge (or rock-hop) at 3.7 mi and again at 4.1 mi. As the canyon becomes narrower, the number of echoes of waterfalls increases. Birch, beech, and rhododendron cover the canyon walls. At 4.8 mi arrive at the most spectacular section of the trail, where it spans a tier of the Upper Falls of Seneca. Across the creek is a R jct with the *Huckleberry Trail,* but 0.2 mi farther downstream on the *Seneca Creek Trail* begins the *Horton Trail.* (See descriptions below.)

Whispering Spruce Trail (0.5 mi); Huckleberry Trail (5.2 mi; USFS #533); Lumberjack Trail (5.3 mi; USFS #534); High Meadows Trail (1.9 mi; USFS #564)

LENGTH: 12.9 mi combined

DIFFICULTY: easy to strenuous

FEATURES: panoramic, heath meadows, nature study, RR history

TRAILHEADS AND DETAILS: (These trails are grouped because of their connections and all begin or end on high elevations of Spruce Mtn.) Spruce

Knob (4,861 ft), the state's highest point, is 8.3 mi E from the Spruce Knob Lake Campground and 11.7 mi W from US-33 near Judy Gap. From the parking area follow the signs on the interpretive loop *Whispering Spruce Trail* to the observation tower. From the deck are views E to the North Fork Mtn Range and 38 mi farther to the Shenandoah Mtn Range. The N views include Picea Peak (4,613 ft), Little Middle Mtn, and Roaring Plains. Scenery to the W spans the Middle Mtn Range, Cunningham Knob (4,450 ft), Spruce Knob Lake, Big Run Grazing Area, Yokum Knob (4,300 ft), Pharis Knob (4,674 ft), and numerous spur ridges and valleys. The S views are to Hunting Ground Mtn and the Big Mtn Range. Continue on the trail through spruce missing limbs on the W side because of the constant and often harsh winds. There are magnificent views at the outcroppings. Rose azalea, fireweed, pink lady-slipper, mtn ash, deciduous hollies, and minnie-bush (*Menziesia pilosa*) provide seasonal beauty. Return to the parking area. To hike the *Huckleberry Trail* begin at the N side of the parking area at the trail sign. The treadway is rocky through spruce, mtn laurel, bleeding heart, huckleberry, and Canada dogwood (*Cornus canadensis*). At 0.2 mi is a faint trail, R, with white blazes, for 150 yd to a spring. Excellent vistas are at 1.0 mi and a heath meadow continues for 0.3 mi. At 1.9 mi are remains of a small-plane crash, L. Shift more to the W side of Spruce Mtn and enter another heath meadow of ferns, grasses, and huckleberry with views W at 2.6 mi. Descend slightly to a shallow saddle and turn L at 3.2 mi. (Here the *Huckleberry Trail*'s distance was extended by the USFS in the early 1990s to replace 2.0 mi of the former *Horton-Horserock Trail* from the top of Spruce Mtn to *Seneca Creek Trail*.) Descend on a rocky, eroded treadway. Pass an open field with a large patch of false hellebore (*Veratrum viride*), a poisonous plant that according to legend was used to select Indian chiefs. If a man survived its consumption, he was considered to be a potential chief.

At 3.8 mi is a jct with *Lumberjack Trail* R and L. (Description follows.) Continue down the slope on the *Huckleberry Trail* to the edge of a grazing field and reach a jct with *Judy Springs Trail*, L, at 4.0 mi. (*Judy Springs Trail* descends 0.7 mi to Judy Springs and *Seneca Creek Trail*.) Continue on the *Huckleberry Trail* through an open hardwood forest to descend steeply on an old woods road. Skirt the R edge of a pasture and descend into hemlock and beech to meet *High Meadows Trail*, R, near a stream at 4.8 mi. Continue descending to parallel and cross a tributary to Seneca Creek. Turn R on a slope above Seneca Creek, then make a sharp L to a jct with *Seneca Creek Trail* at Upper Seneca Creek Falls at 5.2 mi. (To the L *Seneca Creek Trail* goes 4.8 mi to FR-112. To the R it goes 0.2 mi to the jct with the *Horton Trail.*) If hiking the *Lumberjack Trail* R or L from the jct described above and you choose L (S), follow an old RR grade its entire length along the W slope of Spruce Mtn. After 0.4 mi you will notice old RR crossties in a wet area, the first of 12 such places, including 1.0 mi, 1.7 mi, 2.0 mi, and 2.6 mi. There is some evidence of RR trestles. For example, at 1.5 mi yellow birch grows from a rotted log foundation. The RR banks must be followed in a number of areas because of the continuous drainage from the mountainside. Deer and wild turkey are frequently sighted in the hardwood forest of birch and maple. Mtn lettuce (*Saxifraga micranthidifolia*) and orchids in the *Habenaria* genus grow here. Cross the last streamlet at 2.9 mi and arrive at FR-112, the S terminus, at 3.3 mi. From here it is 5.2 mi L on FR-112 and FR-104 to Spruce Knob parking area and 0.6 mi R to the parking area of *Seneca Creek Trail.*

If choosing the R (N) section of *Lumberjack Trail,* follow the straight RR grade and expect it to be wet and rocky. Old crossties are noticeable at 0.4 mi and 1.1 mi. In a hardwood forest some sunshine filters through in the winter, otherwise the only open spaces with some red spruce are at 1.0 mi and at the trail's end at 2.0 mi. At the end the trail forks. To the R is a flat grassy meadow with scattered shrubs and trees. To the L is the beginning of *High Meadows Trail.*

Follow the *High Meadows Trail,* which has some blue blazes or arrows. Make a sharp L off the old road, meander, then briefly follow a fence line at 0.2 mi. Descend steeply among rocks and seepage through yellow birch, beech, cherry, and maple. At 0.6 mi exit the woods on a grassy knoll for an astonishing and unforgettable view of Seneca Creek valley and the W ridges beyond. (Autumn colors are at their peak the first two weeks of October.) Look for blue-blazed posts or cairns in the descent to enter a red spruce and maple grove. Follow an old road in a slight ascent through the forest, but be alert for a sharp R off the road. At 1.3 mi exit the woods on another scenic and grassy slope. Follow cairns SW among gentian, daisy, thistle, goldenrod, and asters. Enter a forest with mosses and sedum. Again enter a pastoral slope with post markers, pass an old cattle salt feeder and reach a jct with *Huckleberry Trail* R and L at 1.9 mi. (*USGS-FS Maps*: Spruce Knob, Whitmer, Onego)

Back Ridge Trail (USFS #526)

LENGTH: 4.6 mi

DIFFICULTY: strenuous, elev gain 1,451 ft

FEATURES: scenic, nature study

TRAILHEAD AND DETAILS: Isolated from the connecting trails described above, the N terminus of *Back Ridge Trail* is 4.1 mi S of the Spruce Knob Lake area using FR-112 and Sawmill Run Rd (CO-28/10). The S terminus is on the W side of the bridge over Big Run on WV-28. Between the termini it is 0.5 mi E on WV-28 and 5.8 mi N on Sawmill Run Rd. If hiking S, park across the road from private property and a Woodlands Institute sign (3,963 ft). The trail, overgrown in sections, follows the ridge line along the USFS boundary with some views E. At 1.0 mi begin a slight descent and skirt the W edge of the ridge. The Big Run Falls, deep in the canyon, can be heard to the R, at 1.5 mi. Follow portions of logging roads with mtn laurel and new growth of oak and beech. Begin a descent, at first gradually, then steeply, on rocky treadway and reach Big Run at 3.1 mi. Rock-hop and reach a jct with old RR grades damaged by flooding. Fishermen use both the R up Big Run and L up Collar Hollow Run. The forest here is chiefly birch, beech, hemlock, and rhododendron. Turn L, downstream, and after 0.1 mi cross Collar Hollow Run. Rock-hop or wade Big Run twice more, the last time at 3.9 mi, where the grade becomes wider. Jewelweed and ground ivy (*Glechoma hederacea*), a creeping herb, are plentiful. Pass a number of small K-dams. Reach WV-28 at 4.6 mi. Parking space is 0.1 mi R on the L side of the highway. (*USGS-FS Maps*: Spruce Knob, Snowy Mtn)

DOLLY SODS AREA
(Tucker, Grant, Randolph, and Pendleton Counties)

The name of Dolly Sods developed from that of the Dahles, a pioneer family who grazed their livestock on sods, meaning "grassy grounds" or pastureland. In 1975, Congress passed the Eastern Wilderness Act, which set aside two areas as wilderness in the MNF. One was the Dolly Sods Wilderness with 10,215 acres, and the other was the 20,000-acre Otter Creek Wilderness in the Cheat District. Adjoining the E boundary of Dolly Sods Wilderness is the 2,400-acre Dolly Sods Scenic Area, which also has restricted usage. On the S boundary, S of FR-19, are more than 11,000 acres of forest on the Flatrock and Roaring Plains. It has a geological, botanical, and wilderness character similar to the other areas, but lacks the same types of restrictions. These combined areas are served by one campground, one picnic area, and an interpretive trail, all of which are outside the Wilderness. The Dolly Sods Picnic Area is on FR-19 0.6 mi SW of the jct of FR-19 and 75. The Red Creek Campground on FR-75 is 5.5 mi N of the picnic area on FR-75, and the *Northland Loop Trail* is 0.4 mi S of the Red Creek Campground on FR-75. The 0.3-mi interpretive trail has stations explaining the flora and how birds and animals use the seeds and fruits, conglomerate rock formations, heath plateaus and bogs with alder thickets. At 0.1 mi on the trail a boardwalk provides views of a glade in Alder Run. North of Red Creek Campground it is 2.6 mi to Bear Rocks on FR-75. Here are sculpted boulders and panoramic views.

The remote and rugged Dolly Sods Wilderness is a popular area for hiking more than 25 mi of trails through northern hardwood and conifer forest, near cascading streams, over rocky plateaus, and around glades and beaver dams. Although permits are not required, it is recommended by the USFS that someone outside the Wilderness know where you are hiking and that you hike with one or more companions. The area is usually wet; there is more than 55 inches of precipitation annually and preparations should be made for rain, thunder, snow, and windstorms. The use of motorized equipment is prohibited and, unless specified otherwise, camping should be 100 ft away from streams and trails and farther away from roads. The rule of "pack it in, pack it out" should be followed devoutly. Horse travel is not suitable.

The Wilderness is replete with wildlife—17 species of amphibians; six species of reptiles (poisonous ones are copperhead and rattlesnake); 38 species of mammals; and 82 species of nesting birds, some of which are not seen in the state's other Wilderness Areas. These species include the marsh hawk (*Circus cyaneus*), upland sandpiper (*Bartramia longicauda*), meadowlark (*Sturnella magna*), kingbird (*Tyrannus tyrannus*), raven, prairie warbler, and Canada goose. The altitude range, from 2,620 to 4,122 ft, provides an environment for hundreds of vascular plant species. Sundew (*Drosera rotundifolia*), cotton grass (*Eriophorum virginicum*), and speckled alder (*Alnus rugosa*) are some of the plants found in the sphagnum bogs. The wilderness is returning to its natural state after a history of forming, lumbering, and military ordinance exercises in WW II. Also returning to its natural state is the Flatrock and Roaring Plains Area.

ACCESS: At the jct of WV-28 and Jordan Run Rd (CO-28/7), near the Smoke Hole Caverns (9.0 mi W of Petersburg), take CO-28/7 N for 1.0 mi, turn L on FR-19, and go 6.0 mi to the jct with FR-75. Trailheads are both R and L. From the W at the jct of WV-32 and Laneville Rd (CO-45), drive 5.8 mi to FR-19 at the North Fork of the Red Creek bridge.

SUPPORT FACILITIES: The Red Creek Campground, 4.9 mi from the jct of FR-19 and FR-75, has 12 campsites, hand-pump drinking water, tables, grills, and vault toilets. It is open usually (depending on snow blizzards) from mid-April to the first weekend in December. The nearest campground with electrical and water hookups and hot showers is at Canaan Valley State Park on WV-32 (304-866-4121), 7.5 mi W from the Red Creek bridge (see chapter 6). The nearest general grocery store is immediately S on WV-32 at its jct with the Laneville Rd entrance to Dolly Sods.

Red Creek Trail (6.1 mi; USFS #514)

CONNECTING TRAILS:
> Little Stonecoal Trail (1.8 mi; USFS #552)
> Dunkenbarger Trail (1.6 mi; USFS #558)
> Big Stonecoal Trail (4.4 mi; USFS #513)
> Rocky Point Trail (1.8 mi; USFS #554)
> Fisher Spring Run Trail (2.3 mi; USFS #510)
> Rohrbaugh Plains Trail (3.5 mi; USFS #508)
> Wildlife Trail (1.2 mi; USFS #560)
> Breathed Mtn Trail (2.5 mi; USFS #553)
> Blackbird Knob Trail (2.2 mi; USFS #511)

TOTAL LENGTH: 27.4 mi

DIFFICULTY: moderate to strenuous

FEATURES: Red Creek drainage, history, nature study

TRAILHEADS AND DETAILS: These trails are described in a group, as if branches from a tree. The trunk is Red Creek Trail with its base entrance on FR-19 at Red Creek. The other trails connect upstream and out from tributaries. A number of circuits can be arranged; some are described below.

Before you begin the trails there are conditions that require attention. One is the danger of flash flooding on the low areas along Red Creek. Because of the steep canyon walls, level space for camping is mainly confined to low areas beside Red Creek, and that space is limited. Some of the desirable sites were washed away or damaged in the November 1985 (or previous) floods or the floods of 1996. All the footbridges have been washed away over a period of time, and there are no plans to rebuild them.

Red Creek is not fordable on the *Red Creek Trail,* near Fisher Spring Run, nor on the *Little Stonecoal Trail,* nor on the *Big Stonecoal Trail* during high water. Additionally, in a flood stage, three tributaries, including Fisher Spring Run, on the E side of Red Creek, are not fordable in a flash flood.

Another concern is that some old mortar shells remain in the area from WW II military exercises. Some shells were detonated in the 1980s and early 1990s. If you find one, the USFS requests that you do not touch it, but visibly mark the site, draw a map, and report your find in person or by telephone to the district office in Petersburg.

In addition to the S trailhead of *Red Creek Trail,* there are three popular access routes from FR-75 on the top of the E ridge of the canyon down to *Red Creek Trail.* They are *Blackbird Knob Trail* (USFS #511); *Fisher Spring Run Trail* (USFS #510); and *Wildlife Trail* (USFS #560). They are briefly described here to assist you in making plans for short or long hikes and camping in Dolly Sods Wilderness.

The 2.2-mi, moderately difficult *Blackbird Knob Trail* begins a few yd N of the Red Creek Campground and parking area. It goes SW, but first more to the W to an outstanding view from sandstone cliffs. It descends to rock-hop Alder Run and Red Creek (when the water level is normal), then to meet the N trailhead of *Red Creek Trail* on the S side of Blackbird Knob.

The 2.3-mi, moderately difficult *Fisher Spring Run Trail* is 2.0 mi S of *Red Creek Trail* (and Red Creek Campground) on FR-75. It descends slightly in the beginning through a hardwood forest 1.2 mi to a jct with the N end of *Rohrbaugh Plains Trail,* L. The trail then follows an old RR grade before dropping steeply on switchbacks along Fisher Spring Run. In a rocky and mossy area the trail turns S in its final crossing of the stream and levels out. As it nears Red Creek you will notice a number of side trails R made by hikers to descend to Red Creek. Ignore these shortcuts and eroded descends. Reach a jct with *Red Creek Trail,* R and L, at 2.3 mi on a high embankment. If going N (upstream) descend for 375 ft to Red Creek. It is here *Red Creek Trail* crosses Red Creek on its route up the W side of the canyon to a jct with *Breathed Mtn Trail.*

The 1.2-mi, easy to moderately difficult *Wildlife Trail* is 1.3 mi S of the *Fisher Spring Run Trail* on FR-75. It gradually descends through beech, birch, cherry, maple, hemlock, and moosewood on an old logging road. At 1.1 mi it stays L of a grazing field and then makes a jct with *Rohrbaugh Plains Trail,* R and L, at 1.2 mi. (To the L on *Rohrbaugh Plains Trail* it is 0.8 mi on the trail's journey S to an escarpment for spectacular views of Red

Creek Canyon.) Turn R on *Rohrbaugh Plains Trail* for 0.4 mi to a jct with *Fisher Spring Run Trail*, R and L. Turn L and follow the description above.

To follow the *Red Creek Trail*, park at the parking area near the wildlife manager's cabin on FR-19, the E side of Red Creek bridge. (It is 5.8 mi E from WV-32 on the Laneville Rd [CO-45] and 10.7 mi W from WV-28 on FR-19.) Hike upstream on an old RR grade under tall hemlock, birch, maple, cherry, and poplar. Rhododendron forms an understory in sections. Club mosses and ferns are among the ground covers. At 0.5 mi is a jct with *Little Stonecoal Trail*, L.

(To hike *Little Stonecoal Trail*, go 0.1 mi to Red Creek, wade, and parallel E of cascading Little Stonecoal Run. Ascend steadily for 1.3 mi on an old wagon road through maple, birch, poplar, and ash. The slope to the gorge is precipitous. Some of the cascades are arbored with rhododendron. After an elev gain of 1,000 ft, reach a jct with the *Dunkenbarger Trail*, R. *Little Stonecoal Trail* continues for 0.4 mi to its W terminus at the forest boundary. The 1.6-mi *Dunkenbarger Trail* crosses the Coal Knob plateau through a spruce forest with thick rhododendron, mtn laurel, and mosses. Wet spots in the trail are usual. Rock-hop Dunkenbarger Run at 0.9 mi, where deer and bear are occasional visitors. Reach a jct with *Big Stonecoal Trail*. It goes L for 2.5 mi to its N terminus at FR-80 and a jct with *Breathed Mtn Trail*, or go R for 1.9 mi downstream to rejoin the *Red Creek Trail* as described below.)

After 1.0 mi on the *Red Creek Trail* there is evidence of past floods that have rechanneled the river and washed away beaver dams and sections of the old RR grade. At 1.5 mi reach a jct with *Big Stonecoal Trail*, L.

(To hike the 4.4-mi *Big Stonecoal Trail*, wade Red Creek and parallel E of the cascading stream of Stonecoal Run in a steady ascent to a jct with *Rocky Point Trail*, R, at 1.3 mi. [The *Rocky Point Trail* goes 1.8 mi to a jct with the *Red Creek Trail*.] Ahead, the *Big Stonecoal Trail* follows the old RR grade. At 1.7 mi pass R of a waterfall, at 1.8 mi rock-hop Stonecoal Run, and at 1.9 mi reach a jct with *Dunkenbarger Trail*, L. For the next 2.0 mi the treadway is generally wet, mossy, and sometimes rocky on and off the old RR grade. The deciduous forest is mixed with groves of red pine and spruce. Cross the stream again at 2.1 mi, 3.2 mi, and 3.9 mi. There may be active beavers at 3.3 mi. At 3.9 mi begin ascent of a rocky area to the N terminus of the trail and a jct with FR-80, L, and the W terminus of *Breathed Mtn Trail*, R. This area is a frequent campsite for those who enter on FR-80, though FR-80 is severely eroded and passable only with a 4WD vehicle. It is 3.2 mi out to Freeland Rd [CO-37], which makes a jct with WV-32 E of Canaan Valley State Park. *Breathed Mtn Trail* goes 2.5 mi E to a jct with the *Red Creek Trail*.)

Continue upstream on the *Red Creek Trail* from the jct with *Big Stonecoal Trail,* but leave the flood plain and ascend to a mountainside footpath to cross the top of a waterfall at 2.1 mi. At 2.5 mi cross another cascading tributary (impossible to rock-hop in high water) and reach a jct with *Fisher Spring Run Trail,* R, at 3.2 mi.

(The *Fisher Spring Run Trail* ascends 2.3 mi to an access point on FR-75, an elev gain of 1,000 ft. Ascend, cross Fisher Spring Run at 0.4 mi [not passable in high water], and ascend on seven switchbacks N of the cascading stream. Reach a jct with the *Rohrbaugh Plains Trail,* R, at 1.2 mi. Stream runs underground in the area. Continue upstream; at 1.6 mi veer R from the stream and ascend in a rocky treadway, sometimes wet. Birch, beech, and maple are prominent. At 2.1 mi pass a small clearing and reach FR-75 parking area at 2.3 mi. From here it is 2.0 mi N on FR-75 to Red Creek Campground.)

(On the *Rohrbaugh Plains Trail,* from the jct with *Fisher Spring Run Trail* follow the old RR grade for 0.4 mi to the jct, L, with the *Wildlife Trail.* [The 1.2-mi *Wildlife Trail* is an abandoned FR that was used for maintaining wildlife food fields. It is now an easy, graded access trail from a parking area on FR-75, 2.2 mi N from the *Rohrbaugh Plains Trail* S terminus at the picnic area, and 1.3 mi S from the *Fisher Spring Run Trail* on FR-75.] Continue on the *Rohrbaugh Plains Trail* past a wildlife food plot at 0.6 mi and a large field at 0.8 mi. Reach scenic outcroppings at 0.9 mi, where for 0.2 mi there are views of Red Creek Canyon and the Stonecamp Mtns. Cross three drains, pass through sections of hemlock and spruce, boggy areas, and open grassy fields before crossing the last drain at 2.7 mi. Cross an old woods road and exit at FR-75 at 3.5 mi near the picnic area.)

To continue on the *Red Creek Trail* from the jct with the *Fisher Spring Run Trail,* make a short descent to Red Creek and wade or rock-hop near the blue blazes at 3.0 mi. Go upstream in a campsite area under hemlock, ash, and birch, and ascend to a jct with *Rocky Point Trail,* L, at 3.6 mi.

(The *Rocky Point Trail* is an old RR grade, exceptionally rocky in places. When the tree leaves are off there are views of Fisher Spring Run falls and the rock formations on the canyon rim of Rohrbaugh Plains. At 1.0 mi the trail curves R at the enormous sandstone cliffs of Breathed Mtn. Thoreau observed in his hikes that the finest stonecutters were not of copper or steel, but of "air and water working at their leisure with a liberal allowance of time." A good example is here on Pottsville sandstone. A climb to some of the higher rock formations provides a magnificent view of Red Creek

Canyon, Stonecoal Gorge, Coal Knob, and as far SW as Roaring Plains. Bear have been seen on the trail from here to the *Big Stonecoal Trail* jct at 1.8 mi. A return to the point of origin at the Red Creek parking area can be made here by turning L on the *Big Stonecoal Trail*, downstream to the *Red Creek Trail*, and to the Red Creek parking area for a circuit of 8.2 mi. Or a longer loop can be made by going upstream to meet *Dunkenbarger Trail*, turning L, making a jct with *Little Stonecoal Trail*, and returning to the Red Creek parking area for a loop of 9.6 mi.)

To continue on the *Red Creek Trail*, follow the canyon on the old RR grade in a deciduous forest and reach a jct with *Breathed Mtn Trail*, L (W), at 5.0 mi.

(The 2.5-mi *Breathed Mtn Trail* ascends steeply and reaches a boggy plateau at 0.3 mi. Numerous beaver ponds are R of the scenic and mesic trail for the next 1.0 mi. The forest is mixed with fir, spruce, yellow birch, maple and cherry, rhododendron, and mtn laurel. Red pine plantations are at 0.8 mi and 1.1 mi. Lycopodium and sphagnum are profuse. Cross the headwaters of Stonecoal Run at 2.3 mi and reach the W terminus of the trail; make a jct with *Big Stonecoal Trail* and FR-80, described above. A loop can be made here on the *Big Stonecoal Trail* to rejoin the *Red Creek Trail* for a return to the parking area at the Red Creek bridge for a total of 13.5 mi, or 13.8 if using the *High Water Trail*.)

Continue on the *Red Creek Trail* and pass over some old RR grade ties with spikes. Reach the confluence of the left fork of Red Creek and Red Creek at 5.2 mi. Rock-hop the left fork to a popular campsite area and follow the blue blazes upstream, L. At 5.3 mi leave the creek bank and ascend steeply into a red spruce forest. Leave the Dolly Sods Wilderness Area at 5.6 mi, but follow the trail through an open field of blueberry, minnie-bush, wintergreen, wildflowers, and mtn laurel. Reach the N terminus of the *Red Creek Trail* at 6.1 mi and a jct with the *Blackbird Knob Trail*. Backtrack, or follow the *Blackbird Knob Trail*, R.

If taking the *Blackbird Knob Trail*, follow a pleasant trail through a hardwood forest to an open area where deer and grouse are frequently seen. Rock-hop or wade Red Creek at 0.5 mi and Alder Creek at 1.1 mi. Ascend gradually in open areas. Follow the path to a rock outcropping with spruce, ferns, and blueberry at 1.8 mi; descend slightly and reach FR-75 at 2.2 mi for a total mileage of 8.3 mi from the Red Creek bridge on FR-19 and an elev gain of 1,267 ft. Across the road is the parking area and to the R is the Red Creek Campground. (*USGS-FS Maps*: The Blackbird Knob, Blackwater

Falls, Laneville, and Hopeville topos [1967–69] have a number of incorrect trail routes.)

FLATROCK AND ROARING PLAINS AREA
(Randolph and Pendleton Counties)

South of Dolly Sods Wilderness and across FR-19 is 17.7 sq mi of scenic grandeur known as Flatrock and Roaring Plains. Geologically similar to Dolly Sods, it has fewer open meadows and rock outcroppings. But like Dolly Sods, it has windswept areas of blueberry, azalea, mtn laurel, and red spruce. Mt Porte Crayon, its highest point at 4,770 ft, has unparalleled views. Gaining access to it and other open places near it is becoming more difficult because of dense red spruce. A gated forest road (FR-70) enters from FR-19 to part of the highlands; it ends between Flatrock Plains (more central to the plateau) and Roaring Plains (more to the S). Four trails penetrate deeper into this wild and rugged bear habitat.

South Prong Trail (5.9 mi; USFS #517); Boar's Nest Trail (2.7 mi; USFS #518)

LENGTH: 8.3 mi combined

DIFFICULTY : strenuous

FEATURES: scenic, balds, nature study

TRAILHEADS AND DETAILS: The E trailhead of the *South Prong Trail* is at a parking area 0.4 mi W of the Dolly Sods Picnic Area on FR-19. Enter the trail on sections of boardwalk in a wet area for 0.5 mi. On drier treadway reach a rocky ridge line at 1.0 mi; vistas follow. Forest has spruce, cherry, Canada dogwood, huckleberry, rhododendron, and fly poison. Pass large cairns at 1.5 mi, followed by a rock formation, L, and a scenic campsite, L, at 1.7 mi. At 1.8 mi make a sharp R through a meadow, cross a drain and descend on a steep, rocky treadway to FR-70 at 2.7 mi. (To the R on FR-70 it is 1.7 mi to a gate and FR-19, and 0.2 mi R to the point of origin for a loop of 4.6 mi. Gated FR-70 is always locked.)

To the L on FR-70 it is 1.4 mi to the SE terminus of *Boar's Nest Trail*. Beyond, on FR-70, it is 0.7 mi to the end of the road, where the 3.0-mi *Roaring Plains Trail* begins.) Cross FR-70, descend to join an old RR grade, and cross the South Fork of Red Creek at 3.1 mi. Turn a sharp R and begin to parallel the creek. The treadway is over conglomerate rocks, and the trees are northern hardwoods. At 4.3 mi leave the RR grade and descend over RR grade switchbacks to rock-hop the South Fork of Red Creek.

Ascend to gated FR-479 and its parking area at 5.7 mi at FR-19. Here is also the N trailhead of *Boar's Nest Trail*. On FR-19 it is 1.0 mi L (W) to Red Creek bridge and 1.5 mi R (E) up the mtn to where you started.

Begin *Boar's Nest Trail* by following the blue blazes. Rock-hop the South Fork of Red Creek and begin a 1,240-ft gain in elev on an old logging road. After 0.7 mi leave the road and ascend steeply for another 0.6 mi to dense sections of spruce, and arrive on a rocky plateau with huckleberry and mtn laurel. Parts of the treadway are wet. Reach FR-70 at 2.7 mi. To the L it is 1.4 mi to crossing the *South Prong Trail* and another 1.7 mi to FR-19. To the R it is 0.4 mi to the *Roaring Plains Trail*. (*USGS-FS Maps*: The Laneville and Hopeville topos [1969] have a number of incorrect trail routes.)

Flatrock Run Trail (5.1 mi; USFS #519); Roaring Plains Trail (3.3 mi; USFS #548)

LENGTH: 8.4 mi combined

DIFFICULTY: strenuous, elev gain 2,380 ft

FEATURES: scenic, geology, isolated

TRAILHEADS AND DETAILS: From the Red Creek bridge drive W on the paved Laneville Rd (CO-45) for 1.5 mi to the first paved road L, and go 0.8 mi to cross a cement bridge (flooded in high water) over Red Creek to a sign and parking area L. From the W, at the jct of WV-32 and Laneville Rd, drive E for 4.3 mi and, immediately after passing a tan metal building on the R, turn R. It is 0.8 mi farther as described above. (The first trail mi is on private property, but the USFS has a trail-use agreement with the landowner.) Climb over the main gate, if it is locked, and follow a cattle pasture road through a field of grasses and such wildflowers as black-eyed Susan, viper's bugloss, chicory, spotted knapweed (*Centaurea masculosa*), daisy, and common tansy (*Tanacetum vulgare*). Pass through two pasture gates and cross small drains at 1.2 mi and 1.4 mi. Pass an abandoned cabin and enter a forest of hemlock. Turn sharply R on an old RR grade at 2.0 mi, away from Flat Rock Run. At 2.3 mi turn L on the RR grade switchback, but go straight at the next two RR grade switchbacks at 2.7 mi and 3.0 mi. Ferns, black cohosh, and white snakeroot are prominent in the forest of cherry, locust, maple, and birch. Deer, wild turkey, grouse, and owls are often seen in this area. Rock-hop cascading and scenic Right Fork of Flat Rock Run at 3.1 mi. A few yd ahead is a large boulder that has walking fern (*Camptosorus*) at eye level. Leave the RR grade, R, at 3.4 mi and ascend steeply for 0.9 mi on a footpath that crosses the old RR grade switchbacks.

Reach a R turn at a RR grade at 4.3 mi. The treadway is wet and mossy with patches of ferns. Spruce becomes dominant. At 5.1 mi reach the E terminus of the trail at a jct with *Roaring Plains Trail,* its W terminus.

(To the R the old RR grade, now soggy and overgrown, leads 0.8 mi to Mt Porte Crayon. ATV traffic has made a new, but also muddy, route.) Although there is not any specific trail to Mt Porte Crayon (4,770 ft) and its rugged surroundings, it is a significant place. It was dedicated on July 5, 1941, in memory of Gen David Hunter Strother, artist, author, diplomat, and outdoorsman, who explored the mountains in this area. His pseudonym was "Porte Crayon." The USFS cut a special trail from the A. B. Wolford farm near Harperton for the dedication party of 40 people. Strother's grandson was there and so was the curly-haired, three-year-old great-grandson, called the "Little General." He was carried to the windswept top on the back of a USFS staff member. Jack Prebble, of *Harper's New Monthly* magazine, said Strother had "inspired our love of the forest, the streams, and the caverns of his native highlands. Seldom is a man so honored."

Turn L at the jct on *Roaring Plains Trail* and ascend (a spring is R) 0.1 mi to a grassy old RR grade. Turn L and follow the wide clearing through high meadows for 0.5 mi before it narrows to a footpath on a rocky bald (4,720 ft). (A stack of rock for a campfire shield is L.) The area has sections of dense grasses, goldenrod, blueberry, mtn ash, and blue gentian (*Gentiana clausa*). Enter a spruce forest at 1.0 mi that is intersected with open meadows and dense groves of rhododendron and mtn laurel. Turn sharply L at 2.5 mi and descend slightly to the headwaters of the South Fork of Red Creek. It is 3.4 mi on FR-70 to its locked gate at FR-19, 0.5 mi W of the Dolly Sods Picnic Area. (*USGS-FS Maps*: The Laneville and Hopeville topos [1969] have a number of incorrect trail routes.)

SECTION 6: WHITE SULPHUR RANGER DISTRICT

This district is the most southern of the Monongahela National Forest. Its western boundary is the Greenbrier River and its eastern boundary is on the crest of the Allegheny Mtn range, along the West Virginia–Virginia state line. The northern boundary crosses the Middle Mtn and Brush Mtn Ranges from the E to the Calvin Price State Forest in the W, only a few miles N of the Greenbrier-Pocahontas county line, where it adjoins the Marlinton District. Within the district's 97,928 acres are two recreation areas—beautiful Lake Sherwood on Meadow Creek and Blue Bend on Anthony Creek. In addition to 81.3 mi of hiking trails, of which 31.2 mi comprise the *Allegheny Trail,* the district has more than 140 mi of forest roads suitable for hiking. Trail usage is frequent to moderate. (At least 12 trails with a total of 30 mi have been abandoned between 1985 and 1995 because of lack of usage or maintenance funding.) Scenic areas with the most outstanding vistas are at the end of Beaver Lick Tower Rd (FR-343); check with the district office to find out if the road is open), the NW section of *Meadow Mtn Trail*, the *Allegheny Mtn Trail*, and the end of FR-139 from Blue Bend Campground to Hopkins Mtn. The Blue Bend Campground is also a good base point for excursions on the *Greenbrier River Trail*, which passes through the community of Anthony (see chapters 1 and 6).

ADDRESS AND ACCESS: District Ranger, White Sulphur Ranger District, PO Box 520, White Sulphur Springs, WV 24986; 304-536-2144. The district office is in the US Post Office Bldg, East Main St, White Sulphur Springs.

MAPS: Numbers 29–32

BLUE BEND RECREATION AREA (Greenbrier County)

There are two campgrounds here: Blue Bend with 22 sites, open year-round, and Blue Meadows Group Campground, open from Memorial Day through Labor Day during the full recreation season. During the summer season there are flush toilets and water fountains, but in the off-season there are vault toilets and hand water pumps. Neither campground has hookups. Each campsite is provided with a table, grill, waste receptacle, and lantern post. At Blue Bend space is allocated on a first-come, first-served basis, with a maximum of eight people per site and a maximum stay of 14 days. The Blue Meadow Group Campground is available by reservation.

The area has 25 picnic tables and two large picnic shelters. The larger picnic shelters may be reserved for groups. Swimming is allowed in the cool Anthony Creek. Bathing clothes, changing facilities, and vault toilet are provided in the day-use area. For anglers, Anthony Creek is stocked with trout and there are trout and bass in the nearby Greenbrier River. For hikers, the area is ideal for a variety of day hikes or backpacking trips. Trail maps are available at the campgrounds.

ACCESS: The eastern access is 3.7 mi W on Little Creek Rd (CO-16) and Big Blue Bend Rd (CO-16/2) from the jct with WV-92 at Alvon. The western access is 8.0 mi E on Anthony Station Rd (CO-21/2) from US-219 at Frankford.

SUPPORT FACILITIES: It is 10.0 mi S on WV-92 to White Sulphur Springs to shopping centers, restaurants, motels, banks, service stations, and a hospital. Green Acres Grocery is 5.0 mi from the campground on WV-92, 1.3 mi S from the Little Creek Rd jct. It has hunting and fishing licenses also (304-536-4510). For a campground with hookup facilities, commercial Paradise Campground is 1.2 mi E on Big Blue Bend Rd from the Blue Bend Recreation Area to Big Draft Rd. Open May 1–Sept 15 (304-536-3223).

Blue Bend Loop Trail (5.0 mi; USFS #614); Anthony Creek Trail (3.8 mi; USFS #618)

LENGTH: 8.8 mi combined

DIFFICULTY: moderate

FEATURES: scenic river and overlooks

TRAILHEADS AND DETAILS: From the parking area in the Blue Bend Picnic Area (1,944 ft), follow the trail signs across the swinging footbridge over Anthony Creek to the *Blue Bend Loop Trail* (once called *Round Mtn Trail*) to a signpost. From the signpost at the fork turn R and follow downstream through an exceptionally scenic forest of hemlock, ash, poplar, sycamore, beech, basswood, maple, and white pine. Rhododendron and spicebush are in patches. Wildflowers include mandrake, stonecrop, cohosh, wild geranium, and ragwort. At 1.6 mi is a jct with the *Anthony Creek Trail* at the mouth of Big Draft. (*Anthony Creek Trail* goes downstream for 3.8 mi to Anthony Station Rd, CO-21/2.) Turn L here on *Blue Bend Loop Trail*, ascend steeply on four switchbacks to the ridge top at 2.7 mi and to an Adirondack shelter that accommodates eight backpackers. A usually dependable spring is 100 yd from the shelter. Continue ahead on an old road across the top of Round Mtn (2,960 ft). Begin the ridge descent through an open forest and at 3.6 mi enter a rhododendron thicket. Continue descent to three precipitous overlooks with superb views of the Anthony Creek valley. Trailing arbutus and wintergreen border sections of the trail. After seven switchbacks complete the descent to the creek side and return to the swinging bridge at 5.0 mi.

To hike the 3.8-mi *Anthony Creek Trail,* turn at the jct mentioned above, cross the mouth of the Big Draft, and go downstream through a hardwood forest, sometimes following an old tram road. Deer are likely to be seen on this trail. At 0.5 mi pass L of a rock cribbing and a good fishing hole. Pass other good fishing spots and a number of excellent camping areas. At 2.7 mi cross Laurel Run, and at 3.1 mi is a jct L with the *South Boundary Trail.* (The *South Boundary Trail*, described below, ascends 5.0 mi to Jericho Draft

Rd, CO-36.) Continue ahead and R to ford the 60-ft-wide Anthony Creek, a stream that is hazardous to cross at high-water times. Wading may be easier upstream about 200 yd. Rock fanciers will find a wide range of color and variety here. After crossing the creek follow the old road around the base of Gunpowder Ridge, where wild orchids and squirrel cups grow on the road banks. Good campsites are by the Greenbrier River. Exit at the bridge on Anthony Station Rd (CO-21/2). Backtrack for a total of 10.8 mi or have a vehicle shuttle for 4.0 mi E to the campground. (Across the Greenbrier River bridge is the *Greenbrier River Trail* described in chapter 6.) (*USGS-FS Map*: Anthony)

South Boundary Trail (5.0 mi; USFS #615)

CONNECTING TRAIL:
> (*Anthony Creek Trail*, 3.8 mi: USFS #618)

TOTAL LENGTH: 10.0 mi round-trip

DIFFICULTY: moderate

FEATURE: forest succession

TRAILHEAD AND DETAILS: The easiest access is to drive E from the campground on Big Blue Bend Rd (CO-21/1) for 1.1 mi to Big Draft Rd (also called Jericho Draft Rd) (CO-36/1) and turn R. Go 3.5 mi on Big Draft Rd to the trailhead and parking space, R (W). (Another access route is from the *Anthony Creek Trail* mentioned above.)

At the trail signs ascend W on the *South Boundary Trail* to a ridge with hardwoods, scattered white pines, rhododendron, mtn laurel, blueberry bushes, and wintergreen. At 0.8 mi cross a forest timber road and follow a jeep trail. At 2.1 mi cross an earthen barrier that prevents vehicular usage of the trail. Follow a private road for 0.4 mi past a hunting cabin, R, to another earthen barrier at the MNF boundary. Cross the barrier in a hardwood forest and reach a knoll (3,121 ft) at 3.1 mi. After 1.0 mi farther begin a steep descent to the jct with *Anthony Creek Trail* at Anthony Creek. Options here are to backtrack, turn R and hike 5.4 mi to the Blue Bend Campground, or ford the creek and go 0.6 mi to the Greenbrier River bridge described above. (*USGS-FS Maps*: Anthony, White Sulphur Springs)

Beaver's Tail Trail

LENGTH: 0.3 mi

DIFFICULTY: easy

FEATURE: trail for the visually handicapped

TRAILHEAD AND DETAILS: Across the road from the Blue Meadow Campground in the parking lot, follow the signs on the loop trail with lettered and Brailled interpretive signs. In a level area, the visually handicapped can hear and wade in the creek; at other places they can smell plants such as wild phlox, spicebush, and wild roses. The trail is a contribution of the USFS, the Lewisburg Lion's Club and clubs of District 29-N, and the YCC of 1974–75. It is a National Recreation Trail. (*USGS-FS Map*: Anthony)

LAKE SHERWOOD RECREATION AREA
(Greenbrier County)

Through cooperative efforts in 1958, the USFS and the West Virginia Department of Natural Resources constructed the Lake Sherwood Recreation Area. Their choice of the Upper Meadow Creek valley at 2,668 ft elev between Meadow Creek Mtn and the Allegheny Mtns has made this beautiful valley one of the Monongahela National Forest's most popular vacation localities. The area is named after the Sherwood Land, Mineral and Timber Company, the former owner.

The appealing 165-acre lake is stocked with largemouth bass, catfish, bluegill, and tiger musky. Deer, turkey, grouse, skunk, red squirrel, fox squirrel, raccoon, and rattlesnakes are in the surrounding forest. (State licenses and USFS stamps are necessary for anglers and hunters.)

There are two sandy beaches, one on the W bank and another on a connecting island. Lifeguards are on duty in the summer months. Boats and canoes are available for rent, and there are three boat launches and docks for public use. Three campgrounds—West Shore Campground, Pine Run Campground, and Meadow Creek Campground—provide 96 family units and 50 units for group camping. During the summer the camping area has restrooms with electricity, running water, and hot showers. Capacity for each campsite is eight people, and a maximum stay is 14 days. Full-season operation is from Memorial Day through Labor Day. During the off-season 25 campsites are available, with vault restrooms and hand water pumps. Campsites are not reserved, but reservations may be made for a group of up to 100 campers. Facilities include grates, tables, trash receptacles, and lantern posts. There are 100 picnic sites on the Pine Knoll and Lakeside Picnic Areas and one large shelter for group or family outings. Reservations are accepted. For hiking enthusiasts, the lake area has eight connecting trails.

ACCESS: At the jct of WV-92 and Sherwood Lake Rd (CO-14/1) in Neola, drive E on the Sherwood Lake Rd for 10.5 mi.

SUPPORT FACILITIES: General stores are in Neola. Grocery, camping foods, firewood, and laundry facilities are available at a seasonal country store 1.7 mi from the campground on Sherwood Lake Rd.

Lake Sherwood Trail (3.7 mi; USFS #601); Virginia Trail (0.6 mi; USFS #685); Allegheny Mtn Trail (3.6 mi; USFS #611); Connector Trail (1.9 mi; USFS #604); Meadow Creek Trail (2.7 mi; USFS #684); Meadow Mtn Trail (3.5 mi; USFS #610); Allegheny Trail (see separate description, USFS #701); Upper Meadow Trail (1.2 mi; USFS #672)

LENGTH: 17.2 mi combined

DIFFICULTY: easy to strenuous

FEATURES: scenic, wildlife, wildflowers

TRAILHEADS AND DETAILS: Base trailhead is Pine Knoll Picnic Area in Lake Sherwood Recreation Area for the purpose of this description. These trails are listed together because they all connect; they will be described individually in the order they are listed, with connecting descriptions to follow. For hikers who wish to go farther into the forest with a day pack, or a backpack for overnight camping, these descriptions will offer distance options for loop combinations.

The 3.7-mi *Lake Sherwood Trail* is probably the most-hiked trail in the district because of scenic beauty and the concentration of summer campers. From the parking lot at Pine Knoll Picnic Area follow the trail sign through tall white pine, hemlock, and oak to the lake. Turn R. Cattails and witch hazel grow in the coves. Reach the dam at 0.5 mi and cross the spillway on a footbridge. At 0.9 mi is a jct with the *Virginia Trail*. (The 0.6-mi *Virginia Trail* ascends to the *Allegheny Mtn Trail*, unrelated to the *Allegheny Trail* on the W ridge of the lake area.) At 1.5 mi cross a small stream, and at 2.3 mi cross a footbridge over Meadow Creek to a fork. The *Lake Sherwood Trail* continues L.

(To the R is easy to moderately difficult *Meadow Creek Trail*. It goes upstream, crossing the creek seven times [no bridges]. The trail is known for its cool and alluring passage. Wildlife such as deer, turkey, grouse, bobcat, and beaver may be seen or heard. Native trout is in the creek pools. In a forest of hardwoods, white pine, and mtn laurel are long dense tunnels of rhododendron. Its N terminus is a jct with *Connector Trail*.)

Continue on the *Lake Sherwood Trail* and after 0.2 mi reach a boat access in Meadow Creek Campground. Here is the nearest space to park for gaining access to the *Meadow Creek Trail*. The parking space is in the loop, opposite campsite #72. Pass another boat access in Pine Run Campground. Follow the trail through the West Shore Campground to the public boat launch and docks and the swimming area, and return to the Pine Knoll and Lakeside Picnic Areas at 3.7 mi.

The shortest access route to the 3.6-mi *Allegheny Mtn Trail* is on the 0.6-mi *Virginia Trail* mentioned above. Follow the *Lake Sherwood Trail* to the *Virginia Trail* and ascend on an old road under tall trees for 0.3 mi; then ascend on a wide footpath for another 0.3 mi to a saddle on the Allegheny Mtn ridge, the West Virginia–Virginia state line. Turn L (N) and ascend from the saddle along the Allegheny Mtn ridge through a hardwood forest. Occasional patches of blueberry, buckberry, wintergreen, flame azalea, and pinxter are noticeable. Deer, grouse, and wild turkey are likely to be seen on this trail. At 1.0 mi the old CCC fire road becomes more of a footpath through rocky sections. At 1.8 mi ascend to a knob (3,214 ft) where a faint trail, R, leads down into Meadow Lick Hollow. Here, and at other places, are E overlooks for scenic views of Lake Moomaw and Bolar Mtn. At 3.6 mi is a jct with the SE terminus of *Connector Trail*.

If continuing for a loop, follow the *Connector Trail* 0.5 mi to the jct with *Meadow Creek Trail*, L. If following the *Meadow Creek Trail* and the W section of *Lake Sherwood Trail* to Pine Knoll Picnic Area, the loop is 9.2 mi.

If planning the longest loop, stay on the *Connector Trail* (an old road) for 1.4 mi to cross streams among mtn laurel, and ascend through a young forest. Pass a wildlife opening before reaching another old road at the top of the mtn. (Here a R goes 1.0 mi to FR-55 at the White Sulphur/Marlinton Ranger District line, and another 6.0 mi N on FR-55 to WV-39.)

Turn L (S) on *Meadow Mtn Trail* in a young forest. Enter an older forest at 0.5 mi, pass a gated timber road R at 1.1 mi, and another timber road R at 1.4 mi. Deer, squirrel, grouse, and skunk are on the ridge. Ascend and descend on knobs, and at 2.7 mi is a superior view of Lake Sherwood. On the R at 3.6 mi is a jct with the *Allegheny Trail* and the S end of *Meadow Mtn Trail*. Follow the *Allegheny Trail* for 0.5 mi to a jct L with *Upper Meadow Trail*. (The *Allegheny Trail* continues S.)

Descend on the *Upper Meadow Trail* on an old road with switchbacks, and among hardwoods and white pine. Cross a stream bordered with rhododendron and continue descent on a foot trail. Arrive to cross FR-14, curve L, and return to Pine Knoll Picnic Area for a loop of 12.3 mi. (*USGS-FS Maps*: Lake Sherwood, Rucker Gap, Mtn Grove)

MIDDLE MOUNTAIN AREA
(Greenbrier and Pocahontas Counties)
Middle Mtn Trail (South) (13.2 mi; USFS #608); (Allegheny Trail); Dock Trail (2.0 mi; USFS #656); Brushy Mtn Trail (2.1 mi; USFS #655)

LENGTH: 17.3 mi combined

DIFFICULTY: moderate

FEATURES: scenic, historic, wildlife

TRAILHEADS AND DETAILS: In Neola at the post office and jct of WV-92 and North Fork Rd (FR-96), go W on FR-96 for 0.5 mi across the Anthony Creek bridge and cross the North Fork on a low-water bridge. Look for parking space for the *Middle Mtn Trail*, R. At the S terminus of *Middle Mtn Trail* wade the North Fork, pass through a grassy meadow, and gradually ascend on a foot trail in and out of coves. At 1.2 mi begin the first of four switchbacks and reach the ridge crest at 1.7 mi. A number of signs on the trail mark watersheds of the hollows. For example, Hatfield Hollow at 2.1 mi, Lynch Hollow at 4.3 mi, Coles Run at 4.6 mi, and Sugar Run at 7.2 mi. At 2.3 mi and 2.7 mi are examples of mtn andromeda (*Pieris floribunda*), a low, white flowering shrub that blooms in early April. There is a water hole at 3.4 mi; at 4.5 mi the trail becomes a jeep road and is gated at 5.0 mi with the jct and W end of Coles Run Rd (FR-875). (It is 3.7 mi on Coles Run Rd to a gated entrance at WV-92, 2.4 mi N of Neola.) Continue ahead on a foot trail through an open forest of hardwoods, flame azalea, rose azalea, mtn laurel, white pine, wildflowers such as gold star, and ferns such as maidenhair. At 7.5 mi reach a low-standard forest road, Divide Rd (FR-790). At 8.9 mi pass a wildlife opening. (The *Allegheny Trail* is R at 9.5 mi. It descends 2.4 mi to a parking area at WV-92, and continues ahead to join the *Dock Trail*.) Reach a jct, L, at 10.8 mi with the *Dock Trail*. Ahead the *Middle Mtn Trail* continues through hardwoods, chiefly an oak and hickory forest, for 2.4 mi to a point where the old FR-790 turned R at the boundary with the Marlinton Ranger District.

(At 0.2 mi ahead reach an intersection with the newly constructed FR-790-B, L. The *Middle Mtn Trail* [N] continues ahead on the ridge, parallels L of the new FR-790-A for a short distance, and gradually descends for 4.6 mi to an exit on WV-39/92, opposite the Laurel Creek Picnic Area. To the R of FR-790-B is a new 1.2-mi section of the 3.0-mi FR-790 that leads down the mtn to a gate at WV-92, 1.4 mi S of the Pocahontas Campground. See section 5.)

The 2.0-mi *Dock Trail* is a woods road (FR-310) that is closed to vehicles year-round. It is also the *Allegheny Trail*. From the *Middle Mtn Trail* it descends for 0.6 mi on a spur ridge, S of the headwaters of Douthat Run, before curving L of the ridge and descending to "the Dock" at Douthat Rd (CO-23). The Dock received its name from a timber loading dock used by early timbermen. (To the R on Douthat Rd it is 7.0 mi to WV-39/72 in Minnehaha Springs. To the L on Douthat Rd it is 0.6 mi to gated Beaver Lick Tower Rd [FR-343], a 4.3-mi scenic road open from early October to Dec 31 and accessible to passenger vehicles. It ascends to a spectacular vista at a dismantled fire tower site [3,645 ft]. Here is the highest point in the district and the E trailhead of the *Beaver Trail* in the Marlinton Ranger District.)

Across Douthat Rd at the W terminus of the *Dock Trail* is the *Brushy Mtn Trail*. Follow an old gated road through a pine plantation to a gate. To the L is a grassy area with beds of mint and violets that is good for campsites. Cross a small drain and reach a fork at 0.4 mi in a meadow of cinquefoil, wild strawberry, and peppermint. At the fork the *Allegheny Trail* continues L for a 1.0-mi route to cross the Beaver Lick Tower Rd and join the *Beaver Creek Trail*. To the R the *Brushy Mtn Trail* crosses the drain to ascend gradually W and then N through rhododendron, oak, locust, maple, mtn laurel, sassafras, and Virginia pine to the N terminus at 2.1 mi for a jct with the Beaver Lick Tower Rd. (From here it is 1.1 mi to the dismantled Beaver Lick Tower mentioned above.) Backtrack. (*USGS-FS Maps*: Alvon, Rucker Gap, Lake Sherwood)

2. George Washington and Jefferson National Forests

Of all exercises, walking is the best
—Thomas Jefferson

GEORGE WASHINGTON NATIONAL FOREST

The George Washington National Forest (GWNF), with its 1,058,727 scenic acres in Virginia (953,866) and West Virginia (104,861), is the largest national forest east of the Mississippi River. It was established by a proclamation from President Herbert Hoover on June 23, 1932. Two of its six districts, Lee and Dry River, are partially in West Virginia. Chiefly on the western slopes of the Shenandoah and Great North Mountain Ranges in Hardy and Pendleton Counties, it is rugged, beautiful, and historic. The West Virginia forest is home for the black bear (the state animal), deer, turkey, grouse, fox, raccoon, squirrel, timber rattlesnake, owl, hawk, and numerous species of songbirds, particularly the warblers. Although a deciduous forest, there are scattered stands of magnificent white pine, Virginia pine, and hemlock. Wildflowers common to the Appalachian region are abundant.

Among its main geological attractions in West Virginia are Lost River sinks, Trout Run sinks, and panoramic ridges of limestone and sandstone cliffs. There are five recreation areas: Brandywine, Camp Run, Trout Pond, Wolf Gap, and Hawk. All have camping units but only Trout Pond has hookups. Brandywine and Trout Pond have facilities for fishing and swimming. There are more than 90 mi of hiking trails.

INFORMATION: The George Washington and Jefferson National Forests have administratively consolidated. See address below. Contact the district offices or the main office. Dry River Ranger District, 112 N River Rd, Bridgewater, VA 22812; 540-828-2591. Lee Ranger District, 109 Molineu Rd, Edinburg, VA 22824; 540-984-4101. George Washington and Jefferson National Forest Hq, 5162 Valley Pointe Pkwy, Roanoke, VA 24019; 540-265-5100.

MAPS: Numbers 33–37

DRY RIVER RANGER DISTRICT

This district has 49,106 acres on the western slopes of the Shenandoah Mtn Range, where dozens of tributaries flow into the South Branch of the Potomac River. The E-W US-33 passes through the center of the forest at 3,450 ft elev on its route between Richmond and Ohio. Two camping areas, Brandywine on US-33 and Camp Run, N of Fort Seybert on Camp Run Rd (CO-3), are in the district. Historic Fort Seybert was the site where pioneers were massacred by the Delaware Indians in 1758. In addition to the district's designated trails, there are more than 85.2 mi of winding forest roads to hike. The district maintains *Saw Mill Trail* annually, but does not have an established maintenance schedule for the other trails.

BRANDYWINE RECREATION AREA (Pendleton County)

Nestled in the picturesque cove of Hawes Run, the Brandywine Recreation Area has 60 picnic units, 30 paved camping units (no hookups), a lake for swimming and fishing, drinking water, flush toilets, and two hiking trails. The area is open from May 15 to Dec 1, and it can be used as a base point to drive to the other five trails in the district.

ACCESS: From the town of Brandywine drive E on US-33 for 2.8 mi to entrance on the R. From Harrisonburg, VA, drive W on US-33 for 27.2 mi to entrance on the L.

SUPPORT FACILITIES: A grocery store, motel, restaurant, and service station are in the town of Brandywine. Privately operated Shenandoah Shadow Campground with hookups and open year-round is nearby; 304-249-5184.

Saw Mill Trail (USFS #1035)

LENGTH: 4.3 mi
DIFFICULTY: moderate
FEATURES: wildlife

TRAILHEAD AND DETAILS: Park in the parking lot, if not camping, and walk 0.4 mi to an old logging road with yellow blazes in the second circle of the campground. Pass through the opening of a wildlife food plot; silverberry is prominent. At 0.3 mi begin the first of four crossings of

Hawes Run, a small tumbling stream. Pass R of an old sawmill site at 1.3 mi in a forest of oak, white pine, and hemlock. Ascend the SW slope of a ridge at 2.3 mi, descend, cross another ridge, and descend to a stream in a hemlock grove at 3.0 mi. Pass through three more wildlife food plots and return to the campground at 4.3 mi. (*USGS Map*: Brandywine)

High Knob Trail (USFS #1021)

LENGTH: 5.4 mi round-trip
DIFFICULTY: strenuous, elev gain 2,120 ft
FEATURES: secluded and scenic
TRAILHEAD AND DETAILS: Park in the parking lot, if not camping, and walk 0.4 mi to a gated wildlife food plot (opposite campsite #28) and go 150 yd along the R edge of a silverberry border to the entrance by a tall white pine. (This trail may be overgrown in sections.) Ascend the steep ridge through a forest of oak, mtn laurel, locust, maple, dogwood, hickory, and white and Virginia pine for the entire ridge length of 2.3 mi. Along the trail are patches of huckleberry, trailing arbutus, and other wildflowers. Near the top of the mountain reach the private road of MacNeff. (It is 0.7 mi L to US-33 at the West Virginia–Virginia state line.) Turn R, go 0.1 mi on the road to a fork, and turn L to High Knob, elev 4,080 ft. The lookout tower has been dismantled. Backtrack. (*USGS Map*: Brandywine)

Road Run Trail (USFS #1023)

LENGTH: 2.8 mi round-trip
DIFFICULTY: strenuous, elev gain 1,400 ft
FEATURE: wildlife
TRAILHEAD AND DETAILS: From Brandywine Recreation Area drive 0.7 mi E on US-33 to jct with West Side Rd (FR-151) on L. Drive 2.7 mi on FR 151 to a small parking area on R in a sharp curve; trail sign is on the R bank before the curve. (Another access is to go 3.1 mi E on US-33 from Brandywine Recreation Area to the jct with FR-85 [Hall Spring Hunter Access Rd] on L. This is a rough, narrow but scenic route; you may have to walk it. After 2.6 mi reach the trailhead on L.) From FR-151 trail sign ascend steeply on an unblazed path of 0.3 mi to the crest of a ridge with leaning chestnut oaks. Bear L and ascend on gradual contour in oak, Virginia pine, and patches of huckleberries. The area is

remote. Reach FR-85 at 1.4 mi. Backtrack or use vehicle shuttle. (*USGS Map*: Brandywine)

Bother Ridge Trail (USFS #1026)

LENGTH: 3.1 mi
DIFFICULTY: strenuous, elev gain 1,820 ft
FEATURES: scenic views of Reddish Knob and little Fork Valley

TRAILHEAD AND DETAILS: From the town of Brandywine jct of US-33 and Sugar Grove Rd (CO-21), drive 9.7 mi S on CO-21 to the jct with Moyers Gap Rd (CO-25). Turn L on CO-25 and drive 3.5 mi to a narrow dirt road on the L for SW trailhead. Park in grassy area of the Transcontinental Cable Route. Trailhead is at the continuing jeep road. For the NE trailhead continue the drive on CO-25, pass FR-61 on R at 0.6 mi, and after 3.4 mi farther reach the mtn summit jct with FR-85. (Ahead in Virginia on SR-924, VA-257, and VA-42 it is 21 mi to Harrisonburg. On the R of this jct is FR-85 S and 2.5 mi to panoramic Reddish Knob, 4,387 ft.) Turn L on FR-85 N and drive 1.7 mi to the fork of FR-85 and FR-85-A. Park here (FR-85-A goes R to Flagpole Knob). Hike L on narrow, rough FR-85 for 0.6 mi to trailhead on L. Descend on yellow-blazed jeep road for 0.7 mi. Turn L off road and follow the ridge, which has excellent views. Wild turkey are often seen here. Also, this area is rich in plant life; Fraser's fir (*Abies fraseri*) and red pine are among the conifers near Bother Knob, and fragrant pennyroyal (*Hedeoma pulegioides*) is on the trail. In the middle of October the green-striped-maple leaves turn to brilliant yellows and gold. Views of Reddish Knob, little Fork Valley, and the US Naval Reservation with huge dishes for radio astronomy and defense purposes are visible from the rock outcrops. At 2.5 mi is a faint red arrow on the L. (Ahead for 0.1 mi is yellow blaze for similar direction.) Descend steeply to a large walnut tree at the jeep road. Turn R, cross a small stream, and reach Transcontinental Cable Route parking area at 3.1 mi. (*USGS Maps*: Brandywine, Reddish Knob, Palo Alto)

Sugar Run Trail (USFS #1025)

LENGTH: 4.5 mi
DIFFICULTY: strenuous, elev gain 2,220 ft
FEATURES: wildlife and wildflowers

TRAILHEAD AND DETAILS: From the town of Brandywine drive S on Sugar Grove Rd (CO-21) for 5.5 mi and turn L on Little Fork Rd (CO-

24). Drive 2.3 mi on CO-24 (crossing unbridged Little Fork) to FR on L. Park here. (FR may be passable for jeep or 4WD vehicle.) Begin hike on an unblazed trail by crossing Little Fork, and reach the forest boundary at 0.2 mi. Cross Sugar Run a number of times; excellent campsites are at 1.4 mi. Oak and white and Virginia pine tower over a carpet of ground ivy and bunches of ferns. Take R fork in a horseshoe curve of road at 1.8 mi and ascend upstream through tall oak, maple, ash, and birch. Wildflowers and wildlife are prominent. Reach headwaters in a deep cove at 3.8 mi; ascend on old road bordered with mtn laurel to FR-85 at 4.5 mi. Backtrack or use vehicle shuttle. (This trailhead can be reached by following directions to the NE trailhead of *Bother Ridge Trail* [see above], but walk 0.1 mi farther on FR-85 to *Sugar Run Trail*, unsigned but marked with a white blaze on L at entrance.) (*USGS-Maps*: Brandywine, Sugar Grove)

Miller Run Trail (USFS #1022)

LENGTH: 4.6 mi

DIFFICULTY: strenuous, elev gain 1,880 ft

FEATURE: mountain streams

TRAILHEAD AND DETAILS: From the town of Brandywine drive S on Sugar Grove Rd (CO-21) for 2.0 mi to Miller Run Rd (CO-21/3), turn L, and drive 2.0 mi to the gate and posted property of Luther Hoover. Request permission to hike upstream to the forest boundary on an old road for 2.6 mi along a pastoral stream with wildflowers. At the end of the road leave the stream L and ascend a ridge to switchbacks at 3.5 mi and again at 3.9 mi. At 4.6 mi reach the summit and rough FR-85. (It is 1.6 mi R on FR-85 to *Bother Ridge* trailhead, described above.) Backtrack or use vehicle shuttle. (*USGS Map*: Brandywine)

LEE RANGER DISTRICT

Three recreational areas—Trout Pond, Wolf Gap, and Hawk—are in the 51,950 acres of this district in West Virginia. Its eastern edge is the crest of the Great North Mountain, the boundary line between the Virginias. Its many tributaries flow into Lost River, which after its 3.0 mi disappearance into Sandy Ridge becomes Cacapon River, a tributary of the Potomac. Two state highways—55 in the N between Strasburg, VA, and Wardensville, WV, and 259 in the S between Harrisonburg and Wardensville—are the major accesses. The district is noted for its highly folded sedimentary rocks of sandstone and limestone, and for such historic communities as Wardensville, a settlement laid out by George Washington for William Warden. Warden and his family were massacred by the Delaware Indians in 1758. Lost River State Park, another historic area, is near the town of Mathias in the SW corner of the district. Black bear, deer, turkey, and raccoon have a wide range in the predominately oak forest, except for conifer stands on some of the rocky ridges. In addition to the district's designated hiking trails, there are more than 85 mi of scenic forest roads.

TROUT POND RECREATION AREA (Hardy County)

This exceptionally attractive recreational area has 50 campsites for tents or RVs; 29 picnic units, some with shelters; Rock Cliff Lake, a 16-acre reservoir for fishing, boating (no outboards), and swimming; bathhouse; dumping station; hot showers; and flush toilets. The season is Apr 1– Dec 1. Trout Pond Recreation Area takes its name from the state's only and largest (1.5-acre) natural lake. It is 300 yd upstream from Rock Cliff Lake. USFS operated; 540-984-4101. Address: Trout Pond Recreation Area, Rte 3, Box 40, Lost River, WV 26811; 304-897-6450.

ACCESS: Drive 6.0 mi N from the town of Mathias or 18.0 mi S from Wardensville on WV-259 to the community of Lost River. Drive 4.5 mi on Mill Gap Rd (CO-16) and turn R on FR-500 for 1.7 mi to the recreation area entrance.

SUPPORT FACILITIES: A grocery store, restaurant, and service station are on the WV-259 highway between Lost River and Mathias.

Rock Cliff Trail (1.0 mi; USFS #1010); Chimney Rock Trail (0.8 mi; USFS #1010B); Fishermen's Trail (0.4 mi; USFS #1010A)

LENGTH: 3.4 mi combined

DIFFICULTY: easy

FEATURE: rare rock outcrops

TRAILHEADS AND DETAILS: From the fishermen's parking lot at Rock Cliff Lake, follow the sign around the lake perimeter on a well-graded trail. Cross the top of the dam at 0.4 mi to a rock formation and jct with *Chimney Rock Trail* on R. *Chimney Rock Trail* descends to a vertical rock outcropping of highly erosion resistant Oriskany sandstone, crosses Trout Run at 0.4 mi, and ascends for another 0.4 mi to a jct with *Trout Pond Trail*. Backtrack. Continue around the lake to a jct with the blue-blazed *Fishermen's Trail*, R, at 0.7 mi. *Fishermen's Trail* ascends to FR-500 for 0.4 mi. Backtrack and turn R toward the bridge across a lake tributary. Complete the combined trails at 3.4 mi. (*USGS Map*: Wolf Gap)

Trout Pond Trail (2.5 mi; USFS #1008); Long Mountain Trail (7.8 mi; USFS #1007)

LENGTH: 10.3 mi combined
DIFFICULTY: moderate
FEATURES: sinkholes, wildlife

TRAILHEADS AND DETAILS: *Trout Pond Trail* is a 2.5-mi purple-blazed trail whose name is derived from the small natural limestone sinkhole pond near the campground. Enter the middle of the trail between campsites #30 and #31. If going S ascend for 1.4 mi to gravel Judge Rye Rd (CO-59) and backtrack. (Or a loop can be made here by ascending Judge Rye Rd for 1.9 mi to the S terminus of yellow-blazed *Long Mtn Trail* on L. Follow *Long Mtn Trail* on an old jeep road for 0.6 mi, then on a foot trail for another 1.8 mi to a jct with *Trout Pond Trail* and *Chimney Rock Trail*. Turn L on *Trout Pond Trail* and go 1.1 mi to complete a circle to the campground for a total of 6.8 mi.) If going N on the *Trout Pond Trail* from campsites #30 and #31, cross creek, pass L of a large sinkhole, and meet the *Long Mtn Trail* at 1.1 mi. (Backtrack, or reverse the loop described above.)

To continue N on the *Long Mtn Trail* (also called *Crack Whip Furnace Trail*) begin here at the jct. Hike along a generally even contour on an old road in a hardwood forest with scattered grassy and brushy areas. At 0.5 mi pass a clearing with W view of Ben's Ridge. At 3.8 mi the road becomes a foot trail for 1.1 mi. Halfway through the foot trail is a wet area between Cherry Ridge and Long Mtn. Reach Trout Run Rd (CO-23/10) on the L side of a private cabin, a few yards W of, and across the road from, the remains of the Crack Whip Furnace, for a total of 7.8 mi from the S terminus on Judge Rye Rd or 6.5 mi from Trout Pond Campground. Backtrack or use vehicle shuttle. (It is 6.5 mi N on CO-23/10 to the town of Wardensville.) On the S terminus of the *Trout Pond Trail* easy connections can be made with the N terminus of *North Mtn Trail* (see below).

North Mountain Trail (USFS #1009)

LENGTH: 6.5 mi
DIFFICULTY: moderate
FEATURES: vistas, wildlife

TRAILHEAD AND DETAILS: To reach the N trailhead from the jct of WV-259 and WV-59 in the community of Lost City, drive E on WV-59 for 7.0 mi to pass the S end of *Trout Pond Trail*, L. Farther E, 0.8 mi on WV-59, is the West Virginia–Virginia state border and the N trailhead, R, of the *North Mtn Trail*. (Ahead, E, it is 1.2 mi on SR-691 to *Long Mtn Trail* [also called *Crack Whip Furnace Trail*], L.) On the Virginia side, drive from Columbia Furnace 9.9 mi (4.5 mi on SR-675, 0.3 mi on SR-789, and 5.1 mi on SR-691). To reach the S trailhead drive from Mathias E 4.8 mi on Upper Cove Rd (CO-20) to Basore jct. Continue 0.3 mi, turn L at a poultry house, and ascend for 2.1 mi on a steep road to the top of the mtn. On the Virginia side, drive from the town of Basye 8.3 mi (3.9 mi on SR-717 and 4.4 mi on SR-720).

There are no springs on this trail. If beginning at N trailhead follow orange blazes (*Laurel Run Trail* also begins here on L, descending) and reach an overlook at 0.8 mi. Purple-blazed *Stack Rock Trail* (also called *Table Rock Trail*) jct is at 2.2 mi, and the yellow-blazed *Falls Ridge Trail* is 100 yd farther on the Virginia side. Parts of hardwood forest are lined with huckleberry, mtn laurel, hawthorn, and bear oak (*Quercus ilicifolia*) thickets at 2.3 mi, 3.3 mi, 4.3 mi, and 5.0 mi. Among the wildflowers are snakeroot, meadow rue, wild geraniums, and woodland sunflowers. Deer, grouse, and turkey may be seen. Large cone-shaped homes of hot-tempered ants are at 3.9 mi and 5.3 mi. Rock outcrops are at 2.7 mi, 3.9 mi, and 4.7 mi. Pass an old homesite at 6.0 mi. Arrive at the gated S terminus at 6.5 mi. (*USGS Maps:* Orkney Springs, Lost City, Wolf Gap)

WOLF GAP RECREATION AREA (Hardy County)

High on the crest of the Virginia–West Virginia state line (2,240 ft) is Wolf Gap Recreation Area with 10 paved camping units, 10 picnic units, a hand pump for drinking water, and vault toilets. It is an excellent base campground open year-round for hikes S to Tibbet Knob and the Trout Pond Recreation Area, and N to Big Schloss and the former *Big Blue Trail*, now *Tuscarora Trail*. By combining trails and some forest and secondary roadways, scenic and challenging loops can be made in Virginia (described in *The Trails of Virginia: Hiking the Old Dominion*, published by the University of North Carolina Press (PO Box 2288, Chapel Hill, NC 27515) or in West Virginia. For example, ascend on the scenic *Mill Mtn Trail* and go 6.0 mi to *Pond Run Trail*. Turn L and go 0.9 mi to a jct with *Half Moon Trail*. Follow *Half Moon Trail* for 3.1 mi to Trout Run Rd (CO-32/10). Turn R on paved CO-32/10 and go 1.3 mi to Crack Whip Furnace; turn L on *Long Mtn Trail* (which makes a jct with trails into Trout Pond Recreation Area) for 7.8 mi. Reach Virginia Lost City Rd (SR-691), which becomes Judge Rye Rd (CO-59) in West Virginia. Turn L on SR-691 and descend for 2.5 mi to *Tibbet Knob Trail* on L. Ascend on *Tibbet Knob Trail* for 2.4 mi and reach the Wolf Gap Recreation Area for a total of 24 mi.

ACCESS: From Wardensville in West Virginia drive SE on Trout Run Rd (CO-23/10) for 13.3 mi. From Edinburg, VA, follow SR-675 W for 12.0 mi.

Mill Mtn Trail (6.0 mi; USFS #1004); Big Schloss Trail (0.3 mi; USFS #1004A); Big Schloss Cutoff Trail (1.3 mi; USFS #415); Pond Run Trail (Tuscarora Trail) (3.9 mi; USFS #1013.2); Peer Trail (3.2 mi; USFS #1002); Half Moon Trail (3.2 mi; USFS #1003); Half Moon Lookout Trail (0.8 mi; USFS #1003A)

LENGTH: 9.8 mi combined
DIFFICULTY: moderate
FEATURES: panoramic Big Schloss, Half Moon Lookout
TRAILHEADS AND DETAILS: Begin the hike near campsite #9, ascend on a wide, orange-blazed jeep road for 0.9 mi to the scenic crest of Mill Mtn. Bear L on rocky trail tread and reach a jct with white-blazed *Big Schloss Trail* at 1.9 mi. Turn R and ascend sharply for 0.3 mi to massive metamorphosed sandstone rock formation (2,964 ft) called the "Castle" by early German settlers. Magnificent views include Trout Run valley and Long Mtn in the W and Little Schloss Mtn and Little Stoney Creek valley in the E. Return to *Mill Mtn Trail*, turn R on the W flank of the Castle to the ridge, and reach a jct with blue-blazed *Big Schloss Cutoff Trail* at 2.8 mi. (This is a 1.3 mi spur trail that descends E to FR-92, 0.5 mi W from the E terminus of *Little Stony Creek Trail*.) Continue ahead and reach Sandstone Spring in a stand of hemlock and a fern glade at 4.5 mi. (This area is the headwaters of a cascading stream W into the canyon of Deep Gutter Run.) On a straight trail through oak and mtn laurel ascend to an airway beacon (3,293 ft, the area's highest peak) at 5.5 mi. Among the trail's wildflowers are fly poison (*Amianthium muscaetoxicum*), with white petals that turn green with age. Descend gradually through open oak forest and reach a jct with *Pond Run Trail* (also a section of *Tuscarora Trail*) at 6.0 mi.

(Right, at this jct, the blue-blazed *Pond Run Trail* descends on a jeep road for 0.6 mi to Sugar Knob Gap and a four-way intersection with yellow-blazed *Little Stony Creek Trail* S and nearby Sugar Knob Cabin owned by the Potomac Appalachian Trail Club (PATC); the purple-blazed, 3.0-mi *Peer Trail*, N, ends on private property in Wilson Cove on Waites Run Rd, 6.7 mi from Wardensville [the USFS and PATC are working on plans to route the trail off private property]; the continuing E blue-blazed rocky *Three Ponds Trail* [also a section of *Tuscarora Trail*] goes 3.0 mi to *Little North Trail* in Virginia, where the *Tuscarora Trail* continues for 48 miles to the *AT* in the Shenandoah National Park.)

Turn L on the *Pond Run Trail* through large oaks and reach Half Moon Spring, R, at 6.7 mi and a jct with *Half Moon Trail* at 6.9 mi. A small, natural wildlife watering hole is here. (Right, the *Pond Run Trail* descends, follows, and crosses the Pond Run stream frequently in hemlock groves for 2.4 mi to Waites Run Rd [CO-5/1], 6.0 mi from the jct with WV-55/259 in Wardensville.) Continue ahead on the *Half Moon Trail*, and arrive at a jct with the *Half Moon Lookout Trail* R at 7.5 mi. (This 0.8-mi, white-blazed spur trail to the remains of a rock lookout provides superb views of Mill Mtn and Trout Run valley. Backtrack.) Continue on the *Half Moon Trail*; descend on a well-graded trail carpeted with moss and banked with mtn laurel to Half Moon Run at 8.3 mi. Curve L, cross stream, and follow a forest road to the gate at Trout Run and CO-32/10 for a total of 10.8 mi. Vehicle shuttle L to Wolf Gap on CR-32/10 is 5.3 mi. (*USGS Maps:* Wolf Gap, Woodstock, Wardensville)

Tuscarora Trail (formerly Big Blue Trail)

Effective January 1, 1997, the *Big Blue Trail* (144 mi) and the *Tuscarora Trail* (119.7 mi) became the *Tuscarora Trail* but continue as a W interstate alternate of the *AT* in Virginia, West Virginia, Maryland, and Pennsylvania. Formerly, the *Big Blue Trail* section was from a jct with the *AT* at Matthews Arm Campground in the Shenandoah National Park W across the Shenandoah Valley and sections of the GWNF into West Virginia. It joined the *Tuscarora Trail* at Hannock, MD, at the Potomac River. The *Tuscarora Trail's* N terminus is at Dean's Gap with the *AT* near Donnellytown, PA. Together the trails provide three long-distance circuit hikes if the C&O Canal Towpath is used, because it cuts across the middle of the long 432-mi loop (making the northern loop 271.1 mi and the southern loop 264.5 mi).

Described below is the 19.3-mi West Virginia segment in the GWNF from Hawk Recreation Area near Capron Springs Rd (N) to *Little North Mtn Trail* in Virginia (S). (The Potomac Appalachian Trail Club has published two pocket-size guidebooks, *The Big Blue, North Half* and *South Half*, with maps of the *Big Blue Trail* by Elizabeth Johnston and Lynn Gallagher. For information contact PATC, 118 Park St, SE, Vienna, VA 22180; 703-242-0693. Also, contact Keystone Trails Assn, PO Box 251, Cogan Station, PA 17728 (for Keystone tel number call ATC at 304-535-6331.)

HAWK RECREATION AREA (Hampshire County)

At a peaceful and remote setting in a hardwood forest, the facilities are 15 campsites (no hookups), a group campground, a 10-unit picnic area, a hand pump for drinking water, and vault toilets. The GWNF made this a primitive nonfee campground in 1985; the season is year-round.

ACCESS: From I-81 in Strasburg, VA, follow VA-55 W for 15.3 mi and turn R on FR-502; from Wardensville, WV, go E on VA-55 for 4.0 mi, turn L on FR-502, turn L on FR-347, and go 0.7 mi to campground entrance on R.

SUPPORT FACILITIES: A grocery store, restaurant, bank, service station, motel, and laundromat are in Wardensville.

Hawk Trail (Tuscarora Trail) (5.2 mi; USFS #1013.4); County Line Trail (Tuscarora Trail) (8.6 mi; USFS #1013.3); Vances Cove Trail (6.3 mi; USFS #400)

LENGTH: 18.1 mi combined

DIFFICULTY: moderate to strenuous

FEATURES: Great North Mtn, Paddy Run

TRAILHEADS AND DETAILS: The former *Big Blue Trail*, now *Tuscarora Trail* system runs through the Hawk Recreation Area. The 5.2-mi *Hawk Trail* (also a section of *Tuscarora Trail*) extends NW 1.6 mi to Hawk Run and cascades, and S 3.6 mi from the Hawk campground entrance gate to WV-55. Described here is the S direction. Ascend the blue-blazed trail for 0.7 mi, where it crosses FR-502, and begin a climb of 18 switchbacks to the ridge of the Great North Mtn at 1.8 mi. Bear R, pass two AT&T towers, and reach WV-VA-55 at 3.6 mi. Cross the highway and begin the 8.6-mi *County Line Trail* (also a section of *Tuscarora Trail*), named for the dividing line between counties in the Virginias. Follow an old road. There are a few overlooks, the best at 3.8 mi and 6.8 mi. At 4.3 mi is the Paul Gerhard Memorial Shelter, built by the Terrapin Trail Club of the University of Maryland in honor of the *AT* hiker and climber. (A blue-blazed spur trail with a spring descends here for 0.6 mi to Paddy Run, FR-371.) At 6.7 mi bear R and begin a descent of a 1,400-ft drop in elev on a series of switchbacks with numerous rock steps. Reach a FR gate at Waites Run Rd (CO-5/1) at 8.6 mi. Here the former *Big Blue Trail* (now *Tuscarora Trail*) continues S on the *Pond Run Trail* (see description above). (It is 6.3 mi R on Waites Run Rd to Wardensville.)

To hike the 6.3-mi *Vances Cove Trail*, turn L on Waites Run Rd, go 0.9 mi to the beginning of a yellow-blazed FR on the L, and follow Cove Run to its end at 2.1 mi. Here the trail continues over a low, flat ridge to follow Paddy Run (a trout-stocked stream) E of FR-371 on an old jeep trail. The area is known for its spring mushrooms and wildflowers. Reach a jct with Gerhard Trail/Road, a 0.6-mi access path to a shelter at 3.7 mi. Continue downstream, crisscrossing Paddy Run on a frequently overgrown and wet treadway. At 4.7 mi the fishermen's trail is easier to follow than the old jeep road. Vegetation is chiefly hardwood with sparse hemlock and white and Virginia pine. Reach the confluence of Paddy Run and Vances Cove Run. Rock-hop to an old campsite and the jct with a 4WD road at 6.3 mi, the N terminus of *Vances Cove Trail*. Access to this point is on FR-93 (suitable for passenger vehicles), 2.7 mi from VA-55 (and 0.8 mi E from the West Virginia–Virginia state line) to a road fork and parking area (R is FR-371). Park here and take a L on the 4WD road, rock-hop the stream, pass under a power line, and at 0.2 mi reach the old campsite and yellow blaze, R. (By using the N access, a round-trip hike of 26.7 mi can be made by turning L on US-55 for 0.8 mi to the jct with the *County Line Trail* and *Hawk Trail*. Turn R on the *Hawk Trail* and return to Hawk Campground.) (*USGS Maps:* Yellow Spring, Wardensville, Mountain Falls)

Squirrel Gap Trail (2.2 mi; USFS #1006); Brushy Hollow Trail (3.0 mi; USFS #1019)

LENGTH: 6.7 mi combined

DIFFICULTY: moderate

FEATURES: site of old whiskey distillery

TRAILHEADS AND DETAILS: From Wardensville go S on WV-55/259 for 2.3 mi to the top of the ridge and turn L on Squirrel Gap Rd (FR-344). Drive 4.0 mi to post-gated road on the R. Park here. Hike the blue-blazed road to a fork at 0.4 mi. Turn L through an open area that has been timbered. Pass R of old sawdust piles at 0.7 mi and at 1.0 mi to a jct with yellow-blazed *Brushy Hollow Trail*, L. Continue ahead to High Top Ridge at 1.5 mi for a fine view of Lost River valley. Descend steeply to Lost River, rock-hop (unless the 125-ft-wide river has high water), and ascend to WV-55/259 at

2.2 mi. A highway pull-off is nearby on R. (From here it is 2.4 mi E on WV-55/259 to a picnic area at Lost River bridge and sinks. West it is 3.0 mi to a jct with WV-29.)

A backtracking hike to *Brushy Hollow Trail* is 1.2 mi; turn R on the 3.0-mi *Brushy Hollow Trail*. Descend on a well-graded foot trail to an old woods road in Ellis Hollow. Pass through a flat area and unseen site of an old whiskey distillery. At 0.6 mi reach a huge spring gushing from a hole in a rock ledge, 50 yds L of the trail. The spring is on private property. To the R is private property with an old farmhouse and outbuildings. Continue ahead under a forest canopy of tall hardwoods and hemlock on an old woods road upstream. Mosses, ferns, and liverwort cover sections of the treadway and rocky areas. Cross the stream a number of times and at 2.7 mi leave the low area and ascend from Brushy Holly to Squirrel Gap Rd. Backtrack or use vehicle shuttle on Squirrel Gap Rd for 4.0 mi to point of origin. (*USGS Map*: Baker)

JEFFERSON NATIONAL FOREST

The Jefferson National Forest (JNF) has six districts and more than 680,000 acres extending in portions from near Kentucky in the W and the Tennessee–North Carolina border in the SW to the James River in the NE. Two of the districts, Blacksburg and New Castle, extend N into the panhandle of Monroe County, for 18,175 acres.

In Virginia, the Jefferson National Forest has more than 1,000 mi of hiking and horse trails, the longest of which is the *Appalachian National Scenic Trail (AT)* with 280 mi. In addition to a vast trail system there are 45 recreational areas. It has several outstanding areas of special significance. One is the 154,000-acre Mt Rogers National Recreational Area, designated by Congress in 1966 to provide multiple recreational opportunities. There are more than 335 mi of hiking and horse trails in this magnificent range of Virginia's highest peaks (Mt Rogers, 5,729 ft, and White Top Mtn, 5,530 ft). Other areas include seven National Recreation Trails and 11 wildernesses. Some of the wilderness areas have remote old roads suitable for trails. Two popular converted RR beds are the Virginia Creeper NRT near Mt Rogers and the *Guest River Gorge Trail* near Coeburn. (Details of the Jefferson National Forest trails are in *The Trails of Virginia: Hiking the Old Dominion*, a comprehensive trail guidebook on more than 1,000 trails, and published by the University of North Carolina Press in Chapel Hill, NC.)

The forest boundaries within Monroe County, WV, are the steep Peters

Mtn ridge on the edge of the St Clair thrust fault in the N and the Potts Mtn ridge in the S along the state line. Potts Creek runs NE through the valley between the ridges. The most scenic area in the county is Hanging Rock, a recently reconstructed fire tower and bird migration observation point, on Peters Mtn. The districts are chiefly hardwood forests with mixed Virginia and white pine, and hemlock. Rhododendron patches are frequent in the coves and mtn laurel and wild azaleas are on the slopes and ridges. Other vascular plants are haw, alder, blueberry, asters, wild orchids, wintergreen, galax, ferns, phlox, yellow violets, shooting star (*Dodecatheon meadia*), goldenrod, pink corydalis (*Corydalis sempervirens*), and Greek valerian (*Polemonium reptans*). A less common plant, turkey beard (*Xerophyllum asphodeloides*), has been seen on Peters Mtn. Its stalks are considered a delicacy by deer. Grasses and sedges are prominent and varied. Wildlife includes bear, deer, grouse, wild turkey, hawks, owls, squirrel, chipmunk, raccoon, rattlesnakes, and songbirds.

BLACKSBURG RANGER DISTRICT

The Blacksburg District has 8,876 acres in West Virginia but does not have any maintained forest roads or recreational areas. There are, however, an estimated 20 mi of abandoned woods road, 6.0 mi of which are on an old RR grade. Adjoining the state line is White Rock Recreation Area with a campground; it is described below. Access to the area is on paved Waiteville Rd (CO-17 and SR-635), a valley road constructed on an old RR grade connecting Pearisburg from the SW to Paint Bank in the NE. Running N-S is gravel and partially paved Limestone Hill Rd, also called Gap Mills Rd (CO-15), crooked and steep in sections, which connects Gap Mills in West Virginia to Maggie and VA-42 in Virginia.

Only portions of two trails in West Virginia, the *Allegheny Trail*, which traverses Peters Mtn (4.5 mi), and the *Virginia's Walk* (0.3 mi), are in the district. Also under the district's management is a third trail, the *Ground Hog Trail*, on the N side of Peters Mtn and S of the community of Lindside. It is a 1.8-mi access route to the *AT* and the S terminus of the *Allegheny Trail*. The *Virginia's Walk* begins in the White Rocks Recreation Area campground, across the road from campsite #9. On a wide and sometimes rocky tread, it goes through a hardwood forest with rhododendron and hemlock in the coves. Ground cedar, wintergreen, and galax are among the ground cover. At 0.6 mi the trail crosses into West Virginia, but it returns to Virginia after crossing Stony Creek. The trail loop is complete on the return to campsite #33 and to the point of origin after 1.2 mi. A 4.6-mi segment of the 5.5-mi *Potts Mtn Trail* borders the state line between Monroe and Craig Counties.

From the White Rock Recreation Area it is 11.7 mi to the *Allegheny Trail*. When leaving the campground, turn R on SR-613, go 0.8 mi, turn R on the Waiteville Rd (SR-635), and go 6.1 mi to Gap Mills Rd (CO-15), L. Ascend for 3.9 mi to the top of Peters Mtn and park at a small parking area, L, under a power line. Follow the yellow-blazed *Allegheny Trail* for 1.0 mi to a spur trail, L, which leads 0.1 mi to Hanging Rock and an observation tower (3,812 ft). Here is a spectacular 360° view of the Peters Mtn Range and far beyond in both states. From the spur jct the *Allegheny Trail* continues SW for another 3.5 mi in West Virginia and 8.1 mi in Virginia to join the *AT*. (See detailed description in chapter 11.) (*USGS-FS Maps:* Lindside, Interior, Waiteville, Gap Mills)

In the Virginia part of the district, there are three campgrounds: Walnut Flats, off SR-606, 12.0 mi NE of Bland; White Pine Horse Camp, off SR-606, also 12.0 mi NE of Bland; and White Rocks, the nearest to West Virginia and described below. Other recreational areas and attractions are the *AT* (and 45 mi on 10 other trails); Interior Picnic Area on SR-635, 13.0 mi NE of Pearisburg; Cascades (70-ft waterfall) on SR-623, 5.0 mi N of Pembroke; Wind Rock Overlook on the *AT* near White Rock Recreation Area; Minnie Ball Hill, Civil War site, near Wind Rock on SR-613; Mountain Lake Wilderness and virgin hemlock stand, off SR-613 near Minnie Ball Hill; Peters Mtn Wilderness; and Mountain Lake (private resort), Virginia's highest natural lake (over 4,000 ft) on SR-613 from US-460 at Hoges Chapel.

NEW CASTLE RANGER DISRICT

The New Castle District has 9,299 acres in West Virginia, all in Monroe County, and three forest roads with a total of 10.9 mi and 2.7 mi of rivers and streams. Only Wilson Branch Rd (FR-5031) on the N slope of Potts Mtn range is open. The other forest roads are closed to vehicle traffic. There are no recreation areas or trails, but probably 15 mi of the *Allegheny Trail* will be located in the district, 7 mi of which will be in West Virginia. Access to the area is the same as described above for the Blacksburg District. (*USGS-FS Maps:* Interior, Waiteville, Paint Bank, Craig Springs, Gap Mills)

SUPPORT FACILITIES: The nearest campground in the Blacksburg and New Castle Districts is White Rock Recreation Area. It has 49 campsites, tent pads, tables, grills, drinking water, and restrooms. Season is Apr 1–Dec 1. (No water after Oct 1.) Access is at the jct of US-460 and SR-635, 3.0 mi E from downtown Pearisburg and 3.0 mi W of Pembroke. Drive 15.7 mi on SR-635 to the jct with SR-613. Turn R, go 0.8 mi to the campground entrance, and turn L. The nearest general store with groceries and gasoline is near the American Gypsum Plant, 4.1 mi after entering SR-635 from US-460. Pearisburg has motels, restaurants, banks, service stations, a hospital, and shopping centers.

INFORMATION: Contact the district offices or the main office. Blacksburg Ranger District, 110 S Park Dr, Blacksburg, VA 24060 (540-552-4641), on US-460 business in Blacksburg; New Castle Ranger District, PO Box 246, New Castle, VA 24127 (540-864-5195), 2.0 mi E of New Castle on SR-615; George Washington and Jefferson National Forests, 5162 Valley Pointe Pkwy, Roanoke, VA 24019-3050 (540-265-5100).

PART TWO

National Park System and Corps of Engineers Trails

3. Appalachian National Scenic Trail

Once you have walked the AT, every subsequent springtime will find you wondering how it would be to hike it again.

—Dorothy Laker

The 2,157-mi *Appalachian National Scenic Trail* (AT) weaves, rises, and falls on ridges and valleys of the Appalachian Mtns in 14 eastern states. A continuous scenic corridor from Maine to Georgia, it is a living, changing masterpiece of incredible dreams, design, and dedication. To hike from end to end, the average number of footsteps is 5,240,000 and the average time it takes is between four and five months. More than 3,000 hikers are known to have completed the world's most famous trail, and millions of other hikers have been lured by its mystique to walk parts of its path.

Earl Shaffer, a WWII veteran from Pennsylvania, was 29 years old when he began his solitary attempt to become the first to hike the *AT* in one trip. At the time (1948), trail leaders thought such a feat impossible. He started at Mt Oglethorpe, GA, on Apr 4 and completed the journey on Aug 5 on Katahdin in Maine. His remarkable adventure is documented in his journal *Walking with Spring*, which was first privately printed in 1981 and later published by the Appalachian Trail Conference (ATC) in 1984. Shaffer hiked the *AT* in the opposite direction in 1965, the first hiker to complete the *AT* in both directions. He started at Katahdin on July 19, and finished at Springer Mtn in Georgia, on Oct 25. (The first person to hike the *AT* in sections was Myron H. Avery, from the 1920s to 1936.) In 1993 it was learned by the ATC staff that six Boy Scouts, aged 15 to 17, from the Bronx in New York City were through-hikers in 1936 from Maine to Georgia. Max Gordon, one of a group of WWI veterans who organized and maintained a food supply line at intervals for the boys, reported the adventure to the ATC.

The first woman to hike the complete distance in one continuous trip was Mrs. Emma Gatewood ("Grandma Gatewood") of Ohio. She started at Mt Oglethorpe on May 3, 1955, and finished at Katahdin on Sept 25. She followed the same route again in 1957, and by 1964, at the age of 77, completed the third trip she had earlier taken in sections. She was dearly loved by the trail world for many reasons. Among them were her stamina, her love for people, and her great sense of humor. For example, on one occasion she was lost and was reminded of it when found by a forest official. "Not lost," she said, "just misplaced." (The first woman to complete the *AT* in sections was Mary Kilpatrick of Philadelphia. She finished in 1939.)

The name and the concept of this supertrail was solely that of Benton MacKaye, a forester and author from Shirley Center, MA. He has said that he thought of it in the early 1900s, before the *Long Trail* was begun in Vermont in 1910.

It was that year that James P. Taylor, a Vermont schoolmaster, established the Green Mountain Club and the concept of the *Long Trail* extending from Canada to Massachusetts. Others who had long-trail and connecting trail concepts were Philip W. Ayres, a New Hampshire forester, and Allen Chamberlain, a Boston newspaper columnist and early president of the Appalachian Mountain Club (founded in 1876). They formed the New England Trail Conference in 1916. One of the conference's goals was to connect the New England trails, a linkage that remarkably resembles the later path of the *AT*.

Two other founding fathers were US forester William Hall, who envisioned a link with the southern Appalachians, and Will S. Monroe, professor and seer of the Green Mountain Club. Monroe's concept was to connect the New England trails to trails in New York and New Jersey. In December 1921, Monroe's friend, J. Ashton Allis, proposed connecting the trails as far as the Pennsylvania state line. Two months before Allis's proposal the *Journal of the American Institute of Architects* carried MacKaye's article "An Appalachian Trail: A Project in Regional Planning."

The response to a singular name for the trails was immediate, and within a year the Palisades Trail Conference (which later became part of the New York–New Jersey Trail Conference) began construction of a 6.0-mi section between Lake Tiorati Circle and Arden to connect with another trail in the Palisades Interstate Park. The trail opened on Sunday, Oct 7, 1923, the first and original section of the *AT*. (The entire *AT* design was initially completed on Aug 15, 1937, but considerable relocation was to follow.)

The leadership of Arthur Perkins of Hartford, CT, began in 1926 to translate MacKaye's dream and proposal into reality, but it was Myron H. Avery of Lubec, ME, who probably more than any other leader was instrumental in implementing MacKaye's proposals. He worked and coordinated agreements with government agencies, including the important Civilian Conservation Corps (CCC), and thousands of volunteers to complete the AT. He was the first president of the Potomac Appalachian Trail Club, formed in November 1927, in Washington, DC, and served as chairman of the Appalachian Trail Conference from 1930 to 1952.

In 1968 Congress created the National Trails System Act and gave further protection to the AT with supplemental amendments in 1970. In 1996 less than 45.0 mi of the AT remained unprotected. Congressional appropriations to the National Park Service for this purpose will determine additional protective purchases.

The AT zigzags along two sections of the West Virginia–Virginia state line for a total of 25.1 mi. The NE section is on the Blue Ridge Mtns between Jefferson County in West Virginia and Loudoun County in Virginia; it is maintained by the Potomac Appalachian Trail Club. The SW section is on Peters Mtn between Monroe County in West Virginia and Giles County in Virginia. It is maintained by the Kanawha Trail Club.

The S entrance to the NE section begins at the corner of Jefferson County in West Virginia and Clarke County in Virginia, 1.3 mi N of Snickers Gap on VA-7 (0.8 mi W of Bluemont). Beginning at the state line it passes the Devil's Racetrack at 2.0 mi, crosses Wilson Gap Rd at 4.8 mi, and reaches Keys Gap Shelter at 12.1 mi. At 13.1 mi it crosses Keys Gap, VA-9 (6.0 mi W of Hillsboro, VA, and 7.0 mi E of Charles Town, WV). At 16.6 mi it forks. Here the old AT went ahead; the new AT goes L into the Harpers Ferry National Historical Park. It descends, passes a R spur to an overlook under a power line, and reaches US-340 at 18.0 mi. Turn L to cross the Shenandoah River bridge, then ahead follow the white blaze over a guardrail to ascend the *Cliff Trail*. Turn L and reach the Appalachian Trail Conference headquarters at the corner of Jackson and Washington Sts at 18.8 mi. From here return to the *Cliff Trail*, turn L, and pass through the lower historic district to the Maryland state line at the Potomac River at 19.4 mi. The AT enters Maryland on the B&O Railroad cantilevered walkway (see section 4).

Access to the state line in the SW section, on Peters Mtn in the Jefferson National Forest, is gained by ascending the AT for 4.1 mi from the New

River bridge (Senator Shumate Bridge) in N Pearisburg. (There is no water on top of Peters Mtn.) For the next 12.5 mi the trail ascends to knobs and descends to gaps between 3,300 ft and 3,700 ft elev. It crosses a number of pipelines and power line swaths from which there are scenic views of Little Mtn N in West Virginia and Angels Rest (3,500 ft) on Pearis Mtn in Virginia. At 9.5 mi it crosses a hunting road that descends, R, for 2.0 mi to FR-972 and out to SR-641 on the Virginia side. It enters Symms Gap Meadow, an exceptionally large and scenic area at 11.3 mi. After another 0.7 mi it crosses a jeep road. At 13.0 mi it meets a jct with the *Ground Hog Trail*, L, a blue-blazed West Virginia access route described below. It passes Dickinson Gap at 14.5 mi and veers L on the slope of Pine Swamp Knob (3,956 ft) at 16.1 mi. At 16.6 mi it leaves the state line and makes a jct with the *Allegheny Trail* (which follows the Peters Mtn ridge NE. See section 11.) The *AT* descends steeply for 1.7 mi, past Pine Swamp Branch Shelter, to an access point on the Waiteville Rd and crosses the road at 20.7 mi. (It is 11.5 mi R to US-460 and another 3.0 mi R on US-460 to Pearisburg.) (*USGS-FS Maps*: Narrows, Petertown, Lindside, Interior. These regular, photo-inspected maps, 1965–79, do not have correct *AT* routes.)

The West Virginia access route on the *Ground Hog Trail* to the *AT* is a direct result of the leadership of Bob Tabor, a trail developer, activist, and founder of the West Virginia Scenic Trails Association (WVSTA). Tabor, Nick Lozano, Charley Carlson, Bruce Bond, and others shared a dream for a trail route more convenient to West Virginians. They contacted landowners S of Lindside in the 1970s for such a purpose. When the Sugar Camp Farm, a picturesque, 159.1-acre tract owned by Cecil B. McKinney, became available, Tabor and associates persisted in having the Appalachian Trail Conference secure funding from the National Park Service to purchase Sugar Camp. In June 1981, Tabor was appointed chairman of a management committee by the West Virginia Scenic Trails Association, and in 1982 the purchase of Sugar Camp was consummated. For continued development and management purposes, a joint arrangement was made between the WVSTA, the Appalachian Trail Conference, the NPS, and the Blacksburg District of the Jefferson National Forest.

Ground Hog Trail

LENGTH: 1.8 mi

DIFFICULTY: easy to strenuous, elev gain 1,325 ft

FEATURES: scenic, wildlife, botanical study

TRAILHEAD AND DETAILS: From the Peterstown jct of US-219 and WV-12 go NE on US-219 for 6.1 mi to Painters Run Rd (CO-219/21), R. (If road sign is missing, notice double blue blazes on a telephone pole, S side of the Full Gospel Assembly church.) Drive 1.2 mi and turn L at the jct with Green Valley Rd (CO-219/24). After 0.5 mi arrive at the Sugar Camp parking lot, R. Another entrance route is from Lindside. Turn S on the Spruce Run Rd (CO-219/19, also called Dunkard Church Rd CO-215/15), and drive 0.8 mi. Turn R at Bradley Cemetery sign and continue R for 2.2 mi to Sugar Camp parking lot, L. Camping is not permitted along *Ground Hog Trail* or on Sugar Camp property.

Begin the hike at the SW corner of the parking lot; pass cairns in the pasture, reach a woods road and turn L, and pass R of a barn at 0.3 mi. Spring water, the only source on the trail, and restroom facilities are available here. Ascend through huge sugar maples and at 0.4 mi pass a large, dead American chestnut (*Castanea dentata*), unique because it is standing, well preserved, and propped by maple and other trees. Adult chestnut trees are now rare. Among the maple are oak, poplar, hickory, locust, and dogwood. Deer are likely to be seen in the area. Cross two spur ridges and at 0.9 mi begin the first of seven major switchbacks to the summit. Pass rock formations covered with mosses and lichens, and earth pockets with ferns, alumroot (*Heuchera americana*), stonecrop, sweet chervil, and rattlesnake orchid (*Goodyera pubescens*). Reach the crest line of Peters Mtn at 1.5 mi and a jct with the *AT*. To the L it is 3.9 mi to the temporary jct and S terminus of the *Allegheny Trail*. To the R it is 1.0 mi to scenic Symms Gap and Meadow, and 12.0 mi farther to US-460 in Pearisburg.

INFORMATION: Appalachian Trail Conference, PO Box 807, Harpers Ferry, WV 25425 (304-535-6331); West Virginia Scenic Trails Association, PO Box 4042, Charleston, WV 25304 (304-755-4878); District Ranger, Blacksburg Ranger District, Jefferson National Forest, 110 S Park Dr, Blacksburg, VA 24060 (540-552-4641).

4. National Recreation Areas and Historical Parks

Mountains are earth's undecaying monuments

—Nathaniel Hawthorne

In addition to the *Appalachian National Scenic Trail* mentioned previously, two other properties in the state under the jurisdiction of the National Park Service have foot trails in use or in the developmental stage. They are Harpers Ferry National Historical Park and the New River National Gorge River.

HARPERS FERRY NATIONAL HISTORICAL PARK

In 1733, Peter Stephens, a pioneer trapper and trader, settled at the confluence of the Potomac and Shenandoah Rivers. To assist his trade and the emigration of other settlers he established a simple ferry service. The service was expanded in 1747 when Robert Harper, an English emigrant from Oxford, purchased Stephen's log cabin and ferry equipment. In 1751 he obtained a land patent for 125 acres from Lord Fairfax. Harper's success as a millwright and ferry operator led to a small settlement named after him by the Virginia General Assembly. It was originally called "Shenandoah Falls at Mr. Harper's Ferry." By the 1790s the area had become more industrialized, particularly after Congress established a national armory. Economic development increased in the 1830s when the Chesapeake and Ohio Canal and the Baltimore & Ohio Railroad were constructed along the Potomac. The development of better transportation also made the armory and rifle factory an important location. It was to this location on Oct 16, 1859, that John Brown, an abolitionist and leader of the Kansas Pottawatomie massacre, led a band of 16 white and five black men in an insurrection. His aim was to liberate the South's slaves, forcing an end to slavery. Two days later Col Robert E. Lee and Lt J. E. B. Stuart, with 91 marines, stormed the armory engine house where Brown and his men had taken refuge. Ten of Brown's followers, including two of his sons, and one of Lee's men were killed. Brown was tried by a jury and hanged in nearby Charles Town on Dec 2 for murder, "treason to the Commonwealth," and insurrection. (Acting as the nation's reporter and artist of the trial for *Harper's* magazine was David Hunter Strother, the famous hiker and outdoorsman, for whom Mt Porte Crayon was named.) Harpers Ferry and John Brown suddenly became national words, as the episode further frayed the ties that held the North and South together. Louise McNeill's poem "John Brown," written in 1979, expressed it this way:

> "Over the South the rumors ran,
> A wild fanatic—his crazy plan—
> ...Over the North the rumors flew,
> A Christian soldier—as brave and true—!"

During the Civil War, Harpers Ferry was a strategic objective for both sides, and it changed hands a number of time. One example is that on Sept 15, 1862, Gen Stonewall Jackson captured the town and 12,419 Union prisoners. Following the war, Storer College for freed blacks was established; it remained in service until 1955 and is now a training center for National Park Service personnel. Otherwise the community declined, its buildings abandoned after the devastating floods of the late 19th century. In 1895, a John Brown Fort monument was erected by the B&O Railroad. Fifty years later Congress authorized a national monument of 1,500 acres. That area, plus 724 more acres, was designated a National Historical Park in 1963 and restoration began.

Hikers interested in history may wish to spend a couple of days here. There are museums, restored buildings, historic sites, the Appalachian Trail Conference headquarters, and trails that connect the tristate area. The new cantilevered walkway on the side of the B&O Railroad connects Harpers Ferry with the C&O Canal National Historical Park and the 3.5-mi *Grant Conway Trail* in Maryland Heights. On Shenandoah St in lower town check the visitor center for a map of Harpers Ferry NHP and information on *Virginius Island Trail*, a 0.8-mi path by the Shenandoah River. A walker's guide map explains sites in a once thriving industrial community. Camping is not permitted in the park. (*USGS Maps:* Harpers Ferry, Charles Town)

ADDRESS AND ACCESS: Superintendent, Harpers Ferry National Historical Park, Harpers Ferry, WV 25425; 304-535-6223. On US-340 turn onto Shenandoah St on the W end of the Shenandoah River bridge.

Support Facilities: Camping is allowed at designated sections of the C&O Canal. A hiker's provision store is in town. The nearest campground area from Harpers Ferry is 1.5 mi up the Potomac River on the C&O Canal at Huckleberry Hill Hiker–Biker Overnighter. It has water, wood, and a restroom. A youth hostel is 1.2 mi downstream on the Sandy Hook Rd that parallels the C&O Canal. Also, the Harpers Ferry KOA Campground is 1.0 mi W of Harpers Ferry on US-340. Its season is Apr 1–Nov 1; 304-535-6895. If choosing a hotel, the Cliffside Inn and Conference Center has two restaurants; 304-535-6302. Other places to eat are within walking distance of the lower town. The nearest grocery store for hikers is a 7/11 convenience store, 1.9 mi up Washington St in the town of Bolivar. For additional information contact West Virginia Information Center, Eastern Gateway Travel Council, Box A, Harpers Ferry, WV 25425; 304-535-2482.

Bolivar Heights Trail

Length: 1.3 mi
Difficulty: easy
Features: scenic, history

Trailhead and Details: At the US-340 and Washington St jct, turn onto Washington St (at the Eastern Gateway Travel Council bldg) and follow the sign, L, to the Bolivar Heights battlefield site and parking area. If driving from the Harpers Ferry historic district, drive 2.0 mi up High St, which becomes Washington St, and turn R to the battlefield site. Follow the scenic loop trail past a series of outdoor exhibits that explain the area's role in the Civil War. Prominent trees are locust, walnut, oak, and hackberry.

Cliff Trail (Jefferson Rock Trail)

Length: 0.8 mi
Difficulty: easy
Features: scenic, history

Trailhead and Details: (This trail is part of the AT.) Park at the visitor center parking area. Near the corner of Shenandoah St and High St, climb the steps that have been cut in the natural rock, pass the restored St Peter's Catholic Church and the ruins of St John's Episcopal Church, and reach the Jefferson Rock at 0.2 mi. (The rock is named after Thomas Jefferson, who visited here in 1783 and wrote that where the Potomac and Shenandoah Rivers meet "they rush together against the mountain, rend it asunder and pass off to the sea. This scene is worth a voyage across the Atlantic." A balancing rock has been stabilized with stone props.) Continue ahead to a spur trail, R, that leads to Robert Harper's grave site. At 0.5 mi reach an access trail that leads 0.2 mi R to the Appalachian Trail Conference head-quarters bldg at the corner of Jackson and Washington Sts. Continue ahead on *Cliff Trail*. To the L a 0.1-mi spur trail descends to Shenandoah St. Ahead, follow the ridge slope to the trail's terminus on a steep descent to US-340 at the W end of the Shenandoah River bridge.

Loudoun Heights Trail

LENGTH: 3.2 mi

DIFFICULTY: moderate to strenuous

FEATURES: scenic, historic

TRAILHEAD AND DETAILS: If on the *AT* hiking N on the ridge line of the West Virginia–Virginia state line, you will reach a jct with the *Loudoun Heights Trail*, ahead (N). (The *AT* descends L [NW] into West Virginia and the crossing of the Shenandoah River bridge.) For *Loudoun Heights Trail* remain on the ridge line. Pass an infantry redoubt of the Civil War, and at 0.8 mi there is a spectacular view of Harpers Ferry and the confluence of the Shenandoah and Potomac Rivers. The trail descends steeply to 2.0 mi, where it follows R on US-340 to the Maryland–Virginia state line at 2.5 mi. After crossing the Potomac River on the Sandy Hook Bridge, the trail reconnects with the *AT* at 3.2 mi near the Harpers Ferry Hostel.

NEW RIVER GORGE NATIONAL RIVER

Congress assigned management responsibility of the New River Gorge National River to the national park system on Nov 10, 1978. The purpose was to conserve an "outstanding natural, scenic, and historic" 50-mi section of the New River Gorge and to preserve a free-flowing segment of the New River "for the benefit and enjoyment of present and future generations." An irregular corridor of 62,000 acres was initially planned to extend from Hinton downstream to Ames near the US-19 bridge. But only 17 percent of the total acreage will be owned by the NPS. Other properties include easement acquisitions, state lands, private land donations, and private ownership. River-use management is the joint responsibility of the NPS and the state's Department of Natural Resources. Zoning and some of the other management responsibilities are shared by the counties (Summers, Raleigh, and Fayette) through which the New River flows.

The park has three management categories. One involves natural zones

I-64 bridge as seen from Glade Creek Trail.

of undeveloped and wilderness-like properties to conserve natural resources. Activities that do not adversely affect the environment are classified in this category; they include hiking, backcountry camping, horseback riding, hunting, and fishing. The historic category protects known cultural resources in the canyon. The third management category of development is the most comprehensive. It includes recreational areas that have picnic units, standard campgrounds, boat ramps, visitor centers, access points and interpretive units, and maintained park roads. In the summer of 1983 the park began visitor service operations with the opening of Canyon Rim Visitor Center (open year-round) at the E end of the US-19 bridge and at the Hinton Visitor Center (open from spring to fall) on WV-3 (the W bank of the river) in Hinton. Since then the Grandview Visitor Center (formerly Grandview State Park) N off I-64, the park headquarters (in Glen Jean), and Thurmond Visitor Center (in Thurmond) offer public services. Although the park headquarters is open year-round, you may wish to inquire about seasonally open visitor centers.

In addition to the centers and their services, the park has advanced from three trails in 1986 to 27 trails in 1996. Among the latter were three under construction and eight undeveloped. Some of the undeveloped trails are described below. Contact the park offices for an update.

At the Canyon Rim Visitor Center a paved walkway, *Canyon Boardwalk Trail*, goes R of the center entrance, but forks for two different views. The L fork descends on 227 steps (228 if you take the L side at the lower observation deck) to an awesome view of the nation's second highest bridge, 876 ft above the New River. (The nation's highest is at Royal Gorge in Colorado.) The R fork extends to an observation deck with a view of the bridge and highway. Either of these trails is 400 yd round-trip. Across US-19 from the visitor center entrance is Burnwood Day Use Area, where the tranquil 1.1-mi *Laing Loop Trail* leads hikers to old-growth hemlock and beech.

The geology and hydrology of the New River are remarkably distinctive. It is part of the nation's longest river system that flows north. A descendant of the prehistoric Teays River system, it may also be the oldest river in North America. Its headwaters of two forks begin in Watauga County, NC, and flow through Ashe and Allegheny Counties before entering Virginia. There, it meanders through Grayson, Carroll, Wythe, Pulaski, Montgomery, and Giles Counties. It cuts its way through the Appalachian Mtns of Virginia to West Virginia's Allegheny Plateau and joins the Gauley River in Fayette County to become the Kanawha River. In this process it drains

6,920 sq mi. Its steepest grade, with a drop of 20 ft per mi, is between Thurmond and the Hawks Nest, a popular stretch for whitewater enthusiasts. Called the "Grand Canyon of the East," its rim is an average of 1,000 ft above the river with a complex of rugged ridges, steep drops from massive quartzite conglomeratic sandstone cliffs, and narrow river channels. Most of the rock formations range in age from 340 million to 280 million years.

Within the park's boundary are 7.1 million tons of coal reserves that could be strip-mined and some currently active gas wells. It is an area rich in deciduous forest and herbaceous flora, at least 1,067 species. Two endemic plants that are endangered in the gorge are Fraser's sedge (*Carex fraseri*) and mountain mint (*Pyenanthemum torrei*). It is estimated that the gorge has 40 species of mammals, 80 species of birds, and 58 species of fish (six of which are endemic).

Although not called a trail, it has to be one of the more rare hikes when once a year, the second Saturday in October, pedestrians are legally allowed to walk 0.6 mi across an engineering wonder, the world's longest steel-arch bridge (US-19). The walk is part of the Bridge Day Festival, when parachutists jump from the bridge to the river and miles of arts and crafts exhibits and food and antique vendors border the S side of US-19.

The park does not provide full-service campgrounds, but there are 23 full-service campgrounds in the surrounding area—including Bluestone and Babcock State Parks. The park has at least two primitive camping areas: the first is across the river from Prince and the second is the five-site area at Glade Creek confluence with the New River. If camping along the trails, choose a place at least 100 ft from the trails. For commercial campgrounds call 800-CALL-WVA.

Guidelines for the gorge are as follows: Avoid use of large vans or trailers on the narrow roads into the gorge; be alert to weather because snow and ice accumulates on the roads in wintertime; stay on the trails; hike with a companion; pets must be leashed; pedestrians have the right of way on the trails; hunting is allowed in the park (wear blaze-orange jacket and cap in seasons); and remember the emergency phone numbers: 256-1700 or 911.

INFORMATION: New River Gorge National River, 246 Main St, Glen Jean, WV 25846; 304-465-0508. Open 8:00 A.M. to 4:30 P.M. Mon through Fri. Fayette Plateau Chamber of Commerce, 310 Oyler Ave, Oak Hill, WV 25901; 304-465-5617.

Glade Creek Area

Glade Creek Trail (5.5 mi); Kates Falls Trail (1.2 mi); Kates Plateau Trail (4.9 mi); Polls Plateau Trail (6.3 mi)

LENGTH: 18+ mi round-trip, combined

DIFFICULTY: moderate to strenuous

FEATURES: remoteness, cascades and waterfalls, wildlife, history, trout fishing

TRAILHEADS AND DETAILS: The best access to *Glade Creek Trail* is from the Hamlet recreation area. Access to Hamlet is on a narrow 6.5-mi gravel road from the W end of Thomas Pugh Bridge off WV-41 at the New River. About halfway on the access road at Mill Creek is the isolated pioneer home of Raymond Hurrah, who lived there for 70 years. The site can be seen also from the main overlook of the park's Grandview Visitor Center off I-64 east of Beckley. At the Hamlet site is a primitive campground for five vehicles, vault toilets, riverside fishing, a footbridge over Glade Creek to an undeveloped trail, and the parking area for access to *Glade Creek Trail*.

The ghost town of Hamlet is at the confluence of the New River and roaring whitewater of Glade Creek. Founded in the early 1920s, it had a post office, boarding house, physician's office, sawmill, and about 30 homes. The settlement's only access was a 750-ft RR bridge constructed by the Chesapeake & Ohio (C&O) Railroad for coal and timber. During the Great Depression, the little village became deserted and in WWII the bridge was dismantled for its steel girders. All that remains of Hamlet are sparse foundation stones and part of a trestle over Glade Creek. The site is symbolic of the rise and fall of bustling communities along the banks of the mighty New River from the 1880s to the 1950s. Hamlet's ghost is mirrored downriver at RR stops such as River View, Beury, Red Ash, Sewell, Nuttal, Kaymoor, and one that had the most to lose, Thurmond. The town's inhabitants came to mine hematite coal, a valuable, nearly smokeless coal known as "black diamond." Now, long freight trains snake through the canyon about a dozen times a day, the whistling echoes and rumbling rails reminders of the towns' days of glory.

In a wilderness environment, *Glade Creek Trail* gradually ascends a narrow-gauge RR bed, parallel with Glade Creek, for its entire distance. It crosses the creek only once, at 2.9 mi on an arched steel footbridge. Along the way are constant thunderous cascades and waterfalls in deep chasms. Tall hemlock and oak tower over rhododendron thickets and pockets of wood betony and maidenhair fern. After crossing the creek there are many species of wildflowers, such as coltsfoot, cohosh, bloodroot, and stonecrop.

At 4.4 mi the trail crosses Kates Creek, and after 170 ft connects with the unsigned and unblazed 1.2-mi *Kates Falls Trail*, L. (It is 150 yd to the falls, where the trail ascends steeply on more than 20 short switchbacks to a grassy road. Here it reaches a jct with an access to the 4.9-mi *Kates Plateau Trail*, which connects with the 6.3-mi (round-trip) *Polls Plateau Trail*, L. To the R on the grassy road, the *Kates Falls Trail* gently descends to its terminus and reconnection with *Glade Creek Trail*.)

After passing the jct with the *Kates Falls Trail,* the *Glade Creek Trail* passes a powerful waterfall and pool and views of the I-64 bridge over the canyon. At the end of the trail is a parking area; *Kates Falls Trail* is L and an extremely rough (unrecommended) county road out 2.0 mi to WV-9. (For high-axle 4WD vehicles attempting this route, exit 129 off I-64 S on WV-9, and after 0.9 mi turn L on a narrow gravel road, opposite a Speed Limit 45 sign.)

If hiking the *Kates Plateau Trail*, where terrain is moderate between 2,600 and 2,800 ft in elev, follow the grassy road N from the *Kates Falls Trail* signpost. At 0.2 mi cross Kates Creek by rock-hopping or wading upstream for 65 yds on the roadbed. At 0.9 mi fork L. In a sylvan and remote hardwood forest the trail passes a bog and former beaver dam before an open area with flat rocks at 1.6 mi. Just beyond, the trail takes an abrupt R turn off the road and steeply up the hill on a footpath.

(If hiking the *Polls Branch Trail*, stay on the old road and continue ahead. At 1.8 mi cross Polls Branch and at 2.0 mi reach a fork. Although the loop part of the trail may be partially undeveloped, it is recommended to take the L fork and make all R turns to return at the loop for the next 2.3 mi. The area is generally flat, pleasant, remote, and ideal for backpack camping. Deer and wild turkey are likely to be seen. After completing the loop return to the jct with *Kates Plateau Trail* at 6.3 mi.)

Continuing on the *Kates Plateau Trail*, reach the top of the ridge at 1.8 mi. Pass through carpets of violets, then under a power line at 2.1 mi to follow an old road. Descend, cross under a power line again, and stay L at a fork. Arrive at an old homesite and apple trees at 2.8 mi. Turn R, level off, and follow an old road parallel to Kates Creek and through beautiful groves of hemlock and rhododendron. Return to the loop at 4.0 mi and stay L to return to the *Kates Falls Trail* jct at 4.9 mi.

Grandview Visitor Center

This area was formerly the 891-acre Grandview State Park, established in 1939 by the Civilian Conservation Corps. It became part of the New River Gorge National River in 1990. It is known for its spectacular views of the river and its geological formations of sandstone, and for *The Hatfields and the McCoys* at the Cliffside Amphitheater, open in June, July, and August. Reservations are recommended. For information contact Theater West Virginia, PO Box 1205, Beckley, WV 25801; 304-253-8313 or 800-642-2766. In addition to the trails described below, a new 2.0-mi trail, *Turkey Spur Trail*, is under construction between picnic shelters #3 and #4 and the Turkey Spur parking area.) (*USGS Map:* Prince)

ADDRESS AND ACCESS: Grandview Visitor Center, 4700 Grandview Rd, Beaver, WV 25813; 304-763-3715. For access E from Beckley follow I-64 5.0 mi to Exit 129B. From Lewisburg go W 40 mi and take Exit 129. Drive N on WV-9 for 6.0 mi to Grandview.

Tunnel Trail (0.4 mi); Castle Rock Trail (0.7 mi); Canyon Rim Trail (1.6 mi)

LENGTH: 2.7 mi round-trip, combined

DIFFICULTY: easy to moderate

FEATURES: natural tunnels, cliffs, scenic views

TRAILHEADS AND DETAILS: From the parking area near the visitor center office, follow the signs to the main overlook for N and S views of the New River. Turn R and descend on a unique trail to caves and through tunnels for a round-trip of 0.4 mi. Back at the main overlook descend to *Castle Rock Trail*, N, and follow the base of the cliffs of sandstone, alum, and coal veins. Reach the jct with the *Canyon Rim Trail* at 0.7 mi. Turn R and follow the *Canyon Rim Trail* to a paved road, turn R, and follow the road 0.1 mi. Enter the forest again, return to the road, and finally, after a number of road contacts, reach post #42 at 1.2 mi from the main overlook.

Backtrack to complete the S end of the *Canyon Rim Trail* to a jct with *Castle Rock Trail*. Follow the numbered posts that designate species of trees, shrubs, and flowers. Among them are flame azalea, Indian cucumber root, teaberry, orchids, hardwoods, and fringe tree (*Chionanthus virginica*). Reach the N overlook, pass L of a water fountain, and return to the main overlook at 1.1 mi—a round-trip total of 2.3 mi.

Big Buck Trail (0.7 mi); Woodland Loop Trail (0.6 mi)

LENGTH: 1.3 mi round-trip, combined

DIFFICULTY: easy

TRAILHEADS AND DETAILS: Drive to the picnic area and park near shelters #2 and #3. Beyond shelter #2 follow a wide road-trail under tall hardwoods. The understory is striped maple, sassafras, arrowwood, and ferns. Loop to a valley and return to the shelter at 0.7 mi. On the S side of the road follow the *Woodland Loop Trail* (formerly *Bridge Trail*) for 0.6 mi through a hardwood forest with mtn laurel and buckberry (*Vaccinium stamineum*).

Sandstone Falls and Brooks Falls

From the jct of I-64 and WV-9 (Exit 129 to Grandview), go E on I-64 10.0 mi to Exit 139 and turn S on WV-20. After 3.0 mi is an overlook, R, of Sandstone Falls. Continue to Hinton, cross a bridge over New River, and after 0.3 mi turn R on Sandstone Falls Rd (CO-26). Drive 3.9 mi on a narrow paved road to Brooks Falls parking area, a popular place for fishing and picnicking. Walk across the road to *Big Branch Loop Trail* and turn L. After 0.2 mi turn R at Big Branch. Ascend by cascades and through an extraordinary abundance of wildflowers garnished with ferns and spicebush. At 0.6 mi ascend near Big Branch waterfalls. After crossing the branch for the last time pass through a hardwood forest with widespread carpets of spring wildflowers (such as lavender phlox and yellow sessile bellwort). Deer and turkey may be seen. At 1.3 mi begin a steep descent to complete the 1.9-mi loop.

Farther downriver, 4.3 mi, is Sandstone Falls, the largest and most awesome waterfalls on the New River. The 0.5-mi *Sandstone Falls Trail* is a wide boardwalk (accessible for wheelchairs) to islands below the 1,500-ft-wide falls. At the main waterfalls on the E side the falls are 25 ft high. Archaeologists estimate the hard sandstone was formed 300 million years ago when West Virginia was a shallow inland sea. The area is popular for fishing (bass and catfish) and observing waterfowl and spring wildflowers. In addition to notable natural history, the area's human history is significant. Native Americans lived here for 15,000 years, and in 1873 the C&O Railroad completed rail transportation into the New River Gorge. Stone from a nearby quarry was used in the Washington Monument to represent West Virginia. (*USGS Maps*: Meadow Creek, Hinton)

> INFORMATION: Hinton Visitor Center is located on WV-20/3, 1.2 mi upriver from the jct of WV-20 and Sandstone Falls Rd (CO-26). It is on the E side of the highway near the New River. Usually open only on week-

ends except intermittently on other days in the summer (9 A.M. to 5 P.M.) Call 304-466-0417 or 304-465-0508 for more information.

Thurmond, Minden, and Cunard Area

Southside Junction to Brooklyn Trail (5.6 mi or 7.0 mi); Southside Junction Connector Trail to Thurmond-Minden Trail (0.4 mi); Thurmond-Minden Trail (3.2 mi); Arbuckle Creek Connector Trail to Thurmond-Minden Trail (0.2 mi); Brooklyn Miner's Trail (1.2 mi)

LENGTH: 10.6 mi or 12.0 mi combined

DIFFICULTY: easy to strenuous

FEATURES: scenic, historic, RR trestles, wildlife

TRAILHEADS AND DETAILS: (The *Southside Junction to Brooklyn Trail* can connect to the *Cunard to Kaymoor Trail* and *Kaymoor Trail* for a distance of 16.6 mi to Fayette Station Rd [WV-82] under the New River Gorge Bridge.) Access to Thurmond is from WV-61 in Glen Jean into the canyon on CO-25 for 6.0 mi. Park at Dun Glen Day Use Area (at the W end of the New River bridge to Thurmond). Ascend an embankment from the parking area to cross the road. At this point the *Southside Junction to Brooklyn Trail* follows a RR grade downriver, but to the L is the unsigned *Southside Junction Connector Trail* to *Thurmond-Minden Trail*. It follows the old RR grade (or up an embankment, then to the old RR grade) and goes W to a jct with the *Thurmond-Minden Trail*.

(The *Thurmond-Minden Trail* officially begins on CO-25 5.1 mi down the mtn from Glen Jean near Dunloup Creek. Park on the N side of the road; pass a gate and a portable toilet. [At 0.4 mi R is a jct with the *Southside Junction Connector Trail* to *Thurmond-Minden Trail*. It ends at the parking area near the river described above.] At 1.0 mi cross a trestle. There are good views of Thurmond at 1.3 mi. The forest is mainly poplar, maple, and oak, with understory of papaw, redbud, and hydrangea. Climb steps over boulders from a large landslide over the RR grade at 1.3 mi. There is another view of Thurmond and the river at 1.4 mi. Reach a jct with the *Arbuckle Creek Connector Trail* to *Thurmond-Minden Trail* at 1.5 mi. Cross trestles at 1.7 mi, 1.9 mi, and 2.3 mi. Arrive at Minden parking lot at 3.2 mi. Backtrack or have a second vehicle. Access from Oak Hill is off WV-16 (across the road from Super American store) W on CO-17, then curve E under WV-16 and go 2.0 mi to a parking lot, R, across a small bridge.)

The blue-blazed *Southside Junction to Brooklyn Trail* is designated for hikers and bikers. In the beginning you will see abandoned rails and crossties, some pinioned by forest growth. At 0.7 mi is a jct with the yellow-blazed (no bikes) *Arbuckle Creek Connector Trail* to *Thurmond-Minden Trail* (described above). Cross a long trestle over Arbuckle Creek, pass a gravel vehicle road, and reach a jct with an undeveloped side trail L at 1.2 mi. The trail is shaded with sycamore, ash, and poplar, and wildflowers are wild geranium, larkspur, fire pink, and bush honeysuckle. On the W side are high rock faces with water seepage, mosses, and ferns. Deer tracks are on the trail. Cross a trestle at 1.3 mi. At 2.3 mi and 2.9 mi are ruins of old buildings. Evidence of camping and fishing are at 4.0 mi near large river sandbars and a big bend in the river. There is an access to the river at 4.9 mi, and the end of the trail is at 5.6 mi.

Here is a jct with (no bikes) *Brooklyn Miner's Trail*, L. (It ascends steeply [600 ft in elev] on switchbacks of old coal roads and stairs for 1.2 mi to a jct with *Brooklyn Mine Access Trail* for equestrians at coal mining sites. To the L is the 4.4-mi equestrian *Brooklyn–Red Ash Trail*, which has a loop. To the R the *Brooklyn Mine Access Trail* N end is at Cunard Rd.)

On the *Southside Junction to Brooklyn Trail* are remains of former buildings. Here was once a tipple for a conveyor up the canyon wall to the mines. (Across the canyon rim, W, is the current community of Brooklyn at the headwaters of Coal Run near Cunard.) If continuing ahead downriver follow a fishermen's road 1.4 mi to a parking area at the riverside end of Cunard Rd. Here is a restroom and river-access boat launch. Backtrack or have a second vehicle. Access to the boat launch from Oak Hill is off WV-16 on CO-14 E 5.4 mi to CO-9, R. After 1.5 mi turn L sharply and L again to an entry road into the park. Pass a parking area with *Cunard to Kaymoor Trail* L, *Brooklyn Mine Access Trail* R, and descend on a narrow and steep road to river-access boat launch and parking area. (*USGS Map:* Thurmond)

INFORMATION: Thurmond Depot (across an old bridge on the New River) at the former RR station. Open weekends through the fall from 9 A.M. to 5 P.M.; intermittently other times. Call 304-465-0508.

Kaymoor Area

Kaymoor Trail (1.9 mi); New River Bridge Trail (1.6 mi); Kaymoor Miner's Trail (0.5 mi); Kaymoor to Cunard Trail (6.5 mi); Long Point Trail (1.8 mi)

LENGTH: 11.4 mi combined

DIFFICULTY: easy to strenuous

FEATURES: scenic, historic, mining sites, mtn climbing

TRAILHEADS AND DETAILS: (This network of trails is also called Canyon Rim Area. It has two trails under construction: 2.5-mi *Fayetteville Trail* and an unnamed, short but steep trail of steps from Kaymoor Mines to the old RR by the New River. [See information below.] The most strenuous trail is *Kaymoor Miner's Trail* and the easy route is *Kaymoor Trail*. Bikers are allowed only on the *Kaymoor to Cunard Trail* (or *Cunard to Kaymoor Trail*, depending on the trailhead of your beginning). All the trails have some magnificent scenery. There are four access points, the least space being at *Kaymoor Trail's* N parking space. For a long hike the *Kaymoor Trail* can be used to connect with *Kaymoor to Cunard Trail*, then L for 1.2 mi on Cunard Rd to the river, upstream on the fishermen's road to *Southside Junction to Brooklyn Trail* for 16.6 mi.)

If beginning on the *Kaymoor Trail* on Fayette Station Rd (WV-82), 2.8 mi from its jct with US-19 in Fayetteville, park in a small space in a curve. To the R is *New River Bridge Trail*. (It ascends steeply among boulders and dangerous cliffs on switchbacks for outstanding views of the New River and the massive bridge overhead. Through rhododendron and hardwoods, ferns and mosses, it reaches the S side of the WV-82 parking area on the Fayette Station Rd, 0.8 mi N of US-19. When the *Fayetteville Trail* is completed the *New River Bridge Trail* will have jct with it near the passage under the bridge.)

The *Kaymoor Trail* turns L in the curve parking space to cross the cascading Wolf Creek on a footbridge. Proceed among oak, hickory, locust, maple, ferns, and wild hydrangea. There are scenic views at 1.4 mi. Arrive at Kaymoor Mines, where a safety board and sign are as real today as in 1962 when the mine closed. An example is Your Family Wants You to Work Safely. On the L (E) are off-limits remnants of a huge conveyor to the Kaymoor coke ovens and tipple near the river. (A pathway with steps is being constructed for the 400-ft descent.) To the R (W) near a stone building is *Kaymoor Miner's Trail*. (It ascends, first on steps, then a hiker's path. Ascend about 400 ft in elev on seven switchbacks, pass bunches of trillium, waterleaf, and ferns. To the L near a waterfall are cliffs used for mountain climbing. Reach the Kaymoor Top #1 parking area at 0.5 mi. Access here from US-19 in Fayetteville is to take WV-16 S through the city for 0.8 mi and turn L abruptly on Gatewood Rd (CO-9). Follow it 1.8 mi to Kaymoor #1 Rd (CO-9/2) L, and go 1.0 mi.)

At the mines continue ahead on the *Kaymoor to Cunard Trail* (also called *Cunard to Kaymoor Trail*), a 6.5-mi hiker/biker RR grade. The elev is generally 1,600 ft in hardwood forest for the entire distance. The trail wiggles in and out of more than 65 ridge curves. There are dips from vacant trestles at a number of places. These spots may be eroded or muddy from bike usage. Pass a small waterfall at 0.6 mi at Craig Branch, and then a jct with an old road, R, that leads up to Kaymoor Top parking area. There are views of the river at 2.0 mi. Pass a bog at 2.7 mi R. At 3.0 mi are steps, wild roses, a waterfall, and a cave with crystal-clear water. At 3.8 mi ignore a road R. (It leads 1.2 mi up the mtn to a boundary gate, then onto private property.)

Cross a small stream, pass a bog R, and pass canyon overlooks at 4.9 mi. There are more bogs, R, from strip mining, for the remainder of the trail; the trail is likely to have wet sections. At 6.2 mi are white pine, Russian olive, and ground cedar. Cross a bridge over cascading Coal Run and arrive at a parking space on Cunard Rd. Backtrack or have a second vehicle. (To the L it is 1.2 mi to the end of Cunard Rd to a parking area, restroom, and boat launch access. (See *Southside Junction to Brooklyn Trail* above.) To the R it is 1.9 mi on CO-9/12 and CO-9, R, to Gatewood Rd (CO-14). Here it is 1.6 mi R on CO-14 to Kaymoor #1 Rd. If L at Gatewood, it is 5.4 mi on CO-14 to Oak Hill and WV-16.

Back at Kaymoor Top #1 parking area the moderate *Long Point Trail* follows a plateau path N through an open area and forests, then descend to cross Butcher branch at 0.6 mi. After 0.1 mi reach a jct with the proposed *Fayetteville Trail,* L. Go R through a hardwood forest to a dead-end trail at cliffs on Long Point Ridge. Views are of the canyon, New River, and the New River Bridge. (*USGS Maps:* Fayetteville, Thurmond)

INFORMATION: Canyon Rim Visitor Center; 304-574-2115. Open daily (except Dec 25 and Jan 1), usually 9 A.M. to 5 P.M., but stays open later in summer. Located on N end of the US-19 New River Bridge.

5. US Army Corps of Engineers Projects

The greatest domestic problem facing our country is saving our soil and water.

—Sam Rayburn

The US Army Corps of Engineers was formed during the early years of the nation's history as part of the Continental army. At the time of the Revolution, West Point, a garrison on the Hudson River, was fortified by an act of Congress—an act that authorized a corps of engineers and artillerymen. In 1798 the corps was enlarged and in 1802 Congress made West Point the military academy for the United States. Since then, Congress has authorized a wide range of projects for the Army Corps of Engineers. Among them have been blazing and building roads, clearing waterways and harbors, building dams for flood control and hydropower, protecting and restoring shorelines, and providing natural disaster relief, fish and wildlife developments, and multiple recreation opportunities. While emphasizing diversity in recreational usage year-round, the Corps enforces zoning regulations to protect the ecology. To enhance this process, the state's Department of Natural Resources has leased project land for additional facilities such as parks and hunting and fishing areas.

The Corps has constructed 10 major recreational lake areas. They are R. D. Bailey Lake, Beech Fork Lake, Bloomington Lake, Bluestone Lake, Burnsville Lake, Easy Lynn Lake, Stonewall Jackson Lake, Summersville Lake, Sutton Lake, and Tygart Lake. The total federally owned land surrounding all 10 projects is 120,000 acres. The total water surface during the summer is 11,300 acres. The Corps's first flood control/recreation project in West Virginia was Tygart Lake on the Tygart River near Grafton, completed in 1938, and the most recent was Stonewall Jackson Lake. (See Stonewall Jackson Lake State Park, section 6.) There are other Corps projects with locks and dams, but recreational usage is limited mainly to fishing and boating.

Recreational facilities include campgrounds, usually with hookups, picnic areas with shelters, restrooms, launching ramps, and marinas. Fishing is a popular sport in all the lakes. Hunting is allowed in specific areas and in accordance with the state game laws. Somewhat less developed are pedestrian, bicycle, horse, snowmobile, and ORV trails, some of which are nonexistent. Foot trails identified by the Corps for this book are described below.

INFORMATION: Public Affairs Office, US Army Engineer District, 502 Eighth St, Huntington, WV 25701; 304-529-5451. Request a directory, "Lakeside Recreation in the Northeast," and brochures on the lakes.

BEECH FORK LAKE (Wayne and Cabell Counties)

Described as a "little jewel," this 720-acre lake was constructed in 1978 for flood control of Twelvepole Creek, recreational purposes, and fish and wildlife management. The total development includes 12,757 acres, with 31 mi of shoreline. The Corps of Engineers has transferred the management of 2,100 acres at the upper end of Beech Fork for the Beech Fork State Park (see chapter 6). Water sports are popular in the summer at the Beech Fork Marina and Boat Launch NE of the dam. Docking facilities, motorboats, canoes, paddle boats, and life jackets are available for visitors at the marina. Picnicking and swimming are allowed at the Stowers Branch area SW of the dam. Here a 4WD-vehicle access road called the *Beaver Pond Trail* leaves the parking lot near the swimming area for 0.6 mi to Stowers Branch. Backtracking is necessary. The full operational period for the lake is from Memorial Day to Labor Day. (*USGS Map:* Lavalette)

ADDRESS AND ACCESS: Resource Manager, Beech Fork Lake, USACE, PO Box 600, Lavalette, WV 25535; 304-525-4831. From I-64 in Huntington drive S on WV-152 for 5.5 mi and turn L on Beech Fork Rd (CO-13). Go 3.0 mi to the lake.

Rock Hollow Trail

LENGTH: 0.5 mi

DIFFICULTY: moderate

FEATURES: scenic, nature study

TRAILHEAD AND DETAILS: Stop at the resource manager's office for a brochure on the trail. Park near the dam, NE, and follow the trail sign across the road. This interpretive loop trail has 16 posts for shrubs, trees, wildflowers, mosses, lichen, and nature lore on a slope with rock formations. At post #13 is a scenic view of the lake.

BURNSVILLE LAKE (Braxton County)

The Corps of Engineers began construction of the 970-acre Burnsville Lake in 1972 and it became operational in 1978. Its main purpose was for flood control of the Little Kanawha River, a stream 167 mi long that drains 2,320 sq mi in parts or all of seven counties. There are nine recreational and scenic areas; among them are areas for picnicking, camping, water sports, fishing, hunting, and hiking. As in the other Corps projects, the state Department of Natural Resources administers the fish-stocking programs and enforces game and conservation laws. Among the fish in the area are bass, crappie, catfish, bluegill, and sunfish. Game species include deer, rabbit, squirrel, raccoon, grouse, and wild turkey.

The property has approximately 60 mi of fire roads and abandoned access roads that can be used for hiking. These road-trails have such names as *Mud Hole Trail*, Long Run Rd, Benny Run Rd, *White-tail Trail,* and *Posey Hollow Trail.* Part of the 19th-century *Weston and Gauley Bridge Turnpike (Trail)* is being restored between here and the new Stonewall Jackson Lake, now being constructed near Weston on the West Fork River. The road-trails can be used only for day hikes. Also, any road-trail originating in either of the two campgrounds—Riffle Run Camp and Bulltown Camping Area—can be used only by campers for access. The project's two well-graded and maintained trails that are open daily to the public are described below. (*USGS Map:* Orlando)

ADDRESS AND ACCESS: Resource Manager, Burnsville Lake, USACE, PO Box 347, Burnsville, WV 26335; 304-853-2371 (for lake conditions, 304-853-2398).

Bulltown Battlefield Trail

LENGTH: 0.3 mi

DIFFICULTY: easy

FEATURES: history, scenic

TRAILHEAD AND DETAILS: From the community of Heaters drive E on US-19/WV-4 to the Bulltown day-use area and turn R (S) to a parking area. The paved loop trail on an open slope with Confederate trenches has an information sign about the Battle of Bulltown, Oct 13, 1863. Here a small contingent of Confederate forces tried unsuccessfully to control the Weston and Gauley Bridge Turnpike.

Bulltown Historic Overlook Trail

LENGTH: 1.0 mi

DIFFICULTY: easy

FEATURES: history, scenic

TRAILHEAD AND DETAILS: On US-19/WV-4 between Bulltown day-use area and Falls Mill, turn N on Millstone Run Rd (CO-19/12) and drive 0.9 mi to the Historical Overlook Area, L. (This is also the route to the Bulltown Camping Area.) From the parking area follow the paved trail to the log St Michael's Catholic Church. Beyond, follow a wood-chip treadway into a forest of walnut, poplar, maple, spicebush, dogwood, and Virginia pine to an overlook and gazebo at 0.4 mi. Wildflowers include ragwort and white snakeroot. Complete the loop and return to the relocated historic village of the Moses Cunningham farm and the Johnson and Fleming houses.

EAST LYNN LAKE (Wayne County)

The Corps of Engineers constructed the East Lynn Lake for flood control of Twelvepole Creek. In the process, recreational areas were provided for water sports, camping, picnicking, hunting, fishing, and hiking. Boats, equipment, and dock space can be rented. There are 169 campsites for tents or trailers, many with hookups; hot showers; and a dumping station. There are also 15 primitive campsites available all year. An unnamed foot trail is within the East Fork Campground. A 1.0-mi trail is planned from near the dam to the marine boat-launch area. Full facilities at the lake are open from May 1 to Oct 15. (*USGS Map:* Nestlow)

ADDRESS AND ACCESS: Resource Manager, East Lynn lake, USACE, HC85, Box 35-C, East Lynn, WV 25512; 304-849-2355. From the community of East Lynn, drive S on WV-37 for 3.0 mi to a turnoff R for 1.5 mi to the Lake Side Marina and Picnic Area.

Lakeside Trail

LENGTH: 1.7 mi

DIFFICULTY: moderate

FEATURES: nature study, scenic

TRAILHEAD AND DETAILS: At the parking lot in the picnic area, follow the trail sign and ascend on a graded yellow-blazed trail in a young hardwood and Virginia pine forest. Ferns and wildflowers are prominent. Reach a knoll at 0.2 mi, turn L, and follow the ridge on an old road to a clearing (formerly a cemetery) at 0.6 mi. Continue ahead and turn to the N side of the ridge. The trail picks up another old road leading past an inactive coal mine and descends to the picnic area about 125 yd from the point of beginning at 1.7 mi.

PART THREE

State-Managed Trails

6. State Parklands and Historic Sites

State parks are priceless and eternal gifts we have given ourselves and future citizens.

—Ronald Barkham

West Virginia has 38 state parks, with a total of 73,728 acres (plus the developing 72-mi *North Bend Rail Trail*). They are protected by law from commercial exploitation of their natural resources. Some of the parks are vacation areas with resort lodges and completely furnished cabins; others are for day use only. While classified as vacation parks because of their developed facilities, they may also encompass significant natural and historical features as well, preserved for the "benefit and enjoyment of future generations." An example is Blackwater Falls State Park, with the state's highest and largest waterfall. The day-use areas primarily feature facilities for sports-associated activities but have no overnight accommodations. Resort state parks offer overnight accommodations, lodges and cabins, golf courses, a complete line of recreational facilities, swimming, tennis, hiking trails, and a year-round recreation and interpretive program. Examples are Pipestem Resort and Valley Falls State Park. Historical areas have been established to preserve locations that have historical, archaeological, or scientific significance. These have day-use facilities, but some recreational facilities may also be available. An example is Watters Smith Memorial State Park, which has a swimming pool and hiking trails in addition to its museum.

The lodge and resort parks are: Blackwater Falls, Cacapon Resort, Canaan Valley Resort, Hawks Nest, North Bend, Pipestem Resort, Twin Falls Resort, and Tygart Lake. Cabin vacation parks are Babcock, Bluestone, Holly River, Lost River, and Watoga. Camping vacation parks are Audra,

Beech Fork, Camp Creek, Cedar Creek, Chief Logan, Moncove Lake, Stonewall Jackson Lake, and Tomlinson Run. Day-use parks are Little Beaver, Pinnacle Rock, and Valley Falls. Also for day use but natural and historical parks are: Beartown, Berkeley Springs, Blennerhassett Historical, Carnifex Ferry Battlefield, Cass Scenic Railroad, Cathedral, Droop Mtn Battlefield, Fairfax Stone, Grave Creek Mound, Point Pleasant Battle Monument, Prickett's Fort, and Watters Smith Memorial. There are two long state park trails: *Greenbrier River Rail Trail* and *North Bend Rail Trail*. Only the parks that have hiking trails are covered in this guidebook. There are 163 named trails; they cover a total of 362 miles.

The state parks system has become one of the state's major tourist attractions. Its development and progress has been outstanding from the beginning, when, on July 1, 1937, four parks (Babcock, Cacapon, Lost River, and Watoga) opened for public use. The total attendance for the 1937–38 season was 75,194; a decade later for the 1947–48 season the attendance had grown to 977,321. When the parks system celebrated its 30th anniversary in 1967, there were 21 parks in operation and three others were under construction. Attendance that year passed 3,000,000. In some parks the demands were exceeding the capacity of the facility. In 1984 attendance had risen to the 7,036,790 mark. In 1996 visitor attendance was 9,329,662, of which 2,972,037 were from out of state. Out-of-state attendance has always been high. For example, in 1984 it was 29.7 percent, and in 1996, 31 percent.

The history of the state parks system began in 1933 when the state legislature established the Division of State Parks. The bill (Chapter 20 of the West Virginia Code) stated that the purpose of the system was to "promote conservation by preserving and protecting" significant natural, scientific, cultural, historic, and archaeological areas. Another purpose was "to provide outdoor recreational opportunities for the citizens of this state and its visitors." Public hunting, mining, and timber harvesting for commercial purposes would not be permitted. The legislative action was a "direct result of the emphasis placed on conservation" by the United States Emergency Conservation Act approved by President Franklin D. Roosevelt on Mar 31, 1933.

The first state park, Watoga, was begun in May 1934, under the provisions of the National Park Service. Watoga was a desirable location to begin because in 1925 the state's Game, Fish, and Forestry Commission had acquired 4,500 acres of timbered hills for a state forest in Pocahontas

County. The intention was to create a state wildlife and forest preserve. A lack of state funds delayed development until 1933, when federal funds appropriated by Congress for emergency conservation work became available from the Federal Forestry Service. A Civilian Conservation Corps (CCC) camp was immediately established, and by 1935 the Watoga area had three such camps.

With an increase in public interest in conservation, the state legislature appropriated $70,000 to purchase other lands for park development. With this funding, acreage was doubled at the Watoga State Park area, and the acquisition of properties for Babcock, Cacapon, Hawks Nest, and Lost River began. Further advancement of these parks began in the spring of 1934 when the state formed the Conservation Commission, an outgrowth of the old Game, Fish, and Forestry Commission. The new commission began an "ambitious program of recreational development" with manpower and funding from the Civilian Conservation Corps.

During the formative years the division operated successfully by coordinating its administrative, central design, and field personnel branches. The designs and plans of the central design office were submitted to the National Park Service. If approved, the office would inspect the facilities under construction to see that government standards were followed. The actual construction process was administered by the CCC, and the field personnel took care of the day-to-day park operation. These early developments were confined to road building; reforestation; and construction of cabins, well and pump houses, hand-dug foot and horse trails, and limited picnic areas. An example of the careful design and grading of a foot trail is the first mile of the *Monongaseneka Trail* in Watoga State Park.

The Carnifex Ferry Battlefield area was acquired in October 1935, the result of preliminary planning by the special Battlefield Park Commission established by the state in 1931. Although the Division of State Parks assumed administrative responsibility for the Droop Mtn Battlefield in 1937, the park was purchased in 1928 and dedicated as a state historic park on July 4, 1929. This early date has led some historians to call it the "granddaddy" of the state parks system.

Pinnacle Rock in Mercer County was purchased in 1938, and the first of two parcels of land for the Grandview State Park (now part of New River Gorge National River) was purchased in 1939. But the main source of funding and manpower through the CCC began to decline in 1940, and on July 2, 1942, Congress passed Public Law 647, the bill that terminated the CCC.

It was the end of a decade of innovative conservation projects to protect natural resources. It was also a change from civilian to military work for thousands of young American men. All the CCC camps were abandoned during WWII. Tomlinson Run CCC camp, completed in 1941, was never occupied, though the camp became a state park in 1939.

After the war, public interest in state parks increased at a time state funding had other priorities. Nevertheless, with the help of the US Army Corps of Engineers, Tygart Lake State Park was established in 1947 and Bluestone State Park in 1955. Purchase of land for Cedar Creek State Park began in 1953 and for the North Bend State Park in 1954. It was during the 1953 session of the state legislature that a major increase in park development was begun through the sale of revenue bonds. In May 1955, the $4,000,000 Revenue Bond Act was signed, and the state park system entered its most progressive period since its early years. Immediate results included the expansion of Blackwater Falls State Park and the opening of Bluestone, Cedar Creek, and North Bend for public use.

On July 1, 1961, a legislative act replaced the Conservation Commission with the Department of Natural Resources and renamed the Division of State Parks the Division of State Parks and Recreation, one of five divisions under the new department. The other four were the divisions of Wildlife, Forestry, Water Resources, and Reclamation, with the later addition of Law Enforcement.

Also in 1961, the Emergency Employment Program (EEP) was created. Its purpose was to improve maintenance and provide recreational renovation and facilities in an expanded program to follow the one-year State Temporary Economic Program (STEP) established in 1960.

Additional assistance to the parks system came in 1963 when the Area Redevelopment Administration (ARA) of the US Department of Commerce allocated approximately $25,000,000 ($16,000,000 of which was a loan) for the future development of six state parks. It was within this year that the land acquisition began for Canaan Valley State Park. Other uses of the ARA funding were: the beginning of land purchases in 1965 for Pipestem State Park; more land for Canaan Valley State Park; land acquisition for Twin Falls State Park in Wyoming County; assistance on the completion of the Cass Scenic Railroad; and additional facilities at Hawks Nest State Park. The purchase of land for Valley Falls State Park began in 1964. In 1967 Pipestem opened, and in 1968, Canaan Valley, Prickett's Fort, and Twin Falls opened also. Little Beaver opened in 1972, and the most recent park to begin operation was Beech Fork in 1979. There is only one new park currently in the planning stage; it is the Stonewall Jackson State Park in Lewis County. In 1985, the Division of State Parks and Recreation was transferred from the Department of Natural Resources to the Department of Commerce.

To make your visit to the state parks an enjoyable and successful experience, the following is suggested. First, write or call for information at the state offices listed at the end of this introduction. Make your lodge or cabin reservations far in advance (in some parks, such as Watoga and Blackwater Falls, you may reserve a campsite), and follow the rules and regulations at the parks.

The campground rules state that campers must register, a campsite can be used for a maximum of two weeks, and no more than two vehicles may be at any one campsite. Quiet hours are observed between 10 P.M. and 7 A.M. It is unlawful to damage or remove any of the natural or man-made objects. In many of the parks, alcoholic beverages are not allowed. Campground facilities are provided for the exclusive use of registered campers. Motorbike riding is prohibited, and pets must be restrained on leashes. Hunting or disturbing wildlife is forbidden. In most parks, camping is not allowed along the hiking trails. Where there are exceptions, such as at Lost River and Holly River, permission must be granted by the park superintendent.

INFORMATION: In addition to the addresses and telephone numbers for each park below, the headquarters is: West Virginia Division of Tourism and Parks, State Capital Complex, 2101 Washington St, E (PO Box 50312), Charleston WV 25305; 800-CALL-WVA.

AUDRA STATE PARK (Barbour County)

Middle Fork River, which flows through beautiful 355-acre Audra State Park, has a mineral acidity that makes it a clear emerald green. The sculpted rocks within the stream make perfect spots for sunbathing. The park has 65 campsites (61 suitable for trailers), a laundry, three picnic areas, and a concrete slab beach by the river. The park is near enough to Volga for adequate supplies. Open Apr 15–Oct 15.

ADDRESS AND ACCESS: Audra State Park, Rte 4, Box 564, Buchannon, WV 26201; 304-457-1162. From Buchannon go E about 2.5 mi on US-33 to Kesling Mill Rd (CO-3), L, and drive 10.0 mi to the park entrance; or, from US-119 in Volga, go 6.0 mi on Audra Park Rd (CO-11) to the park entrance.

Alum Cave Trail

LENGTH: 2.7 mi
DIFFICULTY: moderate
FEATURES: scenic river, Alum Cave

TRAILHEAD AND DETAILS: From the parking area S of the bridge, hike downstream on a paved trail and pass the first 4-H campsite, established in 1919. There is a rhododendron border. Leave the paved trail and follow a footpath through tall hardwoods and hemlock. Reach Alum Cave, L, at 0.4 mi; descend to a boardwalk under the large overhang. Continue downstream with excellent views of the river, turn sharp R at 1.3 mi, and ascend on three switchbacks to the ridge crest. At 1.9 mi is a jct with a spur that leads down the mountain to the cave area. At 2.4 mi pass a picnic area, descend to an overlook at the river, and backtrack to the parking area. (*USGS Map:* Audra)

BABCOCK STATE PARK (Fayette County)

One of the state's oldest parks, Babcock is another spectacular vacation area with a wide range of recreational conveniences. Half of the 4,127 acres is developed and the other half, W of the New River, is wild and scenic where Manns Creek and Glade Creek have cut canyons through a rock formation with cliff lines. Tall hardwoods and hemlock rise above an understory of mtn laurel, rhododendron, buckberry, ferns, and a wide variety of wildflowers. Ferns, mosses, and wintergreen grow near the purple rhododendron (which blooms in May) and the rosebay rhododendron (the state's flower, which blooms in July and early August). Trout are in the cascading creeks, deer roam tranquil trails and ridges, and raccoon visit the campground. Added to all this natural beauty is the Glade Creek Grist Mill, a restored water-powered system with parts and material from a number of other mills, once located near the current park headquarters. Cornmeal and whole-wheat and buckwheat flour are ground and sold here.

There are two short, unblazed trails 300 yd N on the Manns Creek Picnic Area and Campground road from the park entrance road. The 0.3-mi *Mountain Heath Trail* loop has numbered posts (get a guide list from the park office) through a hardwood forest with trailing arbutus and wintergreen. Across the road E is a 255-yd round-trip walk to a natural rock arch among oak, poplar, and dogwood. A new trail, orange-blazed *Manns Creek Gorge Trail,* descends 2.0 mi from campsite #26 in the campground to the first parking lot at Camp Washington Carver on CO-19/33. Along the way are scenic rock outcroppings from a ridge N of Manns Creek among rhododendron, hemlock, and hardwoods. If not backtracking it is 1.5 mi up on CO-19/33 to make a 3.5-mi loop.

Facilities include: 26 cabins; 51 campsites, laundry, and hot showers; dumping station; restaurant; commissary and souvenir shop; swimming pool; boat rentals (nonmotorized); picnic units; game courts; tennis; and nearly 20 mi of hiking trails. Season is Apr 15–Oct 31. (*USGS Maps:* Thurmond, Fayetteville, Winona, Danese)

ADDRESS AND ACCESS: Babcock State Park, HC-35, Box 150, Clifftop, WV 25831; 304-438-3004. From Beckley it is 32 mi N on WV-41; 3.8 mi S on WV-41 from US-60 near Clifftop.

Skyline Trail (2.0 mi); Rocky Trail (0.5 mi); Fisherman's Trail (2.0 mi)

LENGTH: 4.7 mi round-trip, partially combined
DIFFICULTY: easy to moderate
FEATURES: sandstone cliffs, nature study, waterfalls

TRAILHEADS AND DETAILS: These trails, plus part of the *Narrow Gauge Trail*, can make loops. Follow the yellow-blazed *Skyline Trail* from the overlook at Manns Creek Picnic Area. At 0.5 mi reach a jct with the white-blazed *Rocky Trail*, R. For a loop, turn R, descend steeply, cross a stream, turn L on an old RR grade (*Narrow Gauge Trail*), and reach the jct with the *Fisherman's Trail* at 1.0 mi. (The *Fisherman's Trail* is a rocky trail used primarily by fishermen 1.2 mi up and 0.8 mi down the river.) Cross the wood footbridge over Glade Creek and follow *Narrow Gauge Trail* R to a gravel road, Old Sewell Rd, L, at 1.6 mi. Hike L on the road to a paved area and cottage #13 at 2.5 mi. At 2.8 mi turn L near cottage #7 through a dense rhododendron patch to a swinging footbridge. After crossing the bridge follow the trail between cottages #4 and #5 to ascend steeply to *Skyline Trail*. Cross a small bridge over a ravine at 3.1 mi. Wildflowers are prominent in the spring and summer. Scenic views of Glade Creek canyon are at 3.8 mi. Reach a jct with *Rocky Trail* at 4.5 mi and return to the point of origin at the overlook in Manns Creek Picnic Area at 5.0 mi.

Narrow Gauge Trail

LENGTH: 2.4 mi
DIFFICULTY: easy to moderate
FEATURES: RR relics, scenic, swinging bridge, waterfalls

TRAILHEAD AND DETAILS: The N access is on the W side of the park road between the N cabin area and campground; the S access is 1.5 mi down the Old Sewell Rd from the gristmill and park office. (Additionally, the yellow-blazed trail is accessible by taking the *Fisherman's Trail* downstream from the S cabin area #5 near a swinging bridge.) If hiking from the N access begin on the old RR grade with Manns Creek to the R, and among hemlock and rhododendron. Some old crossties remain. At 0.3 mi is a waterfall, L, and creek cascades, R. More cascades are at 0.4 mi. The canyon becomes narrow at 0.5 mi. Curve SE away from Manns Creek at 1.3 mi. At 1.5 mi descend steeply to cross a bridge near a waterfall that splashes through old narrow-gauge-RR wheels. At 1.6 mi is a jct with white-blazed *Rocky Trail*, L. (It ascends steeply 0.5 mi to a jct with *Skyline Trail*, where a L is 0.5 mi to Manns Creek Picnic Area.)

At 1.8 mi jct with orange-blazed *Fisherman's Trail*, R and L. (To the L it is 1.2 mi upstream on a rocky route to S cabin #5 and swinging bridge. To the R it is 0.8 mi downstream to a dead end.) Cross the swinging bridge over Glade Creek and follow a level grassy damp RR grade to a small parking space on Old Sewell Rd at 2.4 mi. Either backtrack, or have a second vehicle waiting for you. (See *Skyline Trail* option described above.)

Island in the Sky Trail (0.4 mi); Wilderness Trail (2.0 mi)

LENGTH: 4.8 mi round-trip, combined
DIFFICULTY: moderate
FEATURES: overlooks, wildlife, remote

TRAILHEADS AND DETAILS: From the parking area of the park office, pass the gristmill and ascend on white-blazed *Island in the Sky Trail*. Turn R onto a rocky area, climb a wood scaffold, and ascend to a ridge and an overlook at 0.3 mi. Follow a spur trail to the road, W, and parking area at 0.4 mi. Turn R on the yellow-blazed *Wilderness Trail* on a serene wilderness road with hardwoods, ferns, and flowering shrubs. Wildflowers include pink lady-slipper and wood betony. Deer are frequently seen on the old road. At 2.2 mi cross a wood bridge; the blaze ends and the trail direction becomes faint at 2.4 mi. Backtrack.

Lake View Trail

LENGTH: 1.2 mi
DIFFICULTY: easy
FEATURES: wildflowers, scenic

Trailhead and Details: From the park office drive W on Sugar Camp Run Rd to the boat dock, L, at Boley Lake. (The lake is named for James C. Boley, who gave 42 years of service to the state parks.) Begin the hike R through a young forest of oak, sassafras, and maple. Along the way are huckleberry, dogwood, pinxter, asters, and wood betony. Cross a branch through mature trees and over some rocky edges. Reach the dam, 1.1 mi. Complete the loop at 1.2 mi.

BEARTOWN STATE PARK
(Pocahontas and Greenbrier Counties)

This day-use educational park of 110 acres is named from a local legend that tells of families of black bear inhabiting a labyrinth of deep crevasses in a sandstone mountainside. The 0.4-mi *Beartown Boardwalk Trail* loop is an easy journey into a massive natural wonder of sculpted stone. The pitted surfaces result from erosion and are covered by rock cap ferns. Trees in the channels are mainly yellow birch and hemlock. Interpretive signs are at the entrance and along the boardwalk.

Address and Access: Beartown State Park, HC 64, Box 189, Hillsboro, WV 24946; 304-653-4254. From Hillsboro on US-219, drive S for 8.0 mi and turn L on Beartown Rd (CO-219/11) at a log church, and drive 1.6 mi to the park entrance.

BEECH FORK STATE PARK (Wayne and Cabell Counties)

Under continuing development, this 3,981-acre park has an exceptionally large campground—275 campsites, many with full-service sites for any size RV. There is a large visitor center, country store, playground and games area, ball fields, picnic shelters, and a boat launching ramp. The major sports activities are fishing, boating, and hiking. There is a 0.8-mi *Physical Fitness Trail* beginning from either the parking lot at the park office or at the entrance of the picnic shelters parking lot. The lake is part of the Beech Fork Dam, constructed by the US Army Corps of Engineers (see chapter 5). Future plans for the park include a total resort-style park with golf course, swimming pool, lodge, and vacation cabins. (*USGS Map:* Winslow)

Address and Access: Beech Fork State Park, 5601 Long Beach Rd, Barboursville, WV 25504; 304-522-0303. From I-64 jct with WV-10, Exit 11, drive S on WV-10 for 1.7 mi to Hughes Branch Rd (CO-43) and follow CO-43 for 7.3 mi to park entrance, R.

Lakeview Trail (1.1 mi); Overlook Trail (1.5 mi)

LENGTH: 2.6 mi round-trip, combined

DIFFICULTY: moderate

FEATURES: wildlife, overlooks, nature study, wildflowers

TRAILHEADS AND DETAILS: The blue-blazed *Lakeview Trail* begins behind the Lakeview camping area bathhouse, near campsite #46. At 0.2 mi cross a stream bed and ascend a hill to where the trail levels out near a cemetery, L, and a ravine, R. At 0.7 mi reach a fork. Veer L to descend a steep hill and end at the campground road and trailhead at 0.9 mi. Or, turn R and follow the trail to the fire circle on the L, an old homestead cabin on the L, and then to the campground road again at 0.9 mi. Another option is to turn R after the cabin and follow the trail back toward the Lakeview bathhouse and exit onto the main road at 1.1 mi, across from the boat launch area.

The trailhead for the red-blazed *Overlook Trail* loop is between the Long Branch bridge and the road to the maintenance area on the N side of the main campground road. A small parking space is on the S side of the road. After entering the trail cross a wooden footbridge in a beautiful grassy area with abundant honeysuckle and clover, and fritillary butterflies. Ascend a slight hill, which gradually becomes a steep incline to a fork in the trail. Turn R to a rock ledge overlooking the park office and picnic area. Follow the ridge for 0.4 mi and then bear L on a N slope of open hardwoods. Descend to a ravine, cross another footbridge, and complete the loop at 1.3 mi. Return to the road at 1.5 mi.

Lost Trail

LENGTH: 2.7 mi

DIFFICULTY: moderate

FEATURES: wildlife, wildflowers, lake views

TRAILHEAD AND DETAILS: This green-blazed trail is a double loop for usage by hikers and mountain-bikers. To reach the trailhead enter between campsites #34 and #35 in the Moxley Branch campground area. Cross a wooden footbridge into a forest of black walnut, redbud, ash, and buckeye. After 0.2 mi is another footbridge and a fork. (The L turn leads to a steep incline.) Turn R near a grove of ash and swamp rose. Quail, songbirds, and deer are often seen here. Pass through a stand of poplar with scattered spicebush, mandrake, and bloodroot. At 1.0 mi cross a third footbridge with another fork in the trail. Go R and walk 0.7 mi along the lake at the water's edge for views of the boat launch area across the lake. Along the way is a natural spring where deer drink. Turn sharply L and ascend to a ridge that loops back to the lower trail. At the top of the ridge come to another fork in the trail. If going R, the trail will descend steeply to the second footbridge mentioned above. (If taking the L fork, descend to the third footbridge and backtrack to the point of origin.)

BLACKWATER FALLS STATE PARK (Tucker County)

This 1,688-acre resort park is a year-round tourist attraction. It is near the state's highest town, Davis, at 3,101 ft elev. The town was founded in 1883 by Senator Henry G. Davis, who established America's first night train in 1848. The park is named for the falls of the Blackwater River, a river that begins in Canaan Valley and whose waters are ambered from the tannin of high-country conifers. The 63-ft Blackwater Falls opens a canyon from the E side of the park that divides the park with a N and S rim. Canyon rim overlooks are at Pendleton Point on the N side and a number of overviews along the S side of the lodge and cabin area. From the parking area at the trading post are stairways and boardwalks that allow visitors a descent to the base of Blackwater Falls. This is an enchanting view any season of the year.

Facilities include: 55 rooms, 25 completely furnished (bring only food and clothes) cabins, 65 tent and trailer campsites (some of which can be reserved), hot showers and laundromat at the campground (but no hookups at campsites), outdoor swimming area, nature and recreation center, restaurant with additional facilities for a private banquet, paddle-boating on Pendleton Lake, horseback riding at the stables, cross-country ski trails, sledding, picnic areas, concessions, playground and naturalist programs, and hiking trails (including sections of the *Allegheny Trail*). (*USGS-FS Maps*: Blackwater Falls, Mozark Mtn)

ADDRESS AND ACCESS: Blackwater Falls State Park, PO Box 490, Davis, WV 26260; 304-259-5216. In Davis on WV-32, turn off at sign on Blackwater Falls Rd (CO-29) to park entrance.

Balsam Fir Trail

LENGTH: 1.5 mi

DIFFICULTY: easy

TRAILHEAD AND DETAILS: After entry into the park, turn R at the first crossroads toward the recreation bldg and its parking lot. If walking clockwise on the blue-blazed trail, go NE near the basketball court and enter a wide forest pathway. Pass first through a grove of dark green balsam fir, but through a predominately maple and beech forest elsewhere. At 0.8 mi curve S to exit between campsites #17 and #18 in the campground area. Turn R, but leave the road R at the playground for a return to the recreation bldg.

Gentle Trail

LENGTH: 100 yd
DIFFICULTY: easy
FEATURES: geology, scenic

TRAILHEAD AND DETAILS: After entry into the park take the Lodge and Cabin Rd, cross the Blackwater River bridge, and park at the first parking area, R. The *Gentle Trail* is a level, wide, asphalt trail, constructed for easy access for the physically handicapped. Nine companies and the Women's Club of Thomas made the trail possible and selected native plants to decorate the trail border. At the observation deck is a sign that reads "So that all may equally enjoy the wonder of God's handiwork." At the lookout is an extraordinary view of the Blackwater Falls and the Blackwater Gorge.

Yellow Birch Trail

LENGTH: 1.5 mi
DIFFICULTY: easy
FEATURE: nature study

TRAILHEAD AND DETAILS: A few yd before arriving at the *Gentle Trail* parking area is a park service and maintenance road, L. At the road entry, R, the yellow-blazed *Yellow Birch Trail* begins. Follow the trail through a mixture of hardwoods and conifers, cross Falls Run and Engine Run, and reach a crossing of Stables Rd and the *Allegheny Trail* at 0.7 mi. (To the L, at the stables, the *Allegheny Trail*, formerly the *Davis Trail*, continues S for 2.8 mi to FR-13. The *Red Spruce Trail* begins at the stables and is used by both equestrians and cross-country skiers.) Continue on the *Yellow Birch Trail*, which parallels the Lodge and Cabin Rd, cross Tank Run, and reach the road across from the lodge after another 0.8 mi for a total distance of 1.5 mi.

Elakala Trail

LENGTH: 0.4 mi
DIFFICULTY: easy
FEATURE: Elakala Falls

TRAILHEAD AND DETAILS: From the parking area of the lodge, SW, follow the red-blazed trail and descend for 0.1 mi to a footbridge over the Upper Elakala Falls on Shay Run. Continue on the trail through an area of huge boulders and a hemlock forest to exit at the Lodge and Cabin Rd. Across the road is the entrance, N, to the *Balanced Rock Trail*. Backtrack or return on the paved road to the lodge.

Balanced Rock Trail (1.0 mi); Rhododendron Trail (0.4 mi); Cherry Lane Trail (0.8 mi)

LENGTH: 2.2 mi combined

DIFFICULTY: easy

FEATURES: Balanced Rock, nature study

TRAILHEADS AND DETAILS: The *Balanced Rock Trail* and the *Rhododendron Trail* directly connect, and the *Cherry Lane Trail's* N terminus is only 0.3 mi N of the *Rhododendron Trail* on the Cabin Rd. The *Balanced Rock Trail* may be entered from the main Lodge and Cabin Rd, across the road from the *Elakala Trail* (0.5 mi W of the lodge), or it can be entered by cabin #13 on the Cabin Rd. If entering by the cabin, follow the orange-blazed trail for 0.2 mi to a jct with the *Rhododendron Trail*. Continue R in a forest of hemlock, rhododendron, birch, and cinnamon fern. Cross Shay Run and go R on the trail that leads to the observation deck on Balanced Rock at 0.4 mi. Backtrack to the jct and continue ahead for 0.6 mi to reach *Elakala Trail*, or turn L at the jct and return on the white-blazed *Rhododendron Trail*, which exits between cabins #9 and #11. The yellow/white-blazed *Cherry Lane Trail* begins on the Cabin Rd 0.3 mi from cabin #9 and below cabin #1. Follow the *Cherry Lane Trail* through beech, yellow birch, maple, cherry, and scattered hemlock to a loop that goes in front of cabin #25 to a cul-de-sac and beyond to a loop jct and point of origin at 0.8 mi.

BLUESTONE STATE PARK (Summers County)

At the confluence of the Bluestone River and the New River in the SE corner of the state is 2,146-acre Bluestone State Park. Rugged, forested mtns surround the park, but views of the state's second largest lake—the 1,800-acre Bluestone Lake—are superb. Facilities include 25 modern cabins (open year-round), 87 tent-trailer campsites with hot showers, swimming pool, gift shop/snack bar, picnic shelter, and dumping station. Rental canoes, boats, water skiing equipment, game courts, and a playground are available. Also, there are areas for picnicking, fishing (for bluegill, largemouth and smallmouth bass, crappie, and catfish), and hiking. Nearby are Pipestem State Resort Park and the Bluestone WMA. (*USGS Map:* Pipestem)

ADDRESS AND ACCESS: Bluestone State Park, HC-78, Box 3, Hinton, WV 25951; 304-466-2805. From Princeton on WV-20, NE, go 28.0 mi. From Hinton go SW on WV-20 for 5.0 mi.

Rhododendron Trail

LENGTH: 0.8 mi

DIFFICULTY: easy

FEATURE: cascading stream

TRAILHEAD AND DETAILS: From the activities bldg follow the red-blazed foot trail through the forest and descend, cross park road, and continue descent on the R side of Surveyors Branch (a stream with cascades unless the summer is dry) to the boat launching ramp. Backtrack or have a vehicle shuttle.

Big Pine Trail (1.7 mi); Riverview Trail (1.6 mi)

LENGTH: 3.3 mi combined

DIFFICULTY: moderate

FEATURES: scenic, wildlife

TRAILHEADS AND DETAILS: To begin the *Big Pine Trail*, drive past the swimming pool to the launching ramp area. Trail is R. Ascend steeply through oak and locust forest on a gradual elev with borders of ferns and mosses. Occasional green blazes remind you of the trail. At 0.9 mi pass the ruins of a log cabin. Spicebush grows nearby. Reach a jct, R, with the *Riverview Trail* at 1.0 mi. (The *Riverview Trail* descends for 0.5 mi to the swimming area.) Continue ahead and reach a jct, L, with the *Boundary Trail* at 1.1 mi. (The *Boundary Trail* is described separately below.) Continue ahead and ascend a narrow ridge, pass under a power line with excellent views at 1.3 mi, and descend slightly. The lake can easily be seen in this area in the wintertime. At 1.5 mi is a trail jct. The *Big Pine Trail* descends L 0.2 mi to a sharp curve in the access road for its terminus at 1.7 mi. The R trail descends 0.2 mi to Meadow Camping Area. (Ahead for 0.2 mi is a spur trail to a rocky area that has an outstanding view of the Bluestone River and the New River convergence. Backtrack to the jct.)

Across the road from the E terminus of the *Big Pine Trail*, begin the E trailhead of the *Riverview Trail*. Cross the road guardrails and follow the blue-blazed trail downstream. At 0.2 mi is a waterfall and in a few yd is a jct with a spur trail, R, that ascends to the access road. Ahead, a section of the trail may be underwater or overgrown. If so, continue on the access road. Pass the campground and reach an old road W of the swimming pool at 1.1 mi. Here the trail ascends for 0.5 mi to a jct with the *Big Pine Trail*. Or hike 0.2 mi on the access road, L, to the point of origin.

Boundary Trail

LENGTH: 1.9 mi

DIFFICULTY: moderate

FEATURES: wildlife, scenic

TRAILHEAD AND DETAILS: In the cabin area, walk in at the cabin #17 entrance but follow the trail sign, R, around the cabin and ascend the ridge. At 0.3 mi pass an open area with a view of the Gib Lilly canyon. Descend on two switchbacks to a stream (which may be dry in the summer) and the park boundary at 0.6 mi. Area has filbert, locust, ash, maple, poplar, ragwort, squirrel cups, and wild rose. At 1.2 mi ascend on a ridge before turning L to flank a deep, open forest cove. Descend on two switchbacks and reach a jct with *Big Pine Trail* at 1.9 mi. One exit option is to turn L on the *Big Pine Trail* and follow it E for 0.6 mi to the main access road, 0.2 mi SW of the park headquarters.

CACAPON RESORT STATE PARK (Morgan County)

Cacapon Resort State Park (ka-KAY-pun) is among the oldest of the state's parks; it opened on July 1, 1937. Its 6,115 acres are mainly on the E side of Cacapon Mtn, stretching from the Virginia state line to within sight of the Potomac River and the state of Maryland. At the widest point are rolling hills and a valley between the communities of Omps and Ridge W of US-522. Although the park has retained its old and rustic charm with facilities constructed of native stone and timber in the Old Inn, it also has the most modern of conveniences in its 50-room lodge overlooking the 18-hole championship golf course. Other facilities are 30 cabins; restaurant (suitable for a banquet); snack bar and gift shop; a lake for swimming, boat rentals, and a sandy beach; picnic areas; courts for tennis and volleyball; children's playground; clubhouse; and riding stables. Fishing is allowed in the lakes, but a license is required. There are six color-coded hiking trails, some of which overlap to form loops and have multiple-color blazes. A separate trail is near the lodge. It is *Piney Ridge Trail*, a 1.0-mi self-guiding nature loop. A printed trail guide is available from the park office. Hikers will pass through a pine and oak/hickory forest. Access to the lodge parking area is off North Fork Cabin area, R. Hikers may not camp in the park, but hikers who wish to rent a horse and arrange a guide from the stable master may camp overnight on the ridge top of Cacapon Mtn. (*USGS Maps:* Ridge, Great Cacapon)

ADDRESS AND ACCESS: Cacapon Resort State Park, Rte 1, Box 304, Berkeley Springs, WV 25411; 304-258-1022. From Berkeley Springs S it is 8.5 mi, R, on US-522, and from Ridge N it is 2.8 mi, L, on US-522.

Ziler Trail (2.3 mi)

CONNECTING TRAILS:
> *Cabin Loop Trail* (0.3 mi)
> *Laurel Trail* (1.8 mi)
> *Central Trail* (5.0 mi)
> *Ziler Loop Trail* (5.1 mi)

Total LENGTH: 14.5 mi

DIFFICULTY: moderate to strenuous

FEATURES: wildlife, wildflowers, scenic rock outcroppings

TRAILHEADS AND DETAILS: The *Ziler Trail* is the park's main through-trail from the park's lowest area to the ridge line of Cacapon Mtn, an elev change of about 1,500 ft. The four connecting trails form succession loops, each providing a distinctive and scenic view of the park's terrain. All the trails have large patches of blueberries and mtn laurel. The forest is mainly hardwoods with scattered Virginia pine. Wildflowers include bird's-foot violet, wild senna, pink lady-slipper, and pipsissewa. Deer and grouse are frequently seen.

To begin the *Ziler Trail* after entering the park, drive 0.7 mi to pass L of the golf course and L again at the fork with the picnic and tennis court signs to a parking area, L. Park near the tennis court. Cross the road to the orange-blazed *Ziler Trail,* the park's only trail that does not loop, and the green-blazed *Laurel Trail,* a jointly running trail for the first 0.9 mi. Pass cabin #25 at 0.1 mi, reach the white-blazed *Cabin Loop Trail* at 0.2 mi, and horse trails soon thereafter. Ascend and veer R at 0.5 mi to arrive at a rock outcropping. Pass through a stand of mtn laurel and reach a jct with the red-blazed *Central Trail* at 0.9 mi.

(The *Central Trail* goes R and L to form a scenic loop on the mountainside. If taking the L, go down a slope, cross the cabin road, and after 0.8 mi cross Middle Fork Indian Run. At 1.0 mi reach a jct with the blue-blazed

Ziler Loop Trail, R. Ahead it is 0.1 mi past the Batt Picnic Area and a park road that leads L for 1.3 mi back to the tennis court. After joining the *Ziler Loop Trail* ascend 0.2 mi before turning R. Go through an open forest of hardwoods, thick patches of blueberries, and mossy rock formations for another 0.9 mi to a spur trail, R, which descends to cabin #1. Continue ahead, pass a rock formation, cross the *Ziler Trail* at a resting bench at 2.1 mi, and pass another spur trail, R, which descends to cabin #10. At 3.1 mi the joint trails part. The *Central Trail* bears R and the *Ziler Loop Trail* ascends L. The *Central Trail* follows a horse trail for 0.3 mi before turning R to later cross the cabin road and the North Fork Indian Run. At 4.7 mi arrive at a jct with the *Laurel Trail.* A turn L on the *Laurel Trail* is 0.3 mi to cabin #22 where another 0.3 mi on the road to the tennis court provides a circuit of 5.3 mi. A turn R on the *Laurel Trail* ascends for 0.3 mi for a return to the *Ziler Trail* and a completion of the *Central Trail* loop at 5.0 mi.)

The *Ziler Trail* follows a partial ridge of Piney Ridge on a wide trail before beginning a steep ascent. The trail is a pioneer route over the Cacapon Mtn. Reach a jct with the *Central* and *Ziler Loop Trails* at 1.3 mi. Continue ahead and ascend steeply to the ridge top of Cacapon Mtn and a jct again at 2.3 mi with the *Ziler Loop Trail.* Backtrack or take a longer route, R or L, as described below for the *Ziler Loop Trail.*

(The blue-blazed *Ziler Loop Trail,* partially described above with the *Central Trail,* leaves the *Central Trail* 0.8 mi N of the *Ziler Trail,* ascends steeply W on a horse trail, and climbs steadily SW to the Cacapon Mtn ridge top with switchbacks and a vista bench along the way. On the ridge top turn S and pass a horse stable, R. Reach a jct with the *Ziler Trail,* L, at 2.3 mi. Descend gradually, pass a rock formation at 3.1 mi and a jct with the *Central Trail* at 3.6 mi. Turn L and reach the spur trail to cabin #1 at 4.7 mi, and return to the mountainside jct with the *Ziler Trail* for a loop of 5.1 mi.)

Ridge Trail

LENGTH: 0.9 mi

DIFFICULTY: easy

FEATURE: rock formations

TRAILHEAD AND DETAILS: From the playground parking lot near the tennis court go across a small stream toward the snack bar and turn R on the yellow-blazed *Ridge Trail.* Go upstream for 0.2 mi before turning L to ascend a moss-covered rocky area with oak and witch hazel. Reach the ridge top of Warm

Spring Ridge at 0.4 mi, curve L, pass viewing areas, descend to the bathhouse, turn L, and return to the snack bar to complete the loop at 0.9 mi.

CAMP CREEK STATE PARK (Mercer County)

About 500 acres of Camp Creek State Forest has been designated a state park. Facilities include a campground with or without electric hookups campsites, picnic area, game courts, playground, and a stream for fishing. Adjoining is the 5,300-plus-acre Camp Creek State Forest with old roads for exploratory hiking. (Visitors should inquire at the park office for a map.) Camp Creek is stocked with trout and deer roam the forest. (*USGS Map:* Odd)

ADDRESS AND ACCESS: Camp Creek State Park, Star Rte, Box 118, Camp Creek WV 25820; 304-425-9481. From US-19 and I-77, Exit 20 (16.0 mi N of Princeton), follow the signs, and go 1.8 mi on Camp Creek Rd (CO-19/5).

Farley Branch Trail

LENGTH: 2.3 mi round-trip

DIFFICULTY: moderate

TRAILHEAD AND DETAILS: Pass the service bldg and park near the picnic area on the L. Enter the forest on the L side of Farley Branch and follow through a mature forest of hardwoods and sparse conifers. Reach a small waterfall at 0.5 mi. (A spur trail goes R across the branch for 0.8 mi to the Blue Jay Camping Area at site #1.) Curve L and reach the ridge top at 0.9 mi (a fire road goes R). Continue ahead on the ridge slope in an oak forest and descend to a scenic waterfall on Mash Fork at 1.7 mi. Turn L on the forest road and walk back to the point of origin at 2.3 mi.

CANAAN VALLEY RESORT STATE PARK (Tucker County)

"A land flowing with milk and honey" (Joshua 5:6). "A wholesome family-type resort in a superb natural setting" (*New York Times*). The first statement refers to the Land of Canaan, between the Jordan River and the Mediterranean Sea, and the second quotation refers to Canaan (Ka-NAN) Valley Resort State Park, in West Virginia. Both are about a "promised land." The West Virginia "Land of Canaan" is a magnificent 5,910-acre highland plateau with facilities for year-round recreation.

Its altitude is ideal for winter sports. A main chairlift extends to a 4,280-ft summit on Cabin Mtn, where 21 slopes provide an 850-ft drop in elev for skiing. Night skiing is scheduled from Tuesday through Saturday. There is an outdoor ice rink for day and night skating, as well as trails for cross-country skiing. Among the summer sports are fishing, swimming, hiking, camping in the 34 full-service campsites, tennis, and golf on an 18-hole course (frequently visited by deer and Canada geese). The 250-room luxury lodge has a restaurant and conference rooms. There are also 23 deluxe cabins. These and other facilities and services make it one of the state's most popular parks. The park is only four hours from Richmond, Baltimore, Charleston, or Washington, DC; only three hours from Pittsburgh; and half a day from Philadelphia or Cleveland. Near the park are Blackwater Falls State Park and the scenic Dolly Sods Wilderness Area in the MNF. (*USGS-FS Maps*: Blackwater Falls, Laneville)

ADDRESS AND ACCESS: Canaan Valley Resort State Park, HC70, Box 320, Davis, WV 26260; 304-866-4121. From Davis go S on WV-32 for 12.0 mi, or from Harman go N on WV-32 for 9.0 mi.

Blackwater River Trail
LENGTH: 0.8 mi
DIFFICULTY: easy
FEATURE: wildlife

TRAILHEAD AND DETAILS: From the parking lot at the golf-course parking area follow the trail sign W through a young forest of hawthorn, then an open forest of maple, big-toothed aspen, and cherry to an old RR grade. At 0.4 mi skirt Blackwater River, where beavers are active. Unique limestone rock formations are here. Deer are likely to be seen.

Middle Ridge Trail (2.3 mi); (Allegheny Trail); Ridge Top Trail (0.1 mi)
Total LENGTH: 2.4 mi
DIFFICULTY: moderate
FEATURES: wildlife, beaver bogs, scenic

TRAILHEADS AND DETAILS: Park at Balsam Swamp Overlook, W of the lodge. Follow the yellow-blazed *Middle Ridge Trail* for 0.2 mi to where the trail forks for a loop. Turn R through a beautiful forest of hemlock, cherry, black and yellow birch, and maple on an old tram road. At 1.1 mi are open bogs and a jct with the *Allegheny Trail* R and L. (The *Allegheny Trail* [listed as *Blackwater Canaan Trail* by the park] goes R 5.9 mi to the boundary of Blackwater State Park. Turn L on the *Middle Ridge Trail*, ascend a knob, and descend to a jct with white-blazed *Ridge Top Trail*, R. (It connects with red-

Marsh boardwalk on Abe Run Trail.

blazed *Club Run Trail* [which may be closed] for a loop to the cabin area.)
Continue on the *Middle Ridge Trail* by staying L, but turn R at the completion of the loop to exit at the parking area.

Bald Knob Trail

LENGTH: 2.3 mi
DIFFICULTY: strenuous (950-ft elev change)
FEATURE: Bald Knob
TRAILHEAD AND DETAILS: Drive to the parking lot at the ski area. Ridge the ski lift to the top of Cabin Mtn and begin into a forest of spruce N of Weiss Knob. Descend on a rocky trail for 0.3 mi to a gas pipeline swath. Turn L and follow an open area to a wet saddle of ferns and wildflowers. Ascend to panoramic Bald Knob (4,308 ft) for views of Canaan Valley at 1.1 mi. In mid-August the mountain is blue with blueberries. Return to the parking lot by descending W on the steep but scenic *Bald Knob Trail* for a round-trip hike of 2.3 mi.

Deer Run Trail (1.3 mi); Abe Run Trail (0.6 mi); Mill Run Trail (0.6 mi); Loop Trail (0.9 mi)

LENGTH: 3.8 mi round-trip, combined
DIFFICULTY: easy
FEATURE: nature study
TRAILHEADS AND DETAILS: After entering the park, turn R at the first road and park at the park headquarters. You will see woodchucks on the wide, manicured road borders. Walk W across the campground entrance road and follow the sign into a lush forest. The orange-blazed interpretive trail has red spruce, hemlock, birch, beech, oak, rhododendron, club mosses, maple, oak, black locust, white ash, yellow iris (*Iris pseudacorus*), and ferns. Cross a boardwalk on Abe Run and parallel the park entrance road. Curve R, leave the roadside, and at 0.6 mi reach a jct with blue-blazed *Abe Run Trail*, R. Continue ahead and meet a jct with *Mill Run Trail*, R, at 0.9 mi. Stay on *Deer Run Trail*, ahead, to trail's end at the swimming pool and tennis courts. Backtrack, and follow *Mill Run Trail*, L. After 0.3 mi there is a side path to a former beaver pond. In a damp forest is a jct with *Abe Run Trail* at 0.6 mi that goes R and L. (To the R it goes to *Deer Run Trail*.) Turn L and follow *Abe Run Trail* to a scenic boardwalk over a marsh. After 0.1 mi is a jct with the *Deer Run Trail*; turn L. Go 0.1 mi to the campground entrance road and sign. From here go to the Nature Center and Ski Touring Center. Follow

the red-blazed *Loop Trail*, at first through a meadow and then around the campground, to rejoin the *Deer Run Trail*.

CARNIFEX FERRY BATTLEFIELD STATE PARK
(Nicholas County)

This historic site of 156 acres has areas mainly for picnicking, hiking, and the study of the Civil War. Scenic, peaceful, and manicured, it even has deer grazing on its fields. It was at this mtn top, Camp Gauley, that on Sept 10, 1861, troops led by Union Brig Gen W. S. Rosecrans engaged the Confederate troops and forced them to evacuate their entrenched positions. The Confederate commander, Brig Gen John B. Floyd, retreated with his 2,000-man force across the Gauley River and E to Meadow Bluff. In the skirmish, the Patterson house, now a museum, was in the line of artillery and musket fire. (*USGS Map*: Summersville Dam)

ADDRESS AND ACCESS: Carnifex Ferry Battlefield State Park, Rt 2, Box 435, Summersville, WV 26651; 304-872-0825. For an E entrance from the jct of US-19 and WV-129 (S of Summersville), go 5.1 mi on WV-129, and turn L on Carnifex Ferry Rd (CO-23) for 0.8 mi. For a W entrance turn on WV-129 from US-33 in Drennen for 5.9 mi.

Carnifex Ferry Trail (1.2 mi); Patterson Trail (2.0 mi); Pierson Hollow Trail (0.8 mi); Fisherman's Trail (0.6 mi)

Total LENGTH: 7.2 mi round-trip, combined

DIFFICULTY: moderate to strenuous

FEATURES: history, scenic overlooks, and forests

TRAILHEADS AND DETAILS: All trailheads and trail intersections are clearly marked with signs. The *Patterson Trail* forms a loop around the park, and all other trails branch from it. It passes through a mixed hardwood forest and features three overlooks of the Gauley River. It is accessible from three points. One is at either side of the road at the Patterson House Museum; another is at either side of the gravel road, one-quarter of a mile W of the picnic area entrance gate, and another is at the main overlook near the historic marker at the picnic area. There are parking areas at each of these access points. The most popular section is the 0.8-mi section starting immediately across the road or E from the museum and ending at the main overlook at the picnic area. The three overlooks of the Gauley River are located along this section.

To reach the *Pierson Hollow Trail,* walk 0.2 mi E on the *Patterson Trail* immediately across the road from the museum. A significant feature of the *Pierson Hollow Trail* is the superb forest of virgin hemlock, oak, and tulip poplar trees. Rhododendron, mtn laurel, and rock formations flank the trail. The trail ends at the Gauley River. Backtrack.

Fisherman's Trail branches off from the *Patterson Trail* 0.1 mi N or to the L of the main overlook at the picnic area. It is an exceptionally steep and rocky descent to Pillow Rapids of the Gauley River. Backtrack.

By following the *Patterson Trail* to the R, S of the main overlook and past picnic shelter #3, the old *Carnifex Ferry Rd* (Trail) can be reached in 0.2 mi. This trail descends gradually along the route Confederate Gen Floyd used for his troops to slip away from Rosecrans's forces after midnight and during the early morning hours of Sept 11, 1861. At 0.9 mi pass a large rock formation on the R that echoes the sounds of the Gauley River, and at 1.2 mi reach the riverbanks where Gen Floyd crossed to the mouth of the Meadow River. It was here the Confederate general destroyed the footbridge and flatboats behind him. As a result of this retreat, the Kanawha Valley was free and the statehood movement enhanced. Backtrack.

CATHEDRAL STATE PARK (Preston County)

One mile E of the historic town of Aurora (1787) is the only large stand of mixed virgin timber left in the state. The stands of hemlock are estimated to be 350 years old, many over 100 ft high and towering like cathedral spires. The largest hemlock in the state (123 ft high, 21.6 ft in circumference, and 66 ft in limb spread) is behind the park headquarters bldg. Purchased by the state in 1942 from Brandon Haas, who had protected the virgin woods, the 133-acre preserve was entered into the National Registry of National Historic Landmarks in 1966. In 1983, the Society of American Foresters recognized the park in the National Areas Program. Among the park slogans are "dedicated to scientific and education purposes...a better understanding of man's environment." Facilities include picnicking, with grates and shelters; camping is not allowed. (*USGS Map:* Aurora)

ADDRESS AND ACCESS: Cathedral State Park, Rte 1, Box 370, Aurora, WV 26705; 304-735-3771. From the jct of WV-24 and US-50, go W on US-50 for 0.5 mi; from Aurora on US-50 go E 1.0 mi.

Cathedral Trail (1.3 mi); Giant Hemlock Trail (0.2 mi); Partridge Berry Trail (0.2 mi); Trillium Trail (0.1 mi); Wood Thrush Trail (0.5 mi)

LENGTH: 2.3 mi round-trip, combined

DIFFICULTY: easy

FEATURES: virgin forest, Rhine Creek

TRAILHEADS AND DETAILS: (It is suggested that you allow time to linger on these trails.) From the parking area follow the trail signs, first on the *Cathedral Trail,* which makes two loops in the forest, and on any of the other trails for connections and loops. The 0.1-mi *Trillium Trail* is usually backtracked. More than 175 species of vascular plants have been identified, including nine fern and 50 wildflower species. Rhododendron is common along Rhine Creek. The *Wood Thrush Trail* loops across US-50 on its return to the parking area.

CEDAR CREEK STATE PARK (Gilmer County)

In one of the Cedar Creek bends is a 2,443 acre park with fine recreational facilities, shale outcrops, tributaries flowing through forested glens, and a tranquil environment. It is Cedar Creek State Park, with facilities that include 48 campsites (most with water and electrical hookups), laundromat, swimming pool, tennis courts, picnic area with shelters, bathhouses, and playground. Fishing (bass and muskellunge) and hiking are other recreational activities. (*USGS Maps:* Glenville, Cedarville)

ADDRESS AND ACCESS: Cedar Creek State Park, Rte 1, Box 9, Glenville, WV 26351; 304-462-7158. From Glenville drive S on US-119/33 for 3.1 mi and turn L on Cedar Creek Rd CO-17) for 3.0 mi. From Cedarville drive NW on Cedar Creek Rd CO-17) for 7.0 mi. (From I-79, Exit 79, go W on WV-5 to Glenville.)

Stone Trough Trail (2.5 mi); Two Run Trail (2.2 mi); North Boundary Trail (1.0 mi)

LENGTH: 6.5 mi round-trip, combined

DIFFICULTY: moderate

FEATURES: history, wildlife

TRAILHEADS AND DETAILS: After crossing the Cedar Creek Bridge turn R at the fork and drive to the parking area nearest campsites #7 and #8. Follow the red-blazed *Stone Trough Trail* upstream along Long Lick Run in a hardwood forest. Papaw, redbud, and dogwood are part of the understory. At 0.8 mi reach a jct with the white-blazed *Two Run Trail,* R. Bear L, pass ruins of an old farmhouse (an old cream separator is a historic reminder), ascend steeply, and reach a unique, hand-chiseled stone watering trough at 1.0 mi. Piped water constantly runs in the trough. Reach the ridge crest at 1.2 mi, veer R at 1.4 mi, and begin a descent. After switchbacks in a rocky area, return to the campground road, turn L, and return to the point of origin at 2.5 mi.

The *Two Run Trail* also begins at the Long Lick Run but branches R and parallels the campground road for 0.2 mi before curving around the ridge to Two Run. Follow upstream to a jct with *North Boundary Trail*, R, at 0.7 mi. Ragwort and other spring flowers are prominent. Deer are likely to be seen. (*North Boundary Trail* ascends to the park boundary in a rocky area, curves L, and descends to rejoin the *Two Run Trail* after 1.0 mi.) Continue upstream on the N side of the ridge and reach a jct with *North Boundary Trail* at 1.3 mi. Turn L, ascend to the ridge top on an old woods road in an oak forest. Descend to the jct with the *Stone Trough Trail* at 2.2 mi. Deer, grouse, and chipmunk are often seen on this trail. Turn L and follow the *Stone Trough Trail* downstream to the campground for a total of 3.0 mi, or 3.5 mi if the *North Boundary Trail* is included.

Park View Trail (1.7 mi); Fisherman's Trail (0.9 mi)

LENGTH: 2.6 mi round-trip, combined
DIFFICULTY: moderate
FEATURES: overlook, Cedar Creek
TRAILHEADS AND DETAILS: Park at the athletic field and hike E at the curve of Cedar Creek Rd. Ascend steeply in a hardwood forest to an overlook of the park and the Cedar Creek area at 0.3 mi. After a long, rugged L curve over the ridge with a number of good views, descend to Cedar Creek Rd at 1.7 mi. Cross the road and hike upstream on *Fisherman's Trail* to the athletic field and point of beginning at 2.6 mi.

CHIEF LOGAN STATE PARK (Logan County)

Before development, the park area was an abandoned coal field and camp. Now it is a popular day-use park of 3,305 acres. It is known mainly for the summer outdoor drama *The Aracoma Story*, the tragic love story of Princess Aracoma, daughter of Indian Chief Cornstalk, and an English scout, Boling Baker. Each summer the park amphitheater also hosts one additional drama along with *The Aracoma Story*. It is also a popular park because of its large restaurant with a dining hall able to provide superb cuisine for parties, proms, and public events. Other facilities are a 280,000-gallon swimming pool and bathhouse, 75 acres of large picnic areas with shelters, miniature golf course, game courts, amphitheater, tennis courts, physical fitness course, and trails for nature study.

The three most recent trails are the *Self-Guiding Interpretive Trail,* an easy 1.0-mi nature study with interpretive pamphlets keyed to trees on the trail. The trailhead is at the lake parking lot. Another nature trail is the 1.1-mi *Guyandotte Beauty Trail.* On a moderately difficult route the trail features the rare and endangered wildflower species Guyandotte beauty (*Synandra hipudula*), which blooms in May. On this trail is an abandoned coal mine fan hole used for ventilation in the mines. Access is at the head of Mud Lick Hollow, which is the first paved road to the L in the main picnic ground; it ends at picnic shelter #4. A third educational trail is *Coal Mine Trail.* A moderately difficult 1.0-mi walk, it features a tram road that passes old mine openings and a tipple site. Access to the trail is behind campsite #2 in the campground. (Because of steep drops, children should not take this trail unsupervised.)

In addition to these trails and others described below are such facilities as a 25-site campground open year-round. The campground accommodates tents and campers, offering water, electricity, and sewage hookups. One of the most recent additions is riding stables that include pony rides for children. Also added is the beautiful Wildlife Exhibit, featuring some wildlife in a zoo environment. The new Chief Logan Lake was completed in 1996, and near the restaurant is an old steam locomotive, a gift from the C&O Railway Company as a monument to coal mining and railroads. (For information on *The Aracoma Story,* contact PO Box 2016, Logan, WV 25601; 304-752-0253.) (*USGS Maps*: Henlawson, Chapmanville)

ADDRESS AND ACCESS: Chief Logan State Park, Logan, WV 25601; 304-792-7127. For entrance to the park drive 3.0 mi N of Logan on WV-10 along the Guyandotte River to the park, L. From Charleston take US-119 to Chapmanville. Turn L on Mitchell Heights Rd.

Lake Shore Trail (0.8 mi); Backbone Trail (2.2 mi); Cliffside Trail (0.6 mi); Buffalo Trail (1.4 mi); Nature Trail (1.0 mi)
LENGTH: 6.0 mi combined
DIFFICULTY: easy to strenuous
FEATURES: wildlife, nature study

TRAILHEADS AND DETAILS: After entering the park go 0.9 mi, turn R at the activities building, and go N for 1.0 mi, R, to a parking area near the dam of a small lake. The *Lake Shore Trail* begins L of the Wolfpen Hollow stream and the *Nature Trail* begins on the R. If taking the *Lake Shore Trail,* follow the service road, pass the lake, cross a meadow L of a gas well, and enter a hardwood forest of large beech, oak, and maple. Circle the hollow on a foot trail and reach a jct with the *Nature Trail,* R, and the *Backbone Trail;* ascend steeply on a graded treadway of the N slope with seven switchbacks for 1.0 mi to the ridge top. At the crest are large oak and hickory. Along the way, in a deciduous forest, are banks of Christmas fern and numerous species of wildflowers. Descend from the ridge on the S side, pass under a power line and reach a jct, R, with the *Cliffside Trail* on the mtn slope, cross under a power line, pass R of a cave and rock overhang, and reach a jct, R, with the *Buffalo Trail* at 3.6 mi. (An access point is L to a picnic and parking area on the main road.) Ascend on the wide *Buffalo Trail* among poplar, oak, and beech. Reach a jct with the *Nature Trail* and the end of the *Buffalo Trail* at 5.0 mi. (A spur trail goes 0.1 mi L to the point of beginning.) Follow the *Nature Trail* for 0.5 mi by the lake to the point of beginning for a loop of 6.0 mi. All of these trails have many wildflowers. Among them are putty-root (*Aplectrum hyemale*), sweet cicely (*Osmorhiza longistylis*), Greek valerian (*Polemonium reptans*), wood betony, asters, and jewelweed.

Woodpecker Trail (1.5 mi); Chief Logan Fitness Trail (1.0 mi)

LENGTH: 2.5 mi combined

DIFFICULTY: easy

FEATURES: nature study, physical fitness

TRAILHEADS AND DETAILS: From the park entrance drive 0.7 mi to a parking area, R, and the sign of the *Woodpecker Trail,* L. Hike across Buffalo Creek on a footbridge, turn R, and go upstream. The forest has yellow buckeye, beech, sycamore, oak, birch, poplar, place locust, elm, and papaw. Cross six small drains (often dry in the summer and fall), parallel an old RR grade part of the way, and reach the trail terminus at 1.5 mi. Backtrack or turn R, then L, to cross Buffalo Creek on an old RR grade trestle. Cross the picnic field to the paved road, turn R, and follow the paved road back to the point of origin for a loop of 2.5 mi. Another choice after crossing the creek is to follow the Vita-Course fitness trail. It is an easy treadway of 15 exercise posts that form a loop; it has its beginning across the road from the C&O steam locomotive.

DROOP MOUNTAIN BATTLEFIELD STATE PARK
(Pocahontas County)

On Nov 6, 1863, Union troops commanded by Gen W. W. Averell defeated Confederate forces under Gen John Echols on Droop Mtn, a high plateau on a ridge W of the Greenbrier River. It was the state's largest battle engagement of the Civil War. In 1929 the area was made a park; it now has 287 acres with picnic areas, a museum with Civil War artifacts, a playground, a lookout tower, and hiking trails. It is a day-use facility and camping is not allowed.

ADDRESS AND ACCESS: Superintendent, Droop Mtn Battlefield State Park, HC 64, Box 189, Hillsboro, WV 24946; 304-653-4254. On US-219, 27.0 mi N of Lewisburg and 15.0 mi S from Marlinton, enter the main gate, W.

Cranberry Trail (0.7 mi); Old Musket Trail (0.5 mi); Tower Trail (0.5 mi); Horse Heaven Trail (0.3 mi); Overlook Trail (0.4 mi); Big Spring Trail (0.3 mi); Minnie Ball Trail (0.2 mi); Old Soldier Trail (0.7 mi)

LENGTH: 3.9 mi round-trip, combined

DIFFICULTY: easy to moderate

FEATURES: history, battlefield, scenic overlooks

TRAILHEADS AND DETAILS: All trails can be connected as loops except *Big Spring Trail*. After entering the park, follow the main road to the park headquarters and parking lot. Follow the trail sign across the road to the *Cranberry Trail*. After a few yd the *Old Musket Trail* goes L (for 0.4 mi to a gravel road), and after another few yd the *Tower Trail* goes L (for 0.5 mi to Lookout Tower). Turn R at a stone shed and rejoin the *Cranberry Trail* at 0.5 mi. (It is 0.2 mi R back to the parking area.) Pass near a cranberry bog in a forest of hardwoods, white pine, mtn laurel, and patches of wintergreen. Cross *Old Soldier Trail*. (It goes R to the main road, S of the museum to the battlefield monuments, and L [NE] to the stone shed near the lookout tower. It passes the spot where Maj Robert Augustus Bailey was shot while trying to rally his men around the Confederate flag.) Here the *Big Spring Trail* descends steeply to a pure mtn spring. Backtrack. Continue ahead and pass Civil War entrenchments to Caesars Mtn Rd. Turn R on the road and return to the parking area. From here, E, downhill and parallel to the gravel road, is the short *Minnie Ball Trail*.

GREENBRIER RIVER TRAIL
(Greenbrier and Pocahontas Counties)

The 950-acre *Greenbrier River Trail* is part of the state's park system, though supervised and maintained by the state's Division of Natural Resources. Often referred to as the "nation's longest state park," it is a narrow (generally 100 ft wide), 75-mi corridor that was formerly the Chesapeake & Ohio Railroad from North Caldwell to Cass. Consistently winding with the banks of the Greenbrier River, it crosses more than 35 bridges, some of which are historically significant, and twice tunnels the mtns to avoid long, horseshoe-shaped curves. It passes tranquil rural communities, pastureland, and groves of flowering plants, and often hugs the slate and sandstone canyon walls. Wildlife are frequently seen on its pathway and along the riverside. Its elev change is approximately 10 ft for each mile.

Motorized traffic is not allowed. In a continuous process of development, the park is used for hiking and backpacking, bicycling, and cross-country skiing. It is also used by bird-watchers and by fishermen as an access route to the river. The Nov 4, 1985, flood damaged trail sections for nearly 30 mi, but the damage was repaired. There was severe flood damage again in the winter and June of 1996. Bicyclists and hikers should contact the address below for current conditions.

Camping is allowed at designated sites as indicated in the trail description below, but for through-hikers staying overnight, camping is permitted within 50 ft of the center of the trail on either side. Campsites must be off the trail and out of sight of road crossings. Care should be used not to park or hike on adjoining private property. At each jct is a trail marker with printed rules and regulations for trail use. Because clean water is rare, hikers should purify all drinking water. Lotions or proper clothing should be used to prevent sunburn on the exposed long sections of the trail. (*USGS-FS Maps*: Lewisburg, White Sulphur Springs, Anthony, Droop, Denmar, Hillsboro, Marlinton, Edray, Clover Lick, Cass)

INFORMATION: Greenbrier River Trail, Watoga State Park, Marlinton, WV 24954; 304-799-4087. Greenbrier River Hike, Bike, and Ski Trail, Inc., PO Box 828, Lewisburg, WV 24901; 304-572-3771.

Greenbrier River Trail

LENGTH: 75.2 mi

DIFFICULTY: easy to moderate

FEATURES: RR history, scenic, wildlife, botanical study, remote

TRAILHEAD AND DETAILS: The following list of mile points, access points, points of interest, and other descriptions is to assist hikers in making plans for short or long treks. The usual highway map may be sufficient for some hikers. Otherwise, a county map provides complete details for the roads, houses, and landmarks. Topo map names are listed above. Some of the C&O mileposts are missing, and others are inconsistently placed. The S terminus of the trail begins at approximately 3.6 mi from the main line in Whitcomb, thus the first C&O milepost, #6, is 2.4 mi on the trail mile point. Access points explain exits to major highways and what facilities are available in the vicinity.

Greenbrier River Trail

MILE POINT		LOCATION AND DESCRIPTION
From S	**From N**	**From North Caldwell to Hooper (2.4 mi)**
0.0	75.2	On Stone House Rd (CO-38), 1.4 mi from US-60 in North Caldwell. First entrance: C&O Railroad crossing
0.1	75.1	Second entrance: Stone House Rd
0.3	74.9	Third entrance: Camp Allegheny Rd (CO-38/1) extends E across the Greenbrier River. Trail banks have ferns, ragwort, wild geranium, pinxter, and bloodroot.
1.1	74.1	S end of islands
1.4	73.8	N end of islands
1.9	73.3	Cottages W and small stream
		From Hooper to Keister (5.3 mi)
2.4	72.8	Access point: Hooper community, cottages W. C&O milepost #6. Harper Rd CO-30/3), 4.8 mi out to US-219
2.8	72.4	Cottage E, on island. Trail banks have trillium, twayblade, soapwort, yellow buckeye, stonecrop.
3.7	71.5	C&O milepost #7
4.3	70.9	Cottages W, cross bridge over small stream
4.7	70.5	C&O milepost #8, waterfall W

MILE POINT		LOCATION AND DESCRIPTION
From S	**From N**	
5.4	69.8	Private road crossing
5.7	69.5	C&O milepost #9; spring W; river islands; sycamore, maple, birch, and poplar near river edge
5.8	69.4	Cottages E, close to the river
6.0	69.2	Private road crossing to cottages. Border of redbud on the trail. *Trillium grandiflorum*, wild ginger, columbine on the rocky banks.
6.7	68.5	C&O milepost #10
7.0	68.2	Private gazebo E
7.2	68.0	Log house E. Telephone Pioneers of America have installed bluebird houses. High slope W.
7.5	67.7	Road crossing to private home E, pastures W
		From Keister to Anthony (3.2 mi)
7.7	67.5	Access point: Keister, houses E and W. C&O milepost #11. Road crossing, Keister Rd (CO-30), 2.2 mi out to Alum Springs, and 3.1 mi farther on Benedict Lane (CO-219/19) to US-219 near the Greenbrier Valley Airport.
8.5	66.7	N end of houses E
8.6	66.6	Cross bridge over small stream
9.2	66.0	River is wide; small cascades W; large beds of wild pink on embankment W
9.5	65.7	C&O milepost #13
9.6	65.6	Private campground
10.2	65.0	C&O milepost #14
10.4	64.8	Cross bridge over small stream
10.7	64.5	Houses W and E, cross private road

MILE POINT		LOCATION AND DESCRIPTION
From S	**From N**	**From Anthony to Spring Creek (7.4 mi)**
10.9	64.3	Access point: Community of Anthony. Anthony Station Rd (CO-21/2), E, is over bridge of the Greenbrier River and to White Sulphur District of the MNF, where camping is allowed by the river on *Anthony Creek Trail*. West is 4.0 mi to US-219 in town of Frankford, W on Anthony Station Rd for 0.3 mi is Anthony General Store, groceries, camping, and fishing supplies; 304-497-2508. Post office.
11.2	64.0	Old bridge foundation. Telephone Pioneers of America have installed bluebird houses.
11.3	63.9	Rhododendron grove
11.6	63.6	C&O milepost #15
11.9	63.3	Views of Greenbrier Youth Camp and river islands. Steep slope W.
12.7	62.5	C&O milepost #16
12.8	62.4	Community of Woodman, cottages E
12.9	62.3	Remnants of old railroad trestle
13.4	61.8	Spring W, near old logging road
14.0	61.2	Old path W
14.1	61.1	Flat area of river bend, potential camping in 0.2 mi of MNF, White Sulphur District, E
14.4	60.8	South edge of horseshoe bend in the river. High peak E
14.8	60.4	Rock formations W
15.9	59.3	Cross two small bridges
16.5	58.7	North edge of horseshoe bend in the river. High peak E.
		From Spring Creek to Renick (3.3 mi)
18.3	56.9	Access point: Community of Spring Creek and Spring Creek Station Rd (CO-13);

MILE POINT		LOCATION AND DESCRIPTION
From S	**From N**	
		W goes 2.0 mi out to US-219 and N 3.1 mi to US-219 in Falling Spring.
18.4	56.8	Cross steel bridge (built by Bethlehem Steel Co. in 1929) over Spring Creek
18.7	56.5	Large grassy meadows E to river
19.5	55.7	Meadows E and W, grassy hillsides W
20.7	54.5	Small limestone cave W
20.9	54.3	Geological survey marker

From Renick/Falling Spring to Horrock (4.8 mi)

21.6	53.6	Access point: Community of Falling Spring (Renick PO), old RR station. Cross Auto Rd (CO-11), W is 0.4 mi to US-219 and grocery store, gasoline, telephone. East goes across the Greenbrier River to Peach Orchard Rd (FR-296) in the White Sulphur District of the MNF.
22.3	52.9	Road crossing
23.0	52.2	Railroad grade is close to the river. Islands E. Civil War route for supplies to Droop Mtn from Virginia through Alvon on WV-92.
24.3	50.9	Cross bridge over small stream
24.8	50.4	Wide lowland E
26.0	49.2	Islands in the rive

From Horrock to Denmar (9.4 mi)

26.4	48.8	Access point: Community of Horrock, cross bridge over small stream. Rorer Rd (CO-7/2) is W for 0.4 mi to a jct with Julia Rd (CO-7/1), L to Brownstone Rd (CO-7), R for 1.4 mi to US-219.
27.4	47.8	Old house W; cross bridge over small stream. Rorer community E.

MILE POINT		LOCATION AND DESCRIPTION
From S	**From N**	
27.6	47.6	South entrance of 430-ft Droop Mtn Tunnel; creosote boards on S entrance; some falling rocks. N entrance has C&O milepost #31.
28.7	46.5	C&O milepost #32
29.7	45.5	C&O milepost #33
30.6	44.6	C&O milepost #34, low river rapids nearby
31.6	43.6	C&O milepost #35
32.1	43.1	Boundary of Greenbrier (S) and Pocahontas (N) Counties. Unmarked ford of river to remote *Spice Ridge Trail* in White Sulphur District, MNF (see section 1).
32.6	42.6	C&O milepost #36
33.6	41.6	C&O milepost #37, W banks have array of wild bleeding heart
34.2	41.0	Steel and wood bridge over Locust Creek. Deer frequently seen here.
34.6	40.6	C&O milepost #38, W banks filled with trillium
34.8	40.4	Meadows, farm, private swinging bridge over the river
35.1	40.1	Access point: House, W; Beard Post Office Rd (CO-31/8) crossing. West for 0.3 mi to Denmar Rd (CO-31), R for 4.9 mi on CO-31 to Hillsboro on US-219.

From Denmar to Seebert (6.4 mi)

35.8	39.4	Access point: Denmar. Access W on Denmar Station Rd (CO-31/7) through Denmar Correctional Center grounds for 0.3 mi to Denmar Rd (CO-31). Right for 4.3 mi to Hillsboro on US-219. East is the fording of the river for connection to the mouth of Laurel Run, the dividing line between the Calvin Price State Forest (S) and the Watoga State Park (N).

MILE POINT		LOCATION AND DESCRIPTION
From S	**From N**	
37.4	37.8	Cross bridge over Mill Run, rows of river birch and purple-flowering raspberry
38.1	37.1	Cross bridge over stream at Burnsides, flat area across the river
38.6	36.6	Excellent view NE of the lookout tower in Watoga State Park
39.3	35.9	Cross road of farm entrance
39.4	35.8	C&O milepost #43
40.1	35.1	Watoga State Park Campground on the other side of the river
40.4	34.8	C&O milepost #44. At low water, the river can be waded here to the campground for fee campsites, showers, restroom, laundry.
41.3	33.9	C&O milepost #45
41.6	33.6	Private homes in Seebert W and E

From Seebert to Buckeye (6.0 mi)

42.2	33.0	Access point: Seebert River Rd (CO-27/3). Right, across the bridge, is Watoga State Park. Numerous facilities (see below). Left in Seebert are groceries, bicycle rentals, and fishing supplies. West on Seebert Rd it is 2.0 mi to US-219, between Hillsboro and Mill point.
42.3	32.9	C&O milepost #46, grove of yellow buckeye
42.6	32.6	Cross Stamping Creek bridge
43.2	32.0	Cross bridge over Stevens Hole Run and Seebert Rd (CO-27); C&O milepost #47
43.3	31.9	Locked gate to exclude motorized vehicles

MILE POINT		LOCATION AND DESCRIPTION
From S	**From N**	
44.0	31.2	Scenic Watoga Bridge crossing of the Greenbrier River. Some of the material made in 1899, constructed in 1925. C&O milepost #48
44.3	30.9	Whistle point
45.1	30.1	C&O milepost #49
45.4	29.8	Cross Beaver Creek bridge in Violet. Islands W. Campsite 100 yds N of bridge.
46.1	29.1	C&O milepost #50; white cedar, yellow buckeye, and ninebark
46.3	28.9	Cross bridge over Griffin Run/Improvement Lick Run
47.0	28.2	C&O milepost #51; viper's bugloss, New Jersey tea (*Ceanothus americanus*), St John's wort
48.0	27.2	Gated to exclude motorized vehicles; farms E

From Buckeye to Marlinton (3.7 mi)

48.2	27.0	Access point: Buckeye Station Rd (CO-219/15) 0.5 mi W across the river on a bridge to community of Buckeye and US-219 for groceries, gasoline, motel
48.9	26.3	C&O milepost #53. Canada geese frequently seen on islands.
49.9	25.3	C&O milepost #54. MNF property, R, across the road to Stillhouse Rd (CO-39/2), L, into Marlinton. Right is to FR 1002 for possible camping sites near Sunday Lick.
50.9	24.3	C&O milepost #55. Cross Stillhouse Run.
51.0	24.2	Marlinton City Park, W, camping allowed for hikers only
51.4	23.8	Water treatment plant W

MILE POINT		LOCATION AND DESCRIPTION
From S	**From N**	
51.5	23.7	Cross Knapp Creek on steel bridge built in 1924
51.8	23.4	To Ninth St and post office

**From Marlinton
to Clover Lick (14.4 mi)**

51.9	23.3	Access point: Marlinton, county seat of Pocahontas County. Restaurants, hotel, motel, grocery stores, service stations, hospital, restored RR depot; Marlinton Ranger District of MNF (304-799-4334); Pocahontas County Historical Museum (304-799-4973); Pioneer Days Festival, second weekend in July (304-799-4315).
53.3	21.9	Old RR water tower. Large stacks of RR trails, ties, cables. Trail gated to prevent motorized vehicles.
53.7	21.5	C&O milepost #58
54.6	20.6	C&O milepost #59, S edge of MNF boundary
56.4	18.8	Cross two bridges; the most N is Halfway Run. Campsites here.
56.5	18.7	Cross Thorny Creek bridge at base of Thorny Creek Mtn
57.5	17.7	C&O milepost #62
58.2	17.0	North edge of MNF boundary. Cross Thorny Creek Mtn Rd (CO-11/2), a road usually in poor condition.
58.5	16.7	C&O milepost #63
59.4	15.8	C&O milepost #64
60.4	14.8	C&O milepost #64
60.7	14.5	South edge of scenic Sharp's Trestle and Tunnel (510 ft). Cuts through a mtn ridge with a sharp horseshoe curve by the river. Most of area in MNF; camping allowed near the river S of bridge.

MILE POINT		LOCATION AND DESCRIPTION
From S	**From N**	
60.9	14.3	North edge of Sharp's Trestle and Tunnel C&O milepost #66, long straight stretch
62.1	13.1	Big Run jeep road W
62.3	12.9	C&O milepost #67, cross Big Run bridge
63.3	11.9	Across the river is Seneca State Forest
64.1	11.1	C&O milepost #69; MNF, L, and curves around Rabbit Knob
66.1	9.1	C&O milepost #71

From Clover Lick to Stony Bottom

66.3	8.9	Access point: Clover Lick community. East is old bridge (washed away in 1985 but being rebuilt) over the river on Laurel Creek Rd (CO-1/4) for 4.1 mi to WV-28, and 2.6 mi S of Dunmore. West is 10.7 mi on Back Mtn Rd (CO-1) to US-219 in Edray, 3.6 mi N of Marlinton.
66.5	8.7	Cross bridge over Clover Creek
67.1	8.1	C&O milepost #72; islands in the river, trail alongside River Rd (CO-1/19)
69.7	5.5	Cross bridge over Elklich Run

From Stony Bottom to Sitlington (1.8 mi)

69.9	5.3	Access point: Stony Bottom with motel, grocery store (304-456-4721); W on Back Mtn Rd (CO-1) it is 5.0 mi N to Cass
71.0	4.2	C&O milepost #73

From Sitlington to Cass (3.5 mi)

71.7	3.5	Access point: Sitlington Crossing. Cross Sitlington Rd (CO-12) and a jct with the *Allegheny Trail*, N and E. East over the river it is 3.1 mi to WV-28 in Dunmore. (The Greenbrier River bridge, damaged by the 1985 flood, is being restored.)

MILE POINT		LOCATION AND DESCRIPTION
From S	**From N**	
		(The *Allegheny Trail* follows Sitlington Rd for 1.1 mi before turning S on its ascent to Thomas Mtn in the Seneca State Forest.)
71.9	3.3	C&O milepost #74
72.8	2.4	C&O milepost #75. South end of original RR with ties and rails remaining.
72.9	2.3	Cross bridge over Moses Spring Creek, N boundary of Seneca State Forest
73.7	1.5	South edge of Greenbrier Ranger District, MNF, across the river
74.0	1.2	Island in the stream
74.2	1.0	Access point: Deer Creek Rd (CO-1/13) N 1.0 mi to Cass
75.2	0.0	Access point: Cass, and Cass Scenic Railroad State Park. North terminus of the Greenbrier River Trail (but the *Allegheny Trail* continues across the bridge and N to Little Mtn). East on WV-7 across the bridge it is 5.5 mi to WV-28. West through Cass to US-219 in Linwood it is 1.6 mi on Back Mtn Rd (CO-1) to Thorny Flat Rd (CO-1/3) for 7.4 mi and Linwood Rd (CO-9) for 2.4 mi. Cass has Whittaker Camping Area with hot showers and RV hookups (304-456-3218), groceries, service station, cafe, and other facilities in season (Memorial Day to Labor Day). Cass Scenic Railroad, Box 107, Cass, WV 24927; 304-456-4300.

HAWKS NEST STATE PARK (Fayette County)

There are many superlatives for the grandeur of this 276-acre park on the New River Gorge—"the Grand Canyon of the East." It has been said that Chief Justice John Marshall admired the views from here more than anywhere else in western Virginia in 1812. The year-round park has a 31-room lodge and restaurant built on the canyon rim. Other facilities are a swimming pool, tennis courts, picnic units, playground, museum with Indian and pioneer artifacts, tramway, paddle boats, jet boats, and a marina for boating and fishing. The tramway descends 446 ft in elev over the Mill Creek Canyon to the marina. The aerial descent is spectacular in itself; to see a C&O train gliding over the Hawks Nest Lake enhances the visual display. (*USGS Maps:* Ansted, Fayetteville, Beckwith)

ADDRESS AND ACCESS: Hawks Nest State Park, PO Box 857, Ansted, WV 25812; 304-658-5212. US-60 (known as Midland Trail Scenic Highway), between US-19 jct E and WV-39 W, passes through the park.

SUPPORT FACILITIES: (See Babcock State Park for campground facilities.) There are a number of private campgrounds in the area. One nearby is on US-60 E of Ansted, with full service. Open May 15–Sept 30. Patty Hill Campground, Victor, WV 25938; 304-658-4784.

Canyon Trail (0.6 mi); Fisherman Access Trail (0.5 mi); Cliffside Trail (1.6 mi); Hawks Nest Loop Trail (0.5 mi); Overlook Trail (0.1 mi)

LENGTH: 4.4 mi round-trip, combined

DIFFICULTY: easy to strenuous

FEATURES: scenic views, cliffs, wildflowers, fishing

TRAILHEADS AND DETAILS: With backtracking and looping, all of these trails can connect. From the lodge parking lot go behind the tennis courts and descend steeply on the strenuous *Canyon Trail* (also called *Governor's Summer Youth Program Canyon Trail*). Wildflowers and ferns are copious. After seven switchbacks arrive at an old road and turn R at 0.3 mi. Pass under the tram line, and reach a jct with a gravel road (CO-60/2, 1.5 mi out to Ansted) and parking lot at 0.5 mi. Here is also a boat launch at Hawks Nest Lake on the New River. Turn L to cross a bridge over Mill Creek to a picnic area and tram entrance at 0.6 mi. Backtrack or take the tram. At the boat launch, described above, the *Fisherman Access Trail* follows lakeside N 0.5 mi to the dam and Turkey Creek waterfalls. Backtrack.

Back at the lodge parking lot walk W to a picnic shelter L, and enter the woods on strenuous *Cliffside Trail*. (Park regulations require children to be accompanied by an adult on this trail.) Descend steeply to overlooks and overhangs of Nuttall sandstone. At 0.2 mi is a very large overhang and at 0.4 mi are bowl-shaped rocks carved by weathering. The New River, dam, and CSX Railroad can be seen at 0.6 mi. Curve N and pass near cascades of Turkey Creek through hemlocks and rhododendron. Ascend steeply to US-60 and turn R; watch carefully for traffic. Arrive at the parking area at 1.0

mi. To the N, across the highway, locate the picnic shelter. Follow easy *Hawks Nest Loop Trail* through an oak/hickory forest with scattered hemlock. Large patches of mandrake and Solomon's seal are in the rich damp cove. Return to the museum. Cross the highway to the parking lot to walk the easy *Overlook Trail* for more views of the New River Gorge. After the overlook walk the highway S for return to the lodge parking lot.

HOLLY RIVER STATE PARK (Webster County)

For many centuries this incomparable land of natural splendor was home for the Shawnee Indians. According to legend, Tecumseh's twin brother, Tenskwatawa, was born here. Relics of their history (including red hematite, which they used for facial decorations, found in the Laurel Fork valley) are on display in the park office. In recognition of these famous Indian leaders, two of the park's four major waterfalls have been named after them. If they returned today they would find the 8,101 acres much as they left them — rich forested mountains with deer and turkey and bobcat; trout darting in the crystal streams; a wide range of such songbirds as the indigo bunting, wood thrush, bluebird, and scarlet tanager; and an incredible paradise of vascular plants. What has been changed is the construction of nine rock-and-log cabins in an "island of rhododendron." There are 88 campsites (211 with electric hookups), a laundromat, swimming pool, picnic areas, game courts, tennis courts, playground, commissary, and restaurant (open from Memorial Day to Labor Day). Cabins are available from the last weekend in April to the fourth Monday in October. Hiking and fishing are additional attractions. There is also a primitive campground for overnight backpackers. The park has two short trails: *Red Spruce Trail* is a 0.2-mi nature trail near campsite #86 and across a sphagnum moss bog with cinnamon ferns to a stand of red spruce at Laurel Fork. The other trail, *Nature's Rock Garden Trail,* is a beautiful 0.5-mi, 25-post, self-guided interpretive trail through rocks, trees, and wildflowers. Among them are papaw, witch hazel, blue cohosh, pink lady-slipper, wild lily of the valley, yellow birch, beech, and hemlock. Some of the ferns are the wood fern, Christmas fern, and lady fern. (*USGS Maps:* Hacker Valley, Goshen)

ADDRESS AND ACCESS: Holly River State Park, PO Box 70, Hacker Valley, WV 26222; 304-493-6353. Access is 2.0 mi N from the post office in Hacker Valley and 6.3 mi S of Cleveland on WV-20.

Tramontane Trail (2.3 mi); Salt Lick Trail (1.2 mi); High Rock Trail (1.3); Oak Ridge Trail (1.8 mi); Wilderness Trail (4.0 mi); Railroad Grade Trail (1.3 mi); Reverie Trail (2.5 mi)

LENGTH: 14.4 mi round-trip, combined

DIFFICULTY: easy to strenuous

FEATURES: wildlife, wildflowers, history, waterfalls

TRAILHEADS AND DETAILS: These connecting trails are described so as to offer a number of loop options from 2.7 mi to 9.1 mi. If you are backpacking overnight at a primitive campsite, plans and permission must be arranged with the park superintendent. A central base point is at the picnic parking area near (W) the park office. Hike across the footbridge of Laurel Fork in a tall hemlock stand on the yellow-blazed *Tramontane Trail* for 125 yd to a jct with the *Salt Lick Trail,* which goes R for 0.4 mi to the campground entrance, and L for 0.8 mi to a jct with the crescent-shaped *Tramontane Trail.*

A turn L begins the shortest loop of combined trails. Follow the scenic *Salt Lick Trail* to the *Tramontane Trail,* turn L, cross the road at cabin #9, cross Laurel Fork again, and pass R of the tennis courts. Cross Pickens Rd to *High Rock Trail,* join the *Reverie Trail* near its terminus at the main park road, cross the road to the campground road, follow the campground road across Laurel Fork to the *Salt Lick Trail,* turn L, and return to the point of origin for a loop of 2.7 mi. For the second loop, continue on the *Tramontane Trail,* ascend in a deep hardwood forest with thick patches of white snakeroot, ragwort, and ground pine. At 0.9 mi arrive at a jct with the blue-blazed *Oak Ridge Trail,* R. (The *Oak Ridge Trail* follows Oak Ridge to an overlook and then descends steeply in sections to the S end of the campground for 1.8 mi.) Turn L; follow a grassy woods road to a fork at 1.2 mi; bear R; cross under a power line; pass ruins of an old homesite, a cinnamon fern patch, and wildlife food plot #9; and at 1.8 mi reach a jct with the blue-blazed *Wilderness Trail.* To the L, with the *Salt Lick Trail,* pass cabin #9, and follow the same directions given above for the 2.7-mi route, except this is a circuit of 4.1 mi.

To hike a third circuit, continue R on the *Wilderness Trail* at the jct with the *Tramontane Trail,* pass through a forest of chestnut tree skeletons and a rusty tub and bed frame from an old homesite. At 2.2 mi are huge boulders of sculpted sandstone; ascend, cross the ridge, descend, and at 2.4 mi reach a jct with a spur trail, R. (It leads 0.5 mi to a view of Tenskwatawa Falls and a gated park fire road. This was an old route of the red-blazed *Potato*

Knob Trail, but there is an easier and more desirable route described below.) At 2.7 mi the *Wilderness Trail* forks. The third and fourth loops go L and the fifth option goes R. (The R fork of the *Wilderness Trail* goes 1.2 mi to its terminus at a former fire tower site and gated fire road. On its route it crosses Crooked Fork and makes an immediate jct with the *Railroad Grade Trail,* L. The *Wilderness Trail* must be backtracked.) To the L at the *Wilderness Trail* fork, follow down Crooked Fork by caves and cascades to make a sharp R near huge cliffs at 3.3 mi. Moss and wood sorrel patches are under tall hemlocks. Squeeze through rocks at 3.5 mi. Cross a footbridge over Laurel Fork in a scenic area of cascades and pools bordered with rhododendron at 3.7 mi. At 3.8 mi the *Wilderness Trail* turns L at a jct with the *Reverie Trail.* The *Wilderness Trail* follows Laurel Fork downstream to the park cabin #1 at 4.6 mi. From here a turn L on the *Tramontane Trail* and a R on the *Salt Lick Trail* take you back to the picnic area for a loop of 5.7 mi.

The fourth loop occurs by taking the yellow-blazed *Reverie Trail* at the jct described above. Ascend, cross Park Rd (also called Pickens Rd) at 3.9 mi, ascend steeply, and reach a primitive campsite at 4.4 mi. From the natural spring begin a steep climb, cross two ridges, and pass under a power line. At 5.1 mi pass under picturesque Tecumseh Falls. Descend steeply, reach Dreamer's Meadow and the jct with *High Rock Trail,* and reach the park's main road at 6.3 mi. Cross the road to the campground road entrance and pass the check-in station. Turn L, cross Laurel Fork, and immediately turn L on the *Salt Lick Trail* to return to the point of beginning for a round trip of 7.0 mi.

The fifth loop can be arranged by taking the R fork of the *Wilderness Trail* described above and turning off L on the *Railroad Grade Trail* for 1.3 mi to a gated fire road at the jct with the gravel Park Rd (CO-10). (At this road jct and confluence of the R, middle, and L forks of the Laurel Fork, the park map may show a much larger loop of the *Railroad Grade Trail.* Hikers interested in this extension should inquire about its condition before attempting the circuit.) Turn L at the jct on the Park Rd and descend for 2.0 mi to a jct with the *Reverie Trail,* R. Follow the *Reverie Trail* as described above for a return to the point of beginning and a round trip of 9.1 mi.

Potato Knob Trail

LENGTH: 2.2 mi round-trip
DIFFICULTY: strenuous
FEATURES: scenic, waterfalls

TRAILHEAD AND DETAILS: From the park entrance drive S on WV-20 for 1.3 mi to the Holly River Rd (CO-3, also called Pickens Rd and Pickens Grade Rd). Drive upstream for 4.2 mi to a Falls sign. Parking is difficult on the main road; depending on the weather, a 4WD vehicle may be necessary to descend to the Left Fork of the Holly River. Walk down the spur road for 0.1 mi to a sign that indicates the Upper Fall is to the L. To the R for 0.3 mi is the "Chute" and the beginning of the climb to Potato Knob. There are three spurs to the Chute, all less than 75 ft from the jeep road. There is a legend that the facial image in the river rocks at the middle spur is that of a Shawnee Indian hunter who drowned in the rapids. The red-blazed *Potato Knob Trail* ascends steeply 640 ft in elev on a rocky and sometimes slippery ridge. Large rock outcroppings on the cone-shaped knob allow for spectacular views of the Holly River canyon. Rhododendron, mtn laurel, oaks, and pines cling to the precipitous slopes. Ferns and mosses mottle the rocks. Reach the summit at 0.7 mi from the base. Backtrack.

LITTLE BEAVER STATE PARK (Raleigh County)

Little Beaver State Park is a 562-acre day-use park for picnicking (with shelters), hiking, fishing, boating, and swimming. It has an 18-acre lake with a 300-ft beach, and offers rentals of paddle and row boats. Fish catches include bass, channel catfish, crappie, bluegill, and trout. (*USGS Maps:* Prince, Shady Spring)

ADDRESS AND ACCESS: Little Beaver State Park, Rte 9, Box 179, Beaver, WV 25813; 304-763-2494. From Exit 129 of I-64, go SW on CO-9 for 0.8 mi, and curve L on WV-307 for 1.3 mi to park entrance L.

Nature Ridge Trail (1.7 mi); Deer Trail (0.9 mi); Railroad Trail (1.8 mi); Beaver Creek Trail (1.7 mi)

LENGTH: 6.1 mi round-trip, combined

DIFFICULTY: easy to moderate

TRAILHEADS AND DETAILS: (Before you begin you may wish to inquire at the park office about the footbridge damaged by flood in 1996 and about an extension trail upstream from the *Beaver Creek Trail*.) Loops can be made on each trail or a combination thereof. If starting with the yellow-blazed *Nature Ridge Trail*, park near the trail sign at the entrance corner of the main parking lot. After 75 yd the trail divides for a loop. If staying L, ascend, and pass a damp area with mandrake and then an old homesite. Chipmunks may scamper across the trail. At 0.2 mi a spur trail goes L to an open field and old road. Stay R on a ridge to a jct with the white-blazed *Deer Trail* at 0.4 mi, R and L.

(The *Deer Trail* descends R 0.3 mi to its W end and a jct with the *Nature Ridge Trail* loop R and L. If you go R on the *Deer Trail* it is 0.2 mi back to the parking area for a loop of 0.9 mi. If taking the *Deer Trail* L, cross a gravel road into a field at 0.1 mi. Descend and stay R of the ball field and R of a pond at 0.5 mi. Descend into a dark forest with huge hemlocks. Cross a small stream to the trail's end and a jct with *Railroad Trail,* R and L, at 0.6 mi. If returning to the parking lot, turn L, parallel the stream among rhododendron and maple to a gravel road. Follow it for a return to a picnic shelter and a loop of 1.4 mi.)

Continue ahead on the *Nature Ridge Trail* among hardwoods and a rocky area. At 0.8 mi, 60 yd before reaching a jct with a gravel road, swing R to descend W, then N, cross *Deer Trail,* and return for a loop of 1.7 mi. At the gravel road (listed above) is the S end of *Railroad Trail.* If following it, cross the gravel road; stay R of a cemetery, but parallel the road to a stream crossing. After crossing curve L and parallel the stream to a jct with *Deer Trail* (described above) at 1.4 mi, and continue downstream to return to the parking lot for a loop of 2.5 mi.

To hike the *Beaver Creek Trail* begin at the park office and follow the E side of the lake 0.5 mi to a crossing of the paved road. (The *Beaver Creek Trail* may also have a sign for *Lake Front Trail.*) Continue upstream among white pine 0.3 mi, where a footbridge crosses Beaver Creek. Return on the W side of the lake. After crossing the paved road you may enter the *Exercise Trail,* which runs jointly with *Beaver Creek Trail.*

LOST RIVER STATE PARK (Hardy County)

This 3,712-acre historic forest park with an abundance of wildlife, wildflowers, and scenic overlooks is named for the Lost River, which disappears for three miles under Sandy Ridge near Wardensville. Formerly owned by the Lee family of Virginia, the restored cottage of Gen "Light-Horse Harry" Lee is now a museum. The area was a CCC camp in the 1930s. Facilities include nine deluxe and 15 standard cabins; restaurant; souvenir store; swimming pool; horse and hiking trails; game and tennis courts; playground and recreation building; and picnic areas. It is open from Apr 1 to Dec 15, but the deluxe cabins are open all year. A private campground adjoins the park on Dove Hollow Rd (CO-14) near the stables. (*USGS Map:* Lost River State Park)

ADDRESS AND ACCESS: Lost River State Park, Mathias, WV 26812; 304-897-5372. In Mathias turn off WV-259 on Howards Lick Run Rd (CO-12) and drive 3.8 mi to the park.

Razor Ridge Trail (1.0 mi); Laurel Trail (0.5 mi); East Ridge Trail (2.5 mi); Howards Lick Run Trail (1.2 mi); Arbutus Trail (0.7 mi); Loblolly Trail (0.8 mi); Staghorn Trail (1.0 mi); Wood Thrush Trail (0.4 mi); Red Fox Trail (0.3 mi); Light Horse Harry Lee Trail (1.3 mi); Covey Cove Trail (0.5 mi); Copse Cove Trail (1.8 mi); Lee Trail (0.5)

LENGTH: 12.5 mi combined

DIFFICULTY: easy to moderate

FEATURES: vistas, Lee's Sulphur Spring

TRAILHEADS AND DETAILS: A variety of short and long loops can be made of these well-graded, color-coded trails. Below is described a combination of trails that loop the ridges around the Cabin Run Rd for 4.5 mi. From cabin #3, at the swimming pool parking lot, begin this loop at the fork of *Razor Ridge Trail* and *Howards Lick Run Trail*. Ascend on the orange-blazed *Razor Ridge Trail* through an oak forest with an understory of buckberry and a floor of moss. At 0.6 mi is a jct R with *Laurel Trail*. (It goes R for 0.5 mi to the Cabin Run Rd.) An open shelter is at 0.9 mi; scenic view is NE. Junction with red-blazed *East Ridge Trail* at 1.0 mi. (Here a loop can be made by taking the *East Ridge Trail* L and descending to the blue-blazed *Howards Lick Run Trail* to follow it back to the swimming pool for a total of 3.3 mi.) Continue R on the *East Ridge Trail*. At 1.3 mi is a jct with the yellow-blazed *Arbutus Trail*. (It goes R for 0.7 mi to *Loblolly Trail*, a horse trail, and to a road at the employee dorm and storage area off Cabin Run Rd.) At 1.5 mi pass the blue-blazed *Staghorn Trail* R. (It descends for 1.0 mi to Cabin Run Rd near cabin #17.) On the L, at 1.7 mi, are huge anthills; a few yd farther is a vista from an open shelter. At 2.1 mi is a jct with the green-blazed *Wood Thrush Trail*. (It descends 0.3 mi to *Staghorn Trail* with an exit out to Cabin Run Rd on the *Staghorn Trail*.) At 2.4 mi is a jct with the *Red Fox Trail*, L, and the *Copse Cove Trail* ahead. The *East Ridge Trail* ends here. (The *Red Fox Trail*, a horse trail, ascends for 0.3 mi to Piney Ridge Rd.) After 0.1 mi on the *Copse Cove Trail*, turn L on the green-blazed *Covey Cove Trail* to the Piney Ridge Rd. At 2.8 mi there is a shelter on the L; turn R on the forest road through chestnut oak and scattered Virginia pine. Turn R off the road at 3.0 mi and after a few yd join the yellow-blazed *Copse Cove Trail*. (To the R it joins the *Light Horse Harry Lee Trail*, a horse trail, which follows the slope downstream to the recreation building.) Continue ahead on the *Copse Cove Trail;* descend to a jct with the orange-blazed *Lee Trail* at 3.4 mi. (The *Lee Trail* is a 0.5-mi spur jct with the *Light Horse Harry Lee Trail* and the *Copse Cove Trail* to Cabin Run Rd and cabin #8.) At 4.1 mi pass another spur, R, which leads to Cabin Run Rd, and continue ahead through a grove of hemlock to Lee's Sulphur Spring and a shelter at 4.3 mi. (Across the stream is the Lee Cabin Museum.) Follow a side trail past cabin #1 to the point of origin at the swimming pool parking lot at 4.5 mi.

White Oak Trail (1.8 mi); Miller's Rock Trail (3.7 mi); Virginia View Trail (0.5 mi); Big Ridge Trail (2.0 mi); Shingle Mill Lake Trail (1.0 mi); Branch Mountain Trail (0.3 mi)

LENGTH: 9.6 mi round-trip, combined

DIFFICULTY: moderate to strenuous

FEATURES: Cranny Crow Lookout, fire tower

TRAILHEADS AND DETAILS: Backpacking is allowed on these trails with permission and registration at the park office. Begin on orange-blazed *White Oak Trail*, a horse trail, at the stables on Dove Hollow Rd. Ascend 0.6 mi to the Firetower Truck Rd. (This road is gated at the bridge on Howards Lick Run Rd, but it is accessible for hiking to connect with all of the above trails.) Cross the road and continue ascent to an open shelter at 1.0 mi. Huckleberries, pennyroyal, goldenrod, and snakeroot are plentiful. At 1.8 mi reach a jct with *Miller's Rock Trail*. Turn R to view the park from the vista at Cranny Crow Lookout (3,250 ft). Allegheny sand myrtle (*Leiophyllum buxifolium*), sundrops (*Oenothera tetragona*), and catnip (*Nepeta cataria*) grow here. (An orange-blazed section of *Miller's Rock Trail* follows the ridge out to Cheeks Rock, S of Cranny Crow.) Along the way pass a jct with *Virginia View Trail*, L, that goes 0.5 mi NE to a jct with *Big Ridge Trail* at a picnic shelter near Firetower Truck Rd. Backtrack past the *Virginia View Trail* jct and *White Oak Trail* jct and reach the Firetower Truck Rd at 2.2 mi. Follow the road R and curve L of the picnic area to restored Mtn Farm Cabin, built in 1840 by William Tusing. Continue ahead to enter the Game Refuge Area. At 3.0 mi reach the 80-step fire tower for views of Cove Mtn and the Shenandoah Mtns in the GWNF. From here it is 0.7 mi ahead to Miller's Rock and more scenic views. Backtrack to the picnic area, enter the yellow-blazed *Big Ridge Trail*, a horse trail, near a large walnut tree R of the picnic area and reach a jct with the *Virginia View Trail*, R. After a descent of 2.0 mi reach the Truck Rd, turn R, ascend to *White Oak Trail*, turn L, and return to the stables for a round trip of 8.2 mi. Another horse trail, *Shingle Mill Lake Trail,* is accessible from the *White Oak Trail,* L and N near the stables to cross Dove Hollow Rd. It descends to the main road near a picnic shelter. On the way, at the ridge top is *Branch Mountain Trail,* R, which descends 0.3 mi to cross a small stream before rejoining *Shingles Mill Lake Trail.*

MONCOVE LAKE STATE PARK (Monroe County)

Referred to as an "outdoorsman's delight," this 895-acre tract in peaceful Sweet Springs Valley has a 144-acre lake filled with largemouth bass, bluegill, trout, and channel catfish. Built on Devil's Creek in 1959, the lake is 2,503 ft in elev. Game hunting is for deer, wild turkey, quail, and woodcock. The campground has 48 tent or trailer campsites (25 with electric hookups) with drinking water, picnic tables, grills, restrooms, and hot showers. Swimming is allowed at designated spots. Other activities are boating, hiking, and picnicking. *Moncove Lake Trail* is an easy nature-study path beginning between campsites #39 and #40 in a white pine forest to an old woods road. At 0.6 mi turn L at an old woods crossroads and enter a swamp area. At another woods road, turn L and cross a small drain at 1.0 mi. Turn sharply L off the woods road, cross the stream and return to campsite #42 for a loop of 1.2 mi. The camping season is almost year-round, but recreation facilities are open from Memorial Day to Labor Day. (*USGS Map:* Paint Bank)

> ADDRESS AND ACCESS: Moncove Lake State Park, Rte 4, Box 73A, Gap Mills, WV 24941; 304-772-3450. From Gap Mills go NE on Devil's Hollow Rd CO-8) for 5.3 mi.

NORTH BEND STATE PARK (Ritchie County)

In this tranquil resort-type park is a trail for the handicapped called "The Extra Mile," but a vacation at this 1,105-acre Eden proves the staff goes an extra mile for everyone. Deluxe vacation cabins, a lodge and restaurant, two campgrounds, a swimming pool, picnic areas, tennis and game courts, playgrounds, and hiking trails are among its facilities. Through the center of this peaceful place flows the North Fork of the Hughes River with its scenic horseshoe bend. Deer roam freely in the park. Adjoining the park, on the NW side, is *North Bend Rail Trail.* It is described below, following North Bend State Park. The park has 11 trails, the longest of which is the 4.0-mi loop *Nature Trail.* Among the short trails is *Giant Pine Trail,* a 0.6-mi loop across the road from the lodge parking area. It descends among white pine and hardwoods in an area severely damaged by wind and ice storms. At 0.2 mi buttercups grow in a damp area. Between the NE road loop of the picnic areas and the playground is 0.3-mi *Giant Tree Trail*. On an easy walkway the trail features large beech, poplar, and oaks. (*USGS Map:* Harrisville)

ADDRESS AND ACCESS: North Bend State Park, Rte 1, Box 221, Cairo WV 26337; 304-643-2931. From the W on US-50 take WV-31 near Nutter Farm (20 mi E of Parkersburg) to Cairo. Turn L on Low Gap Run Rd CO-14) and go 3.3 mi. From the E on US-50 take WV-16 at Ellenboro S to Harrisville. Go W on North Bend State Park Rd (CO-5) for 3.6 mi.

Nature Trail (4.0 mi); Hibbs Cemetery Trail (0.4 mi); Gibbons Trail (0.2 mi); Southern Railroad Trail (0.6 mi); Castle Rock Trail (1.4 mi)

LENGTH: 6.6 mi combined

DIFFICULTY: easy to strenuous

FEATURES: wildlife, botany, geology, scenery

TRAILHEADS AND DETAILS: For the *Nature Trail* begin at the trail sign and orange blaze on the N side of the park road near River Campground site #47 (between the swimming pool and the pond). At the riverside is a large oak and near the steep ascent steps are planned. After 95 yd turn R. Rock formations are L and the hillside has large poplar and beech. Descend to cross a small stream at 0.2 mi. Muddy area has deer tracks. At 0.4 mi is a large sycamore about 17 ft in circumference. Leave the riverside and ascend steps to approach two picnic shelters among oak, pine, and maple at 0.8 mi. Descend steeply, then level out to pass under a power line at 1.0 mi and where woodland sunflowers bloom in the summer. Leave the riverside by turning L and begin to ascend over the toe of a dry ridge. Reach the ridge top, descend, and arrive at Cornwallis Rd at 1.6 mi. (It is 0.5 mi L up Cornwallis Rd to the park entrance.)

Continuing on the trail, turn L, and go 75 ft to re-enter the woods R. Pass caves and cliffs. (To explore, go R and rejoin the trail after 0.1 mi.) Ascend, pass through ferns and make a switchback R at 1.9 mi. Indian pipe grow along a level section of the trail. At 2.4 mi make a switchback, L, among yellow pine at a ridge top. Immediately join an old road and follow it 0.6 mi to a L turn for paralleling the paved road. Pass by old apple trees with a ground cover of white snakeroot, coltsfoot, and day lilies. Cross the paved road (CO-14) at 3.2 mi, ascend, then descend and cross the paved road (now CO-5) at 3.4 mi. (To the L it is 100 yd to the park entrance and R is down the mtn to Jug Handle Campground and on to Harrisville.)

Descend steeply into a hollow to cross two footbridges. Pass through scattered white pine and at 3.6 mi reach a jct with gray-blazed *Hibbs Cemetery Trail*, L. (The 0.4-mi *Hibbs Cemetery Trail* ascends steeply, then levels off behind the park's lodge to a jct with the 0.8-mi *Super Mile Fitness Trail*. [There are 10 exercise stations on the loop.] A turn L is to the parking lot for the lodge.) Continuing on the *Nature Trail*, descend on the E side of the ridge, pass a large rock overhang, and reach a jct with *Gibbons Trail*. (The 0.2-mi *Gibbons Trail* [named for nature-foods writer Euell Gibbons] goes S to exit near the parking area for the swimming pool. On its pathway are tall poplar, oak, birch, white walnut [*Juglans cinerea*], wildflowers, ferns, mosses, and rock outcroppings.) To complete the *Nature Trail* descend to the pond area and return to point of origin.

To begin the green-blazed *Southern Railroad Trail* start either between the check-in station at the pond and the River Run Campground or at the upstream end of the campground. The level walk parallels the river upstream to Jug Handle Campground. Along the way are tall beech, oak, and poplar with ground covers of spicebush, wood mint, and jewelweed. Access to the red-blazed *Castle Rock Trail* loop is near the entrance to the cabin area road loop. If hiking clockwise cross a small stream at 0.2 mi. On the approach to a bend in the river there are sounds from Jug Handle Campground to the L, E. Large rock formations are here and the river bend has rapids. Complete the loop by following downstream before paralleling the cabin road.

Overhanging Rock Trail (0.5 mi); Extra Mile Trail (0.6 mi); North Bend Access Trail (0.6 mi)

LENGTH: 2.9 mi round-trip, combined

DIFFICULTY: easy

FEATURES: nature study, special-population service

TRAILHEADS AND DETAILS: From the River Run camping area, cross the bridge over the river to the sign on the R, N, and ascend on the *Overhanging Rock Trail* (built in 1975 by the YCC). Descend to a ravine in a glen of ferns—silver spleenwort, marginal wood fern, Christmas fern, walking fern—and reach a maintenance shed at 0.5 mi. Exit here at the playground for the handicapped. Turn R on an old RR grade, the paved *Extra Mile Trail* (formerly *Woodland Trail*) for special populations. Both English and Braille are used on 21 information posts. Reach the end of the pavement at 0.3 mi and the trail terminus at 0.6 mi near Bonds Creek and the ruins of an old oil well. Backtrack. A new trail, *North Bend Access Trail* (road) to *North Bend Rail Trail* begins at shelter #3, near *Extra Mile Trail,* and parallels the river and *Extra Mile Trail* to end between a bridge and tunnel. Equestrians and bicyclists use this access route. (See the following description of *North Bend Rail Trail.*)

North Bend Rail Trail

LENGTH: 57.7+ mi

DIFFICULTY: easy to moderate

FEATURES: history, wildlife, wildflowers, tunnels, trestles

TRAILHEAD AND DETAILS: In early 1997 the W trailhead was 0.6 mi E of the post office in Walker, and the E trailhead at the RR crossing in Wolf Summit. Further plans are to open an additional 11.0 mi W from Walker to Parkersburg, a section purchased by North Bend Rails to Trails Foundation from CSX. There are also proposals to complete a section from Wolf Summit to Wilsonburg and extend the trail through Clarksburg. (The current route is part of the *American Discovery Trail*, a cross-country route from California to Delaware.)

The railroad was constructed between 1883 and 1857 by the Northwestern Virginia Railroad, but soon merged with Baltimore & Ohio Railroad. Passenger service declined in the mid-1950s and the last freight train ran in 1984. The track was abandoned in 1988. Bikers, hikers, and equestrians will find sections of the trail to have coarse rough gravel, small gravel, limestone, grass, or combinations. Tunnels may have wet and muddy floors or solid and damp ones. A six-volt flashlight is essential, particularly through the tunnels at Eaton and West Union.

This trail's corridor is narrow, and through-hikers must plan to stay off the trail at motels, inns, designated rustic campsites, or commercial campgrounds. North Bend State Park, 16.6 mi E from the W trailhead, is the only state park on the trail. It has campsites, rooms, and cabins. (See Support Facilities below.) There are grocery stores and restaurants in almost all the towns or communities along the way, but you should take plenty of drinking water for in between. Please do not litter. I have divided the trail into easy day-hike sections, but bikers could complete the entire trail in one day, and hikers could finish in three days. I used a commercial measuring wheel for mileage, more accurate for hikers and bikers than riding the rails.(*County Maps:* Wood, Ritchie, Doddrigde, and Harrison)

ACCESS: For the W trailhead drive 2.5 mi S on I-77 from the I-77 jct with US-50 at Parkersburg. Turn SE on WV-47 and drive 6.8 mi to CO-7, L, and turn E. Drive 4.5 mi to parking and trailhead, L (0.6 mi E of Walker PO). The E trailhead is 0.5 mi N from the jct of US-50 and CO-33 at Wolf Summit (10.7 mi W from the jct of I-79 and US-50 near Clarksburg). After turning onto CO-33 N, immediately turn R to RR crossing.

SUPPORT FACILITIES: For an update on places to stay, camp, buy supplies, dine, have bikes repaired or rented, and shuttle service write or call North Bend Rails to Trails Foundation, Inc., PO Box 206, Cairo, WV 26337; 800-899-NBRT (weekdays).

Section 1:
Parkersburg to Walker (11.0 mi under preparation in 1997)

Section 2:
Walker to Cairo, 13.5 miles

From the Walker Creek parking area and rail gate follow the RR grade E in an open area to cross a tributary of Walker Creek at 0.6 mi. Cross Walker Creek at 1.6 mi. At 2.7 mi the treadway may be rough. Beetree Run parallels L. Enter the first tunnel (#21, 1,840 ft) at 3.0 mi. Cross a road (CO-7) in the community of Eaton at 4.1 mi, and another road (Eaton Rd, CO-13) at 4.8 mi. Cross Goose Creek bridges. At 5.0 mi there is a wide area with a grassy bed and rocky wall L among yellow pine. Cross a trestle over Goose Creek at 5.5 mi. Maple and sycamore are between the trail and creek. Cross a trestle over Goose Creek at 5.7 mi and 5.9 mi. At 6.5 mi are houses, R, and a paved road crossing (CO-18) in the community of Petroleum, a former boomtown with the Jordan Hotel. (CO-18 goes N 6.7 mi to US-50 near Nutter Farm.)

Cross another trestle over Goose Creek at 7.0 mi and pass a beaver pond L at 7.5 mi; the creek is R. Cross a gravel road (CO-18/5) at 7.6 mi and houses R. Cross bridge over Goose Creek at 7.7 mi and more bridges over the creek's oxbows for the next 0.2 mi. Cross a private road at 8.8 mi. Follow a long straight route with soapwort, burdock, azalea, filbert, witch hazel, blackberry, and raspberry. Deer and rabbits are likely seen. There is a slight curve at 10.2 mi among sensitive ferns. Arrive at a tunnel (#19, 1,376 ft) at 10.5 mi. After an exit there is a small beaver dam with hutch, R.

In the community of Silver Run Station, cross Silver Run Rd (CO-31/4) at 11.1 mi. At 11.8 mi is a private road crossing. Cross a bridge over Wildcat Run and through a deep cut at 12.7 mi. At 13.0 mi there are houses, Silver Run Rd and Silver Run, R. Cross North Fork of Hughes River trestle, and reach a jct with Main St (WV-31) R and L in Cairo at 13.5 mi. (Here are a bike shop, PO, stores, restaurants, B&B, and gas station. It is 4.0 mi N to US-50, and 3.9 mi S and E on CO-14 to North Bend State Park. With the use of county maps, Wood and Ritchie, you can drive 16.1 mi back to Walker on gravel and paved road.

Section 3:

Cairo to Pennsboro, 12.5 miles

Pass through a gate at 0.1 mi and at 0.5 mi enter a tall canyon wall with boulders. Among the flowers are joe-pye weed, basil, and Deptford pink. Cross a trestle over North Fork of Hughes River at 0.8 mi. There is a safety deck on the trestle for observing the scenic area. At 2.0 mi is a "black pond" (like others along the trail) formed by original RR grading, L. There is a road jct with Bonds Creek Rd (CO-8) and Bear Run Rd CO-5) at 2.4 mi in the community of Cornwallis (a former boomtown). Bonds Creek Rd goes N 3.1 mi to US-50 (and also downstream to Cairo), and CO-5 also goes to US-50, N, and S across the bridge to ascend 1.2 mi to North Bend State Park entrance, L.

Pass abandoned houses and cross trestled Bonds Creek at 2.8 mi. At 3.0 mi arrive at a signboard, L, with a map of North Bend State Park, and a graveled trail R to the park's campground. Enter tunnel (#13, 353 ft) and exit to rock with scale moss. There is a long black pond between here and the next tunnel. (From tunnel #13 to tunnel #10 there are at least four picnic sites with tables and trash cans.) Enter a tunnel (#12, 577 ft) with brick lining at 3.3 mi. At 3.6 mi parallel Hushers Run. Papaw bushes are at 3.8 mi; dead water is R. At 4.6 mi are large sycamore and cliffs, L.

At 5.1 mi enter the Dick Bias Tunnel (#10, 377 ft). (Bias was the chair of the North Bend Rails to Trails Foundation 1989–94.) Trailsides have large oak, locust, white pine, and sycamore. Pass a church youth camp, R, at 5.7 mi; cross a small cement bridge at 5.8 mi; and enter a rock cut in ridge at 5.9 mi. Hemlock and jewelweed are here. At 6.0 mi you can see US-50, L. Parallel N of Huskens Creek, and at 6.1 mi pass Hales Spring (also known as Hobo Spring), a hand-carved bowl-shaped spring, L. Mosses and cattails are nearby, and large sycamore and yellow poplar are at 6.3 mi. Enter a cut in the ridge at 6.8 mi, then pass under US-50, continuing to parallel Huskens Creek, R. Schofield Stadium of Ritchie County schools is L at 7.1 mi. At 7.3 mi is a specially constructed overpass (highest point of the trail) of WV-16 in Ellenboro. (To the R [S] is US-50 and a fast-food restaurant.)

For the next 1.8 mi the open trail passes between Old US-50 (now CO-50/39) and Huskens Creek with a number of gates and road crossings through Lamberton. Glass outlet buildings and manufacturing companies are along the way. There is a children's ball field, R, at 8.9 mi. Cross a trestle at 9.0 mi. Pass through a cut (former tunnel #9) and under CO-50/39 at 11.1 mi. Cross gravel road (CO-50/20) and at 11.7 mi go through a brick-lined tunnel (#8, 588 ft). Continue paralleling L (N) of CO-50/39. Blue-birds frequent this area in summer. Pass a glass factory, L, at 12.4 mi and Creed Collins Elementary School, L. At 12.5 mi is Pennsboro B&O depot (under restoration) and parking area. (Here are restaurants, bank, B&B, PO, and stores.) Access to US-50 is on CO-50/39, R and W, and then S on CO 50/21, L for 1.5 mi.

Section 4:

Pennsboro to West Union, 12.6 mi

From the depot cross the street to a gated trail. At 0.8 mi reach a tunnel (#7, 779 ft), built in 1862, and a brick lining. Cross transcontinental cable line at 1.2 mi, enter a shady area at 1.7 mi, and pass by large oak and maple forest at 2.4. Deer, squirrel, chipmunk, and rabbit may be seen here. On the L at 2.6 mi are hayfields and then a rustic farm barn. Cross a cement bridge over North Fork of Hughes River and a dirt road. Scenic pastoral area here; songbirds in summer. Pass through the community to Toll Gate (a former boomtown) at 3.4 mi near US-50. Curve N and cross CO-50/30 at 3.8 mi. Pass residential housing. Cross paved road (CO-50/30), then cross Wilhelm Run twice and close to US-50, at 5.7 mi. At 6.0 mi enter a shaded area of willow, oak, and maple, with sumac and cattails in sunny spots.

At 6.5 mi pass through a cut in a rock wall, L. Wildflowers include black-eyed Susan, primrose, lavender, milkweed, yellow snapdragon, and soap-wort. Chipmunk are among the walnut and hickory. After the cut is a bog, L and R. At 7.2 mi is an old farm and barn, L, and elderberry patches, R. Well-landscaped farm follows. Residential houses are at 8.4 mi and 8.7 mi. Cross a paved road (CO-11) in the community of Central Station. Cross a stream and view beautiful meadows, R. Enter a cut at 10.3 mi and the trail's longest tunnel at 10.5 mi (#6, 2,297 ft). The tunnel is mostly solid rock with some brick lining; base is wet. Cross a steel bridge over CO-50/30 at 11.2 mi, followed by crossing Middle Island Creek. At 11.8 mi is a sign for West Union. Cross a paved street at 12.0 mi; pass Trail's Inn Lounge, R; a bike shop. L; then at 12.4 mi cross trestle over WV-18. To the R is the parking area at Cline Stansberry Stadium at 12.6 mi. It is 0.7 mi S out to US-50 on WV-18. (The town has banks, restaurants, lodging, and stores.)

Section 5:

West Union to Salem, 13.2 mi

From the parking area of Cline Stansberry Stadium begin at gate and go E. Cross trestle over Middle Island Creek at 0.1 mi. In the summer the trailsides have Queen Anne's lace, purple thistle, wild rose, and buckeye. Enter a forest of tall sycamore, elm, and maple, and parallel Middle Island Creek. Deer are frequently seen. Cross Middle Island Creek at 1.9 mi. At 2.3 mi enter the town of Smithburg, which has restored Smithburg B&O depot. There is a memorial list of those who drowned in the 1950 flood. Spencer Park has rustic campsites, and to the L is a grocery store and PO.

Pass under US-50 at 2.9 mi. Cross Middle Island Creek at 3.3 mi. Summer birds are prominent in the farm fields and pastureland. Cross Middle Island Creek again at 4.3 mi. Cross a cement bridge at 5.1 mi. Large farming area and hay storage are R, and to the L you can see traffic on US-50 at 5.7 mi. Cross Long Run Rd (CO-15). (To L is access to US-50 and the community of Morgansville; R is Sherwood.) Cross cement bridge at 6.1 mi and enter Long Run Tunnel (#4, 846 ft) at 6.4 mi. Exit into an awesome forest away from the sounds of US-50, but replaced with a cacophony of doves, catbirds, cicadas, and cascades. Leave the cove through a cut. At 7.1 mi houses are R near Middle Island Creek. At 7.7 mi is Crimson River Baptist Church, R, beside the trail.

Pass through a residential area of houses and house trailers. There are road crossings and gateless trail sections. From 9.1 mi to 9.6 mi timber harvesting has caused erosion and damage to the trail. Cross a gas pipeline at 10.0 mi, followed by an isolated graveyard, L. (It may need maintenance.) At 11.8 mi is a grassy area with elderberry, catalpa, jewelweed, and goldenrod. Pass buildings of the state's Department of Corrections, L, at 12.2 mi in the town of Industrial. Ahead is a sign for Salem, chartered in 1794. The trail goes between Main St and the stream, Salem Fork. Pass a day-care center, Salem College, stores, restaurants, banks, lodging, and trail user welcome signs. Arrive at the B&O depot at 13.2 mi. (From Main St N and E on WV 23 it is out to US-50, and NW on CO-50/28 is 1.6 mi to US-50.)

Section 6:

Salem to Wolf Summit, 5.9 mi (10.2 mi if including Wilsonburg)

From the B&O depot in Salem continue E paralleling Salem Fork, R, and WV-23, L. Pass a large grocery store, L, and pass a glassware company at 0.4 mi. Some houses are so close to the trail that residents on the porch greet hikers. Pass a grocery store, L, at 1.2 mi and a neighborhood ball field, R. At 1.6 mi arrive at the Edgar Matthey Shelter, a shady picnic site and floral beds maintained by local citizens.

Cross Raccoon Run Rd (CO-50/6) at 2.0 mi in the community of Bristol. (Inquire to the R about seasonal bike sales and rentals and rustic campsites.) Pass under US-50 at 2.4 mi and parallel a stream. Cross paved road (CO-5/9) at 3.0 mi. Continue in an open area before entering at 3.2 mi the last tunnel of the trail (#2, 1,086 ft), built in 1868. (Water drains out the E end and runs into the tunnel.) End of the ridge cut is at 3.6 mi. At 4.1 mi cross a high cement and steel bridge over CO-5 and Tenmile Creek (all close to US-50). For the next 2.0 mi the grassy trail cuts through two low ridges, and passes private houses to enter the community of Wolf Summit. Pass Wesleyan Methodist Church L. At 5.9 mi the trail currently ends where paved CO-11 crosses. It is 0.5 mi R (S) on CO-11 to US-50. (The ungated and unfinished trail continues about 4.0 mi E paralleling Limestone Run and CO-11 and part of CO-9 to Wilsonburg.)

PINNACLE ROCK STATE PARK (Mercer County)

The state's southernmost park, this 245-acre day-use facility has picnicking, hiking, and fishing. Pinnacle Lake is stocked with trout. Bass, bluegill, and channel catfish are also in the lake. A fishermen's footpath circles the 15-acre lake. Access to the lake is on Pinnacle Rock Rd (CO-52/4), 1.0 mi E of Bramwell on US-52. Electric motors only are allowed on the boats. Camping is prohibited. On US-52 there is a parking area for picnicking and the 0.1-mi *Pinnacle Rock Trail,* which ascends on stone steps to a towering ridge (2,700 ft) of quartzite sandstone, as well as scenic views. (*USGS Map:* Bramwell)

ADDRESS AND ACCESS: Pinnacle Rock State Park, 102 Tremont Pk, Bluefield, WV 24701; 304-589-5307. Drive 5.0 mi NW from Bluefield on US-52 to the park, L, or 1.0 mi E from Bramwell on US-52.

PIPESTEM RESORT STATE PARK
(Mercer and Summers Counties)

It is difficult to find the equal of this magnificent resort park in any state park system. Since the park's opening on Memorial Day 1970, it has become one of the state's most popular vacation resorts. In its 4,023 acres are a wide range of recreational facilities and accommodations that provide exceptional opportunities for enjoyment. All the natural beauty of the Bluestone River Canyon, the rugged mountains, and the waterfalls has been retained in the construction of two luxury lodges (143 rooms); 25 deluxe cottages; three restaurants; 18-hole championship and nine-hole par golf courses; indoor-outdoor Olympic swimming pools; convention center facilities; and lighted tennis courts. The campground is complete with water, electrical and sewage hookups, hot showers, and a laundromat. Additionally, there is a stable for horseback riding and camping, trails for hiking, a nature center, sled run, lake for fishing, cross-country ski trails, and a crafts and gift shop. Mountain bikes are permitted on *River* and *County Line Trails*. A 3,600-ft-long aerial tramway provides access to the Mountain Creek Lodge at the base of the Bluestone River Canyon for a 1,000-ft elev drop. The park's name is from a local white flowering plant (*Spiraea alba*), a close relative of bridal wreath, used by Indians and early settlers as pipestems. The park and facilities are open year-round.

There are a few foot trails with trailheads on the roadside away from designated parking lots. An example is the blue-blazed *Dogwood Trail*. It begins near, but N of, the nature center, and descends on an old road 120 yd to cross a horse trail. At a small pond turn R (an old log cabin is L) and pass through locust, maple, white pine, and oak to a rocky area at 0.2 mi. Return to the road at 0.6 mi. Another example is *Turkey Spur Trail*. Access to the red-blazed, 0.3-mi road-trail is R after turning R toward the lodge from the park headquarters. It descends through shagbark hickory, maple, and white pine. At 0.1 mi reach a jct with *Cottage Trail* L, followed by a jct with multiple-use, blue-blazed *Lake Shore Trail* at 0.3 mi. Backtrack, or turn R and follow *South Side Trail* up to the lodge road and turn R for a loop. (*USGS Maps:* Pipestem, Flat Top)

ADDRESS AND ACCESS: Superintendent, Pipestem Resort State Park, PO Box 150, Pipestem, WV 25979; 304-466-1800. From Princeton take WV-20, NE, for 16.0 mi to the park entrance, L. From Blue Stone Lake take WV-20, SW, for 8.0 mi.

Pipestem Knob Trail

LENGTH: 0.6 mi round-trip

DIFFICULTY: easy

FEATURE: panoramic vista

TRAILHEADS AND DETAILS: After the park entrance stop at the Pipestem Knob parking area. Follow the paved trail up to the observation tower through a forest of maple, oak, hickory, dogwood, sumac, ferns, and wild-flowers. From the top (3,000 ft) are scenic views of Little Mtn and Peter's Mtn, E, and the Allegheny Plateau, W.

Lick Hollow Trail (1.1 mi); Canyon Rim Trail (0.7 mi); River Trail (6.5 mi); Farley Ridge Trail (0.7 mi)

LENGTH: 16.9 mi round-trip, combined

DIFFICULTY: moderate to strenuous

FEATURES: Heritage Point, Bluestone Canyon, wildlife, history

TRAILHEADS AND DETAILS: Except for the first trail in this group, all must be backtracked, thus doubling the walking distance and requiring adequate time allowance. Park at the Canyon Rim Center and enter the *Lick Hollow Trail* at the NW corner of the parking area. Pass large Russian olive bushes, follow a grassy path for 0.1 mi, and turn R on a narrow trail in a young forest. Descend into a forest of mature hardwoods and fern beds. Ascend to a spur trail for a view of the Bluestone River Canyon and the horseback-riding camp at 0.4 mi. Turn L at 0.6 mi where old chestnut railings may be seen. Descend in a shagbark hickory stand and complete the loop back to the parking area at 1.1 mi.

From the visitor center follow the sign at the NE corner on the blue-blazed *Canyon Rim Trail*. Descend and cross the orange-blazed *River Trail* at 0.4 mi. Reach the end of the trail at scenic Heritage Point overlook (2,200 ft) at 0.7 mi. Backtrack to the *River Trail*. Here, ascend to the parking area or take the *River Trail* E or W. If E, follow an old road (used for cross-country skiing) for 1.1 mi to the main road at Pipestem Lodge. If W, follow the old road under the tramway, cross a cascading stream, and pass through a forest of ash, oak, walnut, poplar, maple, and hemlock. Deer and wild turkey are frequent. At 0.8 mi reach a jct with the N terminus of the *County Line Trail*. The *River Trail* becomes a horse/bike/foot trail and descends R to the Bluestone River for another 1.1 mi. Rock-hop or wade. Follow downstream for another 0.9 mi to the Mtn Creek Lodge (1,542 ft). Reach a junction here with the 0.7-mi white-blazed *Farley Ridge Trail*, a rugged footpath that ascends steeply to the patrol cabin. Halfway on the ascent are spectacular views from Raven Rock Overlook. Continue downstream for another 1.2 mi and curve away from the river to ascend and cross Bearwallow Ridge. Arrive at the patrol cabin (2,240 ft) at 5.4 mi from the jct with the *Canyon Rim Trail* or 6.5 mi from the Pipestem Lodge. Backtrack.

County Line Trail

LENGTH: 4.2 mi round-trip
DIFFICULTY: moderate
FEATURE: Indian Branch Falls

TRAILHEAD AND DETAILS: From the parking lot at the nature center follow the red-blazed horse/bike/foot trail on a jeep road and descend for 1.4 mi to scenic Indian Branch waterfalls and cliffsides on the L. Ahead are indications of a former homestead with old chestnut rail fences and tree rows. Some parts of the trail are rocky. Large trees border the road before its jct with the *River Trail* at 2.1 mi. Deer are likely to be seen on this trail. Backtrack or use the *River Trail* described above.

Northside Nature Trail

LENGTH: 0.7 mi
DIFFICULTY: easy

TRAILHEAD AND DETAILS: Park behind the park office. Follow the red-blazed trail signs on a former self-interpretive trail built by the YCC in 1979 through a forest of tall trees, shrubs, and flowers. At one post is a large sugar maple. (The sugar maple is the state tree of West Virginia, as well as that of Vermont and Michigan.) Other trees are hickory, oak, poplar, beech, dogwood, and black cherry. Large (17-in circumference) striped maple (*Acer pennsylvanicum*) is part of the understory. Complete the circle and return to the parking lot.

Den Tree Trail (0.5 mi); Long Branch Trail (0.4 mi); Cottage Trail (0.2 mi); South Side Trail (0.6 mi); Lake Shore Trail (2.3 mi); Lakeview Trail (0.8 mi); Law Hollow Trail (0.5 mi)

LENGTH: 8.3-mi round-trip, combined
DIFFICULTY: moderate
FEATURES: Long Branch Lake, wildlife

TRAILHEADS AND DETAILS: Described below is an example of how these connecting trails may be made into shorter or longer loops. Total mileage includes both loops and backtracking routes. Park at the Long Branch Lake parking area near Pipestem Lodge. (Access to the *Den Tree Trail* is at the SE side of Pipestem Arboretum. Pass a wildlife observation area and descend. Cross a bridge over a bog at 0.1 mi. Descend on a slope where trees have been damaged by wind and ice storms. Cross *Law Hollow Trail* below the dam of Long Branch Lake in an area of hemlock, white pine, skullcap, black cohosh, and yellow violets. Backtrack to the parking area or follow the N side of the lake to join *Long Branch Trail*.) Walk W on the paved road for 0.1 mi; turn L at the trail signs and gated road. Descend on the blue-blazed *Long Branch Trail* in a hardwood forest with scattered white pine and rhododendron. Reach the *Lake Shore Trail* at 0.4 mi, turn R, and pass a jct with the *Cottage Trail*, R, at 0.9 mi. (White-blazed *Cottage Trail* ascends 0.2 mi to cottages #1–#9 and the park road. It is 0.4 mi from here, R, to the *Long Branch Trail*.) Continue ahead to the jct with *Turkey Spur Trail*, followed by a jct with the *South Side Trail* at 1.3 mi. (The yellow-blazed *South Side Trail* goes through a hardwood forest with a ground cover of running cedar to the main road near the park office.) Curve L on the road and re-enter the forest for a loop of 1.2 mi for rejoining the *Lake Shore Trail*. Continue on the *Lake Shore Trail*, cross a stream, and a pass a bee tree in a large white oak on the L at 1.5 mi. Hike through an open area. At 1.6 mi is a jct with the *Lake View Trail*. (This white-blazed trail ascends on an old road for 0.8 mi to the main road, across the road from the nature center.) Continue ahead on the *Lake Shore Trail* with views of the lake on the L; more club moss is in this section. Reach an open space below the dam at 2.6 mi, also a jct with *Law Hollow Trail* on the R. (*Den Tree Trail* is accessible from the *Law Hollow Trail*.) Turn L, ascend, reach the top of the dam, turn L off the paved road, and follow the lake to the jct with the *Long Branch Trail* at 2.9 mi. Return to the gated road and the point of beginning at 3.1 mi. (Mountain bikes are permitted on the *Long Branch Trail* and the *Law Hollow Trail*, and on the small section of *Lake Shore Trail* that connects the two.)

STONEWALL JACKSON LAKE STATE PARK
(Lewis County)

Stonewall Jackson Lake State Park includes a 2,650-acre lake formed by a dam on West Fork River. Its recreational activities include a campground on a scenic peninsula, water sports, fishing, picnicking, hunting, a playground, and a multipurpose building that accommodates about 400 people for meetings. The kitchen is fully equipped. (Call for reservations.) Additionally there are two trails. From the picnic shelter there is the *Fitness Trail* (0.5 mi) and near the maintenance center is *Overlook Trail* (0.25 mi). It ascends to a knoll for an overview of the lake.

ACCESS: On I-79 take Exit 91 to US-19 and follow it S for 2.5 mi to park entrance.

INFORMATION: Stonewall Jackson Lake State Park, Rte 1, Box 0, Roanoke, WV 26423; 304-269-0523.

TOMLINSON RUN STATE PARK (Hancock County)

The state's northernmost park, at the top of the panhandle (NW of Pittsburgh), has 1,401 acres of meadows, lakes, steep hills, and overhanging sandstone cliffs. In the park's center is a 29-acre lake from which Tomlinson Run flows through a gorge to drop into the Ohio River. The park has 100 species of birds and among the animals are deer, wild turkey, raccoon, beaver, squirrel, and fox. Facilities include a swimming pool; 100-acre picnic area, two tent/RV campgrounds with hot showers and laundromat (no hookups); group camp; four bass fishing ponds; rowboat and paddle boat marina; tennis courts; dumping station; nearby grocery store; and hiking trails. The season is Apr 15–Oct 15. (*USGS Map:* East Liverpool South)

ADDRESS AND ACCESS: Tomlinson Run State Park, Box 97, New Manchester, WV 26056; 304-564-3651. From the jct of WV-2 and WV-8 in New Cumberland, take WV-8 for 4.0 mi to the park entrance, L.

Big Foot Trail (1.2 mi); Fern Trail (0.5 mi)

LENGTH: 3.2 mi round-trip, combined

DIFFICULTY: easy

FEATURES: beaver dam, wildflowers

TRAILHEADS AND DETAILS: Begin 100 yd W of the picnic area gate and ascend on the red-blazed *Big Foot Trail* in a young forest of cherry, locust, and maple. Reach the lakeside at 0.3 mi where goldenrod, asters, devil's paintbrush (*Hieracium aurantiacum*), Solomon's seal, monarda, filberts, and sensitive fern grow. At 1.0 mi are signs of active beaver. Cross a swampy area and reach the park road, Shepard Valley Rd (CO-12), at 1.2 mi. Turn L and hike on the road for 1.3 mi to the boat-rental building. Ascend the steps on the R of the road and begin the orange-blazed *Fern Trail.* This is a beautiful trail of young white and Virginia pine, club moss, hay-scented fern, and violets. At the jct with a spur trail turn L, and reach the picnic road at 0.5 mi. Turn R of the lake and return to the point of origin at the picnic area at 3.2 mi.

Laurel Trail (2.5 mi); Beech Trail (1.1 mi)

LENGTH: 3.6 mi round-trip, combined

DIFFICULTY: moderate

FEATURES: sandstone cliffs, gorge vistas

TRAILHEADS AND DETAILS: From the group camp drive W to the road jct with Washington Rd (CO-3) and park near the bridge. Hike R (N) 0.1 mi and enter the forest on a blue-blazed trail. Follow the rim of the gorge on the *Laurel Trail* for scenic views for 1.0 mi. (The white-blazed trail ahead is *White Oak Trail*, which is not maintained.) Turn L, descend to the river, and go downstream to the Boy Scout camp. Wild hydrangea, witch hazel, and spicebush grow at the base of the cliffs. Wade the creek (or ascend to the original trail). Continue downstream to the road and bridge at 2.5 mi. Begin the yellow-blazed *Beech Trail* at the parking area on the S side of the bridge; ascend in an open forest of cherry and maple. Reach the crest of the ridge at 0.3 mi, go up the road past the cliffs on the L, turn L, and take the lower fork. Cross Tomlinson Creek at 0.7 mi. (Wading is necessary, or cross on slippery sycamore.) Ascend to the paved road at 0.8 mi and turn L for a return to the parking area at the bridge for a 1.1-mi loop.

TWIN FALLS RESORT STATE PARK (Wyoming County)

Another of the state's resort-type parks, these 3,776 acres in the southern highlands are outstanding for their natural and man-made beauty. Open year-round, the park is an oasis of recreational activities, luxury accommodations, and historic preservation. Facilities include 13 deluxe cabins; 20-room lodge and restaurant; 50 full-service campsites (25 with electricity) with hot showers, laundromat, and contact center; picnic areas and swimming pool; nature center; tennis courts; playground; historic sites; 18-hole championship golf course; and hiking trails. Additionally, an early-1800s pioneer homestead has been restored on Bower's Ridge, and a museum of county historic relics is near the White Horse Knob Observation Tower, elev 2,330 ft. Wildlife frequently seen in the park are deer, raccoon, wild turkey, and grouse. (*USGS Maps:* McGraws, Mullens)

ADDRESS AND ACCESS: Twin Falls Resort State Park, PO Box 1023, Mullens, WV 25882; 304-294-4000. From Pineville drive 6.0 mi E on WV-97.

Cliffside Trail (2.8 mi); Hemlock Trail (1.2 mi); Falls Trail (0.7 mi); Nature Trail (1.2 mi)

LENGTH: 7.8 mi round-trip, combined

DIFFICULTY: moderate

FEATURES: Twin Falls, nature study

TRAILHEADS AND DETAILS: To enter the *Cliffside Trail* in the campground, go to the Fox Hunter's Point and park between the restroom and campsite #24. Follow the trail sign through a hardwood forest on a ridge; bear R at the Bear Wallow spur trail at 0.5 mi. Turn L at the next jct. The trail becomes narrow; descend and reach a scenic cliff edge at 1.4 mi. Hemlock, rhododendron, and mtn laurel add to the natural beauty. Backtrack to the campground and begin the *Hemlock Trail* behind the contact center. Descend on an old road through a magnificent forest of hardwoods, hemlock, ferns, mandrake, ragwort, and banks of club mosses. At 1.2 mi reach a jct with the *Falls Trail*; turn L, cross the Black Fork stream, and pass a jct with the *Nature Trail* at 1.3 mi, R. (The *Nature Trail* makes a loop of 1.2 mi with an ascent to the park's main road and return to the *Falls Trail*.) Continue downstream; bear L for 0.1 mi to the Black Fork Falls. Continue downstream for another 0.5 mi to the Cabin Creek Falls. (These two falls give the park its name.) Backtrack. (There is a shorter entrance to the falls on a park service road near the park's entrance.) Total mileage for backtracking or making a loop on all four trails is 7.8 mi.

Huckleberry Trail

LENGTH: 1.4 mi

DIFFICULTY: easy

FEATURE: Pioneer Farm

TRAILHEAD AND DETAILS: Drive SW from the campground to the parking area at the Pioneer Farm. This is a loop trail and you can descend from here along the farm fence to the forest or cross the road and ascend E into a young pine and dogwood forest. Either way, the trail will cross the road at the top of the ridge near a grassy field. Along the way are sumac, locust, blackberry, huckleberry, club moss, and wildflowers. Deer are likely to be seen.

Two other trails are in the park. One is the 0.5-mi *Cemetery Trail* (which requires a backtrack) at the N end of the golf course. It ascends on a cemetery road, passes one cemetery on a hillside, and terminates at the road's end. Such names as Cox, Phillips, Clay, and Owens are on the stones.

Another trail is the paved *Twin Oaks Trail,* a loop of 0.3 mi developed by the Mullens Lions Club. It is on the park's main road, 1.3 mi from the entrance. The park has approximately 8.0 mi of fire trails.

TYGART LAKE STATE PARK (Taylor County)

The headwaters of the Tygart Valley River begin at 4,000 ft elev in the Cheat Mtns. Turbulent, cascading, and sometimes still in pools and valleys, it flows N to Elkins and to Philippi before it becomes a lake S of the historic town of Grafton. (Grafton is known for its International Mother's Day shrine, the Andrews Methodist Church, where Anna Reeves Jarvis was a member. It was she who observed the first "Mother's Day," on the second anniversary of her mother's death on May 12, 1907. The following year the first organized Mother's Day for all mothers was observed on May 10, 1908. The church at 11 E Main St is open weekdays and Saturday afternoons, May–Oct. For information call 304-265-1589.)

The lake area is also historic as a result of other events. It was in Grafton that the first Union soldier, T. Bailey Brown, was killed in the Civil War. He is buried in a national cemetery, a 3.2-acre plot at 431 Walnut St. South of Grafton in Philippi, the first land battle of the Civil War (without casualties) was fought on June 3, 1861. For historic and recreational information on this area contact the Grafton-Taylor County Convention and Visitors Bureau, 214 W Main St, Room 205, Grafton, WV 26354; 304-265-3938.

The Tygart was impounded by the Corps of Engineers in the 1930s for flood control. During high water the park's marina may be closed, and *Tygart Dam Trail* and *Lake Trail* may be flooded. The road into the park passes the Corps of Engineers visitor center and parking area. Here is an overlook, walkway on part of the dam, and tour arrangements for elsewhere at the dam's facilities. It is at the dam that the 13.0-mi lake has become part of a 2,134-acre state park. (Its waters also extend SW to the Pleasant Creek WMA, which has a campground with pit toilets and water pumps [no electricity]. Access is 9.0 mi S of Grafton, L off US-119.) The state park is outstanding for its beauty as well as its sport facilities for fishing, boating, water skiing, and swimming. Added to these sport facilities are a marina; a 20-room lodge with a restaurant; picnic units; playground; game courts; and 10 deluxe cabins. The completely furnished cabins are constructed of native wood and have native stone fireplaces. A 40-unit campground has limited level areas for RVs. Most of the tent campsites are not level. The park is open from mid-Apr to Oct 31. (*USGS Maps:* Grafton, Thornton)

ADDRESS AND ACCESS: Tygart Lake State Park, Rte 1, Box 260, Grafton, WV 26354; 304-265-3383 (lodge, -2320). In Grafton at the jct of US-50 and US-119 follow signs and drive S on US-119 for 2.0 mi, turn L on Walnut St, cross bridge, turn R on Park Rd (CO-44) S to Corps of Engineers and ahead to park entrance.

Ridge Trail (0.9 mi); Lake Trail (0.6 mi); Woodland Trail (1.0 mi)

LENGTH: 5.0 mi round-trip, combined
DIFFICULTY: easy to moderate
FEATURE: nature study
TRAILHEADS AND DETAILS: For these trails park at picnic area #3 at the park office parking lot. A loop can be made of the first two trails. Cross the main road to begin the yellow-and-red blazed *Ridge Trail*. Ferns and wildflowers, such as bloodroot (*Sanguinaria canadensis*), used by Native Americans for dyes and insect repellent, border the trail. The forest has beech, oak, sycamore, and birch. At 0.2 mi reach the upper side of the slope, then descend, and after crossing a small footbridge ascend 22 ft to a fork. (To the L a red-blazed spur descends 203 yd to the park road, where a turn L makes a 0.6-mi loop back to the park office.) Continue on the main trail and later descend at 0.9 mi to the S end of picnic area #1. Backtrack, or walk the road, L, to the park office for a loop of 1.5 mi. On the way, near the S entrance to picnic area #2 is a jct with the *Lake Trail*. It descends 0.2 mi to a cove at the lake's edge where a curve L goes upstream to the parking lot for picnic area #3.

For the yellow-blazed *Woodland Trail*, cross the main road on the S side of the park office and ascend steeply. In a hardwood forest dominated by poplar and maple, there are spots of white snakeroot and spicebush on the trailway. After a ridge crest begin to descend at 0.3 mi. Pass a fence and under an electric power line before reaching the N edge of the campground. Backtrack or hike the road for 1.2 mi to make a loop of 2.2 mi.

Dogwood Trail (1.1 mi); Tygart Dam Trail (0.9 mi)

LENGTH: 4.0 mi round-trip, combined
DIFFICULTY: easy to moderate
FEATURES: nature study, scenic lake views

TRAILHEADS AND DETAILS: Park at the lodge parking lot and walk 230 yd S on the main road to *Dogwood Trail,* L, and *Tygart Dam Trail,* R. (There is parking space for about two cars here.) For the *Dogwood Trail* ascend through a young forest of black gum, poplar, dogwood, and sassafras. Ferns and sweet cicely are scattered on the forest floor. Curve around a ridge at 0.4 mi where trees become more maple and cherry. At 0.5 mi pass under an electric power line, turn L, parallel the power line for 0.2 mi, turn R at large oak and poplar, and follow a border of rocks. Descend steeply to an old road and exit at the park road at 1.1 mi. Backtrack, or walk the highway for 0.4 mi to the first entrance to the lodge parking lot.

On the *Tygart Dam Trail* descend on an old road, opposite the *Dogwood Trail's* S trailhead, among oak, beech, poplar, and locust. After 0.2 mi pass downslope of the lodge and at the lake's edge. Leave the park boundary at 0.6 mi, then continue to ascend to an exit at the S end of the Corps of Engineers parking lot. Backtrack, or walk the highway for 0.8 mi for a loop of 1.7 mi.

VALLEY FALLS STATE PARK (Marion and Taylor Counties)

Valley Falls was called the "Evil Spirit Falls" by the Cherokee Indians, and white explorers called it "Hard around Falls" in the early 18th century because of the two-tier 30-ft drop. It was also called "Falls of the Big Muddy," an appropriate title 150 years later when floods washed away a thriving community of more than 125 houses and business establishments. By the 1750s it was called "Tygart Falls" after David Tygart, a pioneer who had settled near the stream N of Elkins. The falls changed owners a number of times, and on each occasion the deeds referred to the "great falls of the Tygart Valley" as part of the land grant. An example was in 1784 when Governor Patrick Henry of Virginia granted 1,000 acres to David Gray and Samuel Hanway. In 1852 the Baltimore & Ohio Railroad completed a branch through the canyon. From then until the great floods of 1884 and 1888 and the disastrous fire of 1886, it was a boomtown with a post office, hotel, mills, factories, a Wells-Fargo office, B&O depot, school, and church. In the early 1960s the state wisely purchased 1,145 acres for a state park. It opened in 1964 as a day-use facility for picnicking, history study, and sightseeing. There are plans for a campground and other facilities as funds become available.

ADDRESS AND ACCESS: Valley Falls State Park, Rte 6, Box 244, Fairmont, WV 26554; 304-367-2719. In Fairmont at I-79 Exit 137, take WV-310,

Tygart Falls at Valley Falls State Park.

S, for 8.7 mi to Valley Falls Rd (CO-31/14). Turn R and go 2.0 mi to Valley Falls.

SUPPORT FACILITIES: The nearest campground is 13.0 mi farther on WV-310 to US-50 in Grafton and S on US-119 to Park Rd (CO-44) and to Tygart Lake State Park.

Rhododendron Trail (2.2 mi); Rocky Trail (1.4 mi); Dogwood Trail (0.7 mi); Wild Turkey Trail (1.2 mi); Red Cardinal Trail (1.1 mi); Red Fox Trail (0.4 mi); Deer Trail (2.2 mi)

LENGTH: 9.2 mi combined

DIFFICULTY: easy to strenuous

TRAILHEADS AND DETAILS: This network of trails provides at least six potential loops. They are described in a suggestive order. The *Rhododendron Trail*, *Wild Turkey Trail*, *Red Fox Trail*, and *Deer Trail* may be used for mountain-bike races in addition to hiking. Races have been managed by Gear Pushers Club. Begin at the far parking lot (W) for the *Rhododendron Trail*. Follow a wide old road through an open hardwood forest. At 0.6 mi turn R uphill on another old road. Descend among ferns and striped green maple. At 0.9 mi is the sound of cascading Glady Creek among rhododendron, L, and a jct with *Rocky Trail*, R. It may not be signed; therefore it is easy to miss.

(The *Rocky Trail* ascends steeply on three switchbacks to cliffs at 0.2 mi. Level out and follow an old woods road through habitat of deer and wild turkey. At 0.5 mi turn L on a gentle ascent to a jct with the end of *Rhododendron Trail*, L, and *Wild Turkey Trail* ahead [E]. *Rocky Trail* goes R to descend another 0.6 mi to a jct with *Red Cardinal Trail* L, then steeply among rocks and moss for another 0.1 mi to the picnic area and parking, where you began the *Rhododendron Trail*. If you decided to take the *Red Cardinal Trail* rather than returning, follow it E, first ascending steeply to level off in a young forest. At 0.2 mi are steps. Cross a ravine, pass under a power line at 0.5 mi, and reach the park's paved entrance road at 0.9 mi. Here is parking space for two vehicles. After crossing the road pass remains of an old shed L, and a spring R a few yd before a jct with *Red Fox Trail*, L, and *Deer Trail* ahead at 1.1 mi.)

Continuing upstream on the *Rhododendron Trail* notice a spur trail L at 1.4 mi. It is 300 yd to a double-tiered waterfall on Glady Creek. Continue on the main trail among boulders, cherry, maple, oak, and poplar trees. Ascend to a ridge top and bear R to a jct with the *Dogwood Trail*, L. (During biking races, this jct may be altered.)

(The *Dogwood Trail* ascends on an old road among old apple trees, locust, and dogwood. Level out at 0.2 mi. At 0.4 mi are superb views, L, of distant mtn ranges. Pass carpets of ground cedar, wild geraniums, and white snakeroot. Reach a jct with *Wild Turkey Trail*, R and L, at 0.7 mi. To the L the *Wild Turkey Trail* goes by the side of the ranger's house and to the park office on the entrance road. To the R the *Wild Turkey Trail* goes 1.0 mi to a jct with the end of *Rhododendron Trail*. Along the way it undulates on a ridge through a hardwood forest.)

Continuing on the *Rhododendron Trail* from its jct with *Dogwood Trail*, follow an easy old road 0.4 mi to its end, where it meets *Wild Turkey Trail* and leads to *Rocky Trail* described above.

If starting on the *Red Fox Trail* at the park office, park on the W side of the road and walk S on the road 140 ft (no parking here) to turn L. After a short level area, descend rapidly on switchbacks to a jct with *Deer Trail* L and *Red Cardinal Trail* R at 0.4 mi. (You may see a sign that implies the *Deer Trail* starts 0.2 mi R at the entrance road.) Continue L on the *Deer Trail*. Cross a ravine, pass mining areas, and reach a jct with an old road at 0.7 mi. Turn R. Follow the road in parallel to the RR and Tygart Valley. At 1.7 mi the trail ends at the park's paved road. To the R is 1.0 mi to park office; to the L is 0.5 mi to the picnic parking area at the river.

WATOGA STATE PARK (Pocahontas County)

The state's largest (10,106 acres) and oldest (begun in 1934) park is bordered on the W by the Greenbrier River. It is "the river of islands," according to the Cherokee Indians who called the area *watauga*. Historic as an old CCC camp, vast and varied in scenic beauty in the Appalachian highlands, and modern in facilities, the N half has a wide range of recreational facilities while the S half is roadless and wild. The S boundary is with the Monongahela National Forest and the Calvin Price State Forest, an area from Rock Run to Laurel Run that is a sanctuary for wildlife. Its chief facility is the Laurel Run Primitive Campground. The state's longest trail, the *Allegheny Scenic Trail*, passes through the NE corner of the park. It is likely that wildlife will be seen on the trails or even on the roads. Among them are deer, grouse, wild turkey, quail, raccoon, woodchuck, squirrel, and chipmunk. Watoga is an excellent base camp for hiking excursions in the Monongahela National Forest, the *Greenbrier River Trail*, Droop Mtn State Park, and Beartown State Park.

Facilities are four cabin areas with a total of 33 cabins; 88 campsites (38 at Beaver Creek Campground and 50 at Riverside), some with electric hookups; hot showers; laundry; dumping station; restaurant (open Memorial Day to Labor Day); commissary; swimming pool; game courts; playground; picnic units; arboretum; stables for horse rentals; boat rentals; a lake for fishing; cross-country skiing areas; and trails for hiking. Additionally, a naturalist is on duty in the summer. The season is Apr 1–Dec 10; open campground dates may differ. (*USGS Maps:* Denmar, Lake Sherwood)

ADDRESS AND ACCESS: Watoga State Park, (HC82, Box 252, Marlinton, WV 24954; 304-799-4087. From the W take Seebert Rd (CO-27) at the jct with US-219 between Mill Point and Hillsboro. From the E take Beaver Creek Rd (CO-21) S from Huntersville.

SUPPORT FACILITIES: Fishing bait and equipment, groceries, and a service station are across the Greenbrier River in the community of Seebert. A restaurant and other stores are in the town of Hillsboro, 3.0 mi W from Seebert.

Laurel Ridge Trail (1.3 mi), Allegheny Trail (1.5 mi); Jacob's Well Trail (1.3 mi); Honeymoon Trail (3.5 mi); Ten-Acre Trail (0.2 mi)

LENGTH: 6.3 mi combined

DIFFICULTY: moderate to strenuous

FEATURE: wildlife

TRAILHEADS AND DETAILS: These trails have exits at other trails or park roads, but they also connect for loop arrangements. The 5.0-mi length is the shortest loop. At the picnic shelter go E on the orange-blazed *Laurel Ridge Trail* for 0.5 mi to the road jct of Pyles Rd (CO-21/3) and Pyles Mtn Rd (CO-21/4), 0.7 mi from the park's E entrance. The *Allegheny Trail* crosses here and runs conjointly S with the *Laurel Ridge Trail*. Follow both through hardwood and hemlock forest with dense buckberry and mtn laurel stands to the red-blazed *Jacob's Well Trail*, L, at 1.2 mi. (The *Jacob's Well Trail* descends 1.3 mi to the park's Beaver Creek Campground, S. There are plans to reroute the *Allegheny Trail* to run conjointly with the *Jacob's Well Trail*.) Continue ahead to join the white-blazed *Honeymoon Trail* at 1.3 mi. (The *Honeymoon Trail* has its origin, R, 0.1 mi from the parking area for cabin #34.) Continue ahead on the *Allegheny Trail* and *Honeymoon Trail* to 2.8 mi, where the *Allegheny Trail* continues on the ridge and the *Honeymoon Trail* bears R. (The *Allegheny Trail* descends to Beaver Creek Rd [CO-21] at 4.5 mi, crosses into Calvin Price State Forest, and joins *Beaver Creek Trail* at 6.4 mi. Here you could turn L, go 0.7 mi to the S area of Beaver

Creek Campground, and follow *Jacob's Well Trail* back to the point of origin for a total loop of 9.1 mi.) Continue ahead on the *Honeymoon Trail* along the Pyle Mtn ridge to the blue-blazed *Ten-Acre Trail*. (The *Ten-Acre Trail* descends steeply 0.2 mi in a grove of white pine to the T. M. Cheek Rd. Left at the road it is 1.0 mi S to the superintendent's residence and the S entrance to the park on Beaver Creek Rd.) Continue on the *Honeymoon Trail* to a number of points parallel with the T. M. Cheek Rd. Pass R of the Ann Bailey Lookout Rd at 3.7 mi (2,036 ft). (Ann Bailey is known as the famous "White Squaw of the Kanawha," a scout and message-carrier in the late 18th century.) Pass R of the T. M. Cheek Memorial at 4.1 mi and reach cabin #21 in the cabin area at 4.7 mi. Turn L to return to the picnic shelter at 5.0 mi or R to cabin #34 and rejoin the *Allegheny Trail*, L, for a loop of 5.7 mi.

Lake Trail (1.1 mi); Beaver Bog Trail (0.3 mi)

LENGTH: 1.4 mi combined
DIFFICULTY: easy
FEATURE: Killbuck Lake
TRAILHEADS AND DETAILS: Park at the park office. Cross the road to the lake and follow the orange-blazed trail R from the boat dock. (If fishing, four trout are the maximum.) Cross the footbridge at 0.4 mi and again at 0.9 mi at the spillway. Excellent view of the lake from the N side. *Beaver Bog Trail* is short—a loop below the dam. The name of the trail is not a guarantee of seeing either a beaver or a bog. Return on the road to point of origin.

Honeybee Trail (4.7 mi); Buckhorn Trail (0.8 mi); Dragon Draft Trail (1.4 mi)

LENGTH: 6.9 mi combined
DIFFICULTY: moderate
FEATURE: nature study
TRAILHEADS AND DETAILS: Park at the Brooks Memorial Arboretum on the park's main road, 1.5 mi E from the Greenbrier River entrance. Follow the loop signs, cross a footbridge, turn R on the red-blazed *Honeybee Trail*, and ascend steeply to the crest of the ridge. An open hardwood forest of oak, maple, and sourwood remains consistent on the trail. Reach the ridge top at 1.0 mi and begin descent E of the ridge to a jct with the *Buckhorn Trail* at 1.1 mi, L. (*Buckhorn Trail* descends 0.4 mi to the spring and the central

Dragon Draft Trail in the loop.) At 1.7 mi at the shelter and spring is a jct with the *Dragon Draft Trail*. (The *Dragon Draft Trail* follows Two-Mile Run for 1.4 mi back to the parking area.) Continue ahead on the *Honeybee Trail* through numerous dead trees, victims of fierce ice storms. At 3.2 mi is a jct with the *Buckhorn Trail,* which descends L for 0.4 mi to the *Dragon Draft Trail*. Pass L of the rocky overhangs and descend to the *Dragon Draft Trail* and the footbridge at 4.5 mi and then 4.7 mi to the parking area.

Jesse's Cove Trail (2.4 mi); Arrowhead Trail (1.0 mi); Turkey Spur Trail (0.4 mi)

LENGTH: 5.1 mi combined

DIFFICULTY: strenuous

FEATURES: wildlife, Ann Bailey tower

TRAILHEADS AND DETAILS: Begin at the S edge of the Riverside Campground and follow the yellow-blazed *Jesse's Cove Trail* downriver for 0.4 mi to where it leaves an old roadbed and ascends. Railings are along the cliff passages. Cross the stream at 0.7 mi and parallel L of the cascading Rock Cove Run through tall hardwoods, hemlock, ferns, and copious wildflowers. Reach the Ann Bailey Lookout Rd at 2.4 mi. Turn L and follow the ridge road to the Ann Bailey log tower at 3.9 mi. Here are magnificent views of the Greenbrier River, the *Greenbrier River Trail* (formerly the C&O Railway), and Droop Mtn. Cleared area has patches of huckleberry and wild phlox. To return to the campground, descend steeply on an old road, the *Arrowhead Trail*. After 0.8 mi reach a jct with the *Turkey Spur Trail,* L. (The yellow-blazed *Arrowhead Trail* goes R for 0.2 mi to cabin #3 and the main park road.) Follow the *Turkey Spur Trail* on an old road for another 0.4 mi back to the campground at site #6 for a loop of 5.1 mi.

Monongaseneka Trail

LENGTH: 8.0 mi round-trip

DIFFICULTY: strenuous

FEATURES: wildlife, rock outcrops

TRAILHEAD AND DETAILS: Monongaseneka means "place of the big stone." At the W entrance of the park at the Greenbrier River, drive 0.6 mi to a small parking area on the R. The trail is on the L. Ascend gradually on the W slope of the mtn. Pass rock overhangs at 0.4 mi. Wild pinks are on the banks. At 1.1 mi leave the original trail made by the CCC and descend to a cove, cross a small stream, begin a steep ascent, and reach the ridge crest at

1.5 mi. (A 0.5-mi loop to the L goes to a potential view of the Greenbrier River.) Turn R and follow the trail to a jct with the *Buck and Doe Horse Trail* at 4.0 mi.) Backtrack.

WATTERS SMITH MEMORIAL STATE PARK
(Harrison County)

This 532-acre park has a surprising trail system filled with wildlife. A day-use park, its main publicized attraction is the pioneer homestead restoration in honor of the Watters Smith family. A large swimming pool is on top of a hill and there are meeting rooms, a museum and souvenir shop, picnic areas, a playground, and hiking trails. The park also has 12 gas wells. It is open from Memorial Day to Labor Day. (*USGS Map:* West Milford)

ADDRESS AND ACCESS: Superintendent, Watters Smith Memorial State Park, Box 296, Lost Creek, WV 26385; 304-745-3081. On US-19 in West Milford, drive S on Duck Creek Rd (CO-25/6) for 1.7 mi. From Lost Creek drive W on West Milford Rd (CO-27) for 4.0 mi to Duck Creek Rd as described above.

White Oak Trail (2.0 mi); Dogwood Trail (0.8 mi)

LENGTH: 2.8 mi combined

DIFFICULTY: moderate

FEATURES: scenic, historic, wildlife

TRAILHEADS AND DETAILS: From the picnic area follow the sign for the white-blazed *White Oak Trail* beside the fence line, pass a huge white oak at 0.2 mi, turn R on an old road, then turn L by a walnut tree. Other trees on the trail are beech, dogwood, cherry, redbud, and a variety of oak species. Reach the ridge top at 0.4 mi and the high point at 0.6 mi. Wildlife that may be seen are deer; wild turkey; grouse; red, gray, and flying squirrels; and rabbit. Pennyroyal and white snakeroot are on the seeded road. Pass a grazing field and begin a descent at 1.3 mi. Wild senna (*Cassia hebecarpa*) grows on the dry rocky area with locust, sycamore, and Virginia pine. Views here are of the strip mines. Cross an old mining road and reach a jct with the *Dogwood Trail* at 1.7 mi. Turn R, wind around a drain, and reach the activity center at 2.0 mi. (The *Dogwood Trail* exits L on the activity center road.) To return to the point of beginning, turn R, follow an old road by a lake full of bluegill, and reach the parking area at the swimming pool at 2.3 mi. (It is 0.4 mi more on an old road behind the swimming pool to the picnic area and parking lot.)

7. West Virginia State Forests

*I must go into the woods to feel a part of what I hold dear; for the
regeneration of spirit that it brings.*

—Bob Beanblossom

Seven of the state's nine forests are in mountainous counties adjoining Virginia, Kentucky, or Pennsylvania. The other two are slightly more central, Kanawha in Kanawha County, and Kumbrabow in Randolph County. (Only one county, Pocahontas, has two state forests, Seneca and Calvin Price.) Their total acreage is 79,018. Coopers Rock State Forest, part of which is leased to the West Virginia University Department of Forests, is the largest (12,713 acres) and Greenbrier State Forest is the smallest (5,130 acres).

The primary use of the forests is for the management of commercial timber sales. In the early 1970s all the state forestlands were inventoried for their potential in timber harvesting. During the development of management plans for individual forests, the public reaction was mixed, but Charles Carlson, Howard and Dorothy Guest, and other conservation and environmental leaders in the Charleston area opposed timber harvesting in the Kanawha State Forest. The result was a legislative victory to preserve Kanawha's natural beauty. In many ways it now resembles a state park.

The state has long been recognized for its remarkable deciduous forests. There are at least 50 indigenous species of trees. Northern hardwoods are dominant in four of the state forests—Coopers Rock, Calvin Price, Kumbrabow, and Seneca. These common species are in a varied upland and cove mixture, depending on the loamy soil and the annual rainfall. Among the species are American beech (*Fagus grandifolia*), red maple (*Acer rubrum*), sugar maple (*Acer saccharum*), yellow birch (*Betula alleghaniensis*), Northern red oak (*Quercus rubra*), black cherry (*Prunus serotina*), and white ash (*Fraxinus americana*). Eastern hemlock (*Tsuga canadensis*) and eastern white pine (*Pinus stobus*) are the major conifers.

Central hardwoods flourish in the other five forests. These species include the hickories: bitternut (*Carya cordiformis*); mockernut (*Carya tomentosa*); shagbark (*Carya ovata*); and pignut (*Carya glabra*). Other trees are the American elm (*Ulmus americana*); slippery elm (*Ulmus rubra*); black gum (*Nyssa sylvatica*); black locust (*Robinia pseudoacacia*); sassafras (*Sassafras albidum*); and the white, red, scarlet, and black oaks. Prominent among the pines are pitch (*Pinus rigida*), Virginia (*Pinus virginiana*), table mountain (*Pinus pungens*), and short leaf (*Pinus echinata*).

Historically, the state forest system runs concurrently with the state parks system. During the 1930s designated forests were established as Civilian Conservation Corps (CCC) camps. Among these were Cabwaylingo, Coopers Rock, Greenbrier, Kanawha, Kumbrabow, and Watoga (which later became the first state park). The CCC crews assisted in the building of roads, cabins, fire towers, picnic areas, and trails; reforestation; and other conservation work. When the CCC was phased out in 1942, the state purchased land in Pocahontas County as a game preserve and for the management of forest resources. The area was Seneca State Forest, the state's first designated forest.

All the state forests, except Calvin Price or Camp Creek, have either campgrounds or cottages, or both. Many of their facilities are similar to state parks', and the same 22 rules and regulations governing public use of the parks are also used for the forests and for the state hunting and fishing areas. The list of rules is posted at all campgrounds and offices, and in other conspicuous places on the public lands. They were carefully created to provide safety and security for visitors, protection of wildlife and plant life, and preservation of the natural environment.

Hikers may find the trails in the state forests to be less crowded than some of the better-known or more popular national forest trails. When the many miles of state-forest jeep, fire, and timber roads are included with the designated trails, the opportunity for study of animal and plant life, geology, and natural scenic beauty may be as much or more rewarding than other public properties. All the forests except Calvin Price and Camp Creek have designated trails, but the *Allegheny Trail* runs through the extreme NE panhandle of Calvin Price. (Camp Creek State Park has a trail.) The 9,482-acre preserve is generally undeveloped. A primitive campground provides a base for hunters and for exploratory hikers. The forest is not described in detail elsewhere in this book; information may be obtained by writing the Superintendent, Calvin Price State Forest, Dunmore, WV 24934; (304-799-4087 Watoga State Park).

INFORMATION: West Virginia Division of Forestry, Bureau of Commerce, State Capitol Bldg, 1900 Kanawha Blvd E, Charleston, WV 25305 (304-558-2788); Wildlife Resources Section, Division of Natural Resources, 1900 Kanawha Blvd E, Charleston, WV 25305 (304-558-2771); Parks and Recreation Section, Division of Natural Resources, 1900 Kanawha Blvd E, Charleston, WV 25305 (304-558-2764).

CABWAYLINGO STATE FOREST (Wayne County)

Although this 8,123-acre forest is in Wayne County (bordering the Kentucky state line), its name is a combination of Cabell, Wayne, Lincoln, and Mingo Counties. Wild, rugged, and remote, the numerous coves have fresh mountain streams that drain into the area's main channel, Twelvepole Creek, a stream stocked with trout. Old lumber and hunting roads wind into the valleys and up to the ridges, where deer and turkey are prominent, and the more than 25 commercial oil wells remind the hiker that the forest provides more than lumber, venison, and pan-fried rainbow trout. Facilities include picnic areas with tables, grills, firewood, drinking water, and restrooms; the campground area has similar facilities and hot showers. A fire tower at the campground provides a panoramic view of the forest and 1.0-mi *Indian Trail* descends from the campground through hardwoods, hemlock, and pine to connect the S edge of the group camp. There are two trails that have gas wells on the route: *Beech Ridge Trail*, off CO-41 in the S part of the forest, and *Long Branch Trail*, off CO-41 at the Long Branch Picnic Area. Inquire at the forest office for information. There are 13 vacation cabins, completely furnished. Other facilities are a children's playground and a swimming pool with a bathhouse. The season is May 1–Oct 15. (*USGS Maps*: Kiahsville, Wilsondale)

ADDRESS AND ACCESS: Cabwaylingo State Forest, Rte 1, Box 85, Dunlow, WV 25511; 304-385-4255. From Dunlow go 2.5 mi S on WV-152 to a jct with Twelvepole Creek Rd (CO-35) and turn L on CO-35, near Missouri Branch.

SUPPORT FACILITIES: Groceries and a service station are nearby on WV-152.

Ash Branch Trail

LENGTH: 2.3 mi
DIFFICULTY: moderate
FEATURE: nature study

TRAILHEAD AND DETAILS: After entering the forest follow upstream and park near cabins #8 and #9. Enter the trail at the sign; after 90 yd begin ascent in a hardwood forest with scattered hemlock and wildflowers. At 0.2 mi are wide beds of crested dwarf iris (*Iris cristata*). Cross a footbridge and follow switchbacks to a ridge crossing. Descend, pass a large rock overhang in a damp area; ferns and stonecrop (*Sedum ternatum*) are here. Enter a hemlock grove, descend on a steep area to a service road, and turn L downstream on Long Branch. Cross the stream at 1.4 mi and twice more before reaching the picnic shelter near stone-crafted trail. Reach the children's playground at 1.6 mi; turn L, cross a bridge to the picnic area, go up steps, and follow upstream to a bridge for a return to point of origin at 2.3 mi.

Copley Trail

LENGTH: 3.0 mi round-trip

DIFFICULTY: moderate

TRAILHEAD AND DETAILS: On CO-41 S of cabin #7 ascend to a ridge at 0.6 mi where a spur trail is L. (It leads to rock formations and caves where it is claimed a family of Copleys used the caves for a home.) Continue on the main trail W, descend on switchbacks to end at the group camp or swimming pool. It is 1.5 mi back on CO-41 to point of origin.

Martin Ridge Trail (1.6 mi); Sleepy Hollow Trail (1.0 mi)

LENGTH: 3.8 mi round-trip, combined

DIFFICULTY: moderate

FEATURES: caves, ferns

TRAILHEADS AND DETAILS: At the end of the picnic area at the swimming area on the main road, ascend N on an old wagon road in a hardwood forest. Pass a rock overhang on the L and R. Curve R at 0.4 mi in a mtn laurel section, then L up the ridge to a logging road at 0.7 mi. (A number of logging roads and seeded roads may confuse you in this area.) At 1.6 mi is a jct with *Sleepy Hollow Trail;* turn R beside a large white oak and a hickory tree, and descend on the *Sleepy Hollow Trail*. Pass a gas pipe, descend to a huge rock formation with caves and overhangs, and in the summer notice the numerous fern and lichen species here. Cross a footbridge, enter a hemlock grove, follow a stream, and reach Sweetwater Branch Rd at 2.6 mi. Turn R, walk to the main road and turn R, and follow downstream to the point of origin for a total loop of 3.8 mi.

Spruce Creek Trail
LENGTH: 2.8 mi round-trip
DIFFICULTY: moderate
FEATURE: nature study
TRAILHEAD AND DETAILS: Drive up the main road and park at the Right Fork Picnic Area (across the road from cabins #11 and #12). Follow the trail sign, ascend through a forest of large hemlock and beech on the L side of the stream to Spruce Fork. Reach the Tick Ridge Rd (CO-35/5) at 1.4 mi. Backtrack. (CO-35/5 leads R [NW] to the campground with spur roads off the ridge. This road and other hunting roads are excellent for hiking but are not recommended for use during the hunting season. Check with the superintendent for exploratory routes in the forest.)

COOPERS ROCK STATE FOREST
(Monongalia and Preston Counties)

The state's largest forest, 12,698 acres, is also large in the dimension of its services and facilities. Purchased in 1936, it serves a concentrated population in Morgantown, Fairmont, and West Virginia University. A multiple-use area, the emphasis is on timber, wildlife, and soil and water management; recreational facilities; and preservation of natural beauty and historic sites. Outstanding features are overlooks to the Cheat River canyon, a virgin hemlock grove, and an old iron-ore furnace. Facilities include cross-country skiing, skating, botanical research, hunting, fishing, picnicking, camping, and hiking. There are 24 campsites (none with hookups, but hot showers are available), a playground, and a concession–gift stand.

In the early part of the 19th century, this area was bought by iron companies to mine ore and limestone and produce charcoal. By the turn of the century the Kendall Lumber Company had purchased large holdings for extensive lumbering. In 1959 approximately 7,500 acres of the forest were leased on a long-term basis to West Virginia University's Division of Forestry. It uses the forest for forest-management field programs, research, recreation, and nature study.

The forest is named for a cooper, a maker of barrel staves who, according to legend, was an escaped convict making his hideout in the forest. The area has an endangered species—the flat-spired, three-toothed snail (*Triodopsis platysayoides*). (*USGS Maps*: Bruceton Mills, Lake Lynn)

ADDRESS AND ACCESS: Coopers Rock State Forest, Rte 1, Box 270, Bruceton Mills, WV 26525; 304-594-1561. Drive 10.5 mi E of Morgantown from the jct of US-48 and WV-7 on US-48, or 8.0 mi W of Bruceton Mills at Exit 15.

Raven Rock Trail (3.6 mi); Clay Run Furnace Trail (3.6 mi); Scott Run Trail (1.6 mi)

LENGTH: 8.8 mi round-trip, combined
DIFFICULTY: moderate
FEATURES: Raven Rock, Clay Iron Furnace

TRAILHEADS AND DETAILS: In the McCullum Campground, R of the bathhouse at the trail sign, ascend to the ridge, then E on slope of the ridge to another ridge. At 0.6 mi cross a fire road; turn L on a jeep road at 0.7 mi and continue ahead at the road jct at 1.0 mi. Area has hickory, poplar, oak, cherry, rhododendron, and copious banks of hay-scented fern. At 1.7 mi reach a ridge crest and the Raven Rock overlook at 1.8 mi. Superb view of Cheat River. (Molten cement and insulation of power line is from lightning in 1984.) Backtrack.

To hike the Clay Run Furnace Trail, cross the paved road at the entrance to the campground and descend to Clay Run. Follow downstream for 1.8 mi to the Henry Clay Iron Furnace, built between 1834 and 1836 by Leonard Lamb for Tassey and Bissell. The furnace produced four tons of pig iron each 24 hours, employed 200 workers, and lasted until 1847. (It is 0.5 mi N on a sled road to a parking area for a shorter hike, but a 3.9-mi drive from the campground is necessary. Also, at the furnace it is 1.0 mi S, ascending on a trail to Rock City at the picnic area, and a 2.0-mi hike downstream, W, along Clay Run to its mouth with the Cheat River Dam at Mont Chateau and the West Virginia Geological and Economic Survey headquarters.) Backtrack to the campground.

Scott Run Trail begins at McCullum Campground gate. Descend on an old logging road to a damp tributary area of Scott Run. Cross a footbridge at 0.4 mi and curve around a dry ridge to Scott Run at 0.8 mi. Bobcat, deer, timber rattlesnakes, and wild orchids have been seen on this trail. Backtrack.

Rock City Trail (1.2 mi); Clay Furnace Hiking Trail (2.0 mi)

LENGTH: 3.2 mi round-trip, combined
DIFFICULTY: easy
FEATURES: rock formations, Clay Iron Furnace

TRAILHEADS AND DETAILS: Drive to the farthest loop of the picnic area and park near the trail signs at shelter #3. Follow the *Rock City Trail* sign on a wide trail among tall trees of cherry, poplar, and oak. Pass two wildlife food plots; reach a picnic shelter at 0.4 mi and a sign for cross-country skiers. Explore rock crevices and outcrops at 0.6 mi. Backtrack. In the curve of the parking lot road is the *Clay Furnace Hiking Trail*. It is orange blazed on a woods road and descends for 1.0 mi to the Clay Run and the Clay Iron Furnace. Along the way are chestnut oak, mtn laurel, hemlock, maple, rhododendron, and wintergreen. Backtrack.

GREENBRIER STATE FOREST (Greenbrier County)

One of the marvels of the Mountain State is that a resort complex with the international reputation of the 650-room Greenbrier Hotel and a pristine forest of 5,130 acres with vacation log cabins can be only 3.5 miles apart. Serving their constituencies with equal professional skill, they share in the history and charm of White Sulphur Springs, settled in 1750. Such diversity has its advantages; a hiker on the *Black Bear Trail* by day can enjoy continental cuisine and social elegance by night.

Facilities at the state forest include a number of picnic units; swimming pool with bathhouse; 16 campsites (more planned); and foot trails. Hunting is allowed at designated forest areas with proper licenses and permits. Fishing is convenient in the nearby Greenbrier River. The forest staff presents a Show-Me Hike the last Saturday in April, beginning at picnic shelter #1 at 10 A.M. Information is also available on such flora as Kate's Mtn clover (*Trifolium virginicum*) and box huckleberry (*Gaylussacia brachycera*), neither of which is as rare as once thought. The latter is used locally for "juniper berry" pies. The Greenbrier State Forest staff also administers the *Greenbrier River Trail* (see section 6). (*USGS Maps*: White Sulphur Springs, Glace)

ADDRESS AND ACCESS: Greenbrier River State Forest, HC-30, Box 154, Caldwell, WV 24925; 304-536-1944. Drive 2.0 mi W of White Sulphur Springs on I-64 or US-60 to Harts Run exit and follow Harts Run Rd (CO-60/14) 1.3 mi to entrance.

Young's Nature Trail (1.7 mi); Black Bear Trail (2.4 mi); Old Road Trail (1.5 mi); Rocky Ridge Trail (2.0 mi)
LENGTH: 7.6 mi combined
DIFFICULTY: moderate

FEATURES: wildflowers, Kate's Mtn Overlook

TRAILHEADS AND DETAILS: From the main picnic area, ascend through a forest of tall oak, white pine, and hemlock on *Young's Nature Trail* to a jct with the *Black Bear Trail*, L, at 0.4 mi. *Young's Nature Trail* continues ahead, ascends R of a usually dry stream bed, and reaches Kate's Mtn Rd at 1.7 mi. Backtrack. (A 0.3-mi turn L on the Kate's Mtn Rd leads to a picnic area with a shelter.) On the *Black Bear Trail*, reach a ridge crest at 0.8 mi. On the trail banks are wild pink, bird's-foot violet, trailing arbutus, flame azalea, and squirrel cup (*Hepatica americana*). Yellow lady-slipper and other wild orchids also grow in this area. Descend on the ridge edge at 1.6 mi and reach a jct with the *Old Rd Trail* at 1.7 mi. (A less-used extension of the *Old Rd Trail* goes R and then curves L down to the swimming pool for another 1.5 mi.) Descend on an old road, pass sections of a fitness trail on the R, and reach the main road at 2.4 mi near the cabin area. Turn L and walk up the road to the beginning point at 2.8 mi.

Another hiking trail, the less-used 2.0 mi *Rocky Ridge Trail*, is accessible on the *Old Rd Trail*, 0.2 mi from the swimming pool. It ascends the mountainside to its E terminus at Kate's Mtn Rd (CO-60/34). A turn L on the road is 0.4 mi to the spectacular Kate's Mtn Overlook (2,700 ft). Access to this point for vehicular traffic is 4.8 mi from White Sulphur Springs (near the Greenbrier Hotel) on Kate's Mtn Rd (CO-60/34). The road is paved as it begins, but becomes rough as it climbs the mtn. Another access is to drive S from the campground area on Harts Run Rd (CO-60/14) to its jct L with the Kate's Mtn Rd for a total of 5.1 mi.

KANAWHA STATE FOREST (Kanawha County)

Within 8.0 mi of the capital city, Charleston, this forest paradise of 9,431 acres is an example of the wisdom of state government and individual citizens, such as Charles Carlson, to preserve some of the state's priceless natural history and beauty. Although it has magnificent hiking opportunities, it also has an excellent four-unit campground with full service; a swimming pool; numerous picnic areas; a playground; and a game area. Hunting and fishing are allowed in specified areas with appropriate licenses and permits. Among the wildlife are bear, deer, gray squirrel, grouse, turkey, bobcat, scores of songbird species, and four species of woodpeckers. There are 1,046 species of flora that have been identified, including 23 species of wild orchids—probably more than in any of the other state forests or parks. The gated hunting and fire roads provide additional miles for the exploring hiker, who may pass as many as 23 natural-gas wells, a reminder that natural resources can be used in conjunction with the protection of other resources. The forest is popular for outings by the Kanawha Trail Club, whose lodge on Middlelick Branch is on adjoining property. (*USGS Maps:* Charleston W, Racine)

A 0.5-mi loop *Interpretive Trail* for the physically handicapped is under construction, with assistance from the Greater Kanawha Valley Foundation; Cross Lanes Junior Woman's Club; the Boy Scouts; White Lincoln-Mercury, Inc.; and the Telephone Pioneers of America. The entrance will be across the main road from the old stables, and the trail will skirt both sides of Davis Creek.

ADDRESS AND ACCESS: Kanawha State Forest, Rte 2, Box 285, Charleston, WV 25314; 304-346-5654. From the jct of I-64 and US-119 (Exit 58-A) in Charleston, drive S on Oakwood Rd (US-119) for 1.2 mi. Turn L on Oakwood Rd (CO-13/10), which becomes State Forest Connell Rd (CO-23), and go 6.5 mi S through Laudendale to the forest entrance. (Also, look for forest route signs.)

Hiking Trail (2.4 mi); Pigeon Roost Trail (2.2 mi)

LENGTH: 5.7 mi combined
DIFFICULTY: moderate
FEATURE: nature study

TRAILHEADS AND DETAILS: From the Davis Creek Campground begin the *Hiking Trail* near campsite #14. On the steep ascent are spicebush and black cohosh among the hardwoods. Reach the ridge crest at 0.3 mi. (To the L, by a large P sign, is the N terminus of the *Pigeon Roost Trail*.) Turn R, by a large D sign, and follow the ridge line to a fork. Either route descends to a gated road. Turn R. At 1.3 mi reach a ball field and picnic area. Turn R at a service road jct and follow it upstream through a forest of maple, oak, cucumber, birch, and beech to the campground at 1.7 mi, and to the point of beginning for a loop of 2.4 mi. To make a loop of the *Pigeon Roost Trail*, walk out to the main road, turn R, pass the picnic area, enter the gated gravel walk and reach another picnic area, R, at 0.8 mi. Here is the S terminus of *Pigeon Roost Trail*. For 0.7 mi follow a wide, white-blazed trail on an old road, cross a ravine and pipeline, turn L off the old road, climb steeply in an eroded area, and reach a hunting road. Turn R on a vehicular road with banks of huckleberries. At 2.1 mi turn R at a road jct and follow the ridge road that makes first a slight decline and then an ascent to a curve at 2.8 mi. Turn R on a foot trail and reach a jct with the *Hiking Trail* at 3.0 mi; turn R, descend, and return to campsite #14 for a loop of 3.3 mi.

Johnson Hollow Trail

LENGTH: 1.6 mi round-trip
DIFFICULTY: moderate
FEATURE: wildflowers

TRAILHEAD AND DETAILS: From the Johnson Hollow Picnic Area parking lot on the main road, ascend to picnic shelter #7. Enter a rich, damp forest; first travel upstream, then R in an ascent on a ridge slope. Prominent among the wildflowers are wild hydrangea, mandrake, black cohosh, jewelweed, and meadow rue. Pass the stream again before final ascent to the gated Middle Ridge Rd at 0.8 mi. Backtrack.

Bowers Trail (2.1 mi); Lookout Trail (0.8 mi)

LENGTH: 2.9 mi round-trip, combined
DIFFICULTY: moderate
FEATURES: scenic, wildflowers

TRAILHEADS AND DETAILS: From the swimming pool area, drive upstream on the main road for 0.5 mi to a picnic and parking area, L. On the L side of the road walk up the road for 230 yd to the trail entrance, L. Cross Davis Creek on a footbridge. Ascend on a white-blazed trail and cross under a power line at 0.5 mi. The forest has huge hardwoods and displays of such wildflowers as crested dwarf iris and trillium. Fern patches include maidenhair fern. Cliffs, caves, and sandstone formations add to the trail's scenic attractiveness. Reach an old road at 0.8 mi; turn R. After another 0.3 mi turn L onto a foot trail for a steep descent to the main road at the Dunlop Hollow play area. Turn R, follow the paved road for 130 yd, turn R off the road, cross a footbridge, and enter an open area (may be weedy in the summer). Turn L at a footbridge and cross Davis Creek at 1.9 mi. Reach the point of beginning for a loop of 2.1 mi. Across the road, but N of the stables, is the *Lookout Trail*. It is a steep trail that ascends 0.2 mi to a forest road, where a R turn for another 0.2 mi leads to a scenic overlook of Davis Creek valley. Backtrack.

Beech Glen Nature Trail

LENGTH: 3.2 mi round-trip
DIFFICULTY: easy
FEATURE: natural history

TRAILHEAD AND DETAILS: Park at the Polly Hollow Picnic Area. (According to legend, Polly was a courageous girl who crusaded for a schoolhouse in the valley.) (At the Polly Hollow Picnic Area is the SE terminus of the unmarked, 30-mi *Wyatt Trail*, a Boy Scout trail that goes W-NW to St. Albans. It was created in honor of Bill Wyatt of Troop 146. See chapter 10 for information on permission and guides to hike this trail.) At the gated road, follow it upstream. Some of the trees are ash, hickory, black birch, oak, Virginia pine, and hemlock. At 0.8 mi turn L off the road at a sign. (The *Wyatt Trail* continues ahead on the forest road. Dead-end roads are on the R and L in its climb to the ridge crest and forest boundary line after 0.5 mi. A sharp turn R leads to a jct with Bee Mtn Rd [CO-15, also called Middle Fork Rd]. Here it turns L, leaves the Kanawha State Forest, and descends to Brier Creek and the community of Olcott after 2.5 mi.) Cross Polly Hollow stream at 1.0 mi, near an old coal mine, and ascend. Bluebead lily, wild sweet potato (*Dioscorea villosa*), coreopsis, and bedstraw grow here. Reach a rock formation of sandstone and iron ore segments and moss-covered cliffs at 1.6 mi. (A faint trail ahead for 130 yd leads to a ridge where a R turn up the ridge leads to the forest boundary road. A turn R on the boundary road connects with the Polly Hollow Rd, which leads, R, down the mtn to rejoin the *Beech Glen Nature Trail* after a loop of 2.1 mi.) Backtrack, but at the road jct bear R on an old RR grade with an excellent treadway that parallels the road to reach the point of origin.

Lake Trail

LENGTH: 1.3 mi
DIFFICULTY: easy
FEATURE: nature study

TRAILHEAD AND DETAILS: From the main entrance to the forest, drive 0.2 mi to the picnic and lake parking lot, L. Cross Davis Creek and follow the trail by the lake, turn L, and ascend to a jct with Middle Ridge Rd at 0.4 mi. Backtrack to the lake, turn L upstream, and reach the forest office at 0.9 mi. Turn R on the main road and walk back to the point of origin for 1.3 mi. Wildflowers include wild orchids, trillium, and twayblade.

Alligator Rock Trail (0.6 mi); Lindy Trail (0.6 mi); Ballard Trail (0.7 mi);
Martin Trail (0.3 mi); Critz Trail (0.6 mi)

LENGTH: 3.2 mi combined

DIFFICULTY: moderate to strenuous

FEATURES: geology, nature study

TRAILHEADS AND DETAILS: From the swimming pool parking area, walk E, cross Shrewsbury Hollow stream, ascend to a gated gravel forest road, and turn R. After 0.3 mi, turn L at a large A sign on the white-blazed *Alligator Rock Trail*. Pass a rock formation, descend to a stream bed, follow upstream, and reach a forest road, Middle Ridge Rd, at 0.9 mi. (Across the road is *Lindy Trail*, which descends steeply 0.6 mi to Middlelick Branch and the Kanawha Trail Club Lodge. From here it is 1.0 mi N, downstream, to the main forest entrance, L.) A turn L on the road also descends to Middlelick Branch. Turn R and follow the road for 0.5 mi to a jct with the *Ballard Trail*, L. (The 0.7-mi *Ballard Trail* is another steep access trail to Middlelick Branch Rd, upstream from the Kanawha Trail Club Lodge.) Continue ahead on the road for another 0.3 mi to *Martin Trail*, L. (The *Martin Trail* descends steeply 0.3 mi to the gated Hoffman Hollow forest road that leads L to a jct with the Middlelick Branch Rd.) On the R is an unnamed, faint forest trail that descends into a hollow. It crosses ravines, follows a S slope, passes rock formations, crisscrosses a stream, and exits at the Shrewsbury Hollow Rd after 0.6 mi. (I have called it the *David Critz Trail* because he guided me on this route. Another route, 1.3 mi, which brings the hiker to this exit, is to follow the Middle Ridge Rd S to the first R turn, the Shrewsbury Hollow Rd.) Turn R on the Shrewsbury Hollow Rd, pass the *Alligator Rock Trail* jct at 3.0 mi, and return to the parking lot for a loop of 3.3 mi.

Rock Camp Trail (1.1 mi); North-South Trail (0.7 mi); District Line Trail (1.5 mi); Left Fork Trail (0.7 mi); Bays Fork Trail (2.1 mi)

LENGTH: 6.2 mi combined

DIFFICULTY: moderate

FEATURE: natural history

TRAILHEADS AND DETAILS: In the NW section of the forest there are a number of access points to gated forest roads and jeep trails. Two of these access points are described below. One is the Rock Camp Branch access, S of Ruth, and the other is the Bays Fork access, S of the Ivydale community. If approaching the Rock Camp Branch area from the main forest entrance, drive 6.7 mi NW, downstream by Davis Creek, to the community of Davis Creek at the jct with US-119. (It is 3.5 mi E on US-119 to Charleston and I-64.) Turn L on US-119 (or WV-214 if US-119 is under construction) and travel 2.6 mi to Ruth and a jct with Trace Fork Rd (CO-11/2). Drive upstream for 1.7 mi on Trace Fork Rd to a fork. (A burgundy-colored house is in the fork across the bridge.) Turn L and park at the first jeep road, R. Hike across Rock Camp Branch and follow the jeep road in a forest of tall poplar, ironwood, oak, and beech. (One tree bears a carved message: Susan loves Doug.) Caves are on the L. At 0.6 mi the jeep road turns R and becomes the *North-South Trail*, which ascends and connects with a hunting road. The *Rock Camp Trail* continues ahead but becomes a foot trail. Ascend in a young forest and reach the trail's terminus at *District Line Trail* on the ridge crest at 1.1 mi. (To the L the *District Line Trail* goes 0.8 mi on a jeep road to private property at Long Branch.) Continue R on the *District Line Trail* for 0.7 mi to its S terminus and a jct with the *Left Fork Trail* and a hunting road on a perpendicular ridge line. Make a sharp L and descend on the 0.7-mi *Left Fork Trail* to its terminus and jct with the *Bays Fork Trail*. (Downstream, the *Bays Fork Trail* goes 1.3 mi to Middle Creek and Bee Mtn Road (CO-15), the other access route mentioned above.) Turn R on the *Bays Fork Trail*, cross the stream, and ascend to the headwaters in a deep hollow. Reach the ridge crest and a jct with a hunting road after 0.8 mi. Here, you may backtrack to the point of origin for a total of 6.6 mi. Or, turn R on the jeep road and follow it for 0.9 mi to the *District Line Trail* jct, R, for a return mileage of 6.0 mi. (Another option is to continue W on the hunting road to a more established road and after 0.7 mi take the first R, the *North-South Trail*. This partial return loop is 6.2 mi.)

The other vehicular access point is through the community of Ivydale. From Davis Creek community and the jct of US-119 and Davis Creek Rd (CO-20), drive 0.5 mi on Davis Creek Rd to the W. J. Watters Bldg and turn R across the bridge onto Bee Mtn Rd (CO-15, also called Middle Fork Rd). (It is 6.2 mi upstream on Davis Creek Rd to the main entrance of the forest.) Follow upstream for 3.6 mi beside Middle Fork, pass through Ivydale, and reach the jct with the Bays Fork and *Bays Fork Trail*, R. After Ivydale, the road becomes a stream bed, easily flooded, and the road beyond this point is narrow, often rough; a 4WD vehicle may be necessary. The *Bays Fork Trail* begins first as a jeep road but becomes more of a footpath after passing under the power line at 0.6 mi. At 1.3 mi it connects with the *Left Fork Trail* as described above.

There are other road-trails beyond the Bays Fork. For example, continue 0.7 mi upstream by Middle Fork and reach a jct with gated Rattlesnake Run hunting road, L. It goes 1.7 mi E, crosses a ridge, and descends through the forest service area for a connection to the forest main road, 0.5 mi N of the swimming pool. (For another 4.5 mi CO-15 continues upstream, ascends a mtn ridge to the forest boundary, and descends to the community of Olcott.) The forest has numerous unnamed hunting roads and jeep trails, many that dead-end at gas wells. Hikers unfamiliar with the forest should have directions from the superintendent before taking long exploratory hikes.

KUMBRABOW STATE FOREST (Randolph County)

Between Holly River State Park (W) and the Monongahela National Forest (E) are 9,431 acres of absolute, pristine delight. You can choose a sequestered vacation in one of the five pioneer cabins within the sound of Mill Creek Falls or at the 12 primitive campsites by a trout stream. More wildlife than people visit these sanctuaries. The forest is named for three prominent families—Kump, Brady, and Bowers—who influenced the forest purchase. Highest of all the state forests, its lowest elev is 2,500 ft and its highest elev is 3,734 ft. With 20 wildlife food plots and swift, pure streams, a hiker has a good chance to see and photograph bear, deer, turkey, grouse, or owls. Once among the state's best forest for hemlock and spruce, the forest now has large stands of second-growth cherry, ash, maple, and yellow and black birch. Rainfall is high, approximately 70 in annually, and substantiates the state's slogan that West Virginia is wild, wet, and wonderful. Recreation activities include fishing, hunting, picnicking, and hiking. (*USGS Maps*: Valley Head, Adolph, Pickens)

ADDRESS AND ACCESS: Kumbrabow State Forest, PO Box 65, Huttonsville, WV 26273; 304-335-2219. East entrance is halfway between the towns of Huttonsville and Valley Head on US-219 and WV-50 to Kumbrabow Forest Rd (CO-219/16). Ascend 3.8 mi to forest entrance. West entrance from Pickens is on Haker Valley Rd (CO-47) and Turkey Bone Rd (CO-45) for 8.0 mi.

SUPPORT FACILITIES: Huttonsville/Mill Creek has groceries, service station, bank, hardware store, motel, restaurant, and other services.

Raven Rocks Trail (1.2 mi); Rich Mountain Fire Trail (3.1 mi); Meatbox Run Trail (1.4 mi); Potato Hole Run Trail (1.5 mi)

LENGTH: 7.2 mi combined

DIFFICULTY: moderate to strenuous

FEATURES: Raven Rocks, woods lore, wildlife

TRAILHEADS AND DETAILS: From the campground go 0.5 mi W on the main road and park. Ascend steeply to a superb view of Mill Creek valley and the campground from Raven Rocks at 0.2 mi. Turn L on a wide ridge trail and at 1.2 mi reach a jct with the *Rich Mtn Fire Trail* (sign is marked 4.0 mi to Pickens-Monterville Rd; it should read 3.1 mi to Turkey Bone Rd). Bear L on a grassy road bordered with a lush array of ferns. Reach a road jct, L, at 2.3 mi (*Meatbox Run Trail* begins 100 yd L on this dead-end road. Descend on the footpath along Meatbox Run and reach the Mill Creek Rd at the picnic area at 3.7 mi. Turn L and walk back to the point of beginning for a 4.0-mi loop.) (Another loop can be made by continuing on the dead-end road mentioned above. After 0.5 mi reach a cul-de-sac. On the S side begin a descent on the *Potato Hole Run Trail* into a damp and deep forest of hemlock and rhododendron to the confluence of a stream with Potato Hole Run at 3.5 mi. Reach the forest office at 4.3 mi. Turn L on the Mill Creek Rd and walk back to the point of beginning at 6.2 mi.) To continue on the *Rich Mtn Fire Trail*, disregard numerous spur roads, R or L; pass R of Buck Knob at 2.8 mi and R of Whitman Knob to reach Turkey Bone Rd (CO-45) at 4.3 mi. Backtrack to point of beginning for 8.6 mi or use a vehicle shuttle.

PANTHER STATE FOREST (McDowell County)

There is a legend in parts of this valley that Tommy Lester, a pre–Civil War inhabitant, met a panther face to face. When Lester's gun failed, he had to fight the beast with a knife and help from his dogs. It is assumed he won the fight. As a result the post office, community, creek, and the 7,810-acre forest are named Panther. This once exceptionally wild and rugged hill country near the corners of Virginia, Kentucky, and West Virginia has numerous streams named after animals—deerskin, crane, fox, cub, and, of course, panther.

Facilities are six campsites; a vault toilet; a playground; a group camp with men's and women's barracks, kitchen, and dining areas; picnic areas; swimming pool; and trails. Hunting and fishing (in a rainbow-stocked stream) allowed with appropriate licenses and permits. Season is April to November. (*USGS Maps*: Panther, Iaeger)

ADDRESS AND ACCESS: Superintendent, Panther State Forest, PO Box 287, Panther, WV 24872; 304-938-2252. At the jct of Greenbrier Mtn Rd (CO-3) and Johnny Cake Rd (CO-1) in Panther, go S for 0.4 mi on the Greenbrier Mtn Rd and turn L on Trap Fork Rd (CO-3/1), which becomes Panther Creek Rd (CO-3/2), for a total of 5 mi.

SUPPORT FACILITIES: The nearest food and other supplies are in Iaeger, 12.0 mi E on US-52.

Drift Branch Trail (1.3 mi); Twin Rocks Trail (0.6 mi)

LENGTH: 3.2 mi round-trip, combined
DIFFICULTY: strenuous
FEATURE: panoramic views

TRAILHEADS AND DETAILS: Park at the Cowshead Picnic Area. Cross a footbridge at the sign and follow up the stream of Drift Branch. Among the wildflowers are trillium, foamflower, black cohosh, bloodroot, and rhododendron. At 0.2 mi is a jct with a 0.6-mi spur trail, *Twin Rocks Trail*, R, that goes to the group camp. Continue ahead through an oak forest, pass remains of an old log cabin, and ascend under a power line to a jct with an old fire road at 1.3 mi. Here is a 45-ft-high fire tower established in 1940 at an elev of 2,065 ft. Views of hills and forests are panoramic. Backtrack.

Crane Branch Nature Trail

LENGTH: 1.3 mi
DIFFICULTY: moderate
FEATURE: overlook

TRAILHEAD AND DETAILS: From the camping area cross the road and begin an interpretive trail with 29 markers of trees, shrubs, and wildflowers. Cross Crane Branch, ascend on switchbacks, and reach scenic Buzzard Roost Overlook at 0.6 mi. Return on the N direction of the trail and descend to George's Fork Picnic Area at 1.3 mi. Turn L on the road and walk back to the campground at 1.5 mi.

SENECA STATE FOREST (Pocahontas County)

The state's oldest (1924) forest is named for the Seneca Indians, a tribe of the Iroquois family, who made peace with the US in 1815. Across the nation there are rivers, lakes, counties, creeks, mountains, and rock formations with the name of Seneca. A few hundred of the Seneca descendants are in a reservation in New York State.

A forest of 11,684 acres, the Seneca is bordered on the W by the historic Greenbrier River and on the E by Michael Mtn. The Greenbrier Ranger District of the MNF adjoins on the N. Only a few miles N are Cass Scenic Railroad State Park and the National Radio Astronomy Observatory. Fishing (bass, trout, bluegill), hunting (deer, grouse, wild turkey, bear), and picnicking are its main recreation activities. Also available are seven rustic, isolated cabins and 10 campsites (without hookups). The *Allegheny Trail* passes through the forest; other trails and old forest roads provide good hiking. (*USGS Map*: Clover Lick)

ADDRESS AND ACCESS: Seneca State Forest, Rte 1, Box 140, Dunmore WV 24934; 304-799-6213. From the town of Dunmore go 5.3 mi S on WV-28, and from Huntersville go N on WV-28 for 10.0 mi.

Crestline Trail

LENGTH: 5.4 mi round-trip

DIFFICULTY: moderate

FEATURE: rock outcrops

TRAILHEAD AND DETAILS: From the picnic area of WV-28, drive (or hike) the steep gravel road for 2.1 mi to a small parking area on Michael Mtn. Begin the hike at the trail sign and follow a narrow, rocky, white-blazed treadway. Hemlock, white pine, and chestnut oak are dominant. Fragrant trailing arbutus, huckleberry, and mosses are between the rocks and on the open banks. Follow the ridge crest over rough ledges and cliffs to the highest point on the trail (3,650 ft) at 1.5 mi. There is an orange blaze from 1.8 mi to the trail end at 2.7 mi. Backtrack.

Great Laurel Trail (0.6 mi); Hill Top Trail (1.5 mi); Scarlet Oak Trail (1.0 mi); Horseshoe Trail (1.1 mi)

LENGTH: 5.1 mi combined

DIFFICULTY: moderate

FEATURE: nature study

TRAILHEADS AND DETAILS: In the campground, from site #8, follow *Great Laurel Trail* through an area of rhododendron, white pine, and ferns. Pass the *Horseshoe Trail*, R. Cross Seven Mile Run and ascend to the ridge crest at 0.5 mi. At 0.6 mi is a jct with the *Hill Top Trail* (R is to Lake Rd). Turn L on the *Hill Top Trail* and descend along the ridge. Turn R at 1.0 mi; descend steeply, go through a stand of white pine, and reach the forest office and parking area at 1.5 mi. Turn R on Lake Rd through a deep forest. At 1.8 mi turn R on *Scarlet Oak Trail*, ascend steeply, and reach a jct with the Loop Rd at 2.4 mi (L is the Lake Rd and spur trail to the lake). Turn R, and return to the *Hill Top Trail* R at 2.5 mi. Reach the *Great Laurel Trail* jct at 2.8 mi; turn L. Reach the *Horseshoe Trail* jct, L, at 3.4 mi near the campground. Turn L, ascend on the *Horseshoe Trail* to a ridge and a young forest with wintergreen and mosses. Descend to the campground for a loop of 4.5 mi.

Black Oak Trail

LENGTH: 1.2 mi

DIFFICULTY: easy

FEATURE: nature study

TRAILHEAD AND DETAILS: From the forest office drive the Lake Rd for 2.4 mi to the fire tower crossroads and park. (The yellow-blazed *Allegheny Trail* crosses here, N-S.) Hike R on the Firetower Rd and *Allegheny Trail* for 0.2 mi to the *Black Oak Trail*, L. (It is another 0.2 mi up the road to the fire tower and panoramic views from 3,458 ft elev.) Descend on a footpath through a mature forest, wildflowers, and Indian pipe (*Monotropa uniflora*). Reach a forest road at 1.2 mi, turn L, and walk up the road to the crossroads and beginning point at 2.2 mi.

Thorny Creek Trail

LENGTH: 5.2 mi

DIFFICULTY: moderate

FEATURES: scenic, wildlife

TRAILHEAD AND DETAILS: From the forest office drive 0.8 mi to a jct with Loop Rd and park. Walk on the Loop Rd R 1.5 mi to a jct with *Thorny Creek Trail*. Turn L and descend into Thorny Creek watershed, eventually reaching an old RR grade lined with rhododendron. Cross a stream at 0.6 mi; from here to the lake at 1.1 mi beavers are in abundance. Follow the trail through lake parking area at 1.3 mi and continue downstream through hemlock, rhododendron, and mtn laurel to a meadow of elderberry and sumac. At 1.8 mi cross Thorny Creek on a footbridge near the ruins of an old cabin. Club moss and wintergreen are prominent. At 3.1 mi is a cow pasture on the R. Deer and grouse are often seen in this area. Ascend L of a fence to a ridge, then climb another ridge to a jeep road at 3.6 mi. Follow the jeep road and reach the top of Little Mtn at 4.0 mi. Jct with the *Little Mtn Trail* at 4.5 mi. (The *Little Mtn Trail* is 0.6 mi R to the forest office.) Continue ahead; reach the jct of the Lake and Loop Rds at 5.2 mi.

8. State Wildlife Management Areas

The wild animals own the forest; we are their stewards.

—George C. Clifton

West Virginia has 58 Wildlife Management Areas (WMAs) (formerly Public Hunting and Fishing Areas [PHFAs]. They cover more than 350,000 acres. Some WMAs have primitive or rustic camping areas with vault restrooms, well water, and cleared campsites. There is a nominal fee. (Some WMAs adjoin state parks or are near commercial campgrounds with full service.) Camping is permitted only at designated areas to protect the natural environment. The campgrounds are usually open year-round, depending on the weather. It is wise to check in advance if dates are other than Memorial Day to Labor Day. Although hunting and fishing are the primary activities, the hunting roads and jeep trails provide an incredible network of mileage for hikers. There is space for all types of outdoor activists and nature lovers, and those who do not hunt should choose a time other than the game-hunting seasons. For the protection of wildlife during the breeding seasons, many hunting roads may be locked. An advance check with the Wildlife Resources Division is recommended. Although there are paths and roads to walk in all the WMAs, some have unnamed trails, particularly around the lakes. Others, such as Laurel Lake WMA may have a name, e.g., *Lakeside Trail*. (It also has a short trail named *Flying Squirrel Trail*.) For the purpose of this book, only WMAs with a planned system of named and marked systems (such as Lewis Wetzel WMA), or named but not necessarily on signposts (such as Sleepy Creek WMA), are included.

INFORMATION: Wildlife Resources, Dept. of Natural Resources, State Capital Complex, Bldg 3, 1900 Kanawha Blvd, Charleston, WV 25305; 304-558-2771.

ELK RIVER WMA (Braxton County)

Located at the geographic center of the state, this exceptionally attractive preserve is the state's oldest public hunting and fishing area. It has a vast area (17,184 acres—6,949 state owned and 10,235 leased from the Corps of Engineers) for hunting, fishing, boating, water skiing, hiking, and nature study. For management purposes, the area is divided into two sections: the Holly on the N side of Sutton Lake, and the Elk on the S side. Because the S side has named trails, it is described below. Approximately 30 mi of "hunting trails" are in the forest, and some of these road-trails lead to coves with virgin trees three to five feet in diameter. Camping is not permitted in the WMA but is allowed at three campgrounds on the adjoining Lake Sutton, a US Army Corps of Engineers project. Game species include deer, squirrel, wild turkey, grouse, and raccoon. Anglers can expect bass, walleyes, channel catfish, bluegill, and crappie. Trout are stocked below Sutton Dam. The forest is popular in early April for its morels (genus *Morchella*). Bird-watchers also will find this forest, with its wildlife food plots and water holes, ideal. It is open year-round. (*USGS Maps*: Sutton, Newville, Little Bush)

ADDRESS AND ACCESS: WV-DNR office, PO Box 38, French Creek, WV 26218; 304-924-6211. From downtown Sutton, cross the bridge on Old Turnpike Rd (CO-19/40) and go S for 3.8 mi to a jct with Wolf Creek–Centralia Rd (CO-17). Turn L on CO-17, go 4.1 mi, and bear L at the Spruce Lick Methodist Church; drive 2.7 mi farther and turn L on Stony Creek Rd (CO-17/9). Go another 2.5 mi to Elk River WMA management office, but first call 304-924-6211.

Hickory Flats Trail (4.8 mi); Dynamite Trail (1.0 mi); Tower Falls Trail (0.8 mi); Woodell Trail (2.2 mi); Canoe River Trail (3.6 mi); Gibson Trail (0.9 mi); Billy Linger Trail (4.4 mi)

LENGTH: 17.7 mi round-trip, combined

DIFFICULTY: easy to strenuous

FEATURES: wildlife, plant life, scenic

TRAILHEADS AND DETAILS: The named and signed grassy road-trails form loops, overlaps, and dead ends. They are well maintained and wide enough for hiking, horseback riding, or 4WD vehicles. In the description below, the main ridge trail is emphasized with the side or spur trails in parentheses. Individual mileage is round-trip, but a wide range of combination mileages can occur.

Some of the trees, shrubs, and wildflowers are pignut hickory, white pine, poplar, red and sugar maple, basswood, cucumber tree, hemlock, locust, papaw, yellow root, redbud, jack-in-the-pulpit, mtn laurel, and rhododendron.

Begin from the headquarters parking lot and follow the main road N for 0.2 mi to a locked gate. Pass the gate, slightly descend, and reach the *Dynamite Trail* at 0.5 mi. (The *Dynamite Trail* goes 0.5 mi toward the headwaters of Oldlick Run. Backtrack.) Continue ahead and reach the *Tower Falls Trail*, R, at 0.7 mi. (The *Tower Falls Trail* goes through a wildlife plot and after 0.5 mi dead-ends. Backtrack or connect with the *Woodell Trail*.) At 1.0 mi is a jct with the *Woodell Trail*, R. (The *Woodell Trail* makes a loop and has a spur among a number of wildlife food plots. Mileage potential is 2.2.) On the main route, *Hickory Flats Trail*, reach a jct with *Canoe Trail*, R, at 1.2 mi. The Hickory Flats Shelter is L. (The *Canoe Trail* adjoins the *Woodell Trail*, but soon turns L and descends to Canoe Run. There it crosses the stream and extends toward Sutton Lake. Backtrack for a total of 3.6 mi.) At 2.4 mi the *Hickory Flats Trail* becomes the *Billy Linger Trail*. To the R is the *Gibson Trail*. (The *Gibson Trail* descends and passes a wildlife food plot and water hole for a loop of 0.9 mi.) Continue ahead on the *Billy Linger Trail* through a gate, pass R of a cabin at 2.6 mi, and reach scenic views of Lake Sutton at 3.0 mi and 3.3 mi. Ahead, curve L on the ridge peninsula and descend toward the lake for another 1.3 mi. Excellent views when the leaves are off the trees. Backtrack.

There are other trails in the area. For example, at the entrance to the area the *Stony Creek Hunting Trail* and the *Cherry Tree Hunting Trail* go W. The *Stony Creek Hunting Trail* is approximately 2.5 mi to Mortons Rd (CO-17/3), where a L turn exits to Wolf Creek Rd (CO-17). (A spur trail goes 0.8 mi downstream on Stony Creek to the lake.) The trail has wildlife food plots. The Cherry Tree area extends 1.7 mi to a variety of food plots W of the WMA office.

LEWIS WETZEL WMA (Wetzel County)

For hikers who desire nearly 35 mi of old woods roads and hunters' trails on steep ridges of 1,500 ft elev, deep and damp hollows, and meadows with trout-stocked streams, this 9,125-acre wildlife area is the place to be. That is, during the hunting off-season, because these hills and valleys have the state's highest ruffed grouse (*Bonasa umbellus*) population. Other managed game species are deer, gray squirrel, raccoon, wild turkey, fox, muskrat, mink, and rabbit. Rattlesnakes are among the reptiles and spring peeper among the amphibians. Some of the streams are stocked with rainbow trout. Vegetation consists of central hardwoods such as oak, hickory, sycamore, black locust, black walnut, buckeye, and beech. There is also cherry, papaw, and white pine. The most recent trail, *Locust Ridge Loop Trail*, is named for black locust (*Robinia pseudoacacia*), whose whitish flowers hang in fragrant clusters. Estimated to be 2.5 mi by the forest staff, it descends from the ridge to Huckleberry Run and loops back to the ridge. Among the wildflowers are black-eyed Susan, bee balm, milkweed, and goldenseal. The Wildlife Division has planted bird's-foot trefoil, ladino clover, and autumn olive (silverberry) for numerous wildlife food plots.

This wildlife management area, and the county, received their names from the famous Indian fighter Lewis Wetzel. He was from a courageous pioneer family of explorers and settlers. Lewis, with his brother Jacob, was captured by the Indians in 1777. One of his three other brothers was killed. After his escape Wetzel became a marksman with vengence on this mind. He was also an expert game hunter and country dance fiddler.

Facilities in the area are 20 primitive campsites at the campground, hand-pump well, and vault toilet. Permission must be granted by the superintendent for overnight camping outside the campground. Hunting roads usually need 4WD vehicles. Open year-round. (*USGS Maps*: Big Run, Center Point, Pine Grove)

ADDRESS AND ACCESS: Lewis Wetzel WMA, 8C62, Box 8, Jacksonburg, WV 26377; 304-889-3497. In Jacksonburg at the jct of WV-20 and Buffalo Run Rd (CO-82) follow the Buffalo Run Rd for 3.2 mi to the forest office and another 1.2 mi to the campground.

SUPPORT FACILITES: Groceries and basic supplies are in Jacksonburg. It is 23 mi NW on WV-20 to New Martinsville.

Horse Run Trail (0.9 mi); High Knob Trail (3.3 mi); Lesin Run Trail (1.1 mi); Hart Ridge Trail (1.0 mi); Nettle Run Trail (1.4 mi); Huss Pen Trail (0.9 mi); Hiles Run Trail (0.7 mi)

LENGTH: 9.3 mi combined

DIFFICULTY: moderate to strenuous

FEATURES: wildlife, history

TRAILHEADS AND DETAILS: These connecting trails are all E of Buffalo Run and are used by hunters and hikers. West of the stream are mainly jeep trails, some of which have rough sections and are used by hunters. From the superintendent's office it is 1.2 mi upstream by Buffalo Run to the campground. Here is a base for a combined circuit of the above trails. From the campground, walk out to the entrance road to the *Horse Run Trail*, R. Walk around the locked gate and follow upstream. There are plenty of wildflowers, such as black-eyed Susans, bellflowers, and daisies. Walnut, cherry, and buckeye are also prominent. At 0.3 mi keep R and at 0.4 mi begin ascent, cross the stream, and reach the crest of the ridge at 0.9 mi to connect with the *High Knob Trail*, L. Follow the *High Knob Trail* L (N) and reach a jct with the *Lesin Run Trail* after 1.1 mi (2.0 mi from the campground). (The *Lesin Run Trail* descends, L, for 1.1 mi to the Buffalo Run Rd. A 0.2-mi L turn on the road back to the campground is a loop of 3.3 mi.) Continue ahead and at 2.3 mi reach a jct with the *Hart Ridge Trail*, L. (The *Hart Ridge Trail* follows the ridge line before making a steep descent to the gate at Buffalo Run Rd at 1.0 mi. A 0.3-mi L turn on the road back to the campground is a loop of 3.6 mi.) Continue on the ridge and pass a jct with the *Nettle Run Trail* at 2.7 mi. (The *Nettle Run Trail* descends for 1.4 mi to the forest office. Along the way it follows an old road; passes under a gas pipeline swath to the headwaters of Nettle Run in a dark, damp hollow; reaches a gate and gravel road; and exits R of the office to Buffalo Run Rd. A L turn up the road for 1.2 mi to the campground is a loop of 5.3 mi.) Continue on the *High Knob Trail* on a grassy hunters' road. At 3.1 mi is a sign, R, to Ashcamp Run. Skirt the E slope of the ridge and reach a road jct at 3.3 mi. *High Knob Trail* forks L and the road continues on the R to connect with *Huss Pen Trail* and *Hiles Run Trail* described below. Follow the *High Knob Trail* on a spur ridge line to a pipeline swath and wildlife food plot, and begin an exceptionally steep descent at 3.7 mi. Reach the Buffalo Run Rd on the N side of Nettle Run by the forest office. (A turn L and walk up the road to the campground is a loop of 5.4 mi.) Along the main ridge from the *High Knob Trail* fork go 0.2 mi to a jct with the *Huss Pen Trail*, L. (The *Huss Pen Trail* descends steeply in sections and L of a stream bed to exit after 0.9 mi at Buffalo Run Rd and a gas pipeline. From here it is 1.9 mi L to the campground for a loop of 6.3 mi.) A final trail from the ridge is another 0.7 mi to a jct with *Hiles Run Trail*. (Descend on the *Hiles Run Trail*, L, steeply in sections for 0.7 mi to a cove and on the L of an abandoned oil well before reaching Buffalo Run Rd. From here, L, it is 2.3 mi back to the campground for a loop of 7.2 mi.)

SLEEPY CREEK WMA (Morgan and Berkeley Counties)

Forty years of management by the state's Conservation Commission and Department of Natural Resources have made an outstanding transformation in this 23,000-acre double mtn range. By 1835 all the deer had disappeared and by 1915 all the wild turkey had been killed. By 1910 all the timber had been ravished, and by 1942 a devastating forest fire further diminished forest life on the ridge and in the Meadow Branch valley.

In 1950 the state began purchasing the property from the Farmers Bank of Pittsburgh for only $152 an acre. Until 1954 it was managed as a state forest. Now the forest is growing with oak, Virginia and white pine, hickory, hemlock, beech, and maple. Deer roam the forest, wild turkey are back, and the grouse, squirrel, and raccoon populations are increasing. There are 42 wildlife food plots.

The forest gets its name from the three-pronged Sleepy Creek in Morgan County. The county line of Morgan and Berkeley runs along the ridge of Sleepy Creek Mtn, but most of the preserve is in Berkeley County. The E mtn ridge is Third Hill Mtn, and in the lower half of the area the two ridges are joined with a crossbeam ridge called Locks-of-the-Mtn. Nearby is the preserve's highest peak, Shanghai Beacon (2,172 ft).

In the center of the forest is a 205-acre lake, opened in 1964, where anglers may catch stocked largemouth bass, bluegill, crappie, northern pike, and channel catfish. In keeping with the tranquillity of the forest, only paddle boats and boats with electric motors are permitted. Primitive campgrounds with 75 units are near the lake or at designated places. Well water and vault toilets are available.

There are more than 50 mi of 12 seasonal-access hunting roads and 16 mi of 12-ft trails that have names, but are not signed or marked. A designated foot trail, the longest, is 20.8 mi of the *Tuscarora Trail* (South) formerly *Big Blue Trail*. It parallels the Little Brush Run in the S, the Meadow Branch in the middle, and the Sleepy Creek Mtn ridge line in the N. It overlaps or connects with a number of other footpaths and hunting roads on its route through Sleepy Creek WMA. Its route through Virginia and other areas of West Virginia is described in chapter 11.

Tuscarora Trail (South) (20.8 mi)

(See connecting trails in Sleepy Creek WMA and chapter 11.)

LENGTH: 20.8 mi

DIFFICULTY: easy to moderate

FEATURES: wildlife, scenic, remote

TRAILHEADS AND DETAILS: To enter from the S, drive 2.5 mi W of Glengary on WV-45 to a parking area. Follow the blue blazes on a dirt road and at 0.6 mi turn R to enter the Sleepy Creek WMA. After 1.5 mi reach wildlife food plot #38 and a jct, R, with the *Big Run Trail*. (The 0.7-mi *Big Run Trail* is an unsigned foot trail that goes to another food plot and the E boundary of the forest.) At 2.5 mi reach a jct with *High Rock Trail*, L, and food plot #34. (The 0.6-mi *High Rock Trail* crosses Brush Creek and ascends to High Rock for a jct with the Sleepy Creek Mtn jeep trail.) Reach a jct with the Sleepy Creek Mtn jeep road, L, at 4.5 mi. Continue ahead to a jct, R, with the Pee Wee Point jeep road, ahead to a camping registration board at 4.8 mi, and the jct with the Locks-of-the-Mtn on Hampshire Grade Rd (CO-7/13). Follow the road for 0.8 mi to a jct with an old jeep road, R, the *High Knob Trail*. (The *High Knob Trail* is an unsigned trail that ascends to the Shanghai Beacon for 1.0 mi.) Ahead, after 0.1 mi on the Hampshire Grade Rd, turn L on the Old Still Rd. It descends and follows a ridge past more wildlife plots. At 8.4 mi reach the Dead Mule jeep trail that goes R and up the slope to gated Third Hill Mtn Rd. Continue ahead between Roaring Run and Meadow Branch, but cross Roaring Run at 9.6 mi. (To the R is a footpath, the 1.0-mi *Roaring Run Trail*, which goes up Roaring Run to Third Hill Mtn Rd.)

Arrive at the gravel lake road at 10.0 mi and pass Upper Campground at 10.9 mi. Pass Myers Place Campground at 11.2 mi and reach a road fork at 11.3 mi. (To the R it is 3.9 mi on the road to the superintendent's office and another 2.3 mi to Back Creek Rd [CO-7] and Jones Springs.) To the L at the fork, continue on the *Tuscarora Trail* (South) and pass Piney Point Campground and Lower Campground. At 13.0 mi leave the lakeside road, cross two small streams, and at 13.8 mi turn L at a fork. (The R fork is *Meadow Branch Trail*, which passes under a power line and turns E to a jct with the *Third Mtn Trail* Rd.) At 14.0 mi cross Meadow Creek, pass under a power line, and begin an ascent. Reach White's Gap and Sleepy Creek Mtn jeep road at 16.0 mi. (To the R is the unsigned *White's Gap Trail*, a footpath that descends 1.0 mi to the crossing of Meadow Branch and a fork. The R fork is the 0.5-mi *White's Knob Trail* and the L fork is *Dug Road Trail*. Both make a jct with the Third Hill Mtn jeep road.) Continue on the *Tuscarora Trail* (South) from White's Gap by ascending to the ridge top and following the ridge for 4.0 mi of undulating treadway. Here, as elsewhere in the forest, are mtn laurel, wild azaleas, and dogwood among the oak. At 20.0 mi reach a jct with the *Devil's Nose Trail*, R. (The 1.5-mi *Devil's Nose Trail* is an unsigned route that descends to and rises from Meadow Creek, but runs along the proboscis-shaped curve of Meadow Creek before ascending to Paines Knob on Short Mtn. There it joins a fire trail, other unsigned foot trails, and the 1.0-mi *Morgan Trail* in the Hedges Mtn area. (There is a vehicular access route to the Hedges Mtn area on partly public and partly private lands. For information on this access, contact the superintendent.)

Continue ahead on the *Tuscarora Trail* (South) and reach the Devil's Nose Knob (1,540 ft) at 20.5 mi. Descend steeply and at 20.8 mi leave the Sleepy Creek WMA to enter private property. Continue the descent, cross Meadow Creek, and reach Spruce Pine Roadside Park by WV-9 at 22.0 mi, 8.3 mi E of Berkeley Springs.

ADDRESS AND ACCESS: Sleepy Creek WMA, Rte 2, Box 109-F, Hedgesville, WV 25427; 304-754-3855. From the jct of WV-9 and Back Creek Rd (CO-7), 1.8 mi W of Hedgesville, turn on Back Creek Rd and drive 6.3 mi to Jones Springs. From there continue S for 0.6 mi to Meadow Branch Rd (CO-7/9) and turn R. It is 2.3 mi to the superintendent's office and another 3.9 mi to the Sleepy Creek Lake. From the jct of WV-45 and Back Creek Rd (CO-7) in Glengary, go N for 8.3 mi to Meadow Branch Rd (CO-7/9) and follow directions as above. (An access road that crosses into Morgan County is Hampshire Grade Rd [CO-7/13], which begins in Shanghai on CO-7, 4.7 mi N of Glengary.)

PART FOUR

County and Municipal Trails

9. County and Municipal Parks and Recreation Areas

Mary Draper Ingles walked without trail or rails.
Now we walk town to town on rail trails.

—Marybeth Finch

The Research and Strategic Planning office of the state's Development Office has reported that more than 50 percent of the towns, cities, and counties have parks-and-recreation boards, commissions, or departments. They operate as separate public administrative units, but occasionally combine their resources; an example is the city of Grafton and Taylor County. Their recreation areas vary in size, facilities, and scope from simple day-use picnic areas to lighted sports fields and courts to elaborate sports centers. Kanawha County Parks and Recreation has one of the most comprehensive park systems, with five localities: Shawnee Regional Park at Institute; Coonskin Park near Charleston; Sandy Brae Golf Course in Clendenin; Big Bend Golf Course at Tornado; and Pioneer Park at East Bank. Among the city parks, Oglesby Park in Wheeling is a remarkable example. Its facilities and trails are described in more detail below. A few parks have designated and signed foot trails covered in this chapter, but other parks have unnamed trails and popular walking paths. Examples are Ritter Park in Huntington and Little Creek Park in South Charleston. Others, such as Princeton City Park, have physical fitness trails.

INFORMATION: For a list of parks and recreation areas contact Research Analyst, Development Office, Community Development Division, Bldg 6, Rm B-553, Capital Complex, Charleston, WV 25305; 304-558-4010.

KANAWHA COUNTY
Coonskin Park
This scenic, 947-acre park on a bend by the Elk River is one of three parks

and four golf courses operated by the Kanawha County Parks and Recreation Commission. Only Coonskin Park has a foot trail. The park has an Olympic-sized heated swimming pool and clubhouse; nine lighted tennis courts at the Ivor F. Boiarsky Tennis Center; 18-hole, par-three golf course; fishing area; 19 picnic areas with shelters; restaurant accommodating 275; 18 exercise stations on a Par-course; and nature trail. In the summer a floral display designed in the shape of the state is opposite the tennis courts. The park is open year-round. (*USGS Map*: Big Chimney)

> ADDRESS AND ACCESS: Director, Coonskin Park, Coonskin Dr, Charleston, WV 25311; 304-341-8000. At the jct of I-77 and WV-114, Exit 99, near the state capitol in downtown Charleston, take WV-114 and drive 2.6 mi to Coonskin Dr (CO-51), L. After 0.8 mi arrive at Coonskin Park entrance.

Coonskin Nature Trail
> LENGTH: 1.0 mi
> DIFFICULTY: moderate
> FEATURE: natural science

TRAILHEAD AND DETAILS: Park on the R at the picnic area gate 0.5 mi from the entrance, and follow the sign. Descend into a cove with tall poplar, maple, beech, and hemlock. At a fork, keep L upstream and pass under a unique rock ledge. At 0.3 mi climb steps to a rock overhang. Cross a footbridge and begin a return of the loop; walk under a small waterfall at 0.7 mi. Among the flora are foamflower, wild ginger, papaw, sourwood, arrowwood, and Solomon's seal. Complete the loop and return to the point of beginning at 1.0 mi.

MARION COUNTY

At the time this edition was going to press, a 70-mi network of trails on abandoned RRs was being developed in Marion, Harrison, Monongahela, and Preston Counties. Led by Ralph La Rue, Marion County Parks and Recreation executive director, the first developed trail was 3.0-mi *McTrail*. It links Fairmont to Prickett's Fort State Park. The 16-mi *West Fork River Trail* is planned from Mary Lou Retton Park in Fairmont to Shinnston. The longest planned trails, 50-mi *Caperton Trail* and the *Monongahela River Trail,* go from Prickett's Fort State Park to Morgantown and to the Pennsylvania border.

> INFORMATION: Marion County Parks and Rec., PO Box 1258, Fairmont, WV 26554; 304-363-7037.

MARSHALL COUNTY

Grand Vue Park

The 600-acre Grand Vue Park overlooking the Ohio River valley is called "heaven on a hill" and is operated by the Marshall County Parks and Recreation Dept. It is open year-round. Its summer facilities include an 18-hole golf course; a lighted driving range; a minigolf course; Olympic-sized swimming pool; eight grass-tex tennis courts; fully equipped picnic shelters; outdoor theater and children's "Red Barn" play area; and a nature trail. Winter activities are chiefly cross-country skiing and sledding. Deluxe vacation cabins are available any season; banquet rooms with professional catering services are also available. The park adjoins Moundsville, an internationally known area for glassware (Fostoria, for example) and for the nation's largest prehistoric Indian (Adena) burial mound (Grave Creek Mound, 79 ft high), on Jefferson Ave. The Delf Norona Museum and Cultural Center is nearby. (*USGS Map:* Moundsville)

ADDRESS AND ACCESS: Manager, Grand Vue Park, PO Box 523, Moundsville, WV 26041; 304-845-9810. In Moundsville on US-250 and WV-88 go E to the Fostoria Glass Co. Turn on Fostoria Ave to Oak Ave and to Grandview Rd for park entrance.

Cabin Trail

LENGTH: 1.8 mi
DIFFICULTY: easy
FEATURE: nature study

TRAILHEAD AND DETAILS: Between picnic shelter #1 and the driving range on the E side of the road is a hiking trail sign. Follow the sign on a mowed field for 0.2 mi to a young forest of ash, cherry, apple, and elderberry. In the summer, large patches of milkweed are frequented by monarch butterflies. Enter another field and woods and descend to a glen at 1.1 mi. Turn L, ascend, return to the main trail, and loop back for 1.8 mi.

MONOGALIA COUNTY

Chestnut Ridge (Regional) Park

The Chestnut Ridge (Regional) Park is a county recreation area adjoining West Virginia University (WVU) Forest and Coopers Rock State Forest. Its proximity to the city of Morgantown enables popular usage of facilities. Among the facilities are a lodge; cabins; electric and nonelectric trailer camping; tent shelter; tent camping; dining hall; shower house; picnic areas; concessions; playgrounds; fishing, swimming, and paddle boats at two lakes; volleyball courts; sledding hill; cross-country skiing routes; an arboretum; and trails.

An *Interpretive Trail* (1.0 mi) has a variety of educational signs. Access is near Klaer Lodge and S of campsite #63 in Camping Area E. *Short Hiking Trail* (0.8 mi) circles Harris Lake. Access is off the main park road near the playground and volleyball courts on Goodspeed Rd for hiking and biking 2.5 mi to Quarry Run in WVU Forest. *Wildlife Plot Trail* (1.0 mi) makes a loop from the parking lot near the park office to a scenic view. In addition the park has plans to connect to other WVU Forest trails. One connector would be to *Johnson Hollow Trail* for about 2.0 mi. It would follow a stream and should be open by 1997. A longer trail, *Darnell Hollow Trail*, is a steep hiking/biking route for 4.0 mi to Rte 857 into WVU Forest. (See WVU Forest in chapter 10 and Coopers Rock State Forest in chapter 7.)

ACCESS: From I-68, Exit 15, go N and turn R on CO-73. After 0.5 mi turn L on Sand Springs Rd. Go 1.5 mi and turn L into Chestnut Ridge Park.

INFORMATION: Chestnut Ridge Park, Rte 1, Box 267, Bruceton Mills, WV 26525; 304-594-1773. (After hours: 594-1774; Nature Center: 594-1787.)

PUTNAM COUNTY

There is a 1.0-mi walking trail in Hurricane City Park which follows a picturesque path along a reservoir. Wildflowers dot the trail among trees, and there are three fitness stations and a picnic area along the route. The trail was made possible by the Greater Kanawha Valley Foundation and the city of Hurricane.

INFORMATION: Putnam County Convention and Visitors Bureau, 1 Valley Park Dr, Hurricane, WVA 25526; 304-562-0518.

WOOD COUNTY

Mountwood Park

The 2,600-acre park has a 50-acre lake for boating (canoes, pedal boats, and rowboats), fishing (stocked with trout and bass five months annually), and swimming. Other facilities are tennis courts, ball fields, minigolf course, 23 mi of ORV/mountain bike (and possibly hike) trails, and a nature-study trail. The park has 81 full-service RV campsites, 16 of which have sewer hookups; group and family cottages; and 18 tent campsites. Park is supervised by Wood County Parks and Recreation Commission.

ADDRESS AND ACCESS: Manager, Mountwood Park, Rte 2, Box 56, Waverly, WV 26184; 304-679-3611 or 304-422-7121. From the jct of US-50 and I-77 in Parkersburg, go E on US-50 for 12.0 mi to Volcano Rd (CO-5), R. Continue E on US-50 for 0.7 mi to the campground, L, on Boreland Spring Rd (CO-20).

Mountwood Lake Trail
LENGTH: 2.2 mi
DIFFICULTY: moderate
FEATURES: geology, scenic
TRAILHEAD AND DETAILS: Begin at Loeb's Boat Dock and follow the paved road for 0.3 mi. Turn L and ascend on a treadway of wood chips. Forest is cherry, Virginia pine, maple, oak, and hickory. Pass Wright's Overlook at 0.5 mi and Wilson's Overlook at 0.8 mi. Maidenhair ferns and spicebush are in the forest and crown vetch is at the dam area. Cross the spillway at 1.2 mi and take a 0.1-mi spur trail to the Devil's Tea Table, a unique rock formation at 1.3 mi. Continue around the lake, pass another overlook at 1.9 mi, and reach the beach parking area at 2.2 mi. It is 0.8 mi from there to the Loeb's Boat Dock.

BRIDGEPORT
There is a walking trail from the parking area at Benedum Civic Center. It crosses Virginia Ave, parially parallels a RR grade through a forest to Bridgeport City Park, and makes a loop. City Park also has picnic shelters and ballfields for baseball, football, and soccer.

INFORMATION: Bridgeport Parks and Rec., 164 W Main St, Bridgeport, WV 26330; 304-842-8240.

DUNBAR
Wine Cellar Park
The 314-acre Wine Cellar Park was dedicated in 1982 by the city of Dunbar and financed by the city and the Land and Water Conservation Fund. It has a lighted picnic shelter with fireplace, picnic tables, playground, restrooms, and drinking water on the W side of the park. Plans are to construct hiking trails in this area. On the E side are the three restored wine

cellars built in the early 1860s, a paved nature trail, and a lake for fishing.

ADDRESS AND ACCESS: Park Manager, Wine Cellar Park, City of Dunbar, Dunbar, WV 25604; 304-766-0223. Turn off I-64 at Exit 53 and go 1.7 mi on Dutch Hollow Rd (CO-25/5).

Wine Cellar Nature Trail
LENGTH: 0.6 mi
DIFFICULTY: easy
FEATURES: botany, wine cellars

TRAILHEAD AND DETAILS: Begin at the roadside sign and follow a paved trail suitable for the physically handicapped. Pass through ash, oak, maple, birch, sycamore, and poplar. Among the wildflowers are jewelweed, tall bellflower, sweet cicely, and asters. Ferns are prominent. The trail criss-crosses the stream on footbridges. At the concave is a spur trail up an embankment to the lake. Complete the loop at the wine cellars.

NITRO

Ridenour Park

This city park has a 24-acre lake for fishing, picnic shelters, playground areas, outdoor amphitheater, restrooms, and a nature trail. It is open year-round, daily dawn to dusk.

ADDRESS AND ACCESS: Director, Nitro Parks and Recreation Dept, City Hall, 20th St and 2nd Ave, Nitro, WV 25143; 304-755-0701. From Exit 45 on I-64 in Nitro, go 2.1 mi on WV-25 to 21st St and turn L to the park entrance.

Ridenour Lake Trail
LENGTH: 1.0 mi round-trip
DIFFICULTY: easy
FEATURE: nature study

TRAILHEAD AND DETAILS: From the parking area on the S side of the lake, hike on a wide gravel trail around the lake through a forest of buckeye, beech, maple, hickory, oak, and arrowwood (*Viburnum acerifolium*). Elephant's foot (*Elephantopus carolinianus*) grows on the slope and ironweed near the lake edge. Descend on 33 steps at 0.3 mi, cross a small bridge, and reach a paved road at Lakeview Estates at 0.5 mi. It is another 0.2 mi on the road to the picnic area or backtrack.

SAINT ALBANS

Saint Albans City Park

The park has a lighted baseball field, petting farm, miniature golf, playgrounds, picnic area with shelters, physical fitness course with 20 stations, and hiking trails. It is open daily from mid-April through October and is operated by the city's Parks and Recreation Dept.

ADDRESS AND ACCESS: Director, Saint Albans Parks and Recreation Dept, 500 Washington St, Saint Albans, WV 25177; 304-722-4625 or 304-727-2101. In Saint Albans on US-60, turn onto Walnut St and go 0.6 mi to Kanawha Terrace. Turn R; go 0.1 mi to Vine St and turn L. Go 0.2 mi to Monmouth Ave and turn R. After 0.4 mi reach the park entrance.

Saint Albans Nature Trail

LENGTH: 0.5 mi

DIFFICULTY: easy

FEATURES: covered bridge, plant life

TRAILHEAD AND DETAILS: After the entrance to the park there is a parking area and display board on the R. Follow the paved *Saint Albans Nature Trail*, suitable for the physically handicapped. After 250 yd cross a small covered bridge, then take a dirt footpath. Descend and weave through a forest of maple, poplar, oak, and ash. Among the wildflowers are jewelweed, celandine poppy, comfrey (*Symphytum officinale*), blue-eyed Mary, asters, and trout lily (*Erythronium americanum*). Complete the loop by ascending to the parking area.

WHEELING

Heritage Trail System

The *Heritage Trail* is part of a multiuse trail system networking former railroad corridors and green spaces in the city. In 1997 10.0 mi were completed along the bank of the Ohio River. Its sections are *Warwood Trail* (3.5 mi) from Pike Island Dam to the S of Warwood; and *North to South Wheeling Trail* (6.5 mi) between Warwood and South Wheeling. There are special parking areas along the way for easy access and for the handicapped. Access is at parking lots off WV-2 and the W end of 35th St in South Wheeling.

The paved and wide trail provides recreational opportunities for walkers, joggers, strollers, bikers, roller skaters, and roller bladers. There are some trail rules: pedestrians have the right of way; the trails are open only from dawn to dusk, no unauthorized motor vehicles; no use of alcoholic beverages; no littering; no graffiti; and no soliciting or panhandling. All animals must be on a leash and all animal waste cleaned up. A major safety concern is motor vehicles that may cross or turn onto the trail from streets.

The unfinished *East Wheeling Trail* (4.5 mi are completed) now runs between the *North to South Wheeling Trail* in downtown Wheeling E to Elm Grove. Plans are to extend this network to other routes and to cross the Ohio River into Belmont County, OH.

In addition to the trail project the Wheeling Heritage plans to emphasize its transportation heritage and its future. Plans are to build an Intermodal Transportation Center at Main and 14th St. It will be a transportation hub for local and regional buses, hikers, and bikers (with storage space for bikes). In addition there are plans for a Heritage Park, the redevelopment of waterfront transportation on the Ohio River in downtown Wheeling.

INFORMATION: City of Wheeling, Dept of Development, 1500 Chapline St., Wheeling, WV 26003; 304-234-3701.

Oglebay Park

One of America's outstanding municipal resort parks, Oglebay is West Virginia's finest for recreational, cultural, and educational activities. The 1,460-acre park was originally Waddington Farm, the country estate of Col Earl W. Oglebay, who was born and grew up in the area, but was better known as a Cleveland industrialist and philanthropist. On his death in 1926, he gave the estate to the city of Wheeling for "as long as the people shall operate it for purposes of public recreation and education," with the stipulation that a quarter of the land remain undeveloped. In 1928 it officially became a park operated by the Wheeling Park Commission.

Of particular interest is the Brooks Nature Center, named in honor of Alonzo B. Brooks, a famed forester, author, and park naturalist whose efforts on behalf of Oglebay's natural beauty were outstanding. When he retired in 1942, the report was made that "he lives in every tree, every flower, every bird, and every scampering furry creature at Oglebay Park." (He was the uncle of another famous naturalist and author, Maurice Brooks, professor emeritus of wildlife management at West Virginia University, and reverently named "Dr. Appalachia" by bird artist Roger Tory Peterson. Uncle and nephew are members of a prominent family from French Creek in Upshur County.) The center is open year-round, and nature walks begin here. In the center is the Oglebay Institute Nature Education Department, which offers courses in ecology and environmental education, as well as a nature camp program at its mountain retreat near Terra Alta. Backpacking courses include studies in vascular plants, mushrooms, herpetology, and wild foods.

Oglebay offers an exceptional range of activities. A partial list includes the Speidel Championship Golf Course (and two others) with associated services; indoor and outdoor swimming pools; 11 lighted tennis courts; horseback riding at the riding academy, forest, and arena; skiing (ski shop and rental equipment); boating and fishing in Schenk Lake; picnicking; and nature study. Among the facilities are the Wilson Lodge with 202 guest rooms, executive conference suites, spa, lounges, and dining rooms that can accommodate up to 700 persons; garden center and greenhouses; 65-acre Good Children's Zoo with Benedum Nature Science Theater and Planetarium; Mansion Museum (this was the summer home of Oglebay) with Burton Galleries; Speidel Observatory; Wigginton Arboretum; Burton Wildlife Sanctuary; and outdoor theater. Additionally, there are festivals, concerts, lecture series, celebrations, tournaments, and exhibitions year-round. (*USGS Map*: Wheeling)

ADDRESS AND ACCESS: Visitors Services, Oglebay Park, Wheeling, WV2 26003; 800-624-6988 (locally 243-4000). At the jct of I-70 and US-40, Exit 2A and Oglebay Park signs, go E on US-40 0.2 mi, turn L on WV-88, and go 2.4 mi to park entrance.

Discovery Trail (0.4 mi); Hardwoods Ridge Trail (0.8 mi); Falls Vista Trail (0.5 mi)

LENGTH: 3.0 mi round-trip, combined

DIFFICULTY: easy to moderate

FEATURES: scenic waterfall, nature study

TRAILHEADS AND DETAILS: Park in front of, and begin hikes behind, the Brooks Nature Center. (It is closed Sunday and Monday.) Examine the kiosk and begin on the *Discovery Trail* loop. At 0.1 mi is a jct with *Hardwoods Ridge Trail*, but turn L. Ascend, then keep L by a fence to return to the parking area. For hiking the *Hardwoods Ridge Trail*, cross a bridge over the stream and stay on the hillside to curve around Camp Russell. Make a loop near the end at a waterfall. The most scenic trail is to branch off *Hardwoods Ridge Trail* a few yd after the bridge. Turn L and descend on a number of platforms, steps, and bridges, on *Falls Vista Trail*. End at a platform for views of Oglebay Falls. Backtrack. Some of the vegetation in the trail system are hemlock, red spruce, oak, cherry, locust, wild ginger, ferns, coltsfoot, swamp buttercup, and stonecrop.

Arboretum Trail

LENGTH: 2.8 mi round-trip
DIFFICULTY: easy to moderate
FEATURES: scenic, botanical study

TRAILHEAD AND DETAILS: The 8-ft-wide asphalt trail can be hiked in short or long loops by using a variety of interconnecting trails, and can be entered near the Speidel Observatory (across the road from the Brooks Nature Center), at the garden center (near the park's main office), at Schenk Lake, or at the Good Zoo. From any point there are outstanding views of flowering shrubs, red and white pine and hemlock groves, manicured hillside lawns, and landscaped hardwood sections. If choosing a 1.4-mi-loop around the perimeter from the Brooks Nature Center, parallel the Falls Rd by Wilson Lodge. After 0.7 mi pass through a pine grove to the garden center and greenhouses. From a stone and wood arbor there is a magnificent view of the lakes and hillsides. Go between the greenhouses and the outdoor theater to an overlook and descend to a road jct at Good Children's Zoo at 1.1 mi. Turn L, descend to Schenk Lake at 1.2 mi, and follow the road past the children's center to Brooks Nature Center for another 0.2 mi.

PART FIVE

Private, College, and Special Property Trails

10. Private and College Trails

Skills that our fathers knew,
Trusts that we still hold true,
Work that our hands can do,
Legends untold.

—Louise McNeill Pease

Of the more than 75 known private trails in West Virginia that have names, only 32 are covered in this chapter, because some private land and homeowners do not wish public traffic on their trails and resort owners require trail users to be registered guests. Examples of the latter are such luxurious resorts as Greenbrier in White Sulphur Springs and Glade Springs in Daniels. The same applies to such rustic localities as private Smoke Hole Lodge (accessible by 4WD vehicles) near Petersburg. Some of the state's private garden trails receive immaculate maintenance. Some woods trails are being developed on abandoned farms. A few trails are on ranches or in large private timber or mining industry lands. Other trails are on Nature Conservancy properties, and a large number of trails are in private camps. In the limestone region there are 14 known cave trails, but at the request of the owners only two are described below. Hikers are requested to respect private boundaries and to announce their presence to their hosts. A few trails are on both public and private lands, such as the *Allegheny Trail* and the *Tuscarora Trail* (South), formerly the *Big Blue Trail*. Also, a few, such as *North Fork Mountain Trail* (23.8 mi), may be traversed in their entirety only by permission from the private landowners. The majority of private trails are not listed in this book by request of the landowners. Colleges and universities have a number of unnamed nature walks, but West Virginia University has a major network of trails (see below). Camping is not allowed in its arboretum or forest.

BOY SCOUTS OF AMERICA

West Virginia has eight Boy Scout councils with 12 camps or reservations that comprise a total of 6,053 acres (5,150 in-state and 903 outside the state). There are also four other councils outside the state that serve West Virginia counties. Hiking, backpacking, and camping have long been a significant part of Scouts' outdoor experiences, and their outdoor code is a model for all hikers. Some excerpts are: "As an American I will do my best to treat the outdoors as a heritage to be improved for our greater enjoyment....I will be careful with fire....I will treat private and public property with respect. I will remember that use of the outdoors is a privilege I can lose by abuse....and I will learn how to practice good conservation of soil, forests, minerals, grasslands, and wildlife...."

Although they hike on their own private trails, they also take long hikes on public and semipublic trails in and out of the state, such as the *Appalachian Trail*, *Chesapeake and Ohio Trail*, *Warrior Trail*, *Anthony Wayne Trail*, *Buckeye Trail*, and *Tuscarora Trail (South)*, formerly the *Big Blue Trail*. Numerous trails in the Monongahela National Forest are also used. Medals, patches, and pins are awarded the Scouts when hiking "accredited scouting trails."

The Tri-State Council, Boy Scouts of America (BSA), has two major private trails open to the public, in Cabell, Mason, and Putnam Counties. Permission and advance notice are required to hike the *Adahi Trail* (19.5 mi) and the *Kanawha Trace* (31.7 mi). Both are accessible from Camp Arrowhead. The *Adahi Trail* has its S terminus here and the *Kanawha Trace* passes through on its E-W route. Access to Camp Arrowhead is on Blue Sulphur Rd (CO-17), N from the community of Blue Sulphur (W of Ona on US-60), and Boy Scout Rd (CO-17/4). The *Adahi Trail* runs jointly for 1.5 mi with the *Kanawha Trace* before the former's N route to the Ohio River. It has a number of historic sites, with an emphasis on pioneer life, Civil War skirmishes, and the Albert Gallatin Jenkins Historical Marker.

The *Kanawha Trace* is actually a combination of trails—the *Midland Trail*, the *James and Kanawha River Turnpike*, and the *Hannan Trace*. The W trailhead of the *Kanawha Trace* is at the Woody Williams Bridge, jct of Merrick Creek Rd (CO-19) and Mud River Rd (CO-21), at the N edge of Barboursville. It reaches Camp Arrowhead at 5.3 mi and Williams Shelter at 5.5 mi, then runs jointly with the *Adahi Trail* from 9.2 mi to 10.7 mi. At 14.6 mi, on Dry Ridge Rd (CO-11), is Meadows Grocery and at 19.9 mi is Blackjack School Camp (use of building requires advance registration). The

E trailhead (31.7 mi) is at Fraziers Bottom on US-35 near the Kanawha River at Sider's Country Store.

INFORMATION: Tri-State Council, BSA, 733 7th Ave, Huntington, WV 25701; 304-523-3408. The council has published the *Guidebook to Hiking the Kanawha Trace*, by Charles Dundas and John Gibson. The guidebook has mileposts, elev points, descriptions, and topo map routes.

A semiprivate trail is the 30-mi *Wyatt Trail* in Kanawha County between Saint Albans and Kanawha State Forest. Created in honor of Bill Wyatt of Troop 146 of the Buckskin Area Council, the trail emphasizes biological life, old RR grades, mining areas, and scenic countryside. Permission, a guide, and advance notice are required. (See Kanawha State Forest, chapter 7.)

INFORMATION: Roger Rassmussen, Troop 146, 2519 Winter St, Saint Albans, WV 25177; 304-727-8492.

COOLFONT RESORT
(Berkeley Springs)

Coolfont is a private, family-owned resort in a scenic valley between Cacapon Mtn and Warm Springs Ridge near historic Berkeley Springs. Open to the public all year, it is a 1,350-acre retreat described as "Re+Creation," meaning it is a center both for recreation and for renewing and restoring the human "mind and senses." The resort has a conference center, the famous Treetop House Restaurant, a lodge, chalets, cabins, deluxe mountain homes, a health spa, and fitness vacations (including one on how to stop smoking). Recreational activities include hiking, fishing (no license required), horseback riding, boating, tennis, biking, summer day camps, summer swimming (and indoor pool), winter cross-country skiing, and ice skating. *Martha's Trail* (a 0.5-mi loop) is at the Swim and Fitness Center. Cultural events are chamber music, a film series, and an artist-in-residence. Its campground has 50 units, 33 with full service. There are central restrooms and hot showers, also a laundry and wood supply. The campground is open Easter through Thanksgiving, and the facility is 6.0 mi NW of Cacapon State Park (which does not have a campground). (*USGS Map*: Great Cacapon)

ADDRESS AND ACCESS: Manager, Coolfont, 1777 Cold Run Valley Rd, Berkeley Springs, WV 25411; 304-258-4500. At the jct of US-522 and WV-9 in Berkeley Springs take WV-9 W for 0.7 mi; turn L on Coolfont

Rd and go 3.7 mi. From Cacapon State Park go N on US-522 for 3.6 mi, turn L on Quarry Rd, and go 2.4 mi.

White Trail (1.8 mi); Green-Orange Trail (1.3 mi); Green Trail (2.5 mi); Blue-Orange Trail (0.8 mi); Blue-Red Trail (0.6 mi); Blue Trail (1.0 mi)

LENGTH: 8.0 mi combined

DIFFICULTY: moderate to strenuous

FEATURES: wildlife, scenic

TRAILHEADS AND DETAILS: No camping is allowed on the trails. At the jct of the Cold Run Valley Rd and the Manor House Rd, turn on the Manor House Rd. To the R begin the *White Trail* and the *Green-Orange Trail*. Follow the bridle trail briefly and then begin ascending on the *White Trail*. (Some sections are exceptionally steep.) Chestnut oak, sassafras, scrub pine, beech, and basswood are in the forest. Reach a jct with *Green Trail*, R, at 0.8 mi. (The 2.5-mi *Green Trail* goes W and gradually ascends the mtn to the scenic Prospect Rock. Along the way it meets a jct with the *Green-Orange Trail*, R, at 0.6 mi.) Continue on the *White Trail*; pass a rocky area and a jct with *Blue-Orange Trail* at 1.6 mi. (The *Blue-Orange Trail* goes R to Prospect Rock.) The *White Trail* goes L for 0.2 mi to its terminus at the beginning of the *Blue-Red Trail*, L, and the *Blue Trail*, R. (The *Blue-Red Trail* ascends steeply to the ridge line and drops acutely to its terminus at Rock Slab, which has a spectacular view of Coolfont and the valley.) The *Blue Trail* also ascends steeply but veers R at the Cacapon Mtn ridge line to Prospect Rock (1,500 ft). From here are views of West Virginia, Virginia, Maryland, and Pennsylvania. Also, there are views of Cacapon River, Potomac River, and the town of Great Cacapon. Return on either the *Blue-Orange Trail* or the *Green Trail* (descent of 3.3 mi to highway). Wildflowers on these trails are mandrake, starry champion, sweet cicely, spearmint, and tall bellflower. Deer, grouse, squirrel, and wild turkey are the most frequently seen animals.

Lake Siri Trail

LENGTH: 1.8 mi

DIFFICULTY: easy

TRAILHEADS AND DETAILS: Begin at Treetop House parking lot near Lake Siri. Follow the unmarked trail S (L) to the Alpine Village chalets. Near a stream leave the paved road and make a loop R on a gravel path. Pass Aspen and Zurich chalets near the campground. Turn L before reaching

Lucerne chalet to descend. Follow steps to the dam; after crossing, turn L and follow the W side of the lake for a return.

FOX FIRE RESORT
(Cabell County)

A private campground "designed with the family in mind," the Fox Fire Resort has 122 full-service campsites and standard facilities. The resort also has some special features—for example, live music on the summer weekends. Other facilities are the Slippery Creek Water Slide, picnic areas, swimming and fishing lakes, sport fields, and tent campground. If you just wish to hike the trail, request a visitor pass. (*USGS Map*: Milton)

> ADDRESS AND ACCESS: Manager, Fox Fire Resort, Rte 2, Box 655, Milton, WV 25541; 304-743-5622. From the town of Milton go W on US-60 for 2.0 mi and turn R.

Fox Fire Nature Trail
> LENGTH: 1.1 mi
> DIFFICULTY: easy
> FEATURE: nature study
> TRAILHEAD AND DETAILS: Park at the old barn in the campground, ascend on a paved road to the top of the hill and an observation tower at 0.2 mi. Bear L; descend in a forest of locust, poplar, oak, and pine at 0.5 mi. Reach the resort main road, turn L, and return to the point of beginning.

HUNTINGTON MUSEUM OF ART
(Huntington)

Huntington Museum of Art is the state's largest professionally accredited art museum; it is also a preserve with an arboreal display and a network of nature trails in its 52 acres. In its cultural complex are elegant exhibits of paintings, silver, artifacts, and glass; an observatory; a plant conservatory; an art library and studios; and an auditorium for film and performing arts. It is open year-round, Tues-Sat 10 A.M.–5 P.M. and Sun 12–5 P.M. There is an admission charge in the galleries, but the trails are open to the public free of charge. Volunteer assistance on the trails comes from the Junior League of Garden Clubs, Women's Club of Huntington, and Tri-State Community. (*USGS Map*: Huntington)

ADDRESS AND ACCESS: Nature Coordinator, Huntington Museum of Art, 2033 McCoy Rd, Huntington, WV 25701, tel: 304-529-2701. From the jct of I-64 and WV-527 (Exit 8) drive 0.1 mi on WV-527 to Miller Rd; turn R. Drive 1.0 mi and turn L on McCullough Rd and go 0.6 mi.

Tulip Tree Trail (1.0 mi); Gentle Oak Trail (0.2 mi); Spicebush Trail (0.3 mi)

LENGTH: 1.5 mi combined
DIFFICULTY: moderate
FEATURE: nature study

TRAILHEAD AND DETAILS: From the parking area walk to the R of the building to the trailhead for *Tulip Tree Trail*. Descend on a well-graded trail, pass R of the *Gentle Oak Trail*, and curve E and N and then SW to a jct with the *Spicebush Trail* (loop) at 0.4 mi. Among the tall hardwoods are sugar maple, red and white oak, yellow poplar (tulip tree), beech, black locust, ash, and hickory. Wildflowers include sweet cicely, May apple, and trillium. Spicebush, ferns, and mosses are prominent. Gray squirrel and chipmunk are likely to be seen on the trails. Ascend, steeply in sections, and reach a jct with the *Gentle Oak Trail*, L, at 0.8 mi. Return on either trail for a total route of 1.5 mi.

PINE HILL CAMPGROUND
(Preston County)

In the NE corner of the state is a quiet, 110-acre scenic nature preserve that has the ideal campground. It reminds you of Roy Lee Harmon's "West Virginia June" with its "hallowed hills" where "plain old troubles just melt away." Franklin and Norma Sparber have designed this retreat with generous care for 30 years, and the care for campers is equally generous. Facilities include 60 campsites (all with water and electric hookups and some with sewage hookups); picnic areas; playground; tent sites; flush toilets and hot showers; and nature trails. The campground is within 30 minutes of Cheat Lake Resort and the Deep Creek lake Resort. (*USGS Map*: Brandonville)

ADDRESS AND ACCESS: Pine Hill Campground, Rte 3, Bruceton Mill, WV 26523; 304-379-4612 or 216-466-1451. From Exit 29 on US-48 in Hazelton drive S on CO-5/18 (look for campground signs) for 3.0 mi to a jct. Turn R on Cherry Grove Mountaindale Rd (CO-5/14) and go 1.3 mi to the entrance, R.

Blackberry Trail; Lone Pine Trail; Red Pine Trail; Overlook Trail

LENGTH: 1.0 mi round-trip, combined

DIFFICULTY: easy

FEATURE: nature study

TRAILHEADS AND DETAILS: Because the manicured trails overlap and inter-loop with each other, they are measured as a unit. Follow the trail signs from the parking area through a network of walkways that may take you on side trails in spruce and pine to an overlook toward Kelly's Knob. The Sparbers may change the trail designs and the names; thus, each visit is a new nature study. The trails are open to the public without charge, but the owners request you notify them if you are on the grounds.

SPELEOLOGY TRAILS

In the eastern Appalachians of the state are large limestone belts estimated to be 395 million years old. In them are thousands of caves, fissures, sub-terranean waters, and sinks. The most geologically significant caves have become commercial. They are Organ Cave, the state's longest (40 mi), near Ronceverte; Lost World Cave, a registered National Landmark near Lewisburg; Seneca Caverns, noted for their flowstone colors; and Smoke Hole Cavern, which has the world's longest ribbon stalactite, near Petersburg. These and other less-known caves, also on private property, are protected by West Virginia state law, Code WV-20/7A. These regulations state: "It is illegal to write, mark, break, or deface, or remove any natural material, or to dump refuse, or to disturb, or harm the bats, or other living creatures, or to disturb any artifacts, or bones." Underground hiking can be dangerous, and inexperienced hikers should have both a guide and proper equipment.

INFORMATION: West Virginia Geological and Economic Survey, PO Box 879, Morgantown, WV 26507; 304-594-2331. (For commercial cave trails open to the public, call 800-225-5982.)

SUNRISE MUSEUMS
(Charleston)

Sunrise Museums is a 16-acre cultural and educational complex with two historic mansions, museum, children's museum and planetarium, gardens, nature center, and nature trails. The privately supported nonprofit Sunrise Foundation, Inc., is funded primarily by membership dues and private contributions. The children's museum is the former home of William A. Mac-Corkle, ninth governor of West Virginia. It was built by him in 1905 and named after his family home in Virginia. On the grounds of the children's museum is an analemmic sundial, the largest in the state. Visiting hours are Wed-Sat 11 A.M.–5 P.M. and Sun 12–5 P.M. (closed Mon-Tues). Guided tours arranged by appointment.

ADDRESS AND ACCESS: Sunrise Museums, 746 Myrtle Rd, Charleston, WV 25314; 304-344-8035. From the jct of Bridge Rd and Virginia St downtown, take Bridge Rd across the river, ascend, and turn R on Myrtle Rd to a parking area. Another access is at the jct of MacCorkle Ave (US-119 and WV-61) and Thayer St, near the Amtrak station.

Garden Trail of the Five Senses (86 yd); Sunrise Carriage Trail (0.7 mi)

LENGTH: 1.5 mi round-trip, combined
DIFFICULTY: easy to moderate
FEATURES: Braille signs, scenic, historic

TRAILHEADS AND DETAILS: From the parking area walk to the L of the children's museum through a rose and herb garden to the old carriage road. Here is the *Garden Trail* of the Five Senses, created chiefly for the visually handicapped by Kanawha Garden Council patrons. Descend on the carriage road. There are scenic views of the city and resting benches along the trail. Natural vegetation includes papaw, hemlock, buckeye, poplar, oak, and rhododendron. At 0.7 mi the carriage road ends at its former entrance near MacCorkle Ave and Bridge Rd. Backtrack.

WARRIOR TRAIL ASSOCIATION

The 68.3-mi *Warrior Trail* has 45.5 mi in Pennsylvania and 22.8 mi in Marshall County, WV. It is named for the Amerind Indians, who had a network of trails in the West Virginia panhandle and SE Pennsylvania. The trail has been developed by the Warrior Trail Association of Waynesburg, PA. Originally the trail had mileposts with the name carved vertically, and aluminum blazes on trees and fence posts, but since the early 1980s the blaze has been of yellow paint. In Pennsylvania the E trailhead is at the W side of the Monongahela River between the communities of Greensboro and Glassworks. It crosses the 27-mi *Catawba Trail* in Greene County, S of Kirby, between US-29 and I-79. (The *Catawba Trail* is another trail developed by the association.) There are shelters midway between mileposts 11 and 12, at milepost 24, and between mileposts 35 and 36. There are no shelters in the West Virginia section.

During much of the 1980s the West Virginia section of the *Warrior Trail*, which was mainly on private property, was not maintained. But during the first half of the 1990s there was a resurrection of interest by hikers and some of the landowners. Leading the cause to reestablish a route has been Doug Wood, a trail activist for the 300-mi *Allegheny Trail* in West Virginia and Virginia. The following description is about the current route, of which 19.0 mi is on backcountry roads. For the entire distance in West Virginia the trail follows ridges, undulating on a few hills and averaging an altitude of about 1,350 ft until it drops to about 620 ft at its end to WV-2 S of Moundsville. The highest point, 1,602 ft in elev is at milepost 46, 0.5 mi W from the Pennsylvania state line. The trail's route is mainly through pastureland, with scattered farmhouses along the way. The only stream crossing is Fish Creek, 1.3 mi before the W trailhead.

INFORMATION: Warrior Trail Association, Rte 1, Box 35, Spraggs, PA 15362; contact Lucille Phillips (412-451-8326), Jim Milinovich Jr. (412-852-2610), or Bill Hewitt (412-128-3729). West Virginia Scenic Trails Association, PO Box 4042, Charleston, WV 25354; 304-755-4878, or 304-466-2724 (Doug Wood).

Warrior Trail (West Virginia section); (Marshall County)

LENGTH: 22.8 mi

DIFFICULTY: moderate

FEATURES: historic, scenic pastoral views, wildflowers

TRAILHEAD AND DETAILS: From the town of Cameron at the jct of US-250 and CO-25 (BP Food Mart), drive S on US-250 1.7 mi to CO-98/1 on the L, and the trail access. (To the L [E], the trail is 0.6 mi on Tunnel Hill [named for the Baltimore & Ohio Railroad tunnel under the ridge] to a jct with Woodruff Rd [CO-98]. In the corner of the fork the trail ascends an embankment to a pasture and 0.9 mi to the Pennsylvania state line.) To begin the trail W continue uphill on US-250 for 0.3 mi and turn R on a narrow road on the N side of a house. Drive 0.2 mi to the home of Alan Reid. He allows vehicle parking and field camping for *Warrior Trail* hikers (RD 5, Box 49, Cameron, WV 26033). (See W trailhead at end of description.)

From the farm barn go W into a grassy field with white yarrow and blackberries. Ascend a knoll, descend, then ascend to a gate on the hill at 0.3 mi. Here are old apple trees before entering an open forest of maple, oak, walnut, sumac, and sensitive fern. Descend, but immediately be alert to a turn in the trail R at a gas line for a descent, first on an old weedy road

Warrior Trail passes through Stoy Whipkey Farm southwest of Cameron.

before a L. Ascend to a knob among small hickory at 1.0 mi. Turn L (look for yellow blazes) and cross a gravel road R of a white house at 1.3 mi. Enter a spruce stand and ascend, veering L to an open field area. Arrive at a fence at 1.4 mi. Turn R, and follow the wood's edge through a hayfield. Arrive at another fence, turn R and descend to a gravel road. A white house is L. Here at the road is the old trail milepost 49 at 1.6 mi. Cross the road, pass in front of a long white garage, turn L, and ascend steeply to a hilltop at 1.8 mi. Turn R through an open pasture with scattered shrubs and old apple trees. Descend to a fence and woods with oak and shagbark hickory to arrive at a paved road at 2.0 mi.

Turn R to the Stoy Whipkey farm, pass a house R and a barn L to a rock pile in a large hayfield (with a blaze) at 2.1 mi. (To the R, down the mtn on CO-23, it is 0.8 mi to Cameron Baptist Church on CO-25.) Ascend NW in the hayfield to the woods edge at 2.2 mi on the hilltop. Follow L for beautiful views of the farm. Enter a small border of trees and descend to a large white oak in the field at 2.4 mi. (N from the tree at the woods edge is a natural spring.) From the tree go W on the ridge to enter the forest at 2.5 mi. Ascend and curve around S of a slope with mandrakes in the woods. At 2.6 mi arrive at a wire fence and the original milepost 50 on the Fry farm. Walk through the pasture, where bunches of wild roses and thistle are scattered among old apple trees. Reach a fence at the edge of the pasture and cross into woods, but quickly exit to descend in a field. Stay near the L border and descend among a few trees to paved CO-25/6 at 2.9 mi. Turn L. (To the R 0.2 mi is Indian Run Farm of Lee Boyd, and 0.8 mi farther down the mtn is CO-25 at Pottery Terrace Apartments in Cameron, 0.6 mi W from Cameron Baptist Church.)

From 2.9 mi the *Warrior Trail* now follows narrow paved or gravel roads for the remainder of the journey to WV-2 near the Ohio River. Some of the points of interest or mileposts along the way are as follow: At 3.3 mi are large oak L in the forest, followed by a sharp turn on CO-62 to pass a barn with metal silos R at 3.5 mi. After an open area there is an old barn L, followed by partial woods. Pass an attractive house L with large oak at 5.0 mi, and another barn, silo, and old farm equipment at 6.3 mi. At 6.8 mi is a scenic pasture L, shaped like an immense amphitheater. A few houses are R and L on the road. A jct with Glen Easton Ridge Rd (CO-60) is at 7.8 mi. Arrive at a stop sign at 9.2 mi. To the L is Salem Church of Christ and its cemetery on a scenic windy hill. (Also from the road L and ahead is emergency WV 2, used if WV 2 by the Ohio River is closed.)

Turn R and cross under a large power line at 9.5 mi and 9.9 mi. In between, on the L and near a barn at 9.6 mi is original trail milepost 57. Pass Bowman Church and cemetery, R, and reach a jct with Big Grove Creek Rd (CO-54) R at 10.5 mi. At 0.9 mi R is Bowman Ridge Community Center. There is another cove shaped like an amphitheater on the L at 11.4 mi, and a barn and farm on the R. The road takes a NW turn after a jct with Games Ridge Rd, L, at 12.3 mi. Continue R and pass wonderful Hills and Hollow at 13.2 mi, then arrive at the welcome sight of Family General Store at 14.5 mi, R on the N side of the road. The store has food and other supplies, drinks, telephone, and much-needed information about neighbors who might allow overnight camping. Across the road is Hilltop, Inc., where a corner fence post is original trail milepost 62. Turn L, and at 14.7 mi turn sharply L uphill on Taylor's Ridge Rd (CO-2/1) and pass houses.

Continuing on a narrow paved road, pass a large barn and silo, L. To the R (W) at 15.2 mi are views of the tall towers of a nuclear power plant by the Ohio River. There are more scenic views on the approach to a cluster of houses on the ridge at 15.8 mi. Just beyond the houses the road forks. (To the R is the former *Warrior Trail* route that followed Taylors Ridge to descend steeply to WV-2.) Turn L on gravel Gatts Ridge Rd (CO-72). Cross a gas pipeline swath and descend to view a red-roofed barn on the R and a two-story white farmhouse on the L at 16.8 mi. In the summer the roadside is bordered with orange butterfly weed and fragrant milkweed. Descend; in a sharp curve at 18.5 mi is milepost 66. Descend steeply on four more switchbacks before the road becomes paved at CO-74 in the community of Grayville at 19.3 mi. Watch for yellow blazes on trees or telephone poles. Keep R until the jct with CO-27, L at 19.5 mi. Here near a telephone pole is milepost 67. Turn L on CO-27, cross a metal-framed bridge, pass a jct with Rines Ridge Rd (CO-76), notice a lake on the R, cross another bridge, and stay R to arrive at a roadside parking space to WV-2 at 20.8. (It is 10.0 mi R, N, on WV-2 to Moundsville Plaza R and a bridge over the Ohio River to OH-7. (*USGS Maps*: Cameron, Glen Easton, Powhatan Point)

WEST VIRGINIA UNIVERSITY
(Morgantown)

West Virginia University, founded in 1867, has more than 22,000 students and is the largest educational institution in the state. The school is located in Morgantown, which was settled in 1772, and received its name from Zackquill Morgan, son of Morgan Morgan, who became the state's first permanent settler in 1731, when he settled in what is now Berkeley County. Although the university is the focal point of the city, the federal government has a number of research centers here, among them the Forest Sciences Laboratory, a Bureau of Mines research center, and the Appalachian Laboratory for Occupational Respiratory Diseases. The university has two major areas of interest to hikers: the Core Arboretum and the University Forest.

The Core Arboretum

This 75-acre arboretum was established in 1948 on a forest slope between Monongahela Blvd and the Monongahela River by the Department of Biology. It was originally designed as an outdoor biology laboratory for study and research and for public educational purposes. In 1954 it was officially dedicated and opened to the public as the West Virginia University Arboretum under the leadership and direction of Earl L. Core, professor of biology at the university. On July 1, 1975, the arboretum was named the Core Arboretum in his honor (Dr. Core and Dr. P. D. Strausbaugh were the authors of a definitive, 1,075-page work titled *Flora of West Virginia,* first published in 1952.)

> ADDRESS AND ACCESS: The Core Arboretum, Department of Biology, Brooks Hall, West Virginia University, Morgantown, WV 26506-6057; 304-293-5201. From Exit 155 on I-79, turn E on US-19/WV-7 (Monongahela Blvd), pass the coliseum, and park R at the arboretum sign.

Circular Trail, Strausbaugh Trail, Sheldon Trail, Nuttall Trail, Granville Island Trail, Rumsey Trail, Taylor Trail, Brown Trail, Cliff Trail, Silver Maple Trail

LENGTH: 3.3 mi round-trip, combined

DIFFICULTY: easy to moderate

FEATURE: botanical study

TRAILHEADS AND DETAILS: These trails all connect in a pattern suitable for short loops (such as the 0.2-mi *Circular Trail*) or extended loops, with some unmarked spurs in between. Elev change is 240 ft. There is a network of 28 interpretive signs dealing with history, botany, ecology, and geology. Brochures are available on-site. Birding is best in spring migration. The longest circuit, 2.1 mi, is described below. Begin on the *Circular Trail*, R, and descend on the *Strausbaugh Trail* (named in honor of Dr. P. D. Strausbaugh, former chairman of the university's Department of Biology). Some trees seen on this trail are black cherry, hackberry, sweet birch, black and sugar maple, and oak. Wildflowers include black cohosh, trillium, twinleaf, celandine poppy (*Stylophorum diphyllum*), and wild blue phlox. Pass the *Sheldon Trail*, L (named in honor of Dr. John L. Sheldon, former professor of botany at the university). This trail is noted for its springtime display of wildflowers, particularly Virginia bluebells (*Mertensia virginica*). Make a jct with the narrow and steep *Cliff Trail*, R, which makes a loop.

Cross the abandoned B&O Railroad at 0.7 mi and pass the *Nuttall Trail*, L. (It parallels the RR in a low area near the lagoon and has a number of aquatic plants.) (The RR tracks have been removed. A right of way is in progress to convert the RR grade into a hiking/biking trail [from Fairmont N to Reedsville in Preston County]. The Star City Riverfront Park is a good access point.) The chinquapin oak near the jct with the *Sheldon Trail* is thought to be the second largest in the state. Parallel the Monongahela River on the *Granville Island Trail*, R of the lagoon, at 0.8 mi. Silver maple, black willow, jewelweed, and ground ivy are prominent. Curve L to the east jct of the *Nuttall Trail* (named for Lawrence W. Nuttall, a distinguished amateur botanist from Fayette County), or continue ahead on the *Silver Maple Trail*. Cross the B&O Railroad again at 1.4 mi and make a jct with the *Rumsey Trail*, L (it is named in honor of William E. Rumsey, a former state entomologist), and R with *Taylor Trail*. Follow the *Rumsey Trail* through a hollow where oak, walnut, and maple tower over natural beds of wildflowers. Ascend, and at 1.8 mi reach a trail jct with the *Brown Trail*, L, and the *Taylor Trail*, R. Among the trees in this area are elm, white ash, shagbark hickory, and red oak. The trail is named for Leland H. Taylor, a former professor of zoology at the university. At 2.1 mi return to the *Circular Trail*, where a wide range of native trees and shrubs have been planted.

West Virginia University Forest
(Monongalia and Preston Counties)

In 1959 the West Virginia University Division of Forestry joined in a long-term lease arrangement with the state's Department of Natural Resources for 7,500 acres in Coopers Rock State Forest (see chapter 7). Conveniently located within 12.0 mi of the university, the forest is used for outdoor classwork, field trips, research and forest management, and recreational activities. School groups and organizations interested in a field trip may contact the forest manager for arrangements. The day-use-only forest is open to the public for licensed fishing and hunting, cross-country skiing, and day hiking. No overnight camping is permitted. The forest headquarters are open weekdays 8 A.M.–5 P.M. (*USGS Maps*: Bruceton Mills, Lake Lynn)

> ADDRESS AND ACCESS: Forest Manager, WVU Forest, Rte 1, Box 269, Bruceton Mills, WV 26526; 304-292-6003. Drive 10.5 mi E of Morgantown from the jct of US-48 and WV-7 on expressway US-48, or 8.0 mi W of Bruceton Mills, Exit 15. Go N on Chestnut Ridge Rd (CO-73/1, also called Sand Springs Rd) for 2.0 mi to WVU Forest headquarters on the L.

Virgin Hemlock Trail

LENGTH: 1.2 mi
DIFFICULTY: easy
FEATURE: virgin hemlock grove

TRAILHEAD AND DETAILS: From Coopers Rock State Forest headquarters (at US-48, Exit 15, N) drive E on CO-73/73 for 2.4 mi and park near a culvert and trail sign. Follow the trail into a rocky area with trillium, rhododendron, and wood sorrel. Cross a footbridge over Lick Run, turn L at 0.2 mi, and follow an old tram road through mtn laurel and rhododendron thickets and groves of tall virgin eastern hemlock (*Tsuga canadensis*). Reach a jct with *Tryon's Trail* at 0.6 mi. (*Tryon's Trail* leads upstream for 0.7 mi to connect with *Ken's Run Trail*.) Cross Little Laurel Run and ascend to a gas pipeline clearing, but turn R after 140 ft at 0.7 mi. Descend on a slope through hardwoods with spots of wintergreen and trailing arbutus. Cross Little Creek, rejoin the trail, and return to the parking area at 1.2 mi. (The state champion hemlock is in Cathedral State Park.)

Ken's Run Trail

LENGTH: 6.3 mi round-trip
DIFFICULTY: moderate
FEATURE: forest study

TRAILHEAD AND DETAILS: From the WVU Forest headquarters drive 0.2 mi N on the Sand Springs Rd and turn R to the old archery range parking area. Follow the trail sign and descend on an old road through a verdant forest of oak, maple, poplar, and hickory to the S side of Little Laurel Run. Cross a gas pipeline at 1.2 mi. Continue downstream on an old RR grade for another 0.6 mi to a Little Laurel Run tributary, L, and *Tryon's Trail*, R. (*Tryon's Trail* is a 0.6-mi connector trail downstream to the *Virgin Hemlock Trail*.) Follow the trail L upstream, parallel with Laurel Run, to an old logging and hunting road (CO-2/3) at 2.8 mi. Turn L on the road, pass under a power line at 4.1 mi, and pass R of the WVU-TV tower to Sand Springs Rd at 4.6 mi. (On the road, L, is an access road for 0.3 mi to the former site of Sand Springs fire tower.) A hike S on the road for 1.7 mi makes a loop back to the parking area at 6.3 mi.

Ryan Nature Trail

LENGTH: 1.7 mi
DIFFICULTY: easy

FEATURE: nature study

TRAILHEAD AND DETAILS: From the old archery range parking area follow the trail signs through white pine, Norway spruce, and red pine plantations, and among such hardwoods as aspen, black cherry, birch, black walnut, hickory, poplar, and maple. Ferns and wildflowers, past land use, forest succession, old iron pits, and wildlife fields are part of a former interpretive trail.

Glade Run Trail (1.4 mi); Lick Run Trail (1.7 mi)

LENGTH: 3.1 mi, combined
DIFFICULTY: moderate
FEATURE: black cherry plantation

TRAILHEADS AND DETAILS: From the jct of Sand Springs Rd and CO-73/73 0.5 mi E from the Coopers Rock State Forest headquarters, drive 1.1 mi N on Sand Springs Rd. *Glade Run Trail* is on the L and *Lick Run Trail* is on the R. (A loop can be made by walking 1.5 mi on CO-73/73 to connect the trails for a combined total of 4.8 mi.) On the beautiful *Glade Run Trail* gradually descend, pass through a black cherry plantation, and at 0.7 mi cross Glade Run. Under a canopy of deciduous trees are rhododendron, mtn laurel, spicebush, and numerous wildflowers such as downy false foxglove (*Aureolaria virginica*) and wild indigo (*Baptisia tinctoria*). Reach Coopers Rock Lake (Trout Pond) at 1.4 mi. Backtrack or walk 0.2 mi around the lake to CO-73/73 (Old 73). It is 2.2 mi L on the Old 73 and Sand Springs Rd to the point of origin for a loop of 3.8 mi.

On the *Lick Run Trail* descend on an old woods road through a forest of tall poplar, cherry, oak, and hickory in a moist treadway to CO-73/73 (Old 73) at 1.7 mi. Backtrack or walk CO-73/73 R and Sand Springs Rd to the point of origin for a loop of 3.2 mi.

Goodspeed's Road (2.7 mi); Johnson Hollow Road (3.5 mi); Darnell Hollow Road (2.4 mi)

LENGTH: 10.6 mi round-trip, combined
DIFFICULTY: moderate to strenuous
FEATURES: wildlife, forest study

TRAILHEADS AND DETAILS: With a combination of old tram roads, jeep roads, and state secondary roads, these trails can form two pleasurable loops from the western half of the forest. The first and shortest loop combines part of *Goodspeed's Rd* and all of *Johnson Hollow Rd* for 5.5 mi. The second and longest loop combines all of *Goodspeed's Rd*; all of *Darnell Hollow Rd*, an old jeep road; and part of *Johnson Hollow Rd* for 8.9 mi.

Begin at the parking area at the W end of CO-73/73 (2.4 mi from Coopers Rock State Forest headquarters at Exit 15 of US-48). Hike 0.3 mi up Quarry Run Rd (CO-69/5) to the joint trailheads of *Goodspeed's Rd* and *Johnson Hollow Rd*. Go R on *Goodspeed's Rd*, the old Glade Ridge Rd, and ascend on a ridge. In the forest are maple, oak, poplar, hickory, cherry, and mtn laurel. Pass under a power line at 0.3 mi, reach the ridge crest N of Quarry Run, and at 2.0 mi make a jct with *Johnson Hollow Rd*, L. (The *Goodspeed's Rd* continues R and is described below.)

Take the *Johnson Hollow Rd* and descend steeply for 0.9 mi to a stream crossing; follow downstream on a slope, R of Johnson Hollow Run, for another 0.7 mi. Cross Johnson Hollow Run and pass a jct with a jeep road, R. Curve L on the *Johnson Hollow Rd* around a ridge and at 4.9 mi cross Birch Hollow Run. Pass under a power line at 5.0 mi and reach the point of beginning at 5.5 mi.

For the longer loop, take the first 2.0 mi of the *Goodspeed's Rd* and pass by the *Johnson Hollow Rd*. After another 0.7 mi arrive at the paved Chestnut Ridge Camp Rd (CO-69/2), W of Harris Lake. (To the R it is 0.4 mi to the jct with Sand Springs Rd and the WVU Forest headquarters.) Turn L on the Chestnut Ridge Camp Rd, pass the restored Cheat Mtn School House (1932–40), and reach a parking area and the E trailhead of the *Darnell Hollow Rd* after 0.4 mi on the road. Descend steeply on a jeep road. The forest is mainly red and white oak, maple, locust, hickory, ash, cherry, and sassafras. Pine, hemlock, rhododendron, dogwood, and mtn laurel are among the other trees and shrubs. Patches of ferns and wintergreen are prominent. Wildlife includes deer, grouse, wild turkey, raccoon, chipmunk, and red squirrel. At 0.5 mi parallel Darnell Hollow Run and pass a field and an abandoned ski slope. Cross the run and remain on the S slope of the canyon for the remainder of the distance. Pass rocky sections and reach a jct with the *Johnson Hollow Rd* (CO-69/18), L. (Ahead it is 0.2 mi to Calvary Church and the jct with paved Fairchance Rd [CO-857]). Turn L on the *Johnson Hollow Rd* and go 0.8 mi to where the road becomes a jeep road. Pass under a power line, cross Johnson Hollow Run, and join the *Johnson Hollow Rd* after another 0.8 mi. Turn R on the *Johnson Hollow Rd* and follow it for 1.8 mi to the point of beginning for a circuit of 8.9 mi.

11. The Allegheny Trail and the Tuscarora Trail (South) (formerly Big Blue Trail)

The two longest trans-state trails in West Virginia have many characteristics in common. They are N-S trails that begin in Virginia and reach Pennsylvania on a traverse of national forest, state properties, and private properties. They overlap some other named trails in the process. They both have sponsoring organizations that had their roots in parent organizations for direction and security, and the organizations have used similar techniques in approaching land easements and using volunteers for trail maintenance. Parts of both trails are on public roads. Both have guidebooks published about them by conservationist-hikers who hiked and measured the trails to write from personal experiences. (See the guidebooks listed below.) And they both have options for extension: the *Allegheny Trail* to the proposed *Trans-Virginia Trail* or other S routes and to the *Laurel Highlands Trail* in Pennsylvania; and the *Tuscarora Trail* (South) (formerly the *Big Blue Trail*) to join the *Allegheny Trail* on the *Great North Mtn Trail* in Virginia. They also have their contrasts. The *Allegheny Trail* is unfinished; it has all the excitement of completion dates, section by section. It will also be 150 mi longer than the *Tuscarora Trail* (South). The topography, ecosystems, and types of forest flora and fauna are of greater variety on the *Allegheny Trail*. Each has special points of interest unduplicated by the other.

ALLEGHENY TRAIL

The ultimate outdoor experience for many of us is building and maintaining trails.

—Bob Tabor

In October 1971, at the close of an Izaak Walton League of America meeting in Charleston, two trail leaders and dreamers, Bob Tabor and Nick Lozano, discussed a "long trail" through West Virginia. Later they shared their thoughts with other trail-oriented leaders and environmentalists, and within a year the concept and initial strategy for both the *Allegheny Trail* and the West Virginia Scenic Trails Association (WVSTA) had begun. Since then, about 180 mi of the *Allegheny Trail* have been completed in a proposed route of 300 mi from Monroe County in the S through Preston County in the N.

Tabor has said that the development of the *Allegheny Trail* has been modeled on that of the *Appalachian Trail* (*AT*), with the West Virginia Scenic Trails Association administratively similar to the Appalachian Trail Conference. "Working all day painting blazes, cutting brush, and moving rocks on the trail makes me feel good about myself," said WVSTA board member Shirley Schweizer. "I feel very fortunate to live in West Virginia and be a part of the *Allegheny Trail*."

The trail is divided into four long sections with a trail coordinator for each. Section I is from the Pennsylvania–West Virginia state line to Blackwater Falls State Park for approximately 95 mi; Section II is from Blackwater Falls State Park to Cass for 95 mi; Section III includes the area from Cass to Meadow Creek near Neola for 62 mi; and Section IV is from Meadow Creek/Lake Sherwood Rd to the *Appalachian Trail* at Pine Swamp Branch near the Virginia–West Virginia state line for approximately 55 mi. (Parts of this section are in Virginia.) It is with Section IV that the following S-N trail description begins.

Section IV: Appalachian Trail to Lake Sherwood Road

There are three access routes, all from the *Appalachian Trail*, to the S terminus of the *Allegheny Trail*. One is 1.7 mi, another is 5.5 mi, and the longest is 16.9 mi. To approach the 1.7-mi access route, drive 0.3 mi E from Pearisburg, VA, on US-460, and turn L at the White Rocks Recreation Area sign on SR-635. Drive 10.0 mi to a small parking area, L, near a bridge over Stony Creek. Hike 40 yd on a spur access to the *AT*, turn L, ascend, pass R of the Stone Pine Swamp branch shelter at 0.4 mi, and continue to ascend on a steep, rocky footpath. Cross Pine Swamp Branch, which may be running underneath the boulders, depending on the season. Reach a leveling-out area arbored with rhododendron. On the L are huge hemlock and on the R is the jct with the *Allegheny Trail* at 1.9 mi.

To use the 5.5-mi access, take the blue-blazed *Ground Hog Trail*, a side trail that ascends the N side of Peters Mtn in Monroe County, WV. It is accessible from the jct of US-219 and Painters Run Rd (CO-219/21), 2.4 mi SW of Lindside on US-219. After 1.2 mi on Painters Run Rd turn L at the jct with Green Valley Rd (CO-219/24) and go 0.5 mi to the parking area on the R. Ascend the *Ground Hog Trail* for 1.8 mi to a jct with the *AT*. Turn L on the *AT* for 3.7 mi to the jct with the *Allegheny Trail* as described above. (See book sections 2 and 3 for more information on the *Ground Hog Trail*.) The longest route, 16.9 mi, follows the *AT* from the Senator Shumate Bridge in N Pearisburg N to the jct with the *Allegheny Trail*.

Follow the *Allegheny Trail* for 0.3 mi on a slight ascent to the Peters Mtn ridge crest and turn R on the ridge. In an open forest of oak, hickory, maple, and cherry follow a wide footpath that becomes a 4WD forest road at 0.7 mi. At 0.8 mi is an old hunters' cabin with twin springs that may be dry in the summer or fall. Continue on the winding road, which is sometimes muddy and rutted by 4WD vehicles; leave the road for a short distance at 2.6 mi. At 3.6 mi FR-945 goes R, down the mtn. Turn L and after 0.2 mi reach a level area with a private cottage, L, and a hunters' road that descends into West Virginia. Turn R at a large buckeye tree. Follow this road for 0.5 mi and reach a foot trail at 4.3 mi. To the L is a private grassy field with apple trees and deer blinds. A pioneer area with remnants of a heating stove and barrel hoops is at 4.8 mi. Nearby is an intermittent drain. Large hunting fields are on the L slope. Pass R of another private hunting area at 5.4 mi. From a wide gap ascend to a scenic rock formation at 5.6 mi; leave the foot trail at 6.3 mi. Follow an old forest road through a forest of hickory, chestnut oak, striped maple, white snakeroot, fern beds, and

Gound Hog Trail, southermost access to the Allegheny Trail, southwest of Lindside.

mtn laurel. Wildlife likely to be seen are wild turkey, grouse, and deer. At 7.5 mi reach a jct with a vehicle-use road, L, that descends into the West Virginia side. At 8.1 mi enter Monroe County, WV. Reach the top of a ridge at 8.2 mi, leave the foot trail, enter an old road at 8.4 mi, and reach the top of another ridge at 9.3 mi. Begin gradual descent on a scenic road to a damp area with mtn laurel and a locked gate at 10.1 mi. To the R is a spring on a vehicle-use road. At 10.2 mi is a water hole; at 10.7 mi pass through a grazing field. Cross the center of the field and follow an old logging road with blueberry bushes and running cedar in an area of saplings. The road becomes a foot trail at 10.9 mi. Creasy salad, mullein, wintergreen, galax, and shooting star are seen throughout this area. Leave the leeward side of the ridge and cross to a rocky area at 11.5 mi. At 11.7 mi, R, is an unmarked spur trail for 0.1 mi to a scenic rock formation and Hanging Rock Raptor Migration Observatory (3,812 ft). Formerly a fire tower, the observatory has a railed deck constructed around a glassed enclosure for full 360-degree viewing. It is maintained by the John W. Handlan Chapter of the A. B. Brooks Bird Club from Saint Albans.

Back on the main trail, continue on the foot trail to the N side of a gap and 4WD entrance from the L at 12.1 mi. To the R is private property and a posted sign. Continue on the N side of the ridge on a rocky treadway; pass under a power line and descend from the ridge to a gap and Gap Mills Rd (CO-15), also called Limestone Hill Rd, at 12.6 mi. Parking space for five vehicles is available in a field under the power line. (*USGS Maps:* Lindside, Interior, Waiteville, Gap Mills)

(It is 3.8 mi R [S] on CO-15 to Waiteville Rd [CO-17], and another 6.9 mi to FR-613, L, to White Rock Campground. It is another 6.0 mi on the paved road [which becomes SR-635] to the *AT* access at Pine Swamp Branch. To return to Sugar Camp, follow the L [N] side of CO-15; it is 1.8 mi to Zenith Rd [CO-29], L. After 9.1 mi the road forks. The R fork goes 10.8 mi to Sugar Camp, for a total of 21.7 mi. If taking the L fork on the Zenith Rd, follow Back Valley Rd [CO-29/2]—the road is narrow—and keep L at all other road jcts to arrive at Sugar Camp with a total of 17.3 mi.)

Continuing on the *Allegheny Trail* from the parking area on Gap Mills Rd (CO-15), descend S to parallel the road for 0.2 mi. Make a sharp L onto a grassy fire road (FR-5057). On a gentle contour descend from about 3,330 ft to 2,870 ft in more than 5.0 mi. At 2.3 mi pass an open area near the crest of Peters Mtn. Although there are not any outcrops for views, this area is beautiful for fall foliage in mid-October. After curving around a few ridges and crossing tributaries that flow to Potts Creek, reach the end of FR-5057 at 5.6 mi (22.9 mi from Sugar Camp). Here is a jct with abandoned Crowder Rd (CO-20, a former access road between Laurel Branch and Gap Mills). The trail turns right on Crowder Rd and after 2.7 mi reaches a parking area near a gravel quarry, 0.2 mi before the road intersects with CO-17 and the temporary end of the trail. Here is the community of Laurel Branch. It is 5.1 mi SW on CO-17 to Gap Mills Rd (CO-15). The community of Paint Bank is 5.5 mi NE from Laurel Branch. (*USGS Map*: Ronceverte)

(From Laurel Branch [Crowder Rd area] the trail will go 8.0 mi through Craig County, VA [in the Jefferson NF], then another 16.0 mi in Allegheny County in the George Washington NF to cross I-64 at Jerry's Run. This section is currently under construction.)

To continue on the *Allegheny Trail* from Jerry's Run drive 12.0 mi W of Covington on I-64 (2.0 mi E from West Virginia state line) and Exit 2. Turn N 0.2 mi to a dead-end road and parking space at trail sign. Follow the yellow-blazed trail in a hardwood forest to the top of a ridge. Descend, cross a stream in Fox's Hollow at 0.9 mi, and pass left of a logging road at 1.1 mi. Ascend on a ridge spine to overlooks at 2.3 mi and 2.4 mi. Views SE are of Brushy Mtn and Jerry's Run hollow (locally called Doe Lick), and N to Smith Knob. Follow the boundary between Virginia and West Virginia on an old woods road, but turn left onto private property and another road at 3.3 mi. Turn R at 3.7 mi. Cross a stream at 4.3 mi, and ascend on switchbacks. Leave private property at 4.6 mi. After following the ridge in and out of private property and USFS property, reach Smith Knob (3,400 ft) at 8.1 mi. From a grassy bald there are outstanding views N to Laurel Run Valley and SE to Panther Ridge. Descend in a rough area to a jct with CO-15/3 (Whites Draft Rd, which descends 5.2 mi down the mtn in West Virginia to WV-92) at 9.7 mi. Curve around a ridge of Allegheny Mtn, leave Virginia, and descend on switchbacks to Laurel Run at 11.1 mi in the Monongahela NF. For the next 4.4 mi there are excellent campsites. The trail crosses Laurel Run six times, and passes by and through wildlife fields and forests of white pine, hemlock, hardwoods, and rhododendron. Reach a parking area at CO-14 (Lake Sherwood Rd) at 15.5 mi. (*USGS Maps*: Jerry's Run, Alvon, Rucker Gap) Here is the N end of Section IV and the beginning of Section III's S end. (It is 2.5 mi W on Lake Sherwood Rd to Neola and WV-92, where there are groceries, gasoline, PO, and telephone.)

Section III: Lake Sherwood Road to Cass

From the parking lot, hike W 0.1 mi on Lake Sherwood Rd to cross a footbridge over Meadow Creek. Ascend on switchbacks for nearly 1,000 ft in elev to a scenic outlook at 1.6 mi. Follow the ridge line of Meadow Creek Mtn through a hardwood forest with scattered evergreens. The trail undulates over more than a dozen knobs. At 7.2 mi cross former *Rider Trail* near Dilley Run. Ascend to the knob and ridge, then reach *Upper Meadow Trail* R at 7.9 mi. (*Upper Meadow Trail* descends 1.2 mi E to Lake Sherwood Campground.) Continue on the *Allegheny Trail*, reach a jct with the *Meadow Mtn Trail*, and leave the ridge, L, at 8.4 mi. Descend on switchbacks among wildlife to cross Anthony Creek footbridge at 10.5 mi. Pass through a meadow of thick grasses and abundant wildflowers to reach WV-92 at 10.7 mi. (To the L on WV-92 is 7.4 mi to Neola.)

Cross the road to an excellent parking lot and information signboard. Continue NW to parallel Bear Creek for 0.6 mi before following switchbacks to the top of Middle Mtn. Ascend steeply, curve around a knoll, and reach a jct with *Middle Mtn Trail* R and L at 13.3 mi. (See White Sulphur Ranger District in part 1, section 6.) Turn R (N) and follow the *Middle Mtn Trail* on an easy treadway. At 15.1 mi leave *Middle Mtn Trail* and turn L (W) on the former *Dock Trail*. Descend and at 17.1 mi cross Douthat Rd (CO-23) at the Dock, a parking area only. (It received its name many years ago when the location was a timber loading dock. From here there is another 1.4 mi of the *Allegheny Trail* in White Sulphur Ranger District before entering the Marlinton Ranger District, but the Dock is the most convenient place to park.) On Douthat Rd it is 7.0 mi N to WV-39 and Minnehaha Springs.

From the Douthat Rd jct follow the *Allegheny Trail* and *Brushy Mtn Trail* jointly on a gated forest road through a pine plantation. After 0.4 mi fork L, ascend and cross Beaver Lick Mtn into the Marlinton District of the MNF, and at 3.0 mi pass a jct with the blue-blazed *Beaver Creek Trail*. (The *Beaver Creek Trail* turns R and goes 0.7 mi to the Beaver Creek Campground of Watoga State Park. Hot showers and a laundry are available from Memorial Day to Labor Day.) Pass through the Calvin Price State Forest, and at 9.1 mi reach a jct with Pyles Mtn Rd (CO-21/4), the main road W to Watoga State Park's multiple facilities. After the park, descend to Beaver Creek and ascend to follow the old *Buckley Mtn Trail* in a deciduous forest, mainly oak, that has understory sections of mtn laurel and buckberry. Descend to Gilden Hollow and reach Beaver Creek Rd (CO-21) at 22.6 mi.

Turn L and reach Huntersville after 1.0 mi. (Here are groceries, PO, and phone.) Turn L on WV-39, but after 0.8 mi turn R on WV-28. After another 0.5 mi turn L and ascend steeply to Marlin Mtn Range. Follow the ridge line and reach an Adirondack shelter at 28.0 mi. Continue on the ridge; reach Marlin Mtn peak (3,326 ft) at 30.2 mi. Turn E, cross the Marlin Lick Run headwaters, and return to WV-28 at 33.4 mi. Turn L and after 0.5 mi turn L to ascend Thorny Creek Mtn; enter a jeep road in Seneca State Forest. At 38.5 mi cross the forest's main road (it is 2.4 mi E to forest headquarters and WV-28), pass a lookout tower, and follow the Loop Rd to the forest boundary at 39.7 mi. Descend to Laurel Run Rd (CO-1/4), turn L, and after 0.3 mi turn R and begin ascent of Thomas Mtn. Descend on a jeep road to Sitlington Rd (CO-12) at 44.1 mi (it is 2.2 mi R to WV-28 and Dunmore). Turn L, cross the Greenbrier River, and join the *Greenbrier River Trail* at 45.2 mi. (Because of flood damage in this area, the trail may have been relocated.) Turn R and reach Cass at 48.7 mi, the N terminus of Section III. (Facilities here include groceries, gasoline, PO, phone, campground [304-456-3218], and other facilities from Memorial Day to Labor Day.) (*USGS-FS Maps*: Rucker Gap, Lake Sherwood, Marlinton, Minnehaha Springs, Clover Lick, Cass)

Section II: Cass to Blackwater Falls State Park

To begin Section II, cross the Greenbrier River bridge, turn L, and follow a private road for 1.5 mi to the Greenbrier Ranger District of the MNF. Cross a stream, ascend by another stream, and reach the crest of Little Mtn at 4.0 mi. The forest is deciduous, with scattered hemlock, Virginia pine, wild azaleas, mtn laurel, and witch hazel. Deer, wild turkey, and grouse are commonplace, and bear have been sighted. Outstanding views of the National Radio Astronomy Observatory are along the ridge line. At 7.2 mi *Hosterman Trail* is L. Begin to follow the old blue-blazed *Little Mtn Trail* and follow it in parts for 6.5 mi. At 8.1 mi is a side trail, L, for 0.2 mi to Little Mtn Knob (3,417 ft). Cross Laurel Fork at 9.2 mi and follow up the W side for nearly 1.0 mi before ascending to another ridge line of scenic Little Mtn. Cross Brush Run at 14.2 mi and Spillman Run at 16.3 mi; ascend to a saddle in Sandy Ridge; and descend to Durbin at 18.3 mi. (Durbin has laundry, groceries, hardware, phone, gasoline, PO, restaurant, and pharmacy. It is 2.5 mi E on US-250 to the Greenbrier Ranger District in Bartow.)

Follow US-250 W for 2.7 mi and turn R into the MNF. Descend to and cross Fill Run; ascend to and cross Simmons Rd (CO-250/1); and continue ascent, steep in places, to Shavers Mtn at 25.4 mi. To the L is a 0.2-mi access from Gaudineer Knob Rd (FR-27). Turn R and for the next 20 mi follow the high scenic ridge line, formerly the blue-blazed *Shavers Mtn Trail* (also called the *North-South Trail*). Elevation averages 4,000 ft; red spruce and hemlock groves are among the deciduous hardwoods of oak, cherry, and maple. Wildlife includes bear, deer, red squirrel, grouse, wild turkey, and plenty of chipmunk. At 26.9 mi enter the Gaudineer Scenic Area and reach FR-27 at 27.1 mi. Immediately turn R and re-enter the forest. Pass through a marshy area at 29.2 mi and reach the Johns Camp Run Shelter at 30.5 mi. (The 0.8-mi *Johns Camp Run Trail* is an access route to FR-317.) Water is plentiful here. Wildlife visits frequently. Arrive at the Wildell Shelter at 37.7 mi. At 38.8 mi is a jct with *High Falls Trail*. (It is 1.0 mi R [E] to Little River Rd [FR-44] and 1.5 mi L [W] to the High Falls on Shavers Fork.) Reach Elliots Ridge Rd (CO-22) at 43.4 mi. Turn R and go 0.3 mi on the paved road to a crossroads in Glady. (A few yd to the R is Shifflett's general store with gasoline, limited groceries, PO, and phone; store hours are irregular, usually from 11 A.M. to 3 P.M.) For the next 1.8 mi follow paved Glady Fork Rd (CO-27), turn R into the forest, descend, and ford Glady Fork at 46.4 mi. (If high water prevents crossing, backtrack to the Glady Fork Rd and go 7.5 mi N on the paved road to Alpena and US-33.) Follow sections of old RR grade, and reach a jct with *McCray Creek Trail* at 49.5 mi. Follow sections of an old RR grade, cross a number of tributaries, and reach US-33 in the community of Evened at 54.4 mi. (It is 1.5 mi R [E] up the mtn on US-33 to Wymer, with a general store of groceries, gasoline, PO, and phone; regular opening hours. It is 1.3 mi L [W] to Alpine Lodge and Restaurant [304-636-1470], and 10.0 mi to Elkins.)

Cross US-33, pass through an old farm for 0.3 mi, and cross a secondary road. Pass a farm area and enter the Cheat Ranger District of the MNF to follow old RR grades, forest roads, and foot trails on an exceptionally scenic route for 17.0 mi along Glady Fork. Water sources and excellent campsites are plentiful. Reach FR-240 at 60.4 mi and leave the road at 63.0 mi on Gladden Rd (CO-12). Turn L, follow the Gladden Rd for 0.2 mi to cross Glady Fork and reach a jct with the *Mylius Trail* at 63.4 mi. From here follow gated FR-162 for the next 8.5 mi to Richard Rd (CO-26), cross a low water bridge over the Glady Fork, and reach a paved road at 72.0 mi in Gladden. Follow the Gladden Rd (CO-35/15) along Dry Fork for 3.2 mi and cross the Jenningston Bridge. Turn R and follow Laneville Rd (CO-45) to

Red Creek community and WV-72. Turn L, go 0.1 mi on WV-72, and turn R on Laneville Rd (CO-45). After 1.5 mi on the gravel road, turn L to enter Canaan Valley State Park at 80.4 mi. Follow trails through the park. (There is access to a campground, lodge, restaurant, and other facilities; open year-round.) Ascend Canaan Mtn in the MNF at 83.7 mi in a scenic area of hardwoods and conifers. Reach the Canaan Loop Rd (FR-13) at 84.9 mi; turn R, go 1.2 mi on the gravel road, and make a L turn on the old *Davis Trail*. The area is chiefly rocky and has red spruce groves and large patches of ferns and mtn laurel. This is also a cross-country ski trail, the only one in the state that connects two major state park lodges. Cross *Plantation Trail* at 87.3 mi and pass R of the Canaan Mtn Shelter and spring. Reach the Blackwater Falls State Park stables parking area at 88.9 mi. (From here it is 0.8 mi L to the lodge and restaurant. To the R is the campground and other facilities. It is 2.3 mi from this point to Davis for motels, restaurants, groceries, gasoline, pharmacy, hardware, PO, and phone.) (*USGS-FS Maps*: Cass, Green Bank, Durbin, Wildell, Beverly East, Glady, Bowden, Harman, Mozark Mtn, Blackwater Falls)

Section I: Blackwater Falls State Park to Pennsylvania State Line

The approximately 95-mi Section I begins at the Blackwater Falls State Park stables parking area. It is mainly on secondary roads, with scenic areas through Tucker and Preston Counties, and it is in the process of development for off-road locations and additional campsites. Roads washed away in the 1985 and 1996 floods have been reconstructed.

Follow the *Allegheny Trail* blazes on the paved road to the first intersection. Turn R and follow the entrance road out to WV-32 in the town of Davis. Turn L, follow WV-32 to Thomas, turn L on Douglas Rd (CO-27), and follow it to cross the bridge over the N fork of Blackwater River. Then follow the scenic Canyon Rim Rd (FR 18) for 8.5 mi in the MNF to US-219. Turn R, go 2.1 mi on US-219, and turn L on paved Sugar Lands Rd (CO-25). (It is 4.0 mi ahead on US-219 to Thomas.)

Follow Sugar Lands Rd for 0.4 mi before a R turn on graveled Close Mtn Rd (CO-16). Descend the W slope of Backbone Mtn to a ridge with pastureland, and after 3.1 mi enter the MNF and descend 1,000 ft for 1.3 mi on an exceptionally steep roadway to Horseshoe Run Rd (CO-7). (To the L it is 0.6 mi to the Horseshoe Rec Area in the Cheat Ranger District. See chapter 1.) Turn R on the paved road and go 0.8 mi to the community of Lead Mine. (A general store with groceries and gasoline is here.) Total trail distance from Blackwater Falls State Park is 20.6 mi.

Continue on Horseshoe Run Rd upstream, pass through the community of Shafer, and at 3.1 mi cross Twelve Mile Run. Turn L, go upstream for 0.8 mi, and reach the Preston County line in the MNF. (Campsites are in this area.) Here the road changes name and number to Twelve Mile Rd (CO-112/1). Follow upstream in a hollow to the headwaters and ascend to a ridge. Follow the ridge past a few private houses to a jct with Stemple Ridge Rd (CO-112) in the community of Sell, 3.0 mi from the county line and a total of 27.5 mi from Blackwater Falls State Park.

Cross Stemple Ridge Rd to Snake Rd (CO-110) and descend through a remote area for 4.0 mi to Hardesty and US-50. Turn L. (To the R on US-50 it is 5.4 mi to Aurora and another 1.0 mi to Cathedral State Park.) Pass a motel, restaurant, grocery store, and Cheat River Campground, and after 1.8 mi on US-50 turn R on Madison Rd (CO-84). Follow Madison Rd for 4.1 mi, turn L on Manheim Rd (CO-80, also called Lantz Ridge Rd), and go 3.9 mi to Rowlesburg. (Here are restaurants, grocery stores, service station, laundromat, phone, and PO.) The total mileage from Blackwater Falls State Park is 41.3 mi.

After crossing the B&O Railroad tracks, go N on Shaver M&K Rd (CO-80/2) and Calver Shaver Rd (CO-80/1) for 5.6 mi to Huffman Rd and go 1.4 mi to Fitchett-Ambersburg Rd (CO-86), L. Ascend and descend on Caddell Mtn and, after 5.6 mi on CO-86, make a jct with WV-7 for a total of 53.9 mi.

Turn R on WV-7 and go 2.4 mi to old Terra Alta Pike (CO-45/3), L, at the edge of Terra Alta. (Restaurants, laundromat, motel, PO, groceries, service station, phone, and other stores are here.) After 2.0 mi and six stream crossings, turn L on Laughry Hollow Rd (CO-7/33); go 1.9 mi, pass through two gates to Crane School West End Rd (CO-3/12), and turn L. Proceed for 1.5 mi to Crane School East End Rd (CO-45/1) and turn L. Reach St Joe/Albright after another 2.3 mi, for a total of 64.2 mi from Blackwater Falls State Park. (Albright has a grocery store, service station, PO, and phone.) (This area was severely damaged by the November 1985 flood.)

The trail goes through Albright for 0.7 mi to a jct with WV-26 and N for 1.3 mi on WV-26 to Beech Run Rd (CO-26/23), L. After 6.3 mi through the countryside, turn L on Harmony Grove Rd (CO-14/5) and go 2.9 mi to Mt Nebo, where CO-14/5 becomes Rockville–Mt Nebo Rd (CO-14). The trail is now 74.9 mi from Blackwater Falls State Park.

Go N on CO-14, cross the Big Sandy Creek bridge, and after 2.2 mi turn L on George Walls Rd (CO-14/1). Go 1.9 mi and turn R on Laurel Run Rd (CO-73/5) for 0.6 mi. Pass under US-48 and reach a jct with old US-48 (CO-73-73). (To the R it is 4.9 mi to Bruceton Mills for groceries, service station, PO, phone, restaurant, and general stores. To the L it is 2.5 mi to Coopers Rock State Forest.) Cross the road to a gravel road that goes through a farm, and after 2.6 mi turn R on Dickie Hill Rd (CO-2/5). Go 0.7 mi to join Bensons Rd (CO-2/2, also called Lake O'Woods Rd). Turn L on Hileman Rd (CO-73/9) and go 1.9 mi; turn L on Bryte Rd (CO-6/2) and go 1.0 mi. Turn R on Mt Grove Rd (CO-4/1) at a church cemetery. Proceed for 1.2 mi and turn L on Clifton Mills Rd (CO-4, also known as State Line Rd) for 0.6 mi to the Pennsylvania state line (the Mason-Dixon Line) for a total of 88.2 mi from Blackwater Falls State Park. (*USGS-FS Maps:* Blackwater Falls, Mozark Mtn, Lead Mine, Aurora, Terra Alta, Kingwood, Valley Point, Bruceton Mills)

INFORMATION: For more information on the sections, write or call the following: (Section I) George Rosier, 633 West Virginia Ave, Morgantown, WV 26505, 304-296-5158; (Section II) Eddy Pride, 70 West Park Ave, Westover, WV 26505, 304-296-4555; (Section III) Vicky Shears, 463 Cobun Ave, Morgantown, WV 26505, 304-296-7249; (Section IV) Doug Wood, HC65, Box 182, Forest Hill, WV 24935, 304-256-6850. For information on the *Hiking Guide to the Allegheny Trail*, write or call WVSTA, PO Box 4042, Charleston, WV 25364; 304-755-4878.

TUSCARORA TRAIL (SOUTH)
(FORMERLY BIG BLUE TRAIL)

I worked on the Big Blue Trail because we need a legacy of Nature for future generations.

—Elizabeth Johnston

Thirty-five years ago there was concern among Appalachian Trail Conference leaders that the continuous route of the *AT* was jeopardized on private lands in northern Virginia. The *Big Blue Trail*, now the *Tuscarora Trail (South),* was a product of that concern. It was designed and constructed, and is maintained, by the Potomac Appalachian Trail Club (PATC). Among the early leaders were James Denton, Woody Kennedy, and Fred Blackburn, who had 54 mi of the Big Blue finished by 1970. Notable in the history of trail building and securing private land easements is Tom Floyd; he constructed the final 66 mi. On October 11, 1981, the final mile was finished near the West Virginia–Virginia state line at the Great North Mtn Range. The joining of the *Big Blue Trail* with the 110-mi *Tuscarora Trail* created an *AT* alternate that runs from Matthews Arm in the Shenandoah National Park to rejoin the *AT* in Dean's Gap, PA.

The former *Big Blue Trail* has 11 sections, numbered from the Potomac River to the Shenandoah National Park. Sections 1,2,5, and 6, and parts of 3,4, and 7 are in West Virginia for a total of 65.9 mi. Only the West Virginia mileage is emphasized in this book; it is described S to N and clarified as *Tuscarora Trail (South)*. The first 19.3 mi, from S to N, is in the George Washington National Forest. (See chapter 1.) That part is in Sections 7 and 6, and is described with its joint trail routes from *Little North Mtn Trail* at the West Virginia–Virginia state line to Hawk Campground in chapter 2.

To reach Hawk Campground by vehicle, go 4.0 mi E from Wardensville on WV-55 and turn L on FR-502. (It is 1.0 mi E on WV-55 to the Virginia state line and another 15.3 mi to I-81 in Strasburg, VA.) Drive 3.0 mi on FR-502, turn L on FR-347, and go 0.7 mi to the rustic Hawk Campground entrance, R. Hike the blue-blazed *Tuscarora Trail (South)* NW for 1.6 mi in the GWNF to Hawk Run. Cross Hawk Run three times, ascend to a ridge, follow a woods road, and cross Capon Spring Rd (CO-16) and bridge at 3.8 mi. Pass near a house, cross Middle Ridge and Dry Run, and pass the historic grave site of Jemima Farmer at 5.7 mi. At 6.6 mi pass under a power line and follow woods and jeep roads to cross Milk Rd (CO-23/11) at 7.5 mi. After passage through rural settings of woods and fields, reach branch of Kump Rd (CO-23/9) at 8.1 mi and pass a deserted schoolhouse. Return to the gravel Kump Rd (CO-23/10) and go E along Lohman branch to a parking area at the asphalt road at 11.3 mi. This is the end of Section 5, S of Lehew. (It is 0.8 mi N on Back Creek Rd [CO-23/3] to Lehew and WV-259.)

Section 4 begins here and goes 1.8 mi in West Virginia before it enters Virginia again for 11.7 mi to its end in the community of Gore. Follow Back Creek Rd, R, cross bridge at 0.5 mi, turn L on Gore Rd (CO-23/11) (SR-704 in Frederick County, VA), but turn off the road after 0.1 mi onto a jeep road. At 1.9 mi leave the jeep road and enter Lucas Woods, the site of a dedication ceremony of the *Big Blue Trail* (now *Tuscarora Trail [South]*) completion in 1981. Camping is allowed. Ascend on switchbacks (approx 1,000 ft elev change) to the scenic ridge line of Great North Mtn at 3.2 mi. Vegetation on the mtn includes mtn laurel, wild azaleas, blueberry, sassafras, Virginia pine, oak, hickory, maple, dogwood, trailing arbutus, wintergreen, and pink lady-slipper. Animal life is mainly deer, wild turkey, grouse, gray squirrel, and chipmunk. At 5.6 mi and at 6.2 mi are jct with the historic, orange-blazed *Frye Path Trail*. Reach Pinnacle Rocks and the Devil's Backbone area at 5.8 mi. Descend on switchbacks and enter a gorge at 6.8 mi. Pass through a rocky area for the next 2.3 mi and join a jeep road at 10.0 mi. At 12.9 mi arrive at a dirt road that becomes paved after 0.1 mi. This is SR-853. Cross Back Creek bridge and Winchester Railroad tracks into Gore at 13.5 mi. Section 4 ends here. (Gore has a grocery store, phone, gasoline, and PO.)

Begin Section 3 at the jct of SR-853 and SR-751, turn R on SR-751, and walk out to US-50. Follow US-50 for 0.9 mi and turn L on SR-688. Go 3.3 mi through a farming area and reach a jct, R, on SR-684 in the community of Gainsboro. Turn L on SR-600, cross US-522, and follow SR-600 to Isaacs Creek. Turn L on SR-689 at 7.0 mi. Pass through meadows, farming areas, and woods to a jct with *Fishing Pond Trail* at 9.0 mi. Pass the Dresel Wayside campsites (a private campground available to through-hikers) and continue through farmland and tranquil woodland of oak and pine. At 10.8 mi, cross SR-600, and again at 12.0 mi. (Artesian water is 40 yd L on SR-600, S of the Siler jct.) Follow the trail to a road jct with SR-681, which becomes WV-45 at 15.1 mi, the state line. Follow WV-45 for 1.4 mi to the end of Section 3 at 16.5 mi. Section 2 begins here (2.6 mi W of Glengary on WV-45).

Section 2 begins at a parking area and dirt road. Follow the road for 0.7 mi and turn R into Sleepy Creek WMA. It ends at the Spruce Pine Roadside Park at 22.0 mi. This section is described in detail in chapter 8 because 20.8 mi of it is in the Sleepy Creek WMA. After it leaves the Sleepy Creek it follows down Sleepy Creek Mtn to WV-9. Pass a backpacking campground and go through Spruce Pine Roadside Park in a 650-acre wilderness area known as the General Adam Stevens Park, a property of the Sons of the American Revolution.

At the Spruce Pine Roadside Park (or the new location) enter Section 1 on the paved road across WV-9 (0.3 mi E of the Sleepy Creek bridge) and make an immediate L turn on a footpath. At 0.8 mi turn L on Burnt Mill Rd

(CO-1/3) and cross Sleepy Creek bridge at 1.9 mi. Reach a jct of paved Potomac River Rd (CO-8) at 2.2 mi, turn R and, after 0.2 mi at a jct with Jim West Rd (CO-6), enter a footpath between the roads. Pass through farms and rolling hills, cross Dugan Hollow stream at 5.6 mi, and enter a forest owned by PATC where camping is allowed. Leave the PATC area after 1.0 mi, cross a stream, enter pastureland, and at 6.6 mi join Culp Rd (CO-1/1). Turn L, and immediately R to cross Culp Rd into a meadow. Arrive at the River Rd (CO-1) at 7.2 mi, turn L and reach US-522 at 9.5 mi. Cross the Potomac River bridge into Hancock, MD, take a sharp L, and go under the bridge and across the RR yard to the C&O Canal Towpath. Here is the end of Section 1 at 10.2 mi. (It is 0.2 mi L to a town park and exit to Hancock, and 8.0 mi E on the C&O Canal Towpath to the jct with the *Tuscarora Trail [North]*.)

For more detail, the *Big Blue Trail Guide*, written by Elizabeth Johnston and published by the PATC, is recommended. The trail guide is in two pocket-size books with maps and photography. Contact PATC, 118 Park St SE, Vienna, VA, 22180; 703-242-0693.

Appendix

ORGANIZATIONS AND CLUBS

Kanawha Trail Club

The Kanawha Trail Club began as the Charleston Daily Mail Hiking Club in July 1942. Sol Padlibsky of the Charleston Daily Mail collaborated with H. M. F. Kinsey, a Boy Scouts executive, in organizing group hiking. In September 1944, the group reorganized with 54 charter members and changed the club name to the Kanawha Trail Club. Three years later the club was incorporated and a charter obtained. Plans followed for a rustic lodge on the Middle Lick Fork of Davis Creek, 7 mi from Charleston, and the lodge that was built has been in use since October 1948. The club maintains 20.7 mi of the *AT,* from the New River north to the Stony Creek Valley on the Waiteville Rd. About 80 percent of the club's outings are in the 9052-acre Kanawha State Forest, an area adjoining the club's lodge. In 1978 several club members, including Charley Carlson and Howard and Dorothy Guest, were active in lobbying for a state bill that prohibits commercial timber cutting in this forest. The club has 150 members, and membership is open to all ages.

INFORMATION: Kanawha Trail Club, PO Box 4474, Charleston, WV 25364; 304-744-6575.

Potomac Appalachian Trail Club

The Potomac Appalachian Trail Club is the largest trail-oriented club in the south with over 5,700 members. It was established in 1927 with seven members who built 19 mi of the *AT.* By 1936 it had completed 250 mi of the *AT* from the Susquehanna River in Pennsylvania to Rockfish Gap in Virginia. Today it maintains 270 mi of the *AT* in which the route into Harpers Ferry and short sections into Jefferson County are included. In addition, the club maintains approximately 1,000 mi of other foot trails in the area, including Pennsylvania, Maryland, the District of Columbia, northern Virginia, and such trails as the *Big Blue Trail* in West Virginia.

Exceptionally active, the club maintains 26 primitive and semi-primitive cabins and 30 shelters for *AT* hikers, as well as several trail work centers, provides roving *AT* patrols to help hikers in the peak seasons, and supervises the hut system for long-distance hikers in the Shenandoah National Park. The club also publishes detailed guidebooks, maps, brochures, and other informational materials on such topics as land acquisition for protecting the *AT* and other trails, and government policies and agencies affecting the trails.

INFORMATION: Contact the main office at 118 Park St, Vienna, VA 22180. This office is open to the public from 7 A.M. to 9 P.M. Mon through Wed, and 12 NOON to 2 P.M. Thur through Fri; 703-242-0693.

The Nature Conservancy

The Nature Conservancy is a national nonprofit organization whose objective is to protect, preserve, and conserve the biological diversity of the nation's natural areas. It cooperates and works with other private and public conservation agencies to attain its objectives. Currently it manages a national system of over 1,300 nature sanctuaries with nearly 10 million acres in all 50 states, Canada, the Caribbean, and South America. The conservancy acquires funding from individual contributors, foundation grants, corporate gifts, and investments. Organized in 1950, it had over 800,000 members in 1996. It publishes *The Nature Conservancy News*.

The West Virginia chapter, formed in 1963, protects more than 36,000 acres in 22 private preserves, some of which provide limited hiking opportunities. Two of the preserves have short designated trails. One is Brush Creek, a scenic area in Mercer County near Pipestem State Park. Its 123 acres encompass a section of Brush Creek canyon and the Bluestone River area. Among its features are cascades, cliffs, and rare plants and animals. An old RR grade has been constructed into an easy 1.0-mi *Brush Creek Trail* that leads to the Bluestone River. It must be backtracked. Access is to take WV-20 N from Athens 2.5 mi to Speedway and turn L onto Camp Creek Rd (CO-3). After 2.8 mi turn L at a fork onto a dirt road. Go 0.5 mi to Brush Creek and park at the bridge.

Another preserve is Cranesville Swamp, a 318-acre boreal bog complex in Preston County, S of Cranesville. It is managed by both the West Virginia and the Maryland chapters. The swamp supports a relic colony of northern plant and animal life at a southern latitude. It has the southernmost colony of American larch (*Larix laricina*), the state's only native deciduous cone-bearing tree. Some of the other trees are red spruce, Canada yew, black ash, black cherry, yellow birch, and hemlock. Access from Cranesville is to take the Cranesville Rd (CO-47) S for 2.2 mi to a jct L with Burnside Camp Rd (CO-49) opposite a church. Go 1.0 mi and turn L on Feather Rd (CO-47/1). Go 0.5 mi to a clearing, R,, and past the power line to a parking area. Follow the *Cranesville Swamp Trail* through the woods for 0.3 mi to the boardwalk. The boardwalk extends 500 ft into the swamp. There are four unnamed interpretive trails. Backtrack.

The other preserves with possible hiking opportunities are Panther Knob, 376 acres in Pendleton County on the top of North Fork Mountain; Yankauer, 107 acres along the Potomac River in Berkeley County; Greenland Gap, 255 acres in Grant County in New Creek Mountain gap; Hungry Beech, 127 acres in Roane County on Paxton Ridge and along Green Creek; and Murphy, 276 acres in Ritchie County, near Pennsboro. As trails are "not a management emphasis at the preserves," the hiker should contact the conservancy at the address below for more information.

INFORMATION: The Nature Conservancy of West Virginia, 723 Kanawha Blvd, East (PO Box 3754), Charleston, WV 25337.

Sierra Club

The Sierra Club was founded in 1892 by John Muir, naturalist, conservationist, and writer. It has over 60 chapters nationwide whose nonprofit programs involve legislation; litigation; public information; wilderness outings; white water expeditions, mountaineering, educational workshops, conferences maintenance of trails, huts, and lodges; and publishing. Additionally, the Sierra Club Foundation was established in 1960 for educational, literary, and scientific projects concerning national and international problems of preserving the natural resources. It also has the Sierra Club Legal Defense Fund to assist citizens' groups in protection of the environment. Its purpose is to explore, enjoy, and preserve the nation's forests, waters, wildlife, wilderness, and other natural resources.

The West Virginia chapter of the Sierra Club was officially formed Oct 1, 1984, with a membership of 650. Its predecessor, the West Virginia Group of the Potomac chapter, was established in 1977. Individual groups have not been established, but one in Morgantown is in the formative stage. The chapter publishes a bimonthly newsletter, the *Mountain State Sierran*.

Chapter activities, past and present, include the evaluation and redrafting of the Monongahela National Forest's 1985 Land and Resources Management Plan; service outings for reconstructing, cleaning, and maintaining USFS trails; lobbying for state and federal environmental issues; organizing and hosting environmental education workshops on preserving the natural environment: and sponsoring campers for attendance at the state's Department of Natural Resources Junior and State Conservation Camps.

INFORMATION: Conservation Committee, West Virginia Chapter, Sierra Club, PO Box 4142, Morgantown, WV 26504; 304-637-4082 or 304-789-6277

West Virginia Highlands Conservancy

Established in 1967, the West Virginia Highlands Conservancy advocates the prudent management and conservation of the state's natural resources with a historical emphasis on the more than 901,000-acre Monongahela National Forest and the surrounding eastern highlands. Traditionally, the conservancy has been active in legislative procedures for wilderness preservation; wilderness designation; protection of public lands and water resources, water and air quality, and river conservation; regulating surface mining; and involvement in other environmental issues that affect the state's quality of life.

As a citizens' group of more than 575 individual members and 26 organizational members, it relies primarily on volunteers to pursue its conservation programs. When necessary, it also retains professional assistance in working with the state legislature and Congress in seminars, reports on technical and public policy issues, litigation, negotiations, formal regulatory proceedings, and public hearings to serve as a citizen's advocate before governmental agencies.

As part of its administrative process, it has two annual conferences with pertinent speakers, workshops, and field trips. Additionally, it sponsors a regular year-round outings program that includes hiking, backpacking, skiing, canoeing, spelunking, and other outdoor activities.

The legacy of the conservancy leadership is remarkably successful. Some of the major examples are: 1965, Spruce Knob/Seneca Rocks Natural Recreation Area; 1973, a federal litigation landmark (National Forest Management Act of 1976) that reformed clear-cutting in national forests nationwide; 1975, Otter Creek (20,000 acres) and Dolly Sods (10,215 acres) Wilderness Areas; 1976, Gauley River Canyon preserved from hydropower dam; 1978, worked with the Izaak Walton League to create the New River

Gorge National River Park, 1979 preservation of 35,000-acre Canaan Valley wetlands area, 1983, USFS withdrawal of proposals for threefold increases in timbering, mining, and road construction in the MNF; 1996, USFS reduction of timbering in sensitive area of Gauley Mountain; 1997, one of the plaintiffs in a suit against Corridor H project, a massive four-land highway from east of Elkins through the northeast area of Canaan Valley.

The conservancy is a nonprofit, tax-exempt West Virginia corporation and has an inviolate endowment fund whose investment income is applied to conservation work. "The endowment fund is dedicated to working for the conservation and wise management of West Virginia's scenic rivers, natural heritage, historical sites, and environmental quality of public lands," said Larry W. George, conservancy president. In addition to cash gifts and bequests, real estate, mineral rights, and stocks and bonds, and other tangible properties are of benefit to its services. The conservancy has a constant need for volunteers in field trips, attorneys, engineers, researchers, speakers, and writers. The conservancy publishes a monthly newsletter, the *Highland Voice*, and has also published a *Hiking Guide to Monongahela National Forest* with details and maps of the trails.

INFORMATION: For information on memberships, endowment, gifts, guidebooks, volunteers, and general information, contact West Virginia Highlands Conservancy, PO Box 306, Charleston, WV 25321; 888-201-6252.

West Virginia Scenic Trails Association

The West Virginia Scenic Trails Association was incorporated August 19, 1974, and work began on its chief commitment, the *Allegheny Trail*, in 1975. The two cofounders, Bob Tabor and Nick Lozano, and others, first discussed the subject in October 1971, and in November 1972, met with a group of about 40 people at St John's Episcopal Church in Charleston. Lozano was elected president of the WVSTA, Tabor was vice president, and Bruce Bond was the secretary-treasurer. Tabor had been on the Board of Managers of the Appalachian Trail Conference from 1961 to 1971; his knowledge of government officials and citizen trail supporters led him to model the *Allegheny Trail* and the WVSTA after the AT and the ATC. Among the other early leaders and associates were Charley Carlson, Frank Pelurie, Norman Williams, Zip Little, and John Ballantine.

In addition to the goals of completing the 300 mi *Allegheny Trail* from SW Virginia to Pennsylvania, the association plans to have chapters such as the Mary Ingles chapter develop a 500 mi trail from SW Virginia to N Kentucky along the New, Kanawha, and Ohio rivers, and the Northwest Passage chapter extend the *Allegheny Trail* jurisdiction into Pennsylvania for a connection with the *Warrior Trail* and *Laurel Highlands Trail*. (See *Warrior Trail*, chapter 10.)

Among the general objectives are to improve and enlarge the state trail system; to communicate with the appropriate local, state, and federal agencies in developing and coordinating the trail establishments; and to create local interest groups to participate in trail development and management. "Our immediate objectives are to attract new members. Whatever we accomplish will be made possible by the enthusiasm of our volunteers," said John Giacalone, 1986 association president. The 180-member association invites individuals and organizations to join, has an annual meeting, conducts weekly outings and trail development projects, and publishes a bimonthly newsletter, *Whoop n' Holler*. It has also published the *Hiking Guide to the Allegheny Trail*, a trail point narrative with detailed maps.

INFORMATION: WVSTA, PO Box 4042, Charleston, WV 25364; 304-755-4878. See chapter 11 for information on addresses and telephone numbers for the four sections of the *Allegheny Trail*. For web site: http://wvonline.com/wvsta; for e-mail: ioof.wv.grand-sec@juno.com. (This number is also for West Virginia Trails Coalition, and Mary Engle Trails/Heritage Trust.)

AGENCIES AND OTHER SOURCES OF INFORMATION

There are more than 100 addresses of national, state, and local forests, parks, agencies, and some private organizations listed under address or information in the narrative. A few other allied government agencies, citizens' groups, and centers whose addresses do not appear elsewhere in the book but are related to West Virginia are listed below.

United States Government Departments

Department of Agriculture
Forest Service
PO Box 96090
Washington, DC 20090
202-205-0957
   Regional Foresters
   Region #9
   310 W Wisconsin Ave
   Milwaukee, WI 53203
   414-297-3600

Department of Agriculture
Natural Resource Consv. Services
PO Box 2890
Washington, DC 200013
202-720-3210
   State Biologist
   75 High St, Rm 301
   Morgantown, WV 26505

Army Corps of Engineers
Pulaski Bldg
20 Massachusetts Ave, NW
Washington, DC 20314
202-761-0002

Department of the Interior
1849 C St, NW
Washington, DC 20240
202-208-7351
   Bureau of Land Management
   202-208-3801

   Bureau of Mines
   202-501-9649

National Park Service
Interior Bldg
PO Box 37127
Washington, DC 20013
202-208-4747
   Regional Directors
   143 S Third St
   Philadelphia, PA 19106
   215-597-7013

US Fish and Wildlife Service
Washington, DC 20240
202-208-4717
   Regional Office
   300 Westgate Center Dr
   Hadley, MA 01035
   413-253-8200

Advisory Council of Historic
Preservation
1100 Pennsylvania Ave, NW
Washington, DC 20004
202-606-8503

Environmental Protection Agency
401 M St, SW
Washington, DC 20460
202-260-2090
   Region III
   841 Chestnut Bldg
   Philadelphia, PA 19107
   215-597-9814

Interstate Organizations
(nongovernment)
American Camping Assoc, Inc.
5000 State Rd
Martinsville, IN 46151
317-342-8456

American Conservation Assoc, Inc.
1350 New York Ave, NW
Washington, DC 20005
202-624-9365

American Fisheries Society
5410 Grosvenor Ln
Bethesda, MD 20814
301-897-8616

American Forests
1516 P St, NW
Washington, DC 20005
202-667-3300

American Hiking Society
PO Box 20160
Washington, DC 20041
703-255-9304

American Nature Study Society
5881 Cold Brook Rd
Homer, NY 13077
607-749-3655

American Rivers
801 Pennsylvania Ave, SE
Washington, DC 20003
202-547-6900

Appalachian Mountain Club
5 Joy St
Boston, MA 02108
617-523-0636

Assoc of Forest Svc Employees
for Environmental Ethics
PO Box 11615
Eugene, OR 97440
503-484-2692

Boy Scouts of America
PO Box 152079
Irving, TX 75015
214-580-2000

Brooks Bird Club, Inc.
707 Warwood Ave
Wheeling, WV 26003

Clean Water Fund
1320 18th St, NW
Washington, DC 20036
202-457-0336

Defenders of Wildlife
1101 14th St, NW
Washington, DC 20005
202-682-9400

Friends of the Earth
1025 Vermont Ave, NW
Washington, DC 20005
202-783-7400

Girl Scouts of USA
420 Fifth Ave
New York, NY 10018
212-853-8000

Izaak Walton League of America
707 Conservation Ln
Gaithersburg, MD 20878
301-548-0150

League of Conservation Voters
1707 L St, NW
Washington, DC 20036
202-785-8683

National Audubon Society
700 Broadway
New York, NY 10003
212-979-3000

National Geographic Society
1145 17th St, NW
Washington, DC 20036
202-857-7000

National Speleological Society
Cave Ave
Huntsville, AL 35810
205-852-1300

National Wildlife Federation
1400 16th St, NW
Washington, DC 20036
202-797-6800
   Region 3
   PO Box 1557
   Waynesboro, VA 22980
   504-942-9453

Nature Conservancy
1815 N Lynn St
Arlington, WV 22209
703-841-5300
   Eastern Region
   201 Devonshire St
   Boston, MA 02210
   617-542-1908
   (304-345-4350 WV)

Rails-to-Trails Conservancy
1400 16th St, NW
Washington, DC 20036
202-797-5400

Sierra Club
85 Second St
San Francisco, CA 94105
415-977-5500
   Appalachia Office
   69 Franklin St
   Annapolis, MD 21401
   410-268-7411

Student Conservation Association
PO Box 550 Charleston, NH 03606
603-5463-1700

Wilderness Society
900 17th St, NW
Washington, DC 20006
202-833-2300

West Virginia Government Agencies
Division of Natural Resources
1900 Kanawha Blvd, E
Charleston, WV 25305
304-558-2754

Geological and Economic Survey
PO Box 879
Morgantown, WV 26507
304-594-2331

State Extension Services
Agriculture, Forestry, and Environment
2080 Agricultural Sciences Bldg
Morgantown, WV 26506
304-293-6131
Wildlife
311-B, Percival Hall
West Virginia University
Morgantown, WV 26506
304-293-4797, ext 2493

WV Bureau of Environment
Division of Environmental
Protection, #10
McJunkin Rd
Nitro, WV 25153
304-759-0515

WV Cooperative Fish and Wildlife
Resource Unit
Division of Forestry, WV University
PO Box 6125
Morgantown, WV 26506
304-292-3794

West Virginia Citizens' Groups
A. B. Brooks Nature Center
Oglebay Institute, Oglebay Park
Wheeling, WV 26003
304-242-6855

American Fisheries Society
(Potomac Chapter)
1 Mumbo Ln, PO Box 83
Bakertown, WV 25410
301-984-1908

Forest Watch Coalition
320 Randolph Ave
Elkins, WV 26241
304-637-4082

Izaak Walton League of America
WV Division
Rte 4, Box 334
Morgantown, WV 26505
304-599-9237

Trout Unlimited
WV Council
Rte 1, Box 109Z
Bristol, WV 26332
304-783-5345

WV Highlands Conservancy
PO Box 306
Charleston, WV 25321
304-252-8733

WV Rails-to-Trails
1202 Ridge Dr
S Charleston, WV 25309
304-768-0528

WV Wildlife Federations, Inc
Box 2928
Clarksburg, WV 26302
304-842-3822

Wildlife Society
WV Chapter
2006 Walnut St
Kenova, WV 25530
304-529-5712

Outdoor Recreation
For information on all outdoor recreation activities and scenic areas in West Virginia call 800-CALL WVA

TRAIL INDEX

Parentheses indicate USFS trail number. Boldface and symbols are used to denote the following trails: † is a trail longer than 20.0 mi, § is an environmental nature trail, and ★ is a trail designed for people with physical disabilities.

[†] = trail longer than 20.0 mi
[§] = environmental nature trail
★ = trail designed for people with physical disabilities

About the Author

Allen de Hart has been hiking, designing, constructing, maintaining, and writing about trails for six decades. Born in Patrick County, Virginia, his family moved to near Beckley, West Virginia while he was an infant, but returned to the county of his birth when he was age three. Beginning at age five his seventeen-year old brother, Moir, began taking him on hiking, camping, and fishing trips in Virginia, and to West Virginia and North Carolina. The experience made an indelible impression and enhanced his interest in natural science and outdoor sports. In the 1930s he and his two younger brothers, Dick and Willie, built trails on their large farm and the Bobwhite Trail to Woolwine School, a shortcut from a long school bus ride. With the Appalachian Trail being constructed by the CCC at Rocky Knob, he and his brothers were among the first local users before 1940. But it was not until 1978 he hiked the entire length of the Appalachian Trail.

De Hart has a master's degree in American history from the University of Virginia in Charlottesville; did doctoral work at North Carolina State University; and two National Science Foundation grants in psychology, at Florida State University and the University of Georgia. He is a graduate of the Adjutant General Corps of the US Army and served overseas during the Korean War. He is a history professor emeritus at Louisburg College, Louisburg, N.C., where he and his wife, Flora (whose discipline was English), began teaching in 1957. He also served as director of public affairs for 27 years and has taught courses in outdoor recreation for 15 years. Active in state and community service organizations he has received three Governor's Awards.

He has hiked in 46 states and 18 foreign countries. By 1995 he had measured more than 30,000 miles of trails. From his journals he has authored eight books and trail guides for West Virginia, Virginia, North and South Carolina, Florida, and the sea islands of Georgia. Other outdoor sports in which he has participated are mountain climbing, whitewater rafting, biking, canoeing, hunting and fishing, diving, water skiing, and spelunking. He and his wife created the De Hart Botanical Gardens in Virginia and North Carolina in 1969. The preserve in North Carolina (south of Louisburg on US-401) is the largest private wildflower garden in eastern North Carolina.

About the AMC

The Appalachian Mountain Club pursues an active conservation agenda while encouraging responsible recreation. Founded in 1876, the club has been at the forefront of the environmental protection movement. We believe that successful long-term conservation depends on firsthand experience of the natural environment. AMC's 72,000 members pursue interests in hiking, backpacking, paddlesports, bicycling, and other activities and—at the same time—help safeguard the environment.

The club operates eight alpine huts in the White Mountains that provide shelter, bunks and blankets, and hearty meals for hiker's. Pinkham Notch Visitor Center, at the foot of Mt. Washington, is base camp to the adventurous and the ideal location for individuals and families new to outdoor recreation. Comfortable bunk rooms, mountain hospitality, and home-cooked, family-style meals make Pinkham Notch Visitor Center a fun and affordable choice for lodging. For lodging reservations only, call 603-466-2727; for general information on other AMC programs please call our Boston office at 617-523-0636.

The most recent efforts in the AMC Conservation program include river protection, Northern Forest lands policy, and support for the Clean Air Act. AMC staff and grassroots supporters work together to promote conservation.

The AMC's Education department offers a wide range of workshops to members and the general public, from introductory camping to intensive Mountain Leadership School taught in the White Mountains. In addition, volunteers in each chapter lead hundreds of activities and excursions.

The AMC's Research department focuses on the forces affecting the ecosystem, including ozone levels, acid rain and fog, climate change, rare flora and habitat protection, and air quality and visibility.

The AMC's trails program maintains more than 1,400 miles of trail (including 350 miles of the Appalachian Trail) and more than 50 shelters in the Northeast. Volunteers, seasonal crews, and program staff contribute more than 10,000 hours of public service work each summer. Hikers can volunteer by contacting the AMC Trails Program, Pinkham Notch Visitor Center, PO Box 298, Gorham NH 03581; 603-466-2721.

The AMC's offices in Boston and at Pinkham Notch Visitor Center stock the entire line of AMC publications, including guidebooks and Appalachia, the country's oldest mountaineering and conservation journal. To order, call 800-262-4455 or write AMC, PO Box 298, Gorham, NH 03581.

How to Find Your Way
in the National Forests

A master map of the detailed maps in this book appears on pp. 330–31. Red rectangles and map numbers correspond with the map numbers that follow. The master map of the Monongahela National Forest and part of the George Washington National Forest shows the locations of map numbers 1 through 37. Map number 38, the last in the book, is not included on the master map because it is isolated from the other trail areas. It is in the Blacksburg Ranger District of the Jefferson National Forest NE of Pearisburg, Virginia. Official highway maps of West Virginia and Virginia are essential for using the maps in this book; they provide entrance options from the major highways.

The following 38 trail maps illustrate the hiking trails in the Monongahela, and George Washington/Jefferson National Forests. With permission from the West Virginia Department of Highways, the 1994 county maps have been used as a background for the trail overlays. The county maps were chosen because they have detailed road information that will assist you to locate trailheads, campgrounds, park and forest boundaries, and other significant points of interest conveniently and accurately.

The original map design has only been modified to add new or to delete closed forest roads. For example, FR-76 and FR- 108, in the Gauley Ranger District, have been deleted because they are now hiking trails in the Cranberry Wilderness Area, new forest roads such as FR-296 and FR-875, in the White Sulphur Ranger District, have been added to assist you in trail access or connections.

Other modifications include boundary lines for the Cranberry, Dolly Sods, Laurel Fork, and Otter Creek wilderness areas, the title and elevation of some mountain peaks, trail shelter locations, closed or new campgrounds, and North directional symbols. No route modification has been made on any of the county, state or federal highways. The county-map legend has not been changed; it precedes the maps.

All trailheads have a red dot, a symbol larger than the red dashes that indicate the trails. Although not drawn to scale, careful effort has been made to show trail-terminus points as accurately as possible. Each trail name and its forest number (if one has been assigned) is marked (in red) near the trail route. Where trails continue at crossings, no trailhead sign is indicated. The maps begin with Number 1, for the Cheat Ranger District of the Monongahela National Forest, and end with Number 38, for the Blacksburg Ranger's District of the Jefferson National Forest. On some maps, sections of the *Allegheny Trail* are included because the trail passes through that area. Trails in the Seneca State Forest have also been added on the appropriate maps, for the convenience of the hiker.

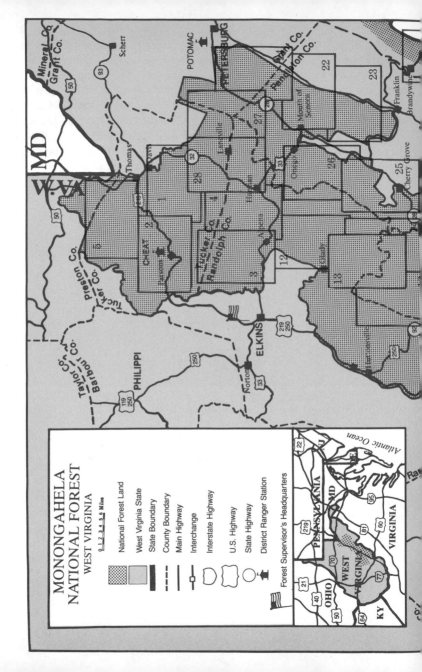

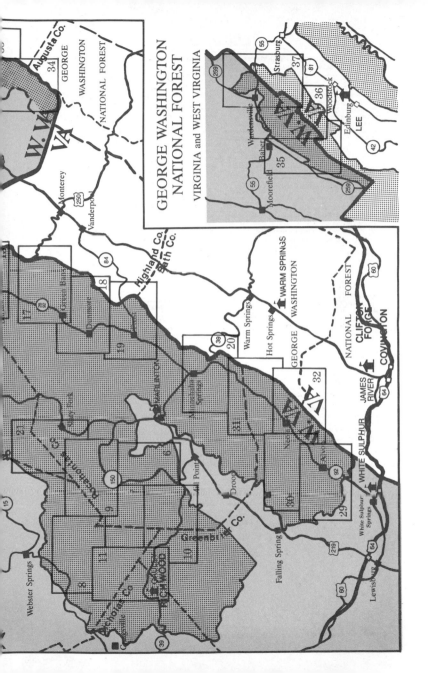

GEORGE WASHINGTON
NATIONAL FOREST
VIRGINIA and WEST VIRGINIA

LEGEND

ROADS AND ROADWAY FEATURES
SURFACE TYPES

TRAIL
IMPASSABLE ROAD
PRIMITIVE ROAD
UNIMPROVED ROAD
GRADED AND DRAINED ROAD
SOIL SURFACED ROAD
GRAVEL OR STONE ROAD
BITUMINOUS ROAD—LOW TYPE
PAVED ROAD
DIVIDED HIGHWAY

HIGHWAY SIGN SYSTEMS

INTERSTATE ROUTE
U.S. NUMBERED HIGHWAY
W. VA. NUMBERED HIGHWAY
W. VA. COUNTY NUMBERED ROUTE
DELTA ROUTE (MAINTENANCE ONLY)

FEDERAL-AID SYSTEMS

FEDERAL AID PRIMARY — FAP
FEDERAL AID SECONDARY — FAS
END OF FAS ROUTE — FAS

FUNCTIONAL SYSTEMS

EXPRESSWAY — X
TRUNKLINE — T
FEEDER — F
STATE LOCAL SERVICE — (ALL OTHERS)

ROADS NOT ON STATE SYSTEM

PUBLIC ROAD — 42
PRIVATE ROAD
SIDE ROADS AND STREETS
  IN INSETS AND MUNICIPALITIES
U.S. FOREST SERVICE ROAD — USFS
W. VA. DEPT. NAT. RESOURCES ROAD — WVNR

RAILROADS

RAILROAD (ANY NUMBER OF TRACKS)
NARROW GAGE RAILROAD
RAILROAD STATION
GRADE CROSSING
RAILROAD ABOVE
RAILROAD BELOW
RAILROAD BRIDGE (WIDE STREAM)
RAILROAD TUNNEL

DRAINAGE

NARROW STREAM
WIDE STREAM
MARSH OR SWAMP
DAM, WITHOUT ROAD

STRUCTURES

HIGHWAY BRIDGE (MORE THAN 20' SPAN)
BRIDGE, GENERAL (WIDE STREAM)
SUSPENSION BRIDGE
TRUSS OR GIRDER BRIDGE
CANTILEVER BRIDGE
DAM WITH ROAD
HIGHWAY TUNNEL
FORD
TOLL BRIDGE — T. Br.

CONSERVATION OR RECREATION

PICNIC GROUND
PLAYGROUND, BALLFIELD
BATHING BEACH OR POOL
SCENIC SITE
CAMPING AREA
CAMP OR LODGE
FOREST RANGER STATION
FISH HATCHERY — (BASIN) (POND)
ZOO
LOOKOUT TOWER
COUNTRY CLUB — CC
GOLF COURSE — GC
DRIVE-IN THEATER
ATHLETIC FIELD — A
AMUSEMENT PARK — AP
FAIRGROUND OR RACE TRACK
RIDING ACADEMY
RIFLE CLUB — RC
ROADSIDE PARK — RP

DWELLINGS, FARM UNITS, ETC.

	(IN USE)	(NOT IN USE)
FARM UNIT		
DWELLING (OTHER THAN FARM)		
ROW OF HOUSES (WITH NUMBER OF DWELLINGS)		
TRAILER PARK	TP	
HOUSE AND STORE (JOINT USE)		
SEASONAL DWELLING		
HOTEL		
MOTEL		
HOSPITAL		
REST HOME		
CHURCH		
CEMETERY		
CHURCH WITH CEMETERY		

EDUCATIONAL

PUBLIC SCHOOL
OTHER EDUCATIONAL INSTITUTIONS
COMMUNITY HALL
MUSEUM

BOUNDARIES

STATE LINE
COUNTY LINE
MAGISTERIAL DISTRICT LINE
INCORPORATED TOWN
PARK OR FOREST BOUNDARY

MISCELLANEOUS

MILITARY POST
MINE
GATE — ×‖×
SINK OR DEPRESSION
LATITUDE AND LONGITUDE — 38°00' 80°00'
HIGHWAY INTERCHANGE

CITY AND VILLAGE CENTERS

STATE CAPITOL
COUNTY SEAT
OTHER CITIES AND VILLAGES — o

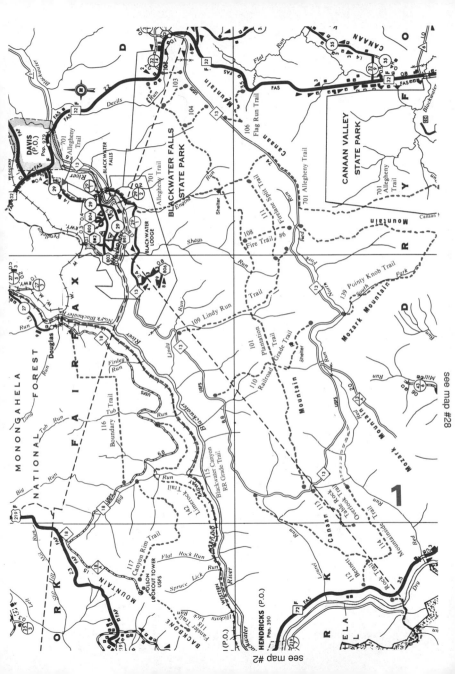

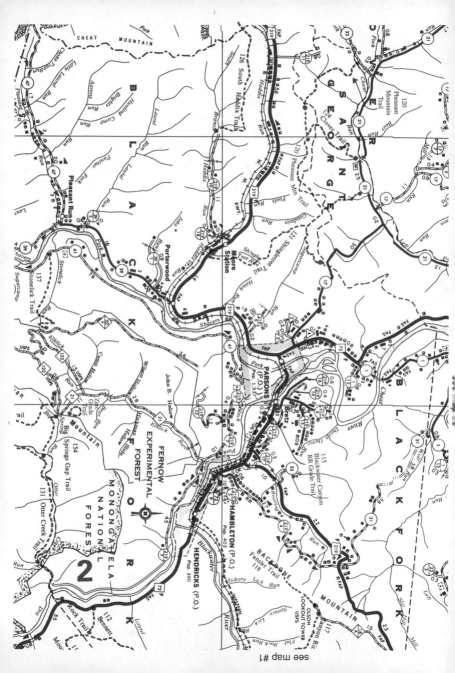

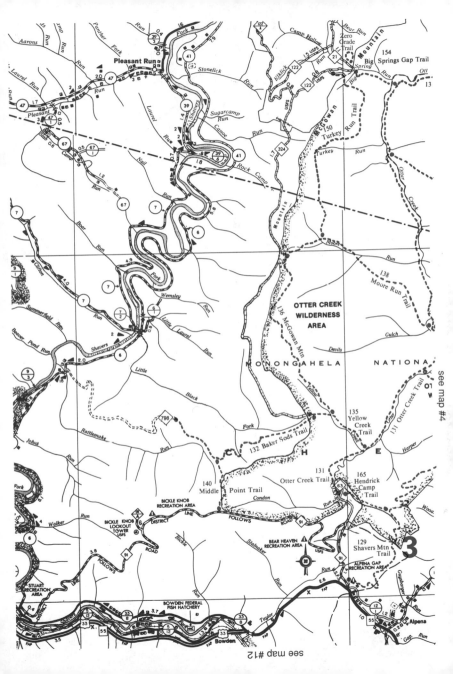

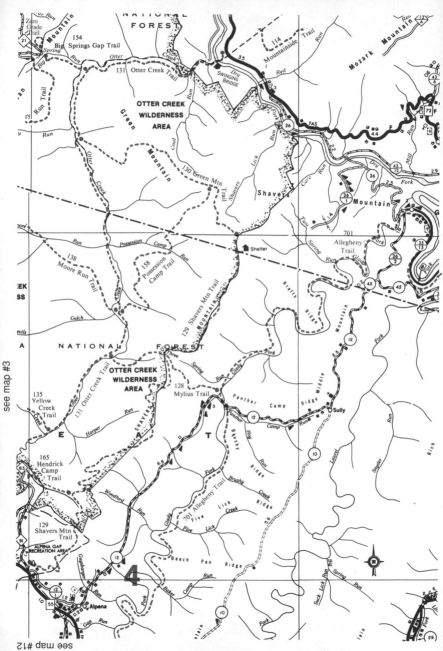

see map #3

see map #12

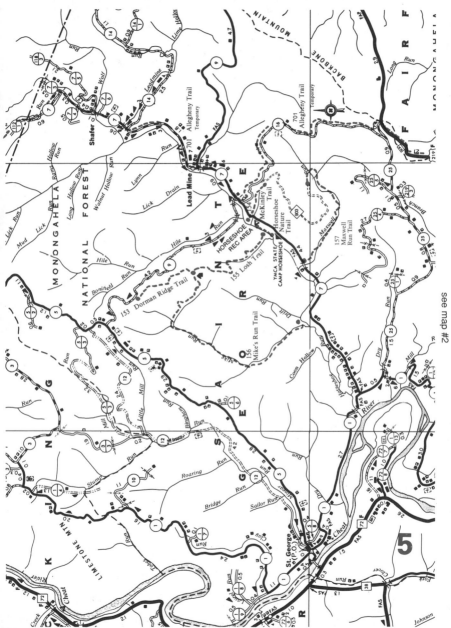

see map #2

5

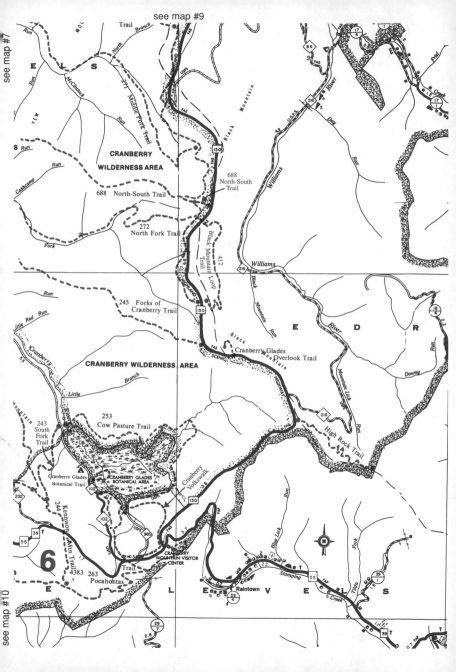

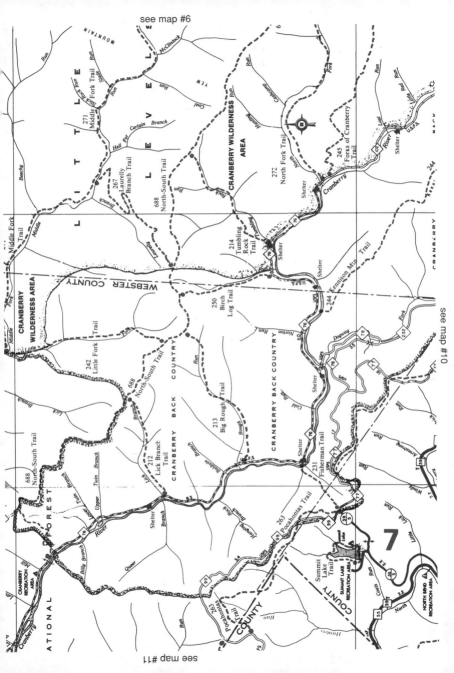

see map #10

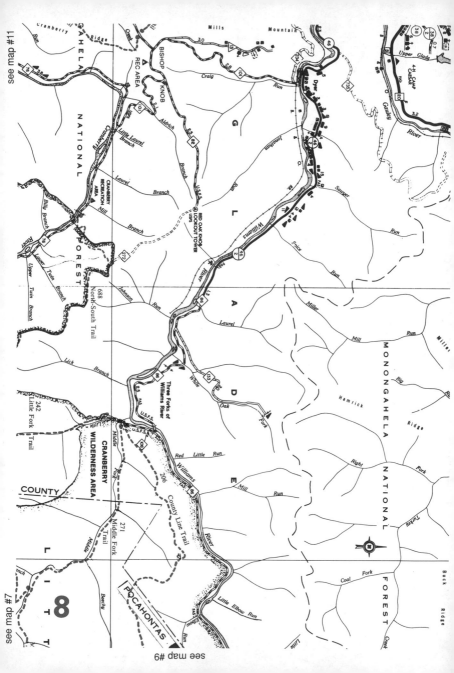

see map #7

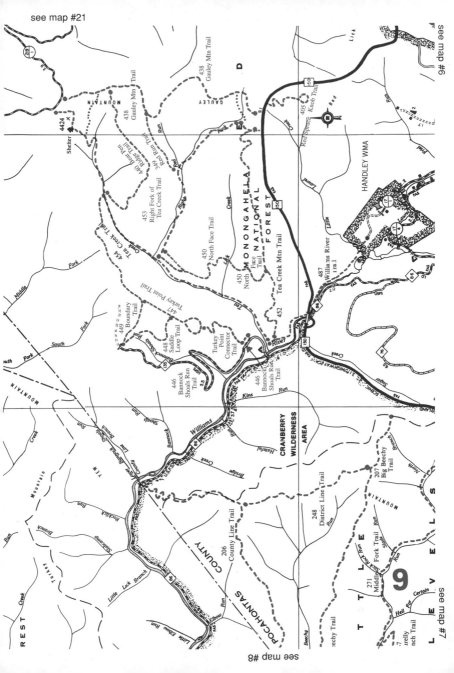

see map #21
see map #6
see map #7
see map #8

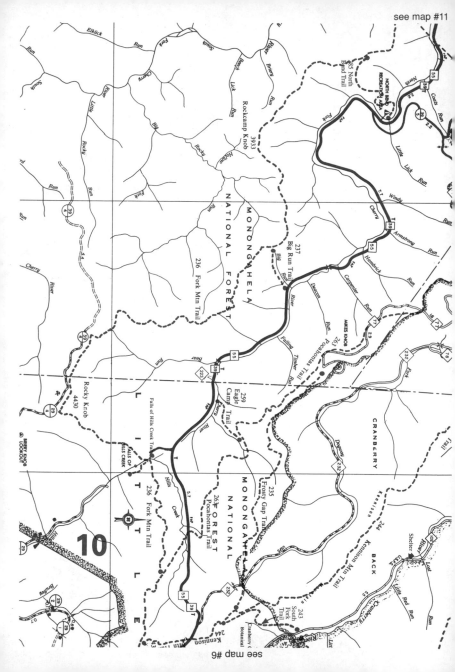

see map #6

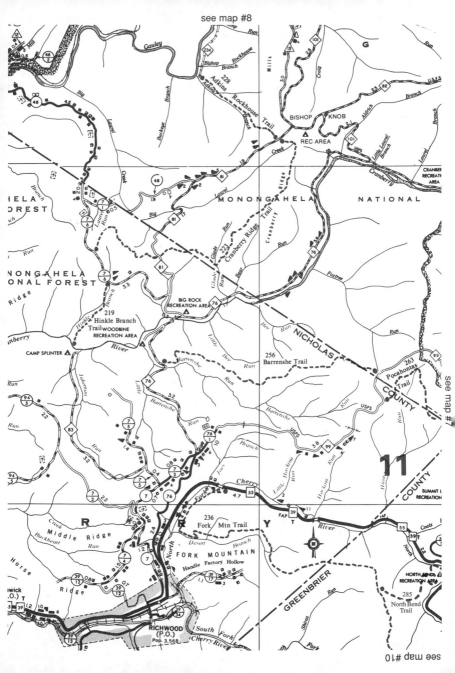

see map #7

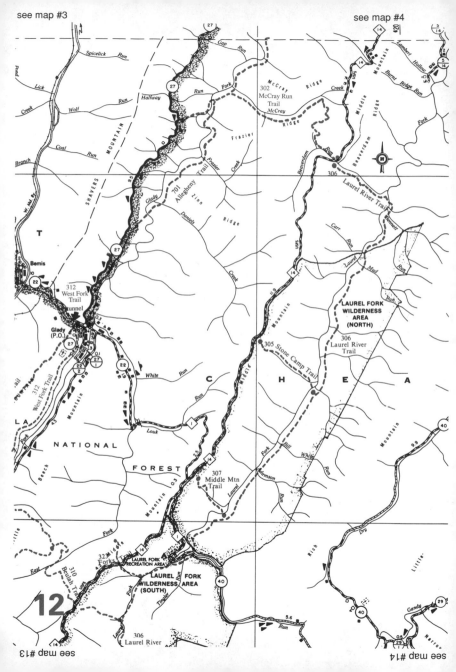

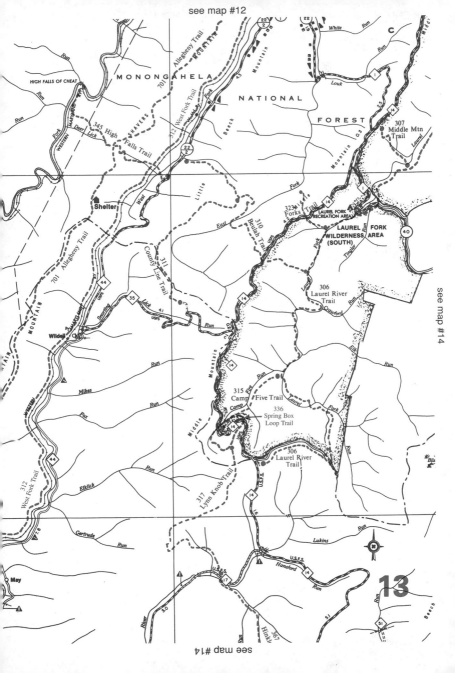

see map #12

MONONGAHELA

NATIONAL

FOREST

HIGH FALLS OF CHEAT

701 Allegheny Trail

312 West Fork Trail

SHAVERS

345 High Falls Trail

Deer Lick

Run

Run

WESTERN

Pork

22
2

Beech

Little

Fork

Louk

Run

White Run

Run

C

Middl

1

307
Middle Mtn
Trail

Mountain 0.3

14

Mountain

Shelter

West

East

Run

310
Beulah Trail

323 Middle
Forks Trail

LAUREL FORK
RECREATION AREA

14

LAUREL
FORK
WILDERNESS
AREA
(SOUTH)

Laurel Fork

River

40

701 Allegheny Trail

311
County Line Trail

MOUNTAIN

WESTERN

Wildell

35

Lick

4.1

USFS

Run

44

306
Laurel River
Trail

Crawford

Laurel Run

Thorny Run

Elk Run

Run

Mikes

Fox

Run

Run

Middle

Mountain

14

315
Camp Five Trail

Camp

Pox

Run

Laurel

Fork

336
Spring Box
Loop Trail

14

Run

312
West Fork Trail

44

7.8

Elklick

Run

317
Lynn Knob Trail

306
Laurel River
Trail

U.S.F.S.

14

16

Bla

Gertrude

Run

14

U.S.F.S.

Hansford

Run

Lukins

Run

N

May

U.S.F.S.
17

River 3.0

Run

Hinkle

Run

167

5.1

Beech

Run

13

see map #14

see map #14

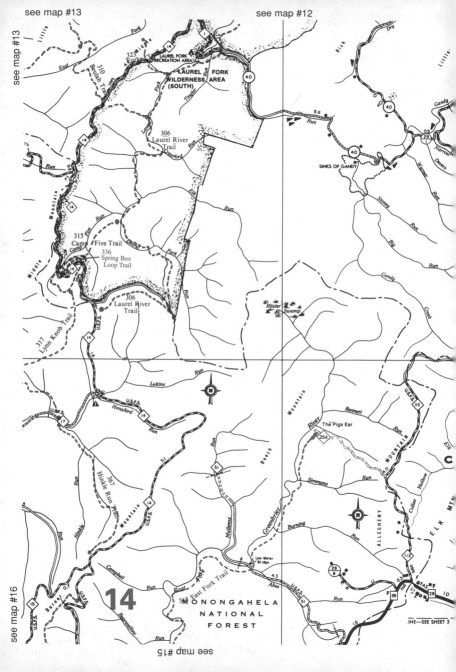

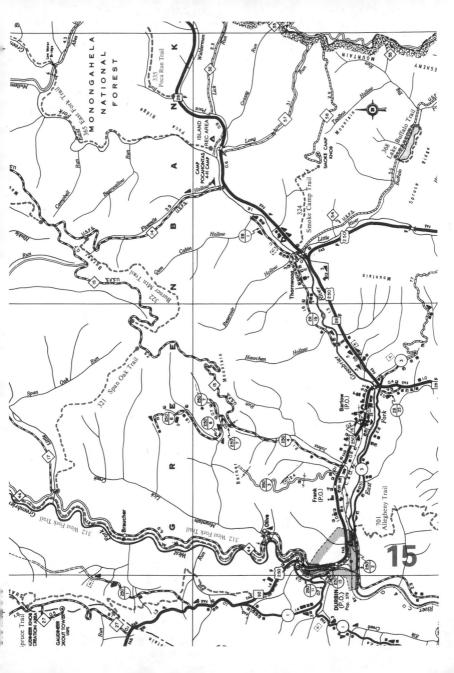

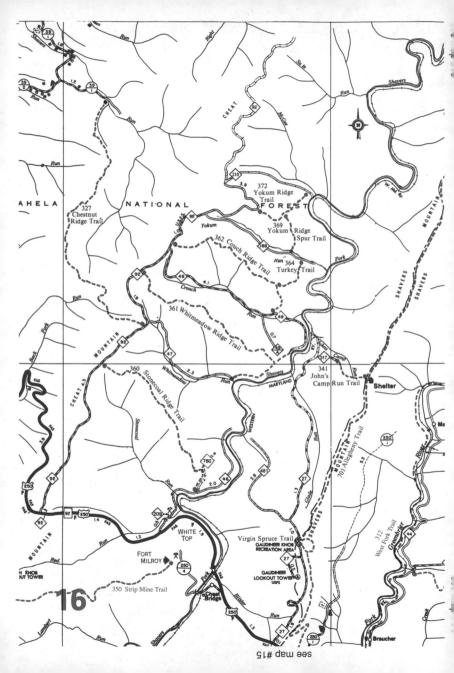

39
1
Shavers

39
2
Run

39
1.2

Run
Right
Run
Su M

CREAT
92
McGe
Run
Shavers
W. Md. Ry.

Run
Run

AHELA

NATIONAL

327
Chestnut
Ridge Trail

210
3.9

372
Yokum Ridge
Trail

FOREST

92
USFS

369
Yokum Ridge
Spur Trail

Yokum

188

MOUNTAIN
SHAVERS
SHAVERS

362 Couch Ridge Trail

92

49

4.1

Run 364
Turkey Trail

Crouch

49

361 Whitmeadow Ridge Trail

Run
0.7

Fork

92
1.9

Run

MOUNTAIN
92

4.7

Whitmeadow
2.3

Run

Shavers

317

341
John's Camp Run Trail

Camp
Run

360
Stonecoal Ridge Trail

MARYLAND

Shelter

CREAT
4.3

Stonecoal

WESTERN

Run

250
1

PAS
PAS

760

2.8

701 Allegheny Trail

250
1

MOUNTAIN

PAS
2.9

250
92

Run

2.0

4.6

4.8

Run

27

1.3

Clark

Run

SHAVERS

Ridge

Ma

250
1

92
250
1.4

209

Run
1.2

White
Top
1.9

Virgin Spruce Trail

GAUDINEER KNOB
RECREATION AREA

SHAVERS

312

West Fork Trail

Greenbrier

Fork

MOUNTAIN
92

PAS

FORT
MILROY

250
4

27

GAUDINEER
LOOKOUT TOWER
USFS

N KNOB
UT TOWER

Red.

350 Strip Mine Trail

Chest
Bridge

Fork
PAS

250

Blister

16

Lambert
Run

Shavers

250
1.3

Run

27

250
1

Fork

Braucher

Creek

see map #15

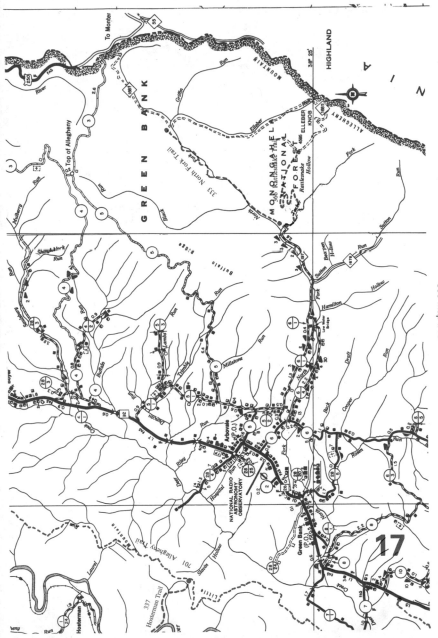

see map #18

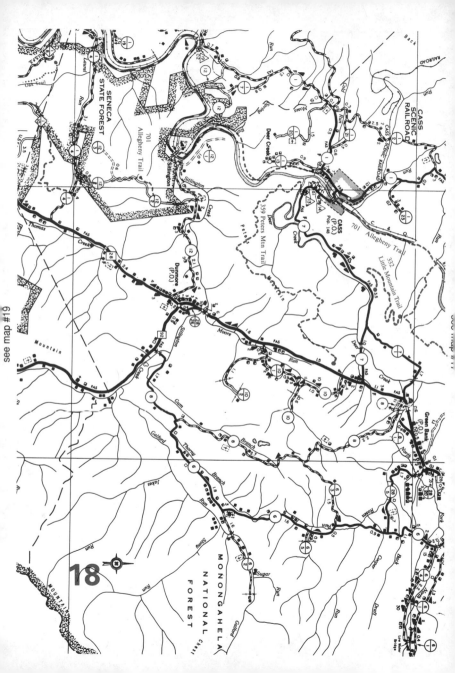

see map #19

SENECA STATE FOREST

701 Allegheny Trail

Stillington

Thomas Creek

Dunmore (P.O.)

Deer Creek

CASS SCENIC RAILROAD

CASS (P.O.) Pop. 146

359 Peters Mtn Trail

332 Little Mountain Trail

701 Allegheny Trail

Mountain

Stillington Creek

Moore Run

Deer Creek

Green Bank (P.O.)

Gum Run

Galford Branch

Jakes Run

Thorny Branch

North Fork

Back

18

MONONGAHELA NATIONAL FOREST

Stump Run

Sugar Run

Run

Galford Creek

Deer

Little River Bridge

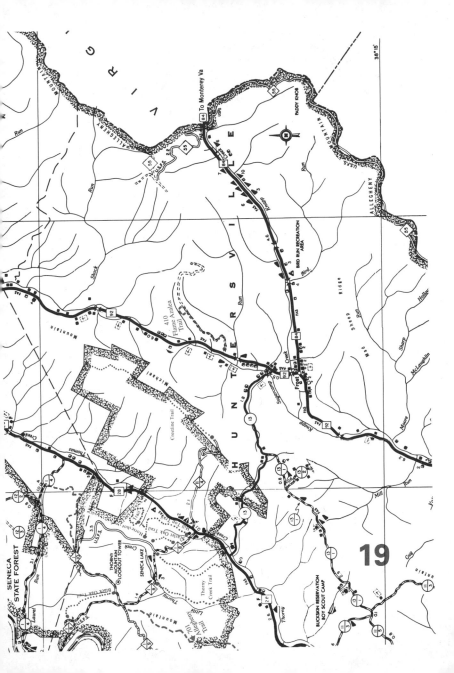

19

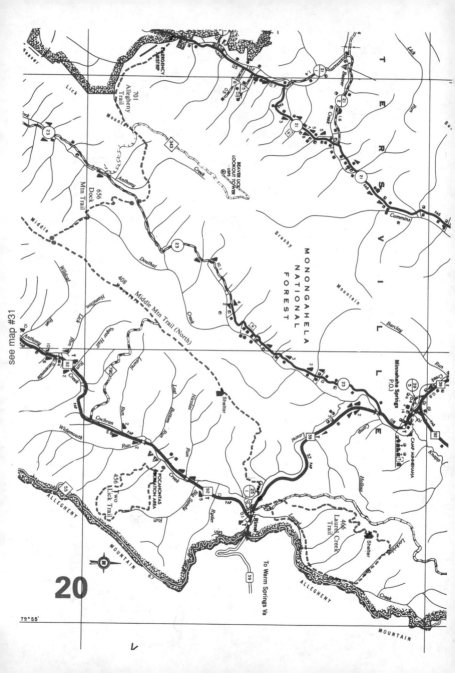

see map #31

20

79°55'

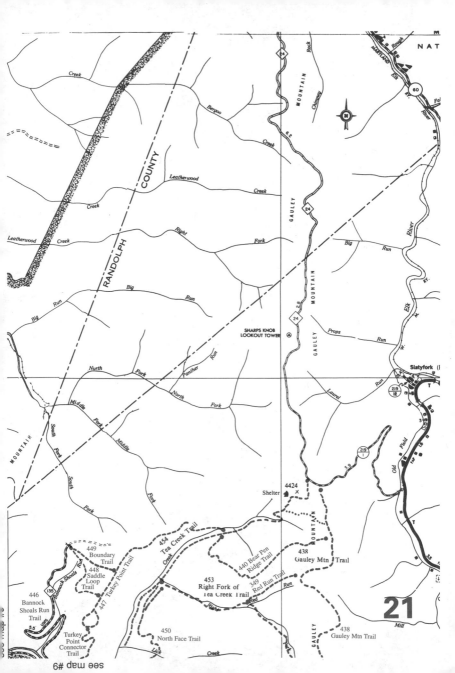

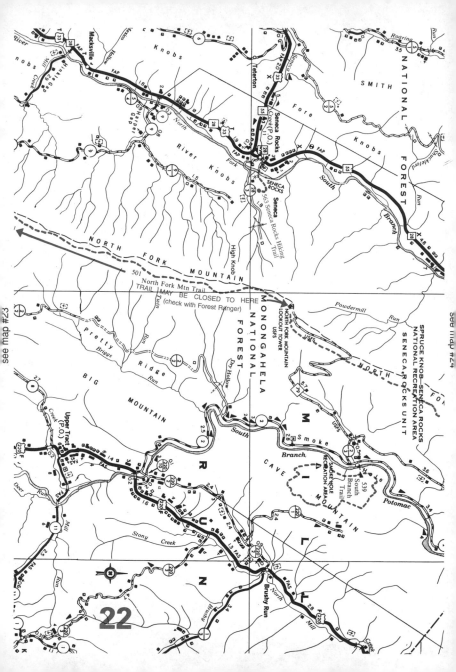

see map #23

see map #24

NORTH FORK MOUNTAIN

North Fork Mtn Trail
TRAIL MAY BE CLOSED TO HERE
(check with Forest Ranger)

501

563 Seneca Rocks Hiking Trail

NORTH FORK MOUNTAIN
LOOKOUT TOWER
USFS

MONONGAHELA NATIONAL FOREST

SMITH NATIONAL FOREST

SPRUCE KNOB-SENECA ROCKS
NATIONAL RECREATION AREA
SENECA ROCKS UNIT

Macksville

Teeterton

Seneca Rocks (P.O.)

SENECA ROCKS

Seneca

Powdermill Run

Pretty Ridge

BIG MOUNTAIN

Briggs Run

Dry Hollow

Upper Tract (P.O.)

Smoke Branch

SMOKE HOLE RECREATION AREA

539 South Branch Trail

CAVE MOUNTAIN

Potomac

Stony Creek

Brushy Run

North Run

Mill Creek

Deer Run

22

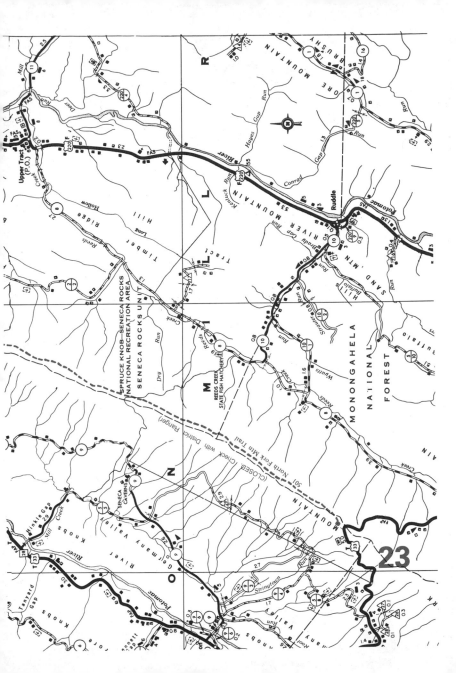

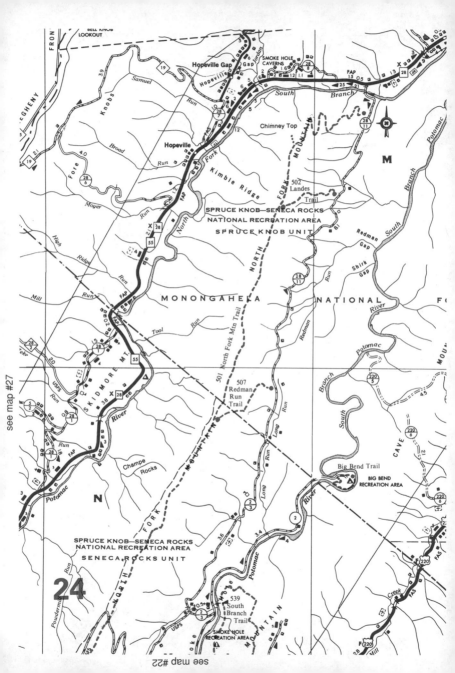

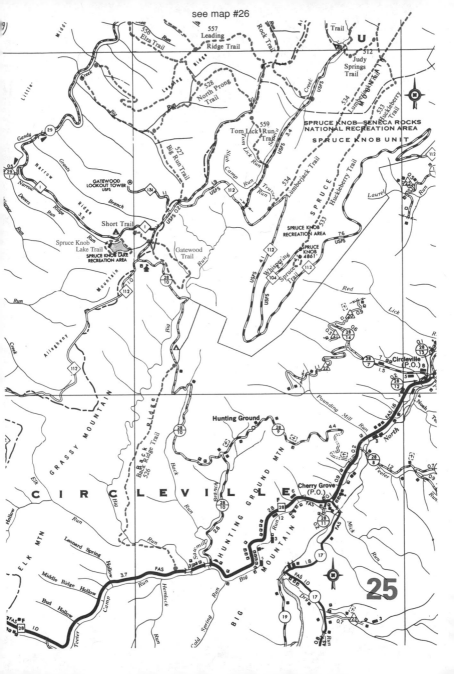

25

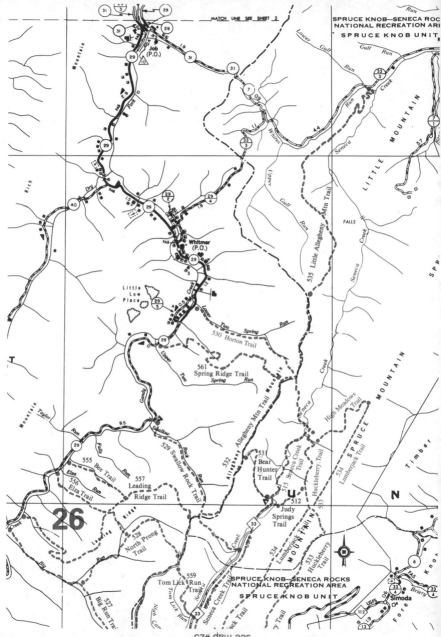

SPRUCE KNOB—SENECA ROC
NATIONAL RECREATION AR
SPRUCE KNOB UNIT

Job (P.O.)

Whitmer (P.O.)

Little Low Place

530 Horton Trail

561 Spring Ridge Trail

535 Little Allegheny Mtn Trail

FALLS

532 Allegheny Allegheny Mtn Trail Mountain

529 Swallow Rock Trail

555 Bee Trail

556 Elza Trail

557 Leading Ridge Trail

531 Bear Hunter Trail

515 Seneca Creek Trail

Huckleberry Trail

534 Lumberjack Trail

High Meadows Trail

SPRUCE MOUNTAIN

TIMBER

26

528 North Prong Trail

512 Judy Springs Trail

33

559 Tom Lick Run Trail

527 Big Run Trail

Seneca Creek Trail

534 Lumberjack Trail

533 Huckleberry Trail

SPRUCE KNOB—SENECA ROCKS
NATIONAL RECREATION AREA
SPRUCE KNOB UNIT

Simoda

FORE KNOB

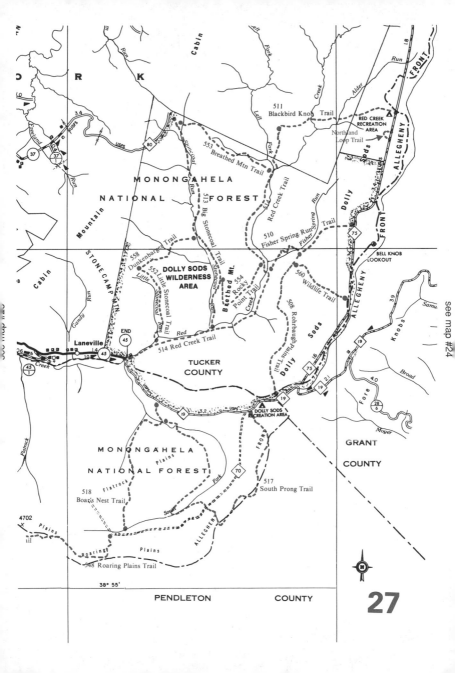

27

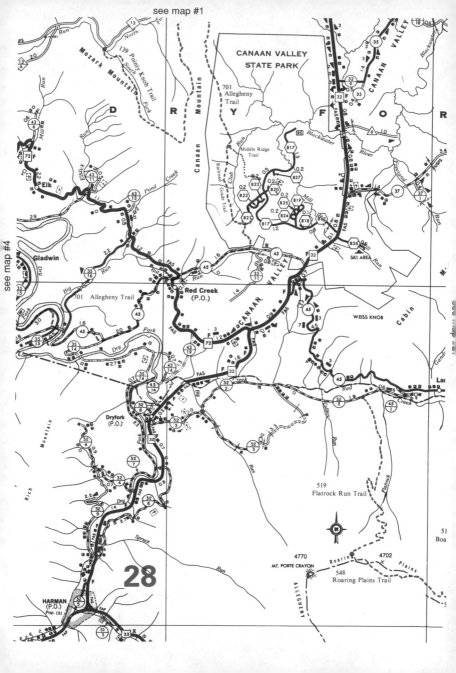

see map #4

CANAAN VALLEY
STATE PARK

701
Allegheny
Trail

Middle Ridge
Trail

Railroad
Grade Trail

Mozark Mountain

139 Pointy Knob Trail

Canaan Mountain

D R Y

F O R

Elk

Gladwin

701   Allegheny Trail

Red Creek
(P.O.)

CANAAN VALLEY

SKI AREA

WEISS KNOB

Cabin

Dryfork
(P.O.)

Rich Mountain

28

519
Flatrock Run Trail

51
Boa

4770
MT. PORTE CRAYON

Roaring Plains

548
Roaring Plains Trail

4702

HARMAN
(P.O.)
Pop. 131

ALLEGHENY

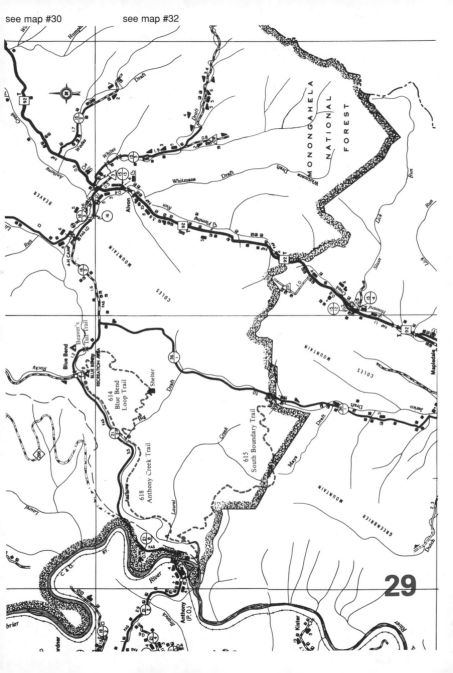

29

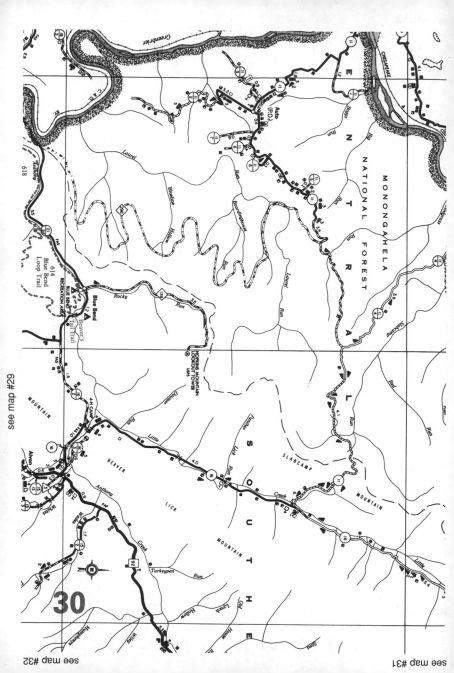

30

MONONGAHELA

NATIONAL FOREST

CENTRAL TRAIL

SOUTH MOUNTAIN

Greenbrier

Auto (P.O.)

Blue Bend
Blue Bend
Loop Trail
614
618
RECREATION AREA
BLUE BEND
Beaver's
Trail Trail

HOPKINS MOUNTAIN
LOOKOUT TOWER
USFS

Laurel Run
Bluelick Run
Roundhouse Run
Laurel Run
Rocky Run
Dawson Run
Little Lick Run
Panther Run
SLABCAMP MOUNTAIN
Red Run

Alvon
Anthony Creek
Wades Creek
Turkeypen Run
Wiley Hollow
Lynch Hollow
BEAVER LICK MOUNTAIN

Humphreys

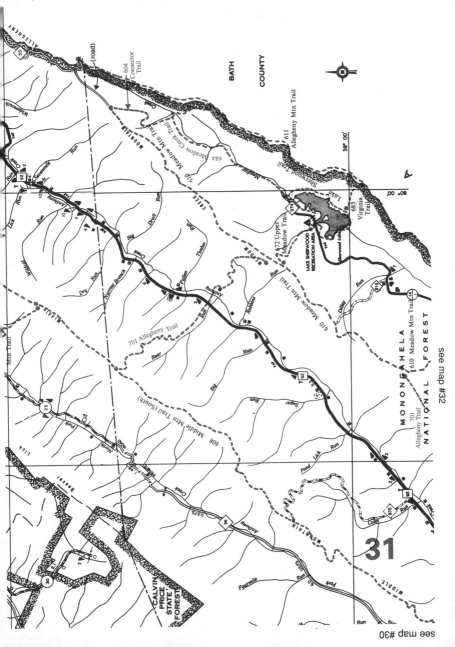

see map #32

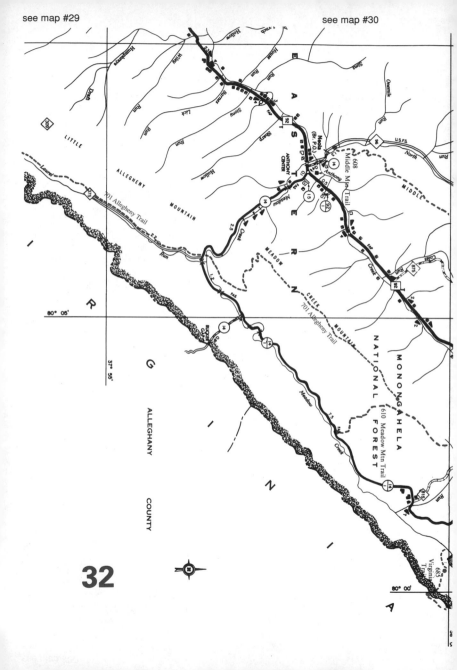

32

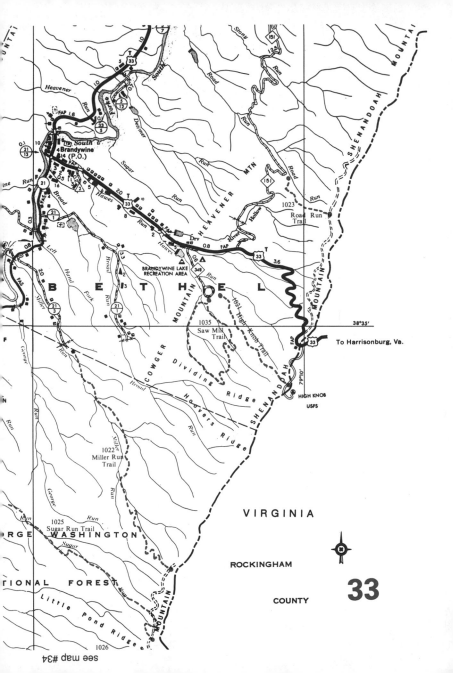

To Harrisonburg, Va.

38°35'

HIGH KNOB
USFS

VIRGINIA

ROCKINGHAM

COUNTY

33

see map #34

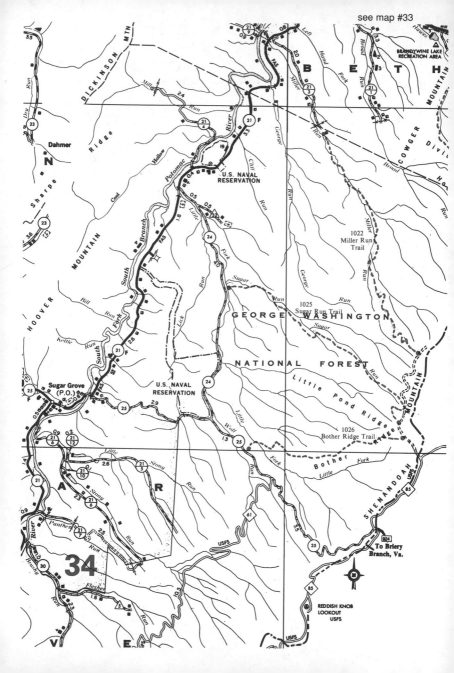

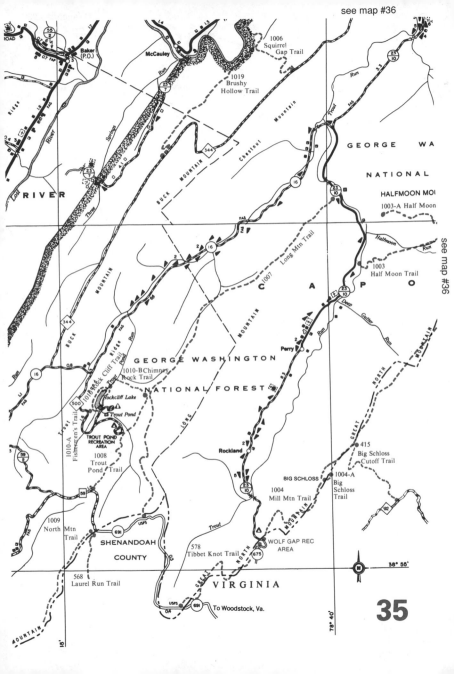

1006 Squirrel Gap Trail

1019 Brushy Hollow Trail

Baker (P.O.)

McCauley

GEORGE WA

NATIONAL

HALFMOON MOI

1003-A Half Moon

1007 Long Mtn Trail

1003 Half Moon Trail

C A P O

RIVER

BUCK MOUNTAIN

Chestnut Mountain

Perry

1010-B Chimney Rock Trail

1010-A Rock Cliff Trail

GEORGE WASHINGTON

NATIONAL FOREST

Rockcliff Lake

Trout Pond

TROUT POND RECREATION AREA

1010-A Fishermen's Trail

1008 Trout Pond Trail

Rockland

LONG MOUNTAIN

NORTH MOUNTAIN

415 Big Schloss Cutoff Trail

BIG SCHLOSS

1004-A Big Schloss Trail

1004 Mill Mtn Trail

1009 North Mtn Trail

SHENANDOAH COUNTY

578 Tibbet Knot Trail

WOLF GAP REC AREA

568 Laurel Run Trail

GREAT NORTH MOUNTAIN

VIRGINIA

To Woodstock, Va.

38° 55'

78° 40'

35

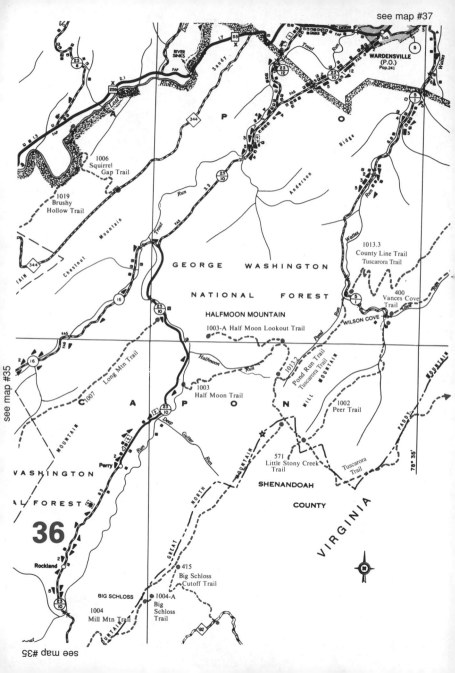

WARDENSVILLE
(P.O.)
Pop.241

1006
Squirrel
Gap Trail

1019
Brushy
Hollow Trail

1013.3
County Line Trail
Tuscarora Trail

GEORGE WASHINGTON

NATIONAL FOREST

400
Vances Cove
Trail

HALFMOON MOUNTAIN

WILSON COVE

1003-A Half Moon Lookout Trail

Long Mtn Trail

1007

1003
Half Moon Trail

1013.2
Pond Run Trail
Tuscarora Trail

1002
Peer Trail

C A P O N

Perry

571
Little Stony Creek
Trail

Tuscarora
Trail

SHENANDOAH

WASHINGTON

COUNTY

V I R G I N I A

A L F O R E S T

36

Rockland

415
Big Schloss
Cutoff Trail

BIG SCHLOSS

1004-A
Big
Schloss
Trail

1004
Mill Mtn Trail

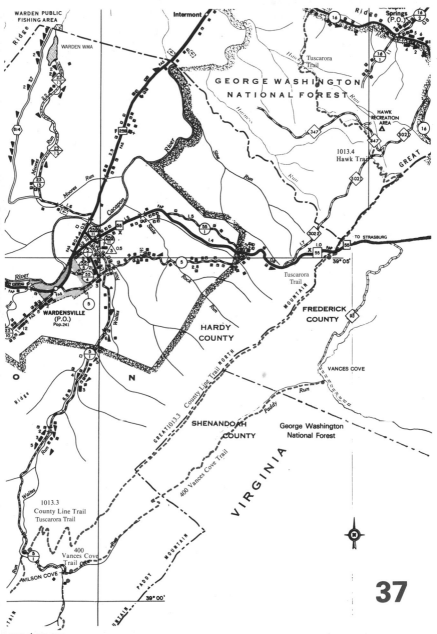

see map #36

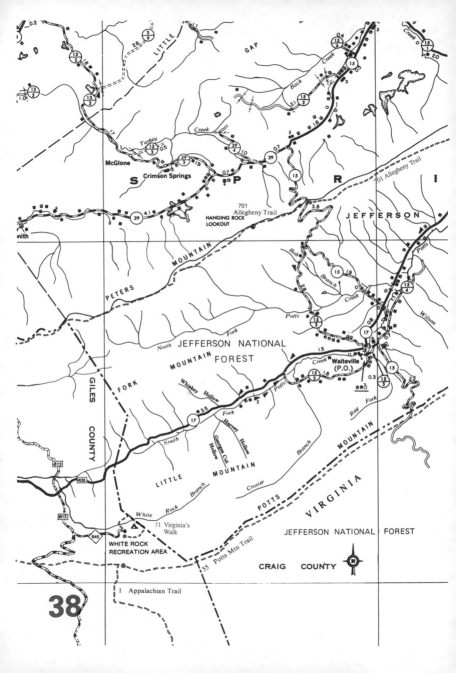